CW00660236

Operational Level

Paper P1

PERFORMANCE OPERATIONS

EXAM PRACTICE KIT

PUBLISHING

WORKING TOGETHER FOR YOU

ELSEVIER

PUBLISHING

CIMA Publishing is an imprint of Elsevier

The Boulevard, Langford Lane, Kidlington, Oxford, OX5 1GB, UK

225 Wyman Street, Waltham, MA 02451, USA

Kaplan Publishing UK, Unit 2 The Business Centre, Molly Millars Lane, Wokingham, Berkshire RG41 2QZ

Acknowledgements

We are grateful to the Chartered Institute of Management Accountants for permission to reproduce past examination questions. The answers to CIMA Exams have been prepared by Kaplan Publishing, except in the case of the CIMA November 2010 answers where the official CIMA answers have been reproduced.

Notice

No responsibility is assumed by the publisher for any injury and/or damage to persons or property as a matter of products liability, negligence or otherwise, or from any use or operation of any methods, products, instructions or ideas contained in the material herein.

British Library Cataloguing in Publication Data

A catalogue record for this book is available from the British Library

ISBN: 978 0 85732 468 9

Printed and bound in Great Britain

11 12 11 10 9 8 7 6 5 4 3 2 1

CONTENTS

Section

Key features in this edition

In addition to providing a wide ranging bank of real past exam questions, we have also included in this edition:

- Paper specific information and advice on exam technique.

- Guidance to make your revision for this particular subject as effective as possible.

- Enhanced tutorial answers packed with specific key answer tips, technical tutorial notes and exam technique tips from our experienced tutors.

You will find a wealth of other resources to help you with your studies on the following sites:

www.EN-gage.co.uk

www.cimaglobal.com

INDEX TO QUESTIONS AND ANSWERS

INTRODUCTION

This new Paper P1 has changed considerably from the old Paper P1, which was predominantly concerned with costing and budgeting methodologies - some 80% of the syllabus weighting was concerned with those areas but now it is 40%.

Areas have been introduced into the new paper P1 from the old Paper P2, covering project appraisal (25%) and uncertainty in analysis (15%). The balance of the paper covers managing short term finance, which was in Paper P7 of the old syllabus.

The direction of the new paper has therefore a much broader view of performance, dealing with details of capital budgeting and treasury management issues. The rather narrow technical approach used in the previous syllabus has been replaced, with the student now required to understand the wider aspects of financial operations. Students should ensure that they cover any deficiencies in their basic costing knowledge, since this new Paper P1 will not spend as much time on this area.

KEY TO THE INDEX

PAPER ENHANCEMENTS

We have added the following enhancements to the answers in this exam practice kit:

Key answer tips

Many answers include key answer tips to help your understanding of each question.

Tutorial note

Many answers include more tutorial notes to explain some of the technical points in more detail.

Top tutor tips

For selected questions, we "walk through the answer" giving guidance on how to approach the questions with helpful 'tips from a top tutor', together with technical tutor notes.

These answers are indicated with the "footsteps" icon in the index.

SECTION A-TYPE QUESTIONS

SECTION B-TYPE QUESTIONS

Cost accounting systems

Standard costing

Budgeting

Risk and decision making

Managing short term finance

SECTION C-TYPE QUESTIONS

Cost accounting systems

Standard costing

Budgeting

Financial information for long term decision making

ANALYSIS OF PAST PAPERS

The table below summarises the key topics that have been tested in the new syllabus examinations to date.

Note that the references are to the number of the question in this edition of the exam practice kit, but the Pilot Paper is produced in its original form at the end of the kit and therefore these questions have retained their original numbering in the paper itself. Where a question has a number in brackets it indicates that the topic appeared more than once in that question and the number in brackets explains how many times it appeared.

Topics from 'Risk and uncertainty' onwards were only introduced to Paper P1 from the May 10 exam sitting. References in the question index to sittings before this date refer to times when these topics appeared in other CIMA papers.

	Pilot	May 08	Nov 08	May 09	Nov 09	May 10	Sep 10
Traditional costing					Q2/Q4		
Modern production environment	Q2	Q2				Q2	Q2
Throughput accounting			Q2				
Activity Based Costing							
Variance analysis	Q4			Q2			
Advanced variances		Q3	Q4	Q2	Q3	Q3	Q3
Budgeting	Q2	Q4		Q2/ Q3		Q2 (2)	Q2 (2)
Forecasting	Q2						
Risk and uncertainty	Q2					Q2	Q2
Investment appraisal	Q3					Q4	Q4
Overall working capital							
Inventory						Q2	Q2
Cash control							
Receivables	Q2 (2)					Q2	Q2
Payables							
Short-term finance/investments							

EXAM TECHNIQUE

- Use the allocated **20 minutes reading and planning time** at the beginning of the exam:
  - read the questions and examination requirements carefully, and
  - begin planning your answers.

  See the Paper Specific Information for advice on how to use this time for this paper.

- **Divide the time** you spend on questions in proportion to the marks on offer:
  - there are 1.8 minutes available per mark in the examination
  - within that, try to allow time at the end of each question to review your answer and address any obvious issues

  Whatever happens, always keep your eye on the clock and **do not over run on any part of any question!**

- Spend the last **five minutes** of the examination reading through your answers, and **making any additions or corrections**.

- If you **get completely stuck** with a question:
  - leave space in your answer book, and
  - **return to it later.** Remember that there is no negative marking, so in Section A questions that offer a multiple choice, you should guess at an answer rather than leaving it out completely.

- Stick to the question and **tailor your answer** to what you are asked.
  - pay particular attention to the verbs in the question.

- If you do not understand what a question is asking, **state your assumptions**.

  Even if you do not answer in precisely the way the examiner hoped, you should be given some credit, if your assumptions are reasonable.

- You should do everything you can to make things easy for the marker.

  The marker will find it easier to identify the points you have made if your **answers are legible**.

- **Written questions**. Your answer should have:
  - a clear structure
  - a brief introduction, a main section and a conclusion.

  Be concise.

  It is better to write a little about a lot of different points than a great deal about one or two points.

- **Computations**:

  It is essential to include all your workings in your answers.

  Many computational questions require the use of a standard format:

  e.g. income tax computations, corporation tax computations and capital gains.

  Be sure you know these formats thoroughly before the exam and use the layouts that you see in the answers given in this book and in model answers.

- **Reports, memos and other documents**:

  Some questions ask you to present your answer in the form of a report, a memo, a letter or other document.

  Make sure that you use the correct format – there could be easy marks to gain here.

PAPER SPECIFIC INFORMATION

THE EXAM

FORMAT OF THE EXAM

		Number of marks
Section A :	A variety of compulsory objective test questions, each worth between two and four marks. Mini scenarios may be given, to which a group of questions relate.	20
Section B:	Six compulsory short answer questions, each worth five marks. A short scenario may be given, to which some or all questions relate.	30
Section C:	One or two compulsory questions. Short scenarios may be given, to which questions relate.	50
		─────
		100
		─────

Total time allowed: 3 hours plus 20 minutes reading and planning time.

SYLLABUS STRUCTURE

		Weighting
A	**Cost accounting systems**	**30%**
B	**Forecasting and budgeting techniques**	**10%**
C	**Project appraisal**	**25%**
D	**Dealing with uncertainty in analysis**	**15%**
E	**Managing short term finance**	**20%**

PASS MARK

The pass mark for all CIMA Qualification examination papers is 50%.

READING AND PLANNING TIME

Remember that all three hour paper based examinations have an additional 20 minutes reading and planning time.

CIMA GUIDANCE

CIMA guidance on the use of this time is as follows:

This additional time is allowed at the beginning of the examination to allow candidates to read the questions and to begin planning their answers before they start to write in their answer books.

This time should be used to ensure that all the information and, in particular, the exam requirements are properly read and understood.

During this time, candidates may only annotate their question paper. They may not write anything in their answer booklets until told to do so by the invigilator.

FURTHER GUIDANCE

As all questions are compulsory, there are no decisions to be made about choice of questions, other than in which order you would like to tackle them.

Therefore, in relation to P1, we recommend that you take the following approach with your reading and planning time:

- **Skim through sections B and C** assessing the level of difficulty of each question.

- **For section C, write down** on the question paper next to the mark allocation **the amount of time you should spend on each part.** Do this for each part of every question.

- **Decide the order** in which you think you will attempt each question:

  This is a personal choice and you have time on the revision phase to try out different approaches, for example, if you sit mock exams.

  A common approach is to tackle the question you think is the easiest and you are most comfortable with first.

  Others may prefer to tackle the longest questions first, or conversely leave them to the last.

  Psychologists believe that you usually perform at your best on the second and third question you attempt, once you have settled into the exam, so not tackling the bigger Section C questions first may be advisable.

  It is usual however that student tackle their least favourite topic and/or the most difficult question in their opinion last.

  Whatever you approach, you must make sure that you leave enough time to attempt all questions fully and be very strict with yourself in timing each question.

- **For each question** in turn, read the requirements and then the detail of the question carefully.

  Always read the requirement first as this enables you to **focus on the detail of the question with the specific task in mind.**

  For computational questions:

  Highlight key numbers / information and key words in the question, scribble notes to yourself on the question paper to remember key points in your answer.

Jot down proformas required if applicable.

For written questions:

Take notice of the format required (e.g. letter, memo, notes) and identify the recipient of the answer . You need to do this to judge the level of financial sophistication required in your answer and whether the use of a formal reply or informal bullet points would be satisfactory.

Plan your beginning, middle and end and the key areas to be addressed and your use of titles and sub-titles to enhance your answer.

- You should not use this time to read **section A**. There will be too much to read and you will achieve little form this.

For all questions:

Spot the easy marks to be gained in a question and parts which can be performed independently of the rest of the question. For example, writing down due dates of payment of tax, due dates for making elections, laying out basic proformas correctly.

Make sure that you do these parts first when you tackle the question.

Don't go overboard in terms of planning time on any one question – you need a good measure of the whole paper and a plan for all of the questions at the end of the 20 minutes.

By covering all questions you can often help yourself as you may find that facts in one question may remind you of things you should put into your answer relating to a different question.

- With your plan of attack in mind, **start answering your chosen question** with your plan to hand, as soon as you are allowed to start.

DETAILED SYLLABUS

The detailed syllabus and study guide written by the CIMA can be found at:

www.cimaglobal.com

APPROACH TO REVISION

QUESTION PRACTICE IS THE KEY TO SUCCESS

Success in professional examinations relies upon you acquiring a firm grasp of the required knowledge at the tuition phase. In order to be able to do the questions, knowledge is essential.

However, the difference between success and failure often hinges on your exam technique on the day and making the most of the revision phase of your studies.

The **Study Text** is the starting point, designed to provide the underpinning knowledge to tackle all questions. However, in the revision phase, pouring over text books is not the answer.

The **online fixed tests** help you consolidate your knowledge and understanding and are a useful tool to check whether you can remember key topic areas.

Revision cards are designed to help you quickly revise a topic area, however you then need to practice questions. There is a need to progress to full exam standard questions as soon as possible, and to tie your exam technique and technical knowledge together.

The importance of question practice cannot be over-emphasised.

The recommended approach below is designed by expert tutors in the field, in conjunction with their knowledge of the examiner and their recent real exams.

The approach taken for the fundamental papers is to revise by topic area. However, with the professional stage papers, a multi topic approach is required to answer the scenario based questions.

You need to practice as many questions as possible in the time you have left.

OUR AIM

Our aim is to get you to the stage where you can attempt exam standard questions confidently, to time, in a closed book environment, with no supplementary help (i.e. to simulate the real examination experience).

Practising your exam technique on real past examination questions, in timed conditions, is also vitally important for you to assess your progress and identify areas of weakness that may need more attention in the final run up to the examination.

In order to achieve this we recognise that initially you may feel the need to practice some questions with open book help and exceed the required time.

The approach below shows you which questions you should use to build up to coping with exam standard question practice, and references to the sources of information available should you need to revisit a topic area in more detail.

Remember that in the real examination, all you have to do is:

- attempt all questions required by the exam

- only spend the allotted time on each question, and

- get them at least 50% right!

Try and practice this approach on every question you attempt from now to the real exam.

EXAMINER COMMENTS

From looking at the post-exam guidance, the common mistakes are as follows :

- misallocation of time;

- running out of time ;

- showing signs of spending too much time on an earlier questions and clearly rushing the answer to a subsequent question;

- Not relating the answer to the scenario / context of the question.

Good exam technique is vital.

THE P1 REVISION PLAN

Stage 1: Assess areas of strengths and weaknesses

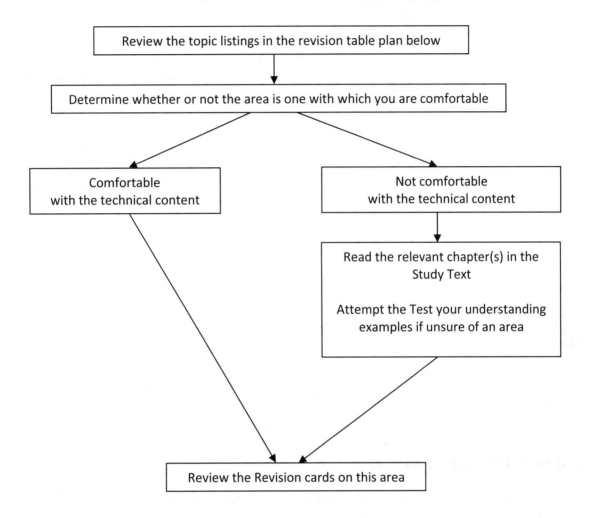

Stage 2: Practice questions

Follow the order of revision of topics as recommended in the revision table plan below and attempt the questions in the order suggested.

Try to avoid referring to text books and notes and the model answer until you have completed your attempt.

Try to answer the question in the allotted time.

Review your attempt with the model answer and assess how much of the answer you achieved in the allocated exam time.

Fill in the self-assessment box below and decide on your best course of action.

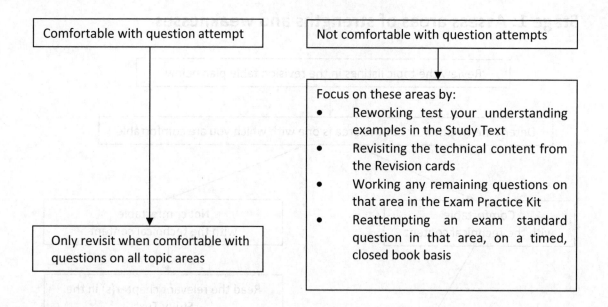

Comfortable with question attempt	Not comfortable with question attempts

Focus on these areas by:
- Reworking test your understanding examples in the Study Text
- Revisiting the technical content from the Revision cards
- Working any remaining questions on that area in the Exam Practice Kit
- Reattempting an exam standard question in that area, on a timed, closed book basis

Only revisit when comfortable with questions on all topic areas

Note that :

 The "footsteps questions" give guidance on exam techniques and how you should have approached the question.

Stage 3: Final pre-exam revision

We recommend that you **attempt at least one three hour mock examination** containing a set of previously unseen exam standard questions.

It is important that you get a feel for the breadth of coverage of a real exam without advanced knowledge of the topic areas covered – just as you will expect to see on the real exam day.

Ideally a mock examination offered by your tuition provider should be sat in timed, closed book, real exam conditions.

THE DETAILED REVISION PLAN

Topic	Study Text Chapter	Questions to attempt	Tutor guidance	Date attempted	Self assessment
Traditional costing	2	262	A lot of this chapter should be familiar to students. The subject matter will form the basis of other questions on areas such as throughput and activity based accounting. Break even principles have been popular in past exams so it is important that you are comfortable with that area.		
Production systems	3	205 206	The areas in this chapter should be no more than a five mark discursive question. Key areas are JIT and TQM.		
Throughput accounting	4	204	Throughput accounting is reasonably straight forward provided you understand the basics of costing from chapter 2 and how to calculate throughput. It is a popular question for students in the exam, but, as the question choice suggests, it is more likely to be examined in section A or B than in section C.		
Activity based accounting	5	198 261	Any long form question on ABC is likely to start with an absorption costing calculation so ensure you are happy with chapter 2 before proceeding onto this topic.		

Topic	Study Text Chapter	Questions to attempt	Tutor guidance	Date attempted	Self assessment
Variances	6 to 8	211 267 268	Variances are a regularly examined area. You need to be comfortable with the basics (Q211), but at this level questions are likely to include either planning variances (Q267) or mix and yield variances (Q268).		
Budgeting	9 to 11	227 232 272	The discursive elements of budgeting as well as forecasting and functional budgets are likely to be limited to sections A and B. Cash budgets (a topic covered again in chapter 17) can become a compulsory section C question. They have a standard technique that you should get comfortable with (see the walkthrough in question 272).		
Uncertainty and risk	12	236 296	In this area you need to be comfortable with drawing decision trees. You also need to be aware that any section C question is likely to involve a sub-requirement on information. But in all section C questions there are likely to be 'easy' marks for criticising the principles of expected values and this is something you should spend some time learning off. Question 296 covers all of this well and you should begin with this question before attempting any other section C questions.		

Topic	Study Text Chapter	Questions to attempt	Tutor guidance	Date attempted	Self assessment
Basic investment appraisal	13	234	It is vital that you master all the techniques on this chapter before proceeding to the next chapter. This chapter (and in particular basic NPV techniques) will give you the skills to pick up the easier marks in the tough questions that follow. Practice as many section A questions as possible to fine tune the techniques that will be required in chapter 14.		
Advanced investment appraisal	14	276 278 281	In dealing with these advanced questions it will be important that you have a proforma that you set up very early in your answer and that you can deal well with areas such as WDA's. Build up your revision by attempting a question with no tax or inflation (Q277), one with tax (Q278), and finally one with tax and inflation (Q281).		
Working capital management	15-18	248 251 257 299	The key here is to understand the balance between profitability (which can come from having a high working capital balance) and liquidity (which comes from keeping working capital low). Question 299 covers all of these areas very well and contains a tutor walkthrough.		

Topic	Study Text Chapter	Questions to attempt	Tutor guidance	Date attempted	Self assessment
Short-term finance and investments	19	246 253 255 305	This is mainly a discursive area that should be a straightforward way to finish your revision. It is probably more likely to appear in sections A or B, but question 305 should be attempted as preparation for a section C question.		

Note that not all of the questions are referred to in the programme above. We have recommended an approach to build up from the basic to exam standard questions.

We have not recommended any **section A** questions as you should attempt as many of these as possible. You should set yourself regular 10 question tests from random chapters. It is better to do, say, every fifth question rather than every question in order as this will test your adaptability better. When you attempt section A questions make sure that you audit the answer – determine why you got it wrong, spot the 'trick' that threw you off, and try to learn from the experience so that you do not repeat the mistake in the future. You will see that in the real exam a lot of the section A questions are similar to those contained in this exam practice kit. Therefore the more you attempt as part of your revision, the higher your recognition rate will be on the day of the exam. You may find that you are attempting questions on the day (albeit with different numbers) which are very similar to ones that you practiced as part of your revision.

The remaining questions are available in the kit for extra practice for those who require more question on some areas.

MATHS TABLES AND FORMULAE

PRESENT VALUE TABLE

Present value of £1, i.e. $(1 - r)^{-n}$ where r = interest rate; n = number of periods until payment or receipt.

Periods (n)	Interest rates (r)									
	1%	2%	3%	4%	5%	6%	7%	8%	9%	10%
1	0.990	0.980	0.971	0.962	0.952	0.943	0.935	0.926	0.917	0.909
2	0.980	0.961	0.943	0.925	0.907	0.890	0.873	0.857	0.842	0.826
3	0.971	0.942	0.915	0.889	0.864	0.840	0.816	0.794	0.772	0.751
4	0.961	0.924	0.888	0.855	0.823	0.792	0.763	0.735	0.708	0.683
5	0.951	0.906	0.863	0.822	0.784	0.747	0.713	0.681	0.650	0.621
6	0.942	0.888	0.837	0.790	0.746	0705	0.666	0.630	0.596	0.564
7	0.933	0.871	0.813	0.760	0.711	0.665	0.623	0.583	0.547	0.513
8	0.923	0.853	0.789	0.731	0.677	0.627	0.582	0.540	0.502	0.467
9	0.914	0.837	0.766	0.703	0.645	0.592	0.544	0.500	0.460	0.424
10	0.905	0.820	0.744	0.676	0.614	0.558	0.508	0.463	0.422	0.386
11	0.896	0.804	0.722	0.650	0.585	0.527	0.475	0.429	0.388	0.350
12	0.887	0.788	0.701	0.625	0.557	0.497	0.444	0.397	0.356	0.319
13	0.879	0.773	0.681	0.601	0.530	0.469	0.415	0.368	0.326	0.290
14	0.870	0.758	0.661	0.577	0.505	0.442	0.388	0.340	0.299	0.263
15	0.861	0.743	0.642	0.555	0.481	0.417	0.362	0.315	0.275	0.239
16	0.853	0.728	0.623	0.534	0.458	0.394	0.339	0.292	0.252	0.218
17	0.844	0.714	0.605	0.513	0.436	0.371	0.317	0.270	0.231	0.198
18	0.836	0.700	0.587	0.494	0.416	0.350	0.296	0.250	0.212	0.180
19	0.828	0.686	0.570	0.475	0.396	0.331	0.277	0.232	0.194	0.164
20	0.820	0.673	0.554	0.456	0.377	0.312	0.258	0.215	0.178	0.149

Periods (n)	Interest rates (r)									
	11%	12%	13%	14%	15%	16%	17%	18%	19%	20%
1	0.901	0.893	0.885	0.877	0.870	0.862	0.855	0.847	0.840	0.833
2	0.812	0.797	0.783	0.769	0.756	0.743	0.731	0.718	0.706	0.694
3	0.731	0.712	0.693	0.675	0.658	0.641	0.624	0.609	0.593	0.579
4	0.659	0.636	0.613	0.592	0.572	0.552	0.534	0.516	0.499	0.482
5	0.593	0.567	0.543	0.519	0.497	0.476	0.456	0.437	0.419	0.402
6	0.535	0.507	0.480	0.456	0.432	0.410	0.390	0.370	0.352	0.335
7	0.482	0.452	0.425	0.400	0.376	0.354	0.333	0.314	0.296	0.279
8	0.434	0.404	0.376	0.351	0.327	0.305	0.285	0.266	0.249	0.233
9	0.391	0.361	0.333	0.308	0.284	0.263	0.243	0.225	0.209	0.194
10	0.352	0.322	0.295	0.270	0.247	0.227	0.208	0.191	0.176	0.162
11	0.317	0.287	0.261	0.237	0.215	0.195	0.178	0.162	0.148	0.135
12	0.286	0.257	0.231	0.208	0.187	0.168	0.152	0.137	0.124	0.112
13	0.258	0.229	0.204	0.182	0.163	0.145	0.130	0.116	0.104	0.093
14	0.232	0.205	0.181	0.160	0.141	0.125	0.111	0.099	0.088	0.078
15	0.209	0.183	0.160	0.140	0.123	0.108	0.095	0.084	0.079	0.065
16	0.188	0.163	0.141	0.123	0.107	0.093	0.081	0.071	0.062	0.054
17	0.170	0.146	0.125	0.108	0.093	0.080	0.069	0.060	0.052	0.045
18	0.153	0.130	0.111	0.095	0.081	0.069	0.059	0.051	0.044	0.038
19	0.138	0.116	0.098	0.083	0.070	0.060	0.051	0.043	0.037	0.031
20	0.124	0.104	0.087	0.073	0.061	0.051	0.043	0.037	0.031	0.026

CUMULATIVE PRESENT VALUE OF £1

This table shows the present value of £1 per annum, receivable or payable at the end of each year for n years $\dfrac{1-(1+r)^{-n}}{r}$

Periods (n)	Interest rates (r)									
	1%	2%	3%	4%	5%	6%	7%	8%	9%	10%
1	0.990	0.980	0.971	0.962	0.952	0.943	0.935	0.926	0.917	0.909
2	1.970	1.942	1.913	1.886	1.859	1.833	1.808	1.783	1.759	1.736
3	2.941	2.884	2.829	2.775	2.723	2.673	2.624	2.577	2.531	2.487
4	3.902	3.808	3.717	3.630	3.546	3.465	3.387	3.312	3.240	3.170
5	4.853	4.713	4.580	4.452	4.329	4.212	4.100	3.993	3.890	3.791
6	5.795	5.601	5.417	5.242	5.076	4.917	4.767	4.623	4.486	4.355
7	6.728	6.472	6.230	6.002	5.786	5.582	5.389	5.206	5.033	4.868
8	7.652	7.325	7.020	6.733	6.463	6.210	5.971	5.747	5.535	5.335
9	8.566	8.162	7.786	7.435	7.108	6.802	6.515	6.247	5.995	5.759
10	9.471	8.983	8.530	8.111	7.722	7.360	7.024	6.710	6.418	6.145
11	10.368	9.787	9.253	8.760	8.306	7.887	7.499	7.139	6.805	6.495
12	11.255	10.575	9.954	9.385	8.863	8.384	7.943	7.536	7.161	6.814
13	12.134	11.348	10.635	9.986	9.394	8.853	8.358	7.904	7.487	7.103
14	13.004	12.106	11.296	10.563	9.899	9.295	8.745	8.244	7.786	7.367
15	13.865	12.849	11.938	11.118	10.380	9.712	9.108	8.559	8.061	7.606
16	14.718	13.578	12.561	11.652	10.838	10.106	9.447	8.851	8.313	7.824
17	15.562	14.292	13.166	12.166	11.274	10.477	9.763	9.122	8.544	8.022
18	16.398	14.992	13.754	12.659	11.690	10.828	10.059	9.372	8.756	8.201
19	17.226	15.679	14.324	13.134	12.085	11.158	10.336	9.604	8.950	8.365
20	18.046	16.351	14.878	13.590	12.462	11.470	10.594	9.818	9.129	8.514

Periods (n)	Interest rates (r)									
	11%	12%	13%	14%	15%	16%	17%	18%	19%	20%
1	0.901	0.893	0.885	0.877	0.870	0.862	0.855	0.847	0.840	0.833
2	1.713	1.690	1.668	1.647	1.626	1.605	1.585	1.566	1.547	1.528
3	2.444	2.402	2.361	2.322	2.283	2.246	2.210	2.174	2.140	2.106
4	3.102	3.037	2.974	2.914	2.855	2.798	2.743	2.690	2.639	2.589
5	3.696	3.605	3.517	3.433	3.352	3.274	3.199	3.127	3.058	2.991
6	4.231	4.111	3.998	3.889	3.784	3.685	3.589	3.498	3.410	3.326
7	4.712	4.564	4.423	4.288	4.160	4.039	3.922	3.812	3.706	3.605
8	5.146	4.968	4.799	4.639	4.487	4.344	4.207	4.078	3.954	3.837
9	5.537	5.328	5.132	4.946	4.772	4.607	4.451	4.303	4.163	4.031
10	5.889	5.650	5.426	5.216	5.019	4.833	4.659	4.494	4.339	4.192
11	6.207	5.938	5.687	5.453	5.234	5.029	4.836	4.656	4.486	4.327
12	6.492	6.194	5.918	5.660	5.421	5.197	4.988	7.793	4.611	4.439
13	6.750	6.424	6.122	5.842	5.583	5.342	5.118	4.910	4.715	4.533
14	6.982	6.628	6.302	6.002	5.724	5.468	5.229	5.008	4.802	4.611
15	7.191	6.811	6.462	6.142	5.847	5.575	5.324	5.092	4.876	4.675
16	7.379	6.974	6.604	6.265	5.954	5.668	5.405	5.162	4.938	4.730
17	7.549	7.120	6.729	6.373	6.047	5.749	5.475	5.222	4.990	4.775
18	7.702	7.250	6.840	6.467	6.128	5.818	5.534	5.273	5.033	4.812
19	7.839	7.366	6.938	6.550	6.198	5.877	5.584	5.316	5.070	4.843
20	7.963	7.469	7.025	6.623	6.259	5.929	5.628	5.353	5.101	4.870

FORMULAE

Probability

$A \cup B$ = A or B
$A \cap B$ = A and B (overlap)
$P(B/A)$ = probability of B, given A

Rules of addition

If A and B are mutually exclusive: $P(A \cup B) = P(A) + P(B)$
If A and B are not mutually exclusive: $P(A \cup B) = P(A) + P(B) - P(A \cap B)$

Rules of multiplication

If A and B are independent: $P(A \cap B) = P(A) \times P(B)$
If A and B are not independent: $P(A \cap B) = P(A) \times P(B/A)$

$E(x)$ $= \sum (\text{probability} \times \text{payoff})$

Quadratic equations

If $ax^2 + bx + c = 0$ is the general quadratic equation, the two solutions (roots) are given by:

$$x = \frac{-b \pm \sqrt{b^2 - 4ac}}{2a}$$

Descriptive statistics

Arithmetic mean

$$\bar{x} = \frac{\sum x}{n} \qquad \bar{x} = \frac{\sum fx}{\sum f} \text{ (frequency distribution)}$$

Standard deviation

$$SD = \sqrt{\frac{\sum (x - \bar{x})^2}{n}} \qquad SD = \sqrt{\frac{\sum fx^2}{\sum f} - \bar{x}^2} \text{ (frequency distribution)}$$

Index numbers

Price relative $= 100 \times P_1/P_0$
Quantity relative $= 100 \times Q_1/Q_0$

Price: $\quad \dfrac{\sum w \times \left(\dfrac{P_1}{P_0} \right)}{\sum w} \times 100$

Quantity: $\quad \dfrac{\sum w \times \left(\dfrac{Q_1}{Q_0} \right)}{\sum w} \times 100$

Time series

Additive model

Series = Trend + Seasonal + Random

Multiplicative model

Series = Trend $\times$ Seasonal $\times$ Random

Linear regression and correlation

The linear regression equation of y on x is given by:

$$y = a + bx \text{ or } y - \bar{y} = b(x - \bar{x})$$

where

$$b = \frac{\text{Covariance}(xy)}{\text{Variance}(x)} = \frac{n \sum xy - (\sum x)(\sum y)}{n \sum x^2 - (\sum x)^2}$$

and

$$a = \bar{y} - b\bar{x}$$

or solve

$$\sum y = na + b \sum x$$

$$\sum xy = a \sum x + b \sum x^2$$

Coefficient of correlation

$$r = \frac{\text{Covariance}(xy)}{\sqrt{\text{Var}(x)\,\text{Var}(y)}} = \frac{n\sum xy - (\sum x)(\sum y)}{\sqrt{\{n\sum x^2 - (\sum x)^2\}\{n\sum y^2 - (\sum y)^2\}}}$$

$$R(\text{rank}) = 1 - \frac{6\sum d^2}{n(n^2 - 1)}$$

Financial mathematics

Compound interest (values and sums)

Future value S, of a sum of X, invested for n periods, compounded at r% interest:

$$S = X\,[1+r]^n$$

Annuity

Present value of an annuity of £1 per annum receivable or payable for n years, commencing in one year, discounted at r% per annum:

$$PV = \frac{1}{r}\left[1 - \frac{1}{[1+r]^n}\right]$$

Perpetuity

Present value of £1 per annum, payable or receivable in perpetuity, commencing in one year, discounted at r% per annum:

$$PV = \frac{1}{r}$$

Section 1

SECTION A-TYPE QUESTIONS

All questions in this section carry two marks each, unless otherwise stated.

COST ACCOUNTING SYSTEMS

1   A business reported a marginal costing profit of $45,000 last period. Its inventory values for the period were as follows:

	$
Opening inventory	16,000
Closing inventory	20,800

If the business had used absorption costing, the inventory values would have been as follows:

	$
Opening inventory	28,000
Closing inventory	36,400

What would have been the reported profit using absorption costing?

A $41,400

B $48,600

C $57,000

D $60,600

2   A company has a budget to produce 5,000 units of Product B in December. The budget for December shows that, for Product B, the opening inventory will be 400 units and the closing inventory will be 900 units. The monthly budgeted production cost data for Product B for December is as follows:

Variable direct costs per unit	$6.00
Variable production overhead costs per unit	$3.50
Total fixed production overhead costs	$29,500

The company absorbs overheads on the basis of the budgeted number of units produced.

The budgeted profit for Product B for December, using **absorption costing**, is:

A $2,950 lower than it would be using marginal costing

B $2,950 greater than it would be using marginal costing

C $4,700 lower than it would be using marginal costing

D $4,700 greater than it would be using marginal costing.

3 A company operates a standard absorption costing system. The budgeted fixed production overheads for the company for the latest year were $330,000 and budgeted output was 220,000 units. At the end of the company's financial year the total of the fixed production overheads debited to the Fixed Production Overhead Control Account was $260,000 and the actual output achieved was 200,000 units.

The under / over absorption of overheads was

A $40,000 over absorbed

B $40,000 under absorbed

C $70,000 over absorbed

D $70,000 under absorbed

4 Company B uses a throughput accounting system. The details of product X per unit are as follows:

Selling price	€50
Material cost	€16
Conversion costs	€20
Time on bottleneck resource	8 minutes

The return per hour for product X is:

A   €105

B   €225

C   €255

D   €375

5 A company produces two products, S and T, which pass through two production processes, X and Y. The time taken to make each product in each process is:

	Product S	Product T
Process X	5 mins	7.5 mins
Process Y	18 mins	12 mins

The company operates a 15-hour day and have an average downtime each day of:

Process X	1.5 hours
Process Y	1.0 hours

The costs and revenue for each unit of each product are:

	Product S	Product T
	$	$
Direct materials	20.00	20.00
Direct labour	18.00	14.00
Variable overhead	4.00	4.00
Fixed costs	5.00	4.00
Total cost	47.00	42.00
Selling price	$95.00	$85.00

Sales demand restricts the output of S and T to 50 and 80 units a day respectively.

(a)   Identify which of the processes is the bottleneck process.   **(2 marks)**

(b)   Determine the daily production plan that would maximise the throughput contribution.   **(3 marks)**

(Total: 5 marks)

6   **What is defined as 'an activity within an organisation which has a lower capacity than preceding or subsequent activities, thereby limiting throughput'?**

A   Bottleneck

B   Constraint

C   Limiting factor

D   Restraint

7   **A company can produce many types of product but is currently restricted by the number of labour hours available on a particular machine. At present this limitation is set at 12,000 hours per annum. One type of product requires materials costing $5 which are then converted to a final product that sells for $12. Each unit of this product takes 45 minutes to produce on the machine. The conversion costs for the factory are estimated to be $144,000 per annum.**

Calculate the throughput accounting ratio for this product and state the significance of the result.   **(3 marks)**

The following data relate to Questions 8 and 9.

A manufacturing company recorded the following costs in October for Product X:

	$
Direct materials	20,000
Direct labour	6,300
Variable production overhead	4,700
Fixed production overhead	19,750
Variable selling costs	4,500
Fixed distribution costs	16,800
Total costs incurred for Product X	72,050

During October 4,000 units of Product X were produced but only 3,600 units were sold. At the beginning of October there was no inventory.

8 **The value of the inventory of Product X at the end of October using marginal costing was:**

A $3,080

B $3,100

C $3,550

D $5,075

9 **The value of the inventory of Product X at the end of October using throughput accounting was:**

A $630

B $1,080

C $1,100

D $2,000

The following data relate to Questions 10 and 11.

The following data relate to a manufacturing company. At the beginning of August there was no inventory. During August 2,000 units of Product X were produced, but only 1,750 units were sold. The financial data for Product X for August were as follows:

	$
Materials	40,000
Labour	12,600
Variable production overheads	9,400
Fixed production overheads	22,500
Variable selling costs	6,000
Fixed selling costs	19,300
Total costs for X for August	109,800

10   The value of inventory of X at 31 August using a marginal costing approach is:

A $6,575

B $7,750

C $8,500

D $10,562

11   The value of inventory of X at 31 August using a throughput accounting approach is:

A $5,000

B $6,175

C $6,575

D $13,725

The following data relate to Questions 12 to 14.

SM makes two products, Z1 and Z2. Its machines can only work on one product at a time. The two products are worked on in two departments by differing grades of labour. The labour requirements for the two products are as follows:

	Minutes per unit of product	
	Z1	Z2
Department 1	12	16
Department 2	20	15

The current selling prices and costs for the two products are shown below:

	Z1	Z2
	$ per unit	$ per unit
Selling price	50.00	65.00
Direct materials	10.00	15.00
Direct labour	10.40	6.20
Variable overheads	6.40	9.20
Fixed overheads	12.80	18.40
	———	———
Profit per unit	10.40	16.20

There is currently a shortage of labour and the maximum times available each day in Departments 1 and 2 are 480 minutes and 840 minutes, respectively.

As part of the budget-setting process, SM needs to know the optimum output levels. All output is sold.

---

12   Calculate the maximum number of each product that could be produced each day, and identify the limiting factor/bottleneck.   **(3 marks)**

13   Using traditional contribution analysis, calculate the 'profit-maximising' output each day, and the contribution at this level of output.   **(3 marks)**

14   Using a throughput approach, calculate the 'throughput-maximising' output each day, and the 'throughput contribution' at this level of output.   **(3 marks)**

15 A business manufactures a single product which sells for $45 per unit. The budgeted data for the latest period are as follows:

Production and sales volume	2,000 units
	$
Material cost	13,500
Direct labour cost	11,800
Production overhead	32,400
Non-production overhead	21,900

Actual production volume and costs were as budgeted for the period but the actual sales volume achieved was 1,800 units. There was no inventory at the beginning of the period. Calculate the profit for the period using:

(a) absorption costing **(2 marks)**

(b) marginal costing **(2 marks)**

(c) throughput accounting. **(2 marks)**

(Total: 6 marks)

16 A company has budgeted breakeven sales revenue of $800,000 and fixed costs of $320,000 for the next period.

The sales revenue needed to achieve a profit of $50,000 in the period would be:

A $850,000

B $925,000

C $1,120,000

D $1,200,000

17 A food-processing company operates an activity based costing (ABC) system. Which of the following would be classified as a facility-sustaining activity?

(i) General staff administration

(ii) Plant management

(iii) Technical support for individual products and services

(iv) Updating of product specification database

(v) Property management

A (i) and (ii)

B (i), (ii) and (v)

C (ii), (iii) and (iv)

D (ii), (iii), (iv) and (v)

E All of them

18 **P operates an activity based costing (ABC) system to attribute its overhead costs to cost objects.**

In its budget for the year ending 31 August 20X6, the company expected to place a total of 2,895 purchase orders at a total cost of $110,010. This activity and its related costs were budgeted to occur at a constant rate throughout the budget year, which is divided into 13 four-week periods.

During the four-week period ended 30 June 20X6, a total of 210 purchase orders were placed at a cost of $7,650.

The over-recovery of these costs for the four-week period was:

A $330

B $350

C $370

D $390

19 **Which of the following statements are correct?**

(i)   A cost driver is any factor that causes a change in the cost of an activity.

(ii)   For long-term variable overhead costs, the cost driver will be the volume of activity.

(iii) Traditional absorption costing tends to under-allocate overhead costs to low-volume products.

A   (i) and (iii) only

B   (ii) and (iii) only

C   (i) and (ii) only

D   (i), (ii) and (iii)

The following data relate to Questions 20 and 21.

DRP has recently introduced an Activity Based Costing system. It manufactures three products:

	Product D	Product R	Product P
Budgeted annual production (units)	100,000	100,000	50,000
Batch size (units)	100	50	25
Machine set-ups per batch	3	4	6
Purchase orders per batch	2	1	1
Processing time per unit (minutes)	2	3	3

Three cost pools have been identified. Their budgeted costs for 20X4 are as follows:

Machine set-up costs $150,000

Purchasing of materials $70,000

Processing $80,000

---

20   Calculate the annual budgeted number of:

(a)   batches

(b)   machine set-ups

(c)   purchase orders

(d)   processing minutes.   **(4 marks)**

21   Calculate the budgeted overhead unit cost for Product R for inclusion in the budget for 20X4.

                                                                                              (4 marks)

22   Explain in less than 50 words, why the costs absorbed by a product using an activity based costing approach could be higher than those absorbed if a traditional labour-based absorption system were used, and identify TWO implications of this for management.

                                                                                              (4 marks)

23   Which of the following statements about JIT is correct?

A   JIT protects an organisation against risks of disruption in the supply chain.

B   A narrow geographical spread in a business makes JIT more difficult to apply.

C   With JIT, there is a risk that stocks could become obsolete.

D   JIT is more difficult to implement when it is not easy to predict patterns of demand.

24   Which feature distinguishes backflush accounting from other systems?

A   Costs are attached when output is completed or sold.

B   Cost records reflect the flow of work through the production process.

C   Entries are not made until the customer pays for goods purchased.

D   Material entries are made when the material is received and moved.

25   Which of the following are aspects of a successful JIT system?

(i)   Demand-driven production

(ii)   Savings in total machine set-up time

(iii)   Grouping machines or workers by product or component rather than by the type of work performed

A   (i) only

B   (i) and (ii) only

C   (i) and (iii) only

D   (ii) and (iii) only

26   T uses a standard labour hour rate to charge its overheads to its clients' work. During the last annual reporting period production overheads were under-absorbed by $19,250. The anticipated standard labour hours for the period were 38,000 hours while the standard hours actually charged to clients were 38,500. The actual production overheads incurred in the period were $481,250.

The budgeted production overheads for the period were:

A $456,000

B $462,000

C $475,000

D   None of the above

27   In the context of quality costs, training costs and reworking costs are classified as:

	Training costs	Reworking costs
A	internal failure costs	external failure costs
B	prevention costs	external failure costs
C	external failure costs	internal failure costs
D	prevention costs	internal failure costs

28   Summary results for Y Limited for March are shown below:

	$000	Units
Sales revenue	820	
Variable production costs	300	
Variable selling costs	105	
Fixed production costs	180	
Fixed selling costs	110	
Production in March		1,000
Opening inventory		0
Closing inventory		150

Using *marginal costing*, the profit for March was:

A $170,000

B $185,750

C $197,000

D $229,250

29   Two CIMA definitions follow:

(1)   A system that converts a production schedule into a listing of the materials and components required to meet that schedule so that adequate inventory levels are maintained and items are available when needed.

(2)   An accounting-oriented information system, generally software-driven, which aids in identifying and planning the enterprise-wide resources needed to resource, make, account for and deliver customer orders.

Which of the following pairs of terms matches the definitions?

	Definition 1	Definition 2
A	Material requirements planning	Enterprise resource planning
B	Manufacturing resource planning	Material requirements planning
C	Material requirements planning	Manufacturing resource planning
D	Manufacturing resource planning	Enterprise resource planning

30   Which of the following statements is/are true?

(i)   Computer-integrated manufacturing (CIM) brings together advanced manufacturing technology and modern quality control into a single computerised coherent system.

(ii)   Flexible manufacturing systems (FMS) are simple systems with low levels of automation that offer great flexibility through a skilled workforce working in teams.

(iii)   Electronic data interchange (EDI) is primarily designed to allow the operating units in an organisation to communicate immediately and automatically with the sales and purchasing functions within the organisation.

A   (i) only

B   (i) and (ii) only

C   (i) and (iii) only

D   (ii) and (iii) only

31   Definition 1: 'A system that converts a production schedule into a listing of materials and components required to meet the schedule so that items are available when needed.'

Definition 2: 'An accounting system that focuses on ways by which the maximum return per unit of bottleneck activity can be achieved.'

Which of the following pairs of terms correctly matches definitions 1 and 2 above?

	Definition 1	Definition 2
A	Manufacturing resources planning (MRP2)	Backflush accounting
B	Material requirements planning (MRP1)	Throughput accounting
C	Material requirements planning (MRP1)	Theory of constraints
D	Supply chain management	Throughput accounting

32 **Which of the following statements is/are true?**

(i) Enterprise Resource Planning (ERP) systems use complex computer systems, usually comprehensive databases, to provide plans for every aspect of a business.

(ii) Flexible Manufacturing Systems (FMS) are simple systems with low levels of automation that offer great flexibility through a skilled workforce working in teams.

(iii) Just-in-time (JIT) purchasing requires the purchasing of large quantities of inventory items so that they are available immediately when they are needed in the production process.

A (i) only

B (i) and (ii) only

C (i) and (iii) only

D (ii) and (iii) only

33 **Overheads will always be over-absorbed when:**

A actual output is higher than budgeted output

B actual overheads incurred are higher than the amount absorbed

C actual overheads incurred are lower than the amount absorbed

D budgeted overheads are lower than the overheads absorbed.

34 **Which of the following definitions are correct?**

(i) Just-in-time (JIT) systems are designed to produce or procure products or components as they are required for a customer or for use, rather than for inventory.

(ii) Flexible manufacturing systems (FMS) are integrated, computer-controlled production systems, capable of producing any of a range of parts and of switching quickly and economically between them.

(iii) Material requirements planning (MRP) systems are computer-based systems that integrate all aspects of a business so that the planning and scheduling of production ensures components are available when needed.

A (i) only

B (i) and (ii) only

C (i) and (iii) only

D (ii) and (iii) only

35 WTD Ltd produces a single product. The management currently uses marginal costing but is considering using absorption costing in the future.

The budgeted fixed production overheads for the period are $500,000. The budgeted output for the period is 2,000 units. There were 800 units of opening inventory at the beginning of the period and 500 units of closing inventory at the end of the period.

If absorption costing principles were applied, the profit for the period compared to the marginal costing profit would be:

A $75,000 higher

B $75,000 lower

C $125,000 higher

D $125,000 lower

36 S Ltd manufactures three products, A, B and C. The products use a series of different machines but there is a common machine, P, that is a bottleneck.

The selling price and standard cost for each product for the forthcoming year is as follows:

	A	B	C
	$	$	$
Selling price	200	150	150
Direct materials	41	20	30
Conversion costs	55	40	66
Machine P – minutes	12	10	7

Calculate the return per hour for each of the products.   **(4 marks)**

37 X Ltd has two production departments, Assembly and Finishing, and two service departments, Stores and Maintenance.

Stores provides the following service to the production departments: 60% to Assembly and 40% to Finishing.

Maintenance provides the following service to the production and service departments: 40% to Assembly, 45% to Finishing and 15% to Stores.

The budgeted information for the year is as follows:

Budgeted fixed production overheads
Assembly	$100,000
Finishing	$150,000
Stores	$50,000
Maintenance	$40,000

Budgeted output   100,000 units

At the end of the year after apportioning the service department overheads, the total fixed production overheads debited to the Assembly department's fixed production overhead control account were $180,000.

The actual output achieved was 120,000 units.

Calculate the under-/over-absorption of fixed production overheads for the Assembly department.   **(4 marks)**

STANDARD COSTING

38 The materials price variance for the month of January was $2,000 (F) and the usage variance was $450 (F). The standard material usage per unit is 6 kg, and the standard material price is $3.00 per kg. 600 units were produced in the period and there was no change in inventory levels during the period.

Material purchases in the period were:

A 2,000 kg

B 2,933 kg

C 3,450 kg

D 3,600 kg

The following data relate to Questions 39 and 40.

X40 is one of many items produced by the manufacturing division. Its standard cost is based on estimated production of 10,000 units per month. The standard cost schedule for one unit of X40 shows that 2 hours of direct labour are required at $15 per labour hour. The variable overhead rate is $6 per direct labour hour. During April, 11,000 units were produced; 24,000 direct labour hours were worked and charged; $336,000 was spent on direct labour; and $180,000 was spent on variable overheads.

39 The direct labour rate variance for April is:

A $20,000 Favourable

B $22,000 Favourable

C $24,000 Adverse

D $24,000 Favourable

40 The variable overhead efficiency variance for April is:

A $12,000 Adverse

B $12,000 Favourable

C $15,000 Adverse

D $15,000 Favourable

41 Which of the following best describes a basic standard?

A A standard set at an ideal level, which makes no allowance for normal losses, waste and machine downtime.

B A standard which assumes an efficient level of operation, but which includes allowances for factors such as normal loss, waste and machine downtime.

C A standard which is kept unchanged over a period of time.

D A standard which is based on current price levels.

The following data relate to Questions 42 and 43.

X Ltd operates a standard costing system and absorbs fixed overheads on the basis of machine hours. Details of budgeted and actual figures are as follows:

	Budget	Actual
Fixed overheads	$2,500,000	$2,010,000
Output	500,000 units	440,000 units
Machine hours	1,000,000 hours	900,000 hours

42 **The fixed overhead expenditure variance is**

A $190,000 favourable

B $250,000 adverse

C $300,000 adverse

D $490,000 favourable

43 **The fixed overhead volume variance is**

A $190,000 favourable

B $250,000 adverse

C $300,000 adverse

D $490,000 favourable)

44 **Y has set the current budget for operating costs for its delivery vehicles, using the formula described below. Analysis has shown that the relationship between miles driven and total monthly vehicle operating costs is described in the following formula:**

$$y = \$800 + \$0.0002x^2$$

where

y is the total monthly operating cost of the vehicles, and

x is the number of miles driven each month

The budget for vehicle operating costs needs to be adjusted for expected inflation in vehicle operating costs of 3%, which is not included in the relationship shown above.

The delivery mileage for September was 4,100 miles, and the total actual vehicle operating costs for September were $5,000.

The total vehicle operating cost variance for September was closest to:

A $713 Adverse

B $737 Adverse

C $777 Adverse

D $838 Adverse

45 The CIMA official definition of the 'variable production overhead efficiency variance' is set out below with two blank sections.

'Measures the difference between the variable overhead cost budget flexed on _____ and the variable overhead cost absorbed by _____ .'

Which combination of phrases correctly completes the definition?

	Blank 1	Blank 2
A	actual labour hours	budgeted output
B	standard labour hours	budgeted output
C	actual labour hours	output produced
D	standard labour hours	output produced

46 **P has the following budget and actual data:**

Budget fixed overhead cost	$170,000
Budget production (units)	42,500
Actual fixed overhead cost	$182,000
Actual production (units)	40,000

The fixed overhead volume variance is:

A $7,500 (A)

B $10,000 (A)

C $10,000 (F)

D $7,500 (F)

47 **R uses a standard costing system and has the following labour cost standard in relation to one of its products:**

10 hours skilled labour at $9.50 per hour = $95.00

During March 20X9, 6,200 of these products were made which was 250 units less than budgeted. The labour cost incurred was $596,412 and the number of direct labour hours worked was 62,890. The direct labour variances for the month were:

	Rate	Efficiency
A	$1,043 (F)	$8,900 (A)
B	$7,412 (F)	$8,455 (A)
C	$1,043 (F)	$8,455 (A)
D	$7,412 (F)	$8,900 (A)

48 L uses a standard costing system. The standard cost card for one of its products shows that the product should use 6 kgs of material P per finished unit, and that the standard price per kg is $6.75. L values its inventory of materials at standard prices.

During November 20X1, when the budgeted production level was 2,000 units, 2,192 units were made. The actual quantity of material P used was 13,050 kgs and material L inventories were reduced by 500 kgs. The cost of the material L which was purchased was $72,900.

The material price and usage variances for November 20X1 were:

	Price	Usage
A	15,185.50 (F)	450.00 (F)
B	11,812.50 (F)	688.50 (F)
C	15,187.50 (F)	450.00 (A)
D	11,812.50 (F)	688.50 (A)

The following data relate to Questions 49 and 50.

Trafalgar budgets to produce 10,000 units of product D12, each requiring 45 minutes of labour. Labour is charged at $20 per hour, and variable overheads at $15 per labour hour. During September, 11,000 units were produced. 8,000 hours of labour were paid at a total cost of $168,000. Variable overheads in September amounted to $132,000.

49 What is the labour efficiency variance for September?

A $5,000 Adverse

B $5,000 Favourable

C $5,250 Favourable

D $10,000 Adverse

50 What is the variable overhead expenditure variance for September?

A $3,750 Favourable

B $,125 Favourable

C $12,000 Adverse

D $12,000 Favourable

51 Operation B, in a factory, has a standard time of 15 minutes. The standard rate of pay for operatives is $10 per hour. The budget for a period was based on carrying out the operation 350 times. It was subsequently realised that the standard time for Operation B included in the budget did not incorporate expected time savings from the use of new machinery from the start of the period. The standard time should have been reduced to 12 minutes.

Operation B was actually carried out 370 times in the period in a total of 80 hours. The operatives were paid $850.

The operational labour efficiency variance was:

A $60 adverse

B $75 favourable

C $100 adverse

D $125 adverse

52 The fixed overhead volume variance is defined as:

A   the difference between the budgeted value of the fixed overheads and the standard fixed overheads absorbed by actual production

B   the difference between the standard fixed overhead cost specified for the production achieved, and the actual fixed overhead cost incurred

C   the difference between budgeted and actual fixed overhead expenditure

D   the difference between the standard fixed overhead cost specified in the original budget and the same volume of fixed overheads, but at the actual prices incurred

53 A company operates a standard absorption costing system. The following fixed production overhead data are available for the latest period:

Budgeted Output	300,000 units
Budgeted Fixed Production Overhead	$1,500,000
Actual Fixed Production Overhead	$1,950,000
Fixed Production Overhead Total Variance	$150,000 adverse

The actual level of production for the period was nearest to:

A   277,000 units

B   324,000 units

C   360,000 units

D   420,000 units

The following data relate to Questions 54 and 55.

Z sells PCs that it purchases through a regional distributor. An extract from its budget for the 4-week period ended 28 March 20X8 shows that it planned to sell 600 PCs at a unit price of $500, which would give a contribution to sales ratio of 25%.

Actual sales were 642 PCs at an average selling price of $465. The actual contribution to sales ratio averaged 20%.

54   The sales price variance (to the nearest $1) was:

      A $22,470   (F)

      B $1,470   (A)

      C $1,470   (F)

      D $22,470   (A)

55   The sales volume contribution variance (to the nearest $1) was:

      A $5,050   (F)

      B $5,150   (F)

      C $5,250   (F)

      D $5,350   (F)

The following data relate to Questions 56 and 57.

SW manufactures a product known as the TRD100 by mixing two materials. The standard material cost per unit of the TRD100 is as follows:

				$
Material X	12 litres	@	$2.50	30
Material Y	18 litres	@	$3.00	54

In October 20X3, the actual mix used was 984 litres of X and 1,230 litres of Y. The actual output was 72 units of TRD100.

56   Calculate the total material mix variance for October 20X3.   (3 marks)

57   Calculate the total material yield variance for October 20X3.   (3 marks)

The following data relate to Questions 58 and 59.

A cleaning material, X2, is manufactured by mixing three materials. Standard cost details of the product are as follows.

Cost per batch of 10 litres of X2

				$
Material C	6 litres	@	$3	18
Material D	3 litres	@	$1	3
Material E	1 litre	@	$5	5
	10			26

In the latest period, the actual mix used was 200 litres of C, 75 litres of D and 25 litres of E. The output achieved was 280 litres of cleaning material X2.

58 **Using the average valuation basis, calculate the material mix variance for each material and in total.** **(4 marks)**

59 **Calculate the total material yield variance.**

60 **A company has a process in which the standard mix for producing 9 litres of output is as follows:**

	$
4.0 litres of D at $9 per litre	36.00
3.5 litres of E at $5 per litre	17.50
2.5 litres of F at $2 per litre	5.00
	58.50

A standard loss of 10% of inputs is expected to occur. The actual inputs for the latest period were:

	$
4,300 litres of D at $9.00 per litre	38,700
3,600 litres of E at $5.50 per litre	19,800
2,100 litres of F at $2.20 per litre	4,620
	63,120

Actual output for this period was 9,100 litres.

Calculate:

(a) the total materials mix variance **(2 marks)**

(b) the total materials yield variance. **(2 marks)**

(Total: 4 marks)

61 Which of the following events would help to explain an adverse material usage variance?

(i) The standard allowance for material wastage was set too high.

(ii) Material purchased was of a lower quality than standard.

(iii) Lower grade and less experienced employees were used than standard.

(iv) More material was purchased than budgeted for the period because output was higher than budgeted.

A (i), (ii) and (iii) only

B (ii), (iii) and (iv) only

C (ii) and (iii) only

D (ii) and (iv) only

62 Which of the following is the most likely to result in an adverse variable overhead efficiency variance?

A Higher bonus payments to employees than standard

B Less experienced employees were used than standard

C The use of more expensive, higher quality materials than standard

D Machine power costs per hour were higher than standard

63 PQR Ltd operates a standard absorption costing system. Details of budgeted and actual figures are as follows:

	Budget	Actual
Sales volume (units)	100,000	110,000
Selling price per unit	$10	$9.50
Variable cost per unit	$5	$5.25
Total cost per unit	$8	$8.30

(i) Calculate the sales price variance. **(2 marks)**

(ii) Calculate the sales volume profit variance. **(2 marks)**

(Total: 4 marks)

The following data relate to Questions 64 to 66.

The following data relate to Product Z and its raw material content for September:

Budget

Output	11,000 units of Z
Standard materials content	3 kg per unit at $4.00 per kg

Actual

Output	10,000 units of Z
Materials purchased and used	32,000 kg at $4.80 per kg

It has now been agreed that the standard price for the raw material purchased in September should have been $5 per kg.

---

64   The materials planning price variance for September was:

A $6,000 Adverse

B $30,000 Adverse

C $32,000 Adverse

D $33,000 Adverse

65   The materials operational usage variance for September was:

A $8,000 Adverse

B $9,600 Adverse

C $9,600 Favourable

D $10,000 Adverse

66   The materials operational price variance for September was:

A $6,000 Adverse

B $6,400 Favourable

C $30,000 Adverse

D $32,000 Adverse

67   A company manufactures a fruit flavoured drink concentrate by mixing two liquids (X and Y). The standard cost card for ten litres of the drink concentrate is:

			$
Liquid X	5 litres	@ $16 per litre	80
Liquid Y	6 litres	@ $25 per litre	150
	11 litres		230

The company does not hold any inventory. During the last period the company produced 4,800 litres of the drink concentrate. This was 200 litres below the budgeted output. The company purchased 2,200 litres of X for $18 per litre and 2,750 litres of Y for $21 per litre.

The materials mix variance for the period was:

A $150 adverse

B $450 adverse

C $6,480 favourable

D $6,900 favourable

The following data relate to Questions 68 and 69.

A company has a process in which three inputs are mixed together to produce Product S. The standard mix of inputs to produce 90 kg of Product S is shown below:

	$
50 kg of ingredient P at $75 per kg	3,750
30 kg of ingredient Q at $100 per kg	3,000
20 kg of ingredient R at $125 per kg	2,500
	─────
	9,250
	─────

During March 2,000 kg of ingredients were used to produce 1,910 kg of Product S. Details of the inputs are as follows:

	$
1,030 kg of ingredient P at $70 per kg	72,100
560 kg of ingredient Q at $106 per kg	59,360
410 kg of ingredient R at $135 per kg	55,350
	186,810

68 Calculate the materials mix variance for March. **(3 marks)**

69 Calculate the materials yield variance for March. **(3 marks)**

The following data relate to Questions 70 and 71.

Q plc uses standard costing. The details for April were as follows:

Budgeted output	15,000	units
Budgeted labour hours	60,000	hours
Budgeted labour cost	$540,000	
Actual output	14,650	units
Actual labour hours paid	61,500	hours
Productive labour hours	56,000	hours
Actual labour cost	$522,750	

70 Calculate the idle time variance for April.

71 Calculate the labour efficiency variance for April.

The following data relate to Questions 72 to 74.

A company uses standard absorption costing. The following information was recorded by the company for October:

	Budget	Actual
Output and sales (units)	8,700	8,200
Selling price per unit	£26	£31
Variable cost per unit	£10	£10
Total fixed overheads	$34,800	$37,000

72 **The sales price variance for October was:**

A $38,500 Favourable

B $41,000 Favourable

C $41,000 Adverse

D $65,600 Adverse

73 **The sales volume profit variance for October was:**

A $6,000 Adverse

B $6,000 Favourable

C $8,000 Adverse

D $8,000 Favourable

74 **The fixed overhead volume variance for October was:**

A $2,000 Adverse

B $2,200 Adverse

C $2,200 Favourable

D $4,200 Adverse

75 **The production volume ratio in a period was 95%.**

Which statement will always be true?

A   Actual hours worked exceeded the budgeted hours

B   Actual hours worked exceeded the standard hours of output

C   Budgeted hours exceeded the standard hours of output

D   Budgeted output was less than the actual output

76 PP Ltd operates a standard absorption costing system. The following information has been extracted from the standard cost card for one of its products:

Budgeted production	1,500 units
Direct material cost: 7 kg × $4.10	$28.70 per unit

Actual results for the period were as follows:

Production	1,600 units
Direct material (purchased and used): 12,000 kg	$52,200

It has subsequently been noted that, owing to a change in economic conditions, the best price that the material could have been purchased for was $4.50 per kg during the period.

(a) Calculate the material price planning variance.

(b) Calculate the operational material usage variance. **(4 marks)**

77 SS Ltd operates a standard marginal costing system. An extract from the standard cost card for the labour costs of one of its products is as follows:

Labour cost	
5 hours × $12	$60

Actual results for the period were as follows:

Production	11,500 units
Labour rate variance	$45,000 adverse
Labour efficiency variance	$30,000 adverse

Calculate the actual rate paid per direct labour hour. **(4 marks)**

BUDGETING

78 Which of the following can be identified as purposes of budgeting?

(i)   Communication

(ii)   Authorisation

(iii)   Sales maximisation

(iv)   Co-ordination

A   (ii) and (iv) only

B   (i) and (ii) only

C   (i), (ii) and (iv) only

D   All of them

79 **An incremental budgeting system is:**

A   a system which budgets only for the extra costs associated with a particular plan

B   a system which budgets for the variable manufacturing costs only

C   a system which prepares budgets only after the manager responsible has justified the continuation of the relevant activity

D   a system which prepares budgets by adjusting the previous year's values by expected changes in volumes of activity and price/inflation effects.

80 **EFG uses an Activity Based Budgeting system. It manufactures three products, budgeted details of which are set out below:**

	Product E	Product F	Product G
Budgeted annual production (units)	75,000	120,000	60,000
Batch size (units)	200	60	30
Machine set-ups per batch	5	3	9
Purchase orders per batch	4	2	2
Processing time per unit (minutes)	3	4	4

Three cost pools have been identified. Their budgeted costs for the year ending 30 September 20X3 are as follows:

Machine set-up costs	$180,000
Purchasing of materials	$95,000
Processing	$110,000

Calculate the budgeted machine set-up cost per unit of product F.   **(3 marks)**

The following data relate to Questions 81 and 82.

A division of LMN operates a fleet of minibuses that carries people and packages for other divisions.

In the year ended 31 October 20X3, it carried 4,420 people and 30,500 kgs of packages. It incurred costs of $850,000.

The division has found that 60% of its total costs are variable, and that 50% of these vary with the number of people and the other 50% varies with the weight of the packages.

The company is now preparing its budget for the three months ending 31 January 20X4 using an incremental budgeting approach. In this period it expects:

•   All prices to be 2% higher than the average paid in the year ended 31 October 20X3.

•   Efficiency levels to be unchanged.

•   Activity levels to be:

        –   1,150 people

        –   8,100 kgs of packages.

81 **The budgeted people-related cost (to the nearest $100) for the three months ending 31 January 20X4 is:**

A $55,300

B $6,400

C $66,300

D $67,700

82 **The budgeted package-related cost (to the nearest $100) for the three months ending 31 January 20X4 is:**

A $56,400

B $57,600

C $67,800

D $69,000

83 **The following details relate to product X in two accounting periods:**

Number of units	500	800
	$/unit	$/unit
Direct materials	2.00	2.00
Direct labour	1.50	1.50
Production overhead	2.50	1.75
Other overhead	1.00	0.625
	7.00	5.875

The fixed cost per period and variable cost per unit are:

	Period fixed cost	Variable cost/unit
	$	$
A	1,000	1.125
B	1,000	4.00
C	1,500	3.50
D	1,500	4.00

84 PP Ltd is preparing the production and material purchases budgets for one of their products, the SUPERX, for the forthcoming year.

The following information is available:

SUPERX

Sales demand (units)	30,000
Material usage per unit	7 kgs
Estimated opening inventory	3,500 units
Required closing inventory	35% higher than opening inventory

How many units of the SUPERX will need to be produced?

A 28,775

B 30,000

C 31,225

D 38,225

85 The following cost per unit details have been extracted from a production overhead cost budget:

Output (units)	6,000	10,000
Production overhead ($/unit)	3.20	3.00

The budget cost allowance for production overhead for an activity level of 7,350 units is:

A $20,505

B $21,765

C $22,845

D $23,515

86 Which of the following definitions best describes 'Zero-Based Budgeting'?

A A method of budgeting where an attempt is made to make the expenditure under each cost heading as close to zero as possible.

B A method of budgeting whereby all activities are re-evaluated each time a budget is formulated.

C A method of budgeting that recognises the difference between the behaviour of fixed and variable costs with respect to changes in output and the budget is designed to change appropriately with such fluctuations.

D A method of budgeting where the sum of revenues and expenditures in each budget centre must equal zero.

87 The overhead costs of RP have been found to be accurately represented by the formula:

$$y = \$10,000 + \$0.25x$$

where y is the monthly cost and x represents the activity level measured as the number of orders.

Monthly activity levels of orders may be estimated using a combined regression analysis and time series model:

$$a = 100,000 + 30b$$

where a represents the de-seasonalised monthly activity level and b represents the month number.

In month 240, the seasonal index value is 108.

Calculate the overhead cost for RP for month 240 to the nearest $1,000. **(3 marks)**

The following data relate to Questions 88 and 89.

H is forecasting its sales for next year using a combination of time series and regression analysis models. An analysis of past sales units has produced the following equation for the quarterly sales trend:

$$y = 26x + 8,850$$

where the value of x represents the quarterly accounting period and the value of y represents the quarterly sales trend in units. Quarter 1 of next year will have a value for x of 25.

The quarterly seasonal variations have been measured using the multiplicative (proportional) model and are:

Quarter 1   – 15%

Quarter 2   – 5%

Quarter 3   + 5%

Quarter 4   + 15%

Production is planned to occur at a constant rate throughout the year.

The company does not hold inventories at the end of any year.

---

88 The difference between the budgeted sales for quarter 1 and quarter 4 next year are:

    A   78 units

    B   2,850 units

    C   2,862 units

    D   2,940 units

89 The number of units to be produced in each quarter of next year will be nearest to:

    A   9,454 units

    B   9,493 units

    C   9,532 units

    D   9,543 units

90   Monthly sales of product R follow a linear trend of $y = 9.72 + 5.816x$, where y is the number of units sold and x is the number of the month. Monthly deviations from the trend follow an additive model.

The forecast number of units of product R to be sold in month 23, which has a seasonal factor of plus 6.5 is, to the nearest whole unit:

A   134

B   137

C   143

D   150

91   Nile is preparing its sales budget . Estimated sales are 120,000 units if the Summer is rainy, and 80,000 units if the Summer is dry. The probability of a dry Summer is 0.4.

What is the expected value for sales volume?

A   96,000 units

B   100,000 units

C   104,000 units

D   120,000 units

92   The budgeted total costs for two levels of output are as shown below:

Output	25,000 units	40,000 units
Total cost	$143,500	$194,000

Within this range of output it is known that the variable cost per unit is constant but fixed costs rise by $10,000 when output exceeds 35,000 units. Calculate for a budgeted output of 36,000 units:

(i)   the variable cost per unit and (ii) the total fixed costs.   **(3 marks)**

93   Which of the following best describes 'budgetary slack'?

A   The difference between what has been set as a budgetary objective and what has been achieved for the period.

B   The demotivating impact of a budgetary target that has been set too high.

C   The deliberate over-estimation of expenditure and/or under-estimation of revenues in the budgetary planning process.

D   Accumulated favourable variances reported against a specific item of budgeted expenditure.

94 A company is preparing its maintenance budget. The number of machine hours and maintenance costs for the past six months have been as follows:

Month	Machine hours	$
1	10,364	35,319
2	12,212	39,477
3	8,631	31,420
4	9,460	33,285
5	8,480	31,080
6	10,126	34,784

The budget cost allowance for an activity level of 9,340 machine hours, before any adjustment for price changes, is nearest to:

A $21,000

B $30,200

C $33,000

D $34,000

95 Z plc has found that it can estimate future sales using time series analysis and regression techniques. The following trend equation has been derived:

$$y = 25,000 + 6,500x$$

where

y is the total sales units per quarter

x is the time period reference number

Z has also derived the following set of seasonal variation index values for each quarter using a multiplicative (proportional) model:

Quarter 1   70

Quarter 2   90

Quarter 3   150

Quarter 4   90

Using the above model, calculate the forecast for sales units for the third quarter of year 7, assuming that the first quarter of year 1 is time period reference number 1.

96   A company is preparing its cash budget for February using the following data. One line in the cash budget is for purchases of a raw material, J. The opening inventory of J in January is expected to be 1,075 units. The price of J is expected to be $8 per unit. The company pays for purchases at the end of the month following delivery.

One unit of J is required in the production of each unit of Product 2, and J is only used in this product. Monthly sales of Product 2 are expected to be:

January	4,000 units
February	5,000 units
March	6,000 units

The opening inventory of Product 2 in January is expected to be 1,200 units.

The company implements the following inventory policies. At the end of each month the following amounts are held:

Raw materials: 25% of the requirement for the following month's production

Finished goods: 30% of the following month's sales

Calculate the value for purchases of J to be included in the cash budget for February.

(4 marks)

The following data relate to Questions 97 and 98.

K makes many products, one of which is Product Z. K is considering adopting an activity-based costing approach for setting its budget, in place of the current practice of absorbing overheads using direct labour hours. The main budget categories and cost driver details for the whole company for October are set out below, excluding direct material costs:

Budget category	$	Cost driver details
Direct labour	128,000	8,000 direct labour hours
Set-up costs	22,000	88 set-ups each month
Quality testing costs*	34,000	40 tests each month
Other overhead costs	32,000	Absorbed by direct labour hours

* A quality test is performed after every 75 units produced

The following data for Product Z is provided:

Direct materials	Budgeted cost of $21.50 per unit
Direct labour	Budgeted at 0.3 hours per unit
Batch size	30 units
Set-ups	2 set-ups per batch
Budgeted volume for October	150 units

---

97   Calculate the budgeted unit cost of Product Z for October assuming that a direct labour-based absorption method was used for all overheads.

98   Calculate the budgeted unit cost of Product Z for October using an activity-based costing approach.

(3 marks)

99 If the budgeted fixed costs increase, the gradient of the line plotted on the budgeted Profit/Volume (P/V) chart will:

A increase

B decrease

C not change

D become curvi-linear

100 XYZ Ltd is preparing the production budget for the next period. The total costs of production are a semi-variable cost. The following cost information has been collected in connection with production:

Volume (units)	Cost
4,500	$29,000
6,500	$33,000

The estimated total production costs for a production volume of 5,750 units is nearest to

A $29,200

B $30,000

C $31,500

D $32,500

101 A company uses time series and regression techniques to forecast future sales. It has derived a seasonal variation index to use with the multiplicative (proportional) seasonal variation model. The index values for the first three quarters are as follows:

Quarter	Index value
Q1	80
Q2	80
Q3	110

The index value for the fourth quarter (Q4) is:

A −270

B −269

C 110

D 130

102 **RF Ltd is about to launch a new product in June 2007. The company has commissioned some market research to assist in sales forecasting. The resulting research and analysis established the following equation:**

$Y = A x^{0.6}$

Where Y is the cumulative sales units, A is the sales units in month 1, x is the month number.

June 2007 is Month 1. Sales in June 2007 will be 1,500 units.

Calculate the forecast sales volume for each of the months June, July and August 2007 and for that three month period in total.   **(4 marks)**

103 **A company has the following budgeted sales figures:**

Month 1 $90,000

Month 2 $105,000

Month 3 $120,000

Month 4 $108,000

80% of sales are on credit and the remainder are paid in cash. Credit customers paying within one month are given a discount of 1.5%. Credit customers normally pay within the following time frame:

Within 1 month   40% of credit sales

Within 2 months   70% of credit sales

Within 3 months   98% of credit sales

There is an expectation that 2% of credit sales will become irrecoverable (bad) debts.

Outstanding receivables at the beginning of month 1 includes $6,000 expected to be received in month 4.

Calculate the total receipts expected in month 4.   **(4 marks)**

104 **D plc operates a retail business. Purchases are sold at cost plus 25%. The management team is preparing the cash budget and has gathered the following data:**

1   The budgeted sales are as follows:

Month	$000
July	100
August	90
September	125
October	140

2   It is management policy to hold inventory at the end of each month which is sufficient to meet sales demand in the next half month. Sales are budgeted to occur evenly during each month.

3   Creditors are paid one month after the purchase has been made.

Calculate the entries for 'purchases' that will be shown in the cash budget for:

(i)   August

(ii)   September

(iii)   October   **(3 marks)**

105 S plc produces and sells three products, X, Y and Z. It has contracts to supply products X and Y, which will utilise all of the specific materials that are available to make these two products during the next period. The revenue these contracts will generate and the contribution to sales (C/S) ratios of products X and Y are as follows:

	Product X	Product Y
Revenue	$10 million	$20 million
C/S ratio	15%	10%

Product Z has a C/S ratio of 25%.

The total fixed costs of S plc are £5.5 million during the next period and management has budgeted to earn a profit of $2 million.

Calculate the revenue that needs to be generated by Product Z for S plc to achieve the budgeted profit. **(3 marks)**

106 A master budget comprises the:

A   budgeted income statement and budgeted cash flow only

B   budgeted income statement and budgeted balance sheet only

C   budgeted income statement and budgeted capital expenditure only

D   budgeted income statement, budgeted balance sheet and budgeted cash flow only

107 CJD Ltd manufactures plastic components for the car industry. The following budgeted information is available for three of its key plastic components:

	W $ per unit	X $ per unit	Y $ per unit
Selling price	200	183	175
Direct material	50	40	35
Direct labour	30	35	30
Units produced and sold	10,000	15,000	18,000

The total number of activities for each of the three products for the period is as follows:

Number of purchase requisitions	1,200	1,800	2,000
Number of set ups	240	260	300

Overhead costs have been analysed as follows:

Receiving/inspecting quality assurance	$1,400,000
Production scheduling/machine set up	$1,200,000

Calculate the budgeted profit per unit for each of the three products using activity-based budgeting. **(4 marks)**

108 S Company has been investigating the time taken to produce one of its products, and found that a 90% learning curve appears to be applicable. If the time taken for the first unit is 7 hours, the total time taken in hours for units 5 to 8 only is:

A   17.078

B   18.144

C   19.590

D   20.142

109 A company has recently completed the production of the first unit of a new product. The time taken for this was 12 minutes. The company expects that there will be a 75% learning rate for this product.

Calculate the total time expected to produce the first four units.

110 FH is an electronics company that has developed a new product for the video conferencing market. The product has successfully completed its testing phase and FH has now produced the first four production units. The first unit took three hours of labour time and the total time for the first four units was 8.3667 hours.

Calculate the learning curve improvement rate (rate of learning) to the nearest 0.1%.

(3 marks)

111 PT has discovered that, when it employs a new test engineer, there is a learning curve with a 75% rate of learning that exists for the first 12 customer assignments. A new test engineer completed her first customer assignment in 6 hours.

Calculate the time that she should take for her 7th assignment to the nearest 0.01 hours.

Note: The index for a 75% learning curve is −0.415.

112 Q Company has developed a new product, the QX9. The time taken to produce the first unit was 21 minutes. Assuming that a 80% learning curve applies, the time allowed for the sixth unit (to 2 decimal places) should be:

A   5.24 minutes

B   8.25 minutes

C   11.65 minutes

D   11.80 minutes

Note: For an 80% learning curve $y = ax^{-0.3219}$

FINANCIAL INFORMATION FOR LONG-TERM DECISION MAKING

113 A company is evaluating a new product proposal. The proposed product selling price is $220 per unit and the variable costs are $55 per unit. The incremental cash fixed costs for the product will be $190,000 per annum. The discounted cash flow calculations results in a positive NPV:

		Cash flow $	Discount rate	Present value $
Year 0	Initial outlay	(2,000,000)	1.000	(2,000,000)
Year 1–6	Annual cash flow	450,000	4.623	2,080,350
Year 6	Sale of assets	75,000	0.630	47,250
Net present value				127,600

What is the percentage change in selling price that would result in the project having a net present value of zero?

A   3.2%

B   4.6%

C   5.9%

D   7.0%

114 The details of an investment project are as follows:

Cost of asset bought at the start of the project	$80,000
Annual cash inflow	$25,000
Cost of capital, after tax	5% each year
Life of the project	8 years

Corporation tax is 25% and is paid in equal quarterly instalments in the 6th and 9th months of the year in which the profit was earned and in the 1st and 3rd months of the following year.

Writing down allowances of 20% reducing balance will be claimed each year.

(Assume the asset is bought on the first day of the tax year and that the company's other projects generate healthy profits.)

The present value of the cash flows that occur in the *second year* of the project is:

A $17,006

B $19,053

C $20,271

D $25,940

The following data relates to Questions 115 and 116.

A company is considering investing in a project that would have a four-year life span. The investment would involve an immediate cash outflow of $250,000 and have a zero residual value. In each of the four years, 6,000 units would be produced and sold. The contribution per unit, based on current prices, is $12. The company has an annual cost of capital of 10%. It is expected that the inflation rate will be 4% in each of the next four years.

115 **The net present value of the project (to the nearest $100) is:**

A $800

B $1,300

C $1,800

D $2,300

116 **If the annual inflation rate is now projected to be 6%, the maximum monetary cost of capital for this project to remain viable is (to the nearest 0.5%):**

A   11.0%

B   11.5%

C   12.0%

D   12.5%

117 **B Company is deciding whether to launch a new product. The initial outlay for the product is $60,000. The forecast possible annual cash inflows and their associated probabilities are shown below:**

	Probability	Year 1	Year 2	Year 3
Optimistic	0.25	$35,000	$40,000	$32,000
Most likely	0.55	$20,000	$26,000	$28,000
Pessimistic	0.20	$18,000	$24,000	$22,000

The company's cost of capital is 8% per annum.

Assume the cash inflows are received at the end of the year and that the cash inflows for each year are independent.

The expected net present value for the product is:

A   ($500)

B $8,634

C $10,189

D $12,348

The following data relates to Questions 118 and 119.

A company is considering investing in a manufacturing project that would have a three-year life span. The investment would involve an immediate cash outflow of $50,000 and have a zero residual value. In each of the three years, 4,000 units would be produced and sold. The contribution per unit, based on current prices, is $5. The company has an annual cost of capital of 8%. It is expected that the inflation rate will be 3% in each of the next three years.

118 The net present value of the project (to the nearest $500) is:

  A $4,500

  B $5,000

  C $5,500

  D $6,000

119 If the annual inflation rate is now projected to be 4%, the maximum monetary cost of capital for this project to remain viable is (to the nearest 0.5%):

  A   13.0%

  B   13.5%

  C   14.0%

  D   14.5%

The following data relates to Questions 120 and 121.

A company is carrying out sensitivity analysis on an investment project. The initial DCF analysis, at a cost of capital of 10%, is as follows:

Year	Item	Cash flow $	DF @ 10%	PV $
0	Cost of machine	(50,000)	1.000	(50,000)
1	Net cash flow from sales	22,000	0.909	19,998
2	Net cash flow from sales	22,000	0.826	18,172
3	Net cash flow from sales	10,000	0.751	7,510
3	Residual value of the machine	10,000	0.751	7,510
	NPV			+ 3,190

The investment is in a machine that will make a product, Product Q. Product Q will sell for $40 per unit, and will have a variable cost of $10 per unit. Annual sales will be 1,000 units in years 1 and 2, and 600 units in year 3. Additional fixed cost expenditure on cash items will be $8,000 each year.

The residual value of the machine will be 20% of the initial cost of the machine.

120 To the nearest 0.1%, by how much could the selling price per unit of the product fall short of the expected $40 without the project ceasing to be viable, given no change in any of the other cash flow estimates?

  A   3.6%

  B   6.0%

  C   6.1%

  D   7.0%

121 To the nearest $1,000, what is the maximum amount that the machine can cost, without the project ceasing to be viable, given no change in any of the other cash flow estimates?

    A $53,000

    B $54,000

    C $55,000

    D $56,000

122 A project has a net present value of $320,000.

The sales revenues for the project have a total pre-discounted value of $900,000 and a total present value of $630,000 after tax.

The sensitivity of the investment to changes in the value of sales is closest to:

    A $310,000

    B $580,000

    C   51%

    D   36%

The following data relates to Questions 123 and 124.

An education authority is considering the implementation of a CCTV (closed circuit television) security system in one of its schools.

Details of the proposed project are as follows:

Life of project	5 years
Initial cost	$75,000
Annual savings:	
Labour costs	$20,000
Other costs	$5,000
Cost of capital	15% per annum

123 Calculate the internal rate of return for this project.

124 Calculate the percentage change in the annual labour cost savings that could occur before the project ceased to be viable. **(3 marks)**

The following data relates to Questions 125 and 126.

CC Company is considering an investment of $300,000 which will earn a contribution of $40,000 each year for 10 years at today's prices. The contribution will rise at the rate of 6% per year because of inflation. The company's cost of money is 11% per annum.

125 Calculate the company's real cost of capital.

126 Calculate the net present value of the project.

127 The management accountant of Bar Company has estimated that the cash flows for Project X would be as follows:

Year	Investment $	Running costs $	Savings $
0	(120,000)		
1		(80,000)	150,000
2		(100,000)	160,000
3		(120,000)	170,000
4		(150,000)	180,000

The project has a positive NPV of $22,900 when discounted at the company's cost of capital, which is 20% per annum.

On reviewing the cost estimates, the management accountant decides that the running costs will in fact be 20% higher each year than originally estimated, although savings will be higher too.

Calculate the minimum percentage that annual savings must be higher than originally estimated for the project to remain viable.

(4 marks)

128 JAH Company is about to invest $400,000 in machinery and other capital equipment for a new product venture. Cash flows for the first three years are estimated as follows

Year	$000
1	210
2	240
3	320

JAH Company requires a 17% return for projects of this type. The above cash flows do not include expenditure on an advertising campaign, which will be incurred in equal annual amounts at the beginning of years 1, 2 and 3.

Ignoring any residual values of the capital equipment, calculate the maximum annual amount that can be spent on advertising, to the nearest $000.

(3 marks)

129 X Company takes on a five-year lease of a building for which it pays $27,200 as a lump sum payment. X Company then sub-lets the building for five years at a fixed annual rent, with the rent payable annually in arrears.

Calculate the annual rental charge, if the rent is set at a level that will earn a DCF yield of 17% for X Company.

130 A company is evaluating a new product proposal. The proposed product selling price is $180 per unit and the variable costs are $60 per unit. The incremental cash fixed costs for the product will be $160,000 per annum. The discounted cash flow calculation results in a positive NPV:

		Cash flow $	Discount rate	Present value $
Year 0	Initial outlay	(1,000,000)	1.000	(1,000,000)
Years 1–5	Annual cash flow	320,000	3.791	1,213,120
Year 5	Working capital released	50,000	0.621	31,050
Net present value				244,170

What is the percentage change in selling price that would result in the project having a net present value of zero?   **(4 marks)**

131 A company is considering investing in a project that requires an initial outflow of $500,000 and will generate expected cash inflows in terms of today's $ of $130,000 over each of the next four years. The company's monetary cost of capital is 7% and inflation is predicted to be 4% over the next four years.

Calculate the company's real cost of capital and the net present value of the project.
(4 marks)

132 The details of an investment project are:

Life of the project	10 years
Cost of asset bought at the start of the project	$100,000
Annual cash inflow	$20,000
Cost of capital, after tax	8% each year

Corporation tax is 30% and is paid in equal quarterly instalments in the 7th and 10th months of the year in which the profit was earned and in the 1st and 4th months of the following year.

Writing down allowances of 25% reducing balance will be claimed each year.

(Assume the asset is bought on the first day of the tax year and that the company's other projects generate healthy profits.)

(Round all cash flows to the nearest $ and discount end of year cash flows.)

Calculate the present value of the cash flows that occur in the second year of the project.
(4 marks)

133 An investment project that requires an initial investment of $500,000 has a residual value of $130,000 at the end of five years. The project's cash flows have been discounted at the company's cost of capital of 12% and the resulting net present value is $140,500. The profitability index of the project is closest to:

A   0.02

B   0.54

C   0.28

D   0.26

134 CC Company is considering an investment of $300,000 which will earn a contribution of $40,000 each year for 10 years at today's prices. The contribution will rise at the rate of 6% per year because of inflation. The company's cost of money is 11% per annum.

Calculate the net present value of the project. **(4 marks)**

135 A company has determined that the net present value of an investment project is $12,304 when using a 10% discount rate and $(3,216) when using a discount rate of 15%.

Calculate the internal rate of return of the project to the nearest 1%.

136 A five-year project has a net present value of $160,000 when it is discounted at 12%. The project includes an annual cash outflow of $50,000 for each of the five years. No tax is payable on projects of this type.

The percentage increase in the value of this annual cash outflow that would make the project no longer financially viable is closest to:

A 64%

B 89%

C 113%

D 156%

The following data relates to Questions 137 and 138.

An investment project with no residual value has a net present value of $87,980 when it is discounted using a cost of capital of 10%. The annual cash flows are as follows:

Year	$
0	(200,000)
1	80,000
2	90,000
3	100,000
4	60,000
5	40,000

137 Calculate the Accounting Rate of Return (ARR) of the project using the average investment value basis. **(2 marks)**

138 Calculate the Internal Rate of Return (IRR) of the project. **(3 marks)**

The following data relates to Questions 139 to 141.

M plc is evaluating three possible investment projects and uses a 10% discount rate to determine their net present values.

Investment	A	B	C
	$000	$000	$000
Initial investment	400	450	350
Incremental cash flows			
Year 1	100	130	50
Year 2	120	130	110
Year 3	140	130	130
Year 4	120	130	150
Year 5*	100	150	100
Net present value	39	55	48

* Includes $20,000 residual value for each investment project.

139 **Calculate the payback period of investment A.**

140 **Calculate the discounted payback period of investment B.** **(3 marks)**

141 **Calculate the Internal Rate of Return (IRR) of investment C.** **(3 marks)**

142 **X is considering the following five investments:**

Investment	J	K	L	M	N
	$000	$000	$000	$000	$000
Initial investment	400	350	450	500	600
Net present value	125	105	140	160	190

Investments J and L are mutually exclusive; all of the investments are divisible and none of them may be invested in more than once.

The optimum investment plan for X assuming that the funding available is limited to $1m is:

A $400,000 in J plus $600,000 in N

B $400,000 in M plus $600,000 in N

C $500,000 in M plus $500,000 in N

D $350,000 in K plus $600,000 in N plus $50,000 in M.

143 A company is considering an investment of $400,000 in new machinery. The machinery is expected to yield incremental profits over the next five years as follows:

Year	Profit ($)
1	175,000
2	225,000
3	340,000
4	165,000
5	125,000

Thereafter, no incremental profits are expected and the machinery will be sold. It is company policy to depreciate machinery on a straight line basis over the life of the asset. The machinery is expected to have a value of $50,000 at the end of year 5.

Calculate the payback period of the investment in this machinery to the nearest 0.1 years.

144 An investment company is considering the purchase of a commercial building at a cost of $0.85m. The property would be rented immediately to tenants at an annual rent of $80,000 payable in arrears in perpetuity.

Calculate the net present value of the investment assuming that the investment company's cost of capital is 8% per annum.

Ignore taxation and inflation.

THE TREATMENT OF UNCERTAINTY IN DECISION MAKING

The following data relates to Questions 145 and 146.

X Company can choose from five mutually exclusive projects. The projects will each last for one year only and their net cash inflows will be determined by the prevailing market conditions. The forecast annual cash inflows and their associated probabilities are shown below.

Market conditions	Poor	Good	Excellent
Probability	0.20	0.50	0.30
	$000	$000	$000
Project L	500	470	550
Project M	400	550	570
Project N	450	400	475
Project O	360	400	420
Project P	600	500	425

145 Based on the expected value of the net cash inflows, which project should be undertaken?

A   L

B   M

C   N

D   P

146 The value of perfect information about the state of the market is:

A   Nil

B $5,000

C $26,000

D $40,000

The following data relates to Questions 147 and 148.

P Company currently sells 90,000 units of product Y per annum. At this level of sales and output, the selling price and variable cost per unit are $50 and $21 respectively. The annual fixed costs are $1,200,000. The management team is considering lowering the selling price per unit to $45.

The estimated levels of demand at the new price, and the probabilities of them occurring, are:

Selling price of $45

Demand	Probability
100,000 units	0.45
120,000 units	0.55

It is thought that at either of the higher sales and production levels, the variable cost per unit, and the probability of it occurring, will be as follows:

Variable cost (per unit)	Probability
$20	0.40
$18	0.60

---

147 Calculate the probability that lowering the selling price to $45 per unit would increase profit.   (4 marks)

148 Calculate the expected value of the company profit if the selling price is reduced to $45 per unit.   (4 marks)

149 The daily demand for a perishable product has the following probability distribution:

Demand (units)	Probability
100	0.25
200	0.40
300	0.35

Each item costs $4 and is sold for $8. Unsold items are thrown away at the end of the day.

If orders must be placed before the daily demand is known, calculate how many units should be purchased at the beginning of each day in order to maximise expected profit?

(4 marks)

150 A company has estimated the selling prices and variable costs of one of its products as follows:

Selling price per unit		Variable cost per unit	
$	Probability	$	Probability
40	0.30	20	0.55
50	0.45	30	0.25
60	0.25	40	0.20

Given that the company will be able to supply 1,000 units of its product each week irrespective of the selling price, and that selling price and variable cost per unit are independent of each other, calculate the probability that the weekly contribution will exceed $20,000. **(4 marks)**

The following data relates to Questions 151 and 152.

A company expects to sell 1,000 units per month of a new product but there is uncertainty as to both the unit selling price and the unit variable cost of the product. The following estimates of selling price, variable costs and their related probabilities have been made:

Selling price		Unit variable cost	
$ per unit	Probability	$ per unit	Probability
20	25%	8	20%
25	40%	10	50%
30	35%	12	30%

There are specific fixed costs of $5,000 per month expected for the new product.

---

151 The expected value of monthly contribution is:

A $5,890

B $10,300

C $10,890

D $15,300

152 The probability of monthly contribution from this new product exceeding $13,500 is:

A   24.5%

B   30.5%

C   63.0%

D   92.5%

153 A baker is trying to decide the number of batches of a particular type of bread that he should bake each day. Daily demand ranges from 10 batches to 12 batches. Each batch of bread that is baked and sold yields a positive contribution of $50, but each batch of bread baked that is not sold yields a negative contribution of $20.

Assuming the baker adopts the *minimax regret* decision rule, calculate the number of batches of bread that he should bake each day. You must justify your answer.   **(4 marks)**

MANAGING SHORT TERM FINANCE

154 If an entity regularly fails to pay its suppliers by the normal due dates, it may lead to a number of problems:

(i)   having insufficient cash to settle trade payables

(ii)   difficulty in obtaining credit from new suppliers

(iii)   reduction in credit rating

(iv)   settlement of trade receivables may be delayed.

Which TWO of the above could arise as a result of exceeding suppliers' trade credit terms?

A   (i) and (ii)

B   (i) and (iii)

C   (ii) and (iii)

D   (iii) and (iv)

155 A conservative policy for financing working capital is one where short-term finance is used to fund:

A   all of the fluctuating current assets, but no part of the permanent current assets

B   all of the fluctuating current assets and part of the permanent current assets

C   part of the fluctuating current assets and part of the permanent current assets

D   part of the fluctuating current assets, but no part of the permanent current assets

156 ABC has produced the following sales forecast:

	$000
January	750
February	760
March	770
April	780
May	790
June	800

Currently 20% of customers pay in cash. Of the credit customers (excluding those who become irrecoverable debts), 60% pay in one month, 30% pay in two months and 10% in three months. Irrecoverable debts are 2%. This payment pattern is expected to continue.

What are the forecast cash receipts in April?   **(3 marks)**

157 If the current ratio for a company is equal to its acid test (that is, the quick ratio), then:

    A   the current ratio must be greater than one

    B   the company does not carry any inventory

    C   trade receivables plus cash is greater than trade payables minus inventory

    D   working capital is positive

158 In October, a company made credit purchases of $18,000 and credit sales of $24,000. All sales are made on the basis of cost plus 25%. By how much will working capital increase in October as a result of these transactions?

159 The following items have been extracted from a company's budget for next month:

	$
Sales on credit	240,000
Expected increase in inventory next month	20,000
Expected decrease in trade receivables next month	12,000

What is the budgeted receipt from trade receivables next month?   **(3 marks)**

160 DY had a balance outstanding on trade receivables at 30 September 20X6 of $68,000. Forecast credit sales for the next six months are $250,000 and customers are expected to return goods with a sales value of $2,500.

Based on past experience, within the next six months DY expects to collect $252,100 cash and to write off as irrecoverable debts 5% of the balance outstanding at 30 September 20X6.

Calculate DY's forecast trade receivables days outstanding at 31 March 20X7.   **(4 marks)**

161 A company has annual sales of $40 million, annual cost of sales of $30 million and makes annual purchases of $15 million. Its balance sheet includes among assets and liabilities the following:

Trade receivables	$4 million
Trade payables	$3 million
Inventory	$8 million

What is its cash conversion cycle?

    A   206.5 days

    B   60.8 days

    C   36.5 days

    D   97.3 days

162 XYZ's annual sales are $100m of which 95% are made on credit. Receivables at the beginning of the year were $10 million and at the end of the year total receivables were $12 million. 10% of receivables were non-trade related.

What is XYZ's average collection period?

A   36.5 days

B   40 days

C   38 days

D   46 days

163 DY's trade receivables balance at 1 April 2006 was $22,000. DY's income statement showed revenue from credit sales of $290,510 during the year ended 31 March 2007.

DY's trade receivables at 31 March 2007 were 49 days.

Assume DY's sales occur evenly throughout the year and that all balances outstanding at 1 April 2006 have been received.

Also, it should be assumed all sales are on credit, there were no irrecoverable debts and no trade discount was given.

How much cash did DY receive from its customers during the year to 31 March 2007?

A $268,510

B $273,510

C $312,510

D $351,510

164 The following items were extracted from a company's budget for next month:

	$
Purchases on credit	360,000
Expected decrease in inventory during the month	12,000
Expected increase in trade payables during the month	15,000

What is the budgeted payment to trade creditors for the month?

A $333,000

B $345,000

C $357,000

D $375,000

165 The trial balance of EH at 31 October 2007 showed trade receivables of $82,000 before adjustments.

On 1 November 2007 EH discovered that one of its customers had ceased trading and was very unlikely to pay any of its outstanding balance of $12,250.

On the same date EH carried out an assessment of the collectability of its other trade receivable balances. Using its knowledge of its customers and past experience EH determined that the remaining trade receivables had suffered a 3% impairment at 31 October 2007.

What is EH's balance of trade receivables, as at 31 October 2007?

A $66,202

B $67,290

C $67,657

D $79,540

166 EV had inventory days outstanding of 60 days and trade payables outstanding of 50 days at 31 October 2007.

EV's inventory balance at 1 November 2006 was $56,000 and trade payables were $42,000 at that date. EV's cost of goods sold comprises purchased goods cost only. During the year to 31 October 2007, EV's cost of goods sold was $350,000.

Assume purchases and sales accrue evenly throughout the year and use a 365-day year. Further assume that there were no goods returned to suppliers and EV claimed no discounts.

Calculate how much EV paid to its credit suppliers during the year to 31 October 2007.

(4 marks)

167 DX had the following balances in its trial balance at 30 September 20X6:

Trial balance extract at 30 September 20X6

	$000	$000
Revenue		2,400
Cost of sales	1,400	
Inventories	360	
Trade receivables	290	
Trade payables		190
Cash and cash equivalents	95	

Calculate the length of DX's working capital cycle at 30 September 20X6.   **(4 marks)**

168 An enterprise commenced business on 1 April 20X2. Revenue in April 20X2 was $20,000, but this is expected to increase at 2% a month. Credit sales amount to 60% of total sales. The credit period allowed is one month. Irrecoverable debts are expected to be 3% of credit sales, but other customers are expected to pay on time. Cash sales represent the other 40% of revenue.

How much cash is expected to be received in May 20X2?   **(3 marks)**

169 Which of the following is LEAST likely to characterise overtrading?

A   Increased borrowing

B   Increased cash balances

C   Increased turnover

D   Reduced working capital

170 An aged creditors analysis (aged trade payables analysis) is:

A   a listing of trade payables by date of invoicing

B   a listing of trade payables with whom you are in arrears

C   the proportion of purchases by value which are overdue

D   a breakdown of trade payables according to length of time elapsing since the purchase was made

171 FGH requires a rate of return of 12.85% each year.

Two of FGH's suppliers, P and Q, are offering the following terms for immediate cash settlement:

Supplier	Cash settlement discount	Normal settlement period
P	1%	1 month
Q	2%	2 months

Which of the discounts should be accepted to achieve the required rate of return?

A   The discounts offered by both P and Q

B   The discount offered by P only

C   The discount offered by Q only

D   Neither of them

172 WM's major supplier, INT, supplies electrical tools and is one of the largest companies in the industry, with international operations. Deliveries from INT are currently made monthly, and are constant throughout the year. Delivery and invoicing both occur in the last week of each month.

Details of the credit terms offered by INT are as follows:

Normal credit period	Cash discount	Average monthly purchases
40 days	2% for settlement in 10 days	$100,000

WM always takes advantage of the cash discount from INT.

Calculate the annual rate of interest (to two decimal places) implied in the cash discount offered by INT. Assume a 365-day year. **(3 marks)**

173 What are the three main services provided by a without recourse factor? **(3 marks)**

174   Invoice discounting normally involves:

A   offering a cash discount for early settlement of invoices

B   selling an invoice to a discount house at a profit

C   selling an individual invoice for cash to a factor organisation at a discount

D   writing off an invoice, partly or in total, as an irrecoverable debt

175   XYZ has $1 million to invest for one year. It can lock it away at a fixed rate of 7% for the full year, or invest at 6.5% for a three-month term, speculating on an increase in interest rates. Assume the rate available increases to 7.5% after three months and XYZ invests at this rate for the rest of the year.

By how much is XYZ better off from its gamble on interest rates?

A $2,500

B $12,836

C $73,414

D $3,414

176   After a bill of exchange has been accepted, there are a number of possible actions that the drawer could take.

Which ONE of the following is NOT a possible course of action?

A   Ask the customer for immediate payment

B   Discount the bill with a bank

C   Hold the bill until the due date and then present it for payment

D   Use the bill to settle a trade payable

177   The bank accepts the instrument drawn upon it by its customer, and then sells it into a secondary market at a discount, including a commission, passing the proceeds to its client. The bank then pays the bill at face value. Which description best describes this instrument?

A   A letter of credit

B   A forfaiting agreement

C   An acceptance credit

D   A commercial bill

178   Which of the following most appropriately describes forfaiting?

A   It is a method of providing medium-term export finance

B   It provides short-term finance for purchasing fixed assets which are denominated in a foreign currency

C   It provides long-term finance to importers

D   It is the forced surrender of a share due to the failure to make a payment on a partly paid share

179 List FOUR forms of short-term finance generally available to small entities.   **(4 marks)**

180 AL's customers all pay their accounts at the end of 30 days. To try and improve its cash flow, AL is considering offering all customers a 15% discount for payment within 14 days.

Calculate the implied annual (interest) cost to AL of offering the discount, using compound interest methodology and assuming a 365-day year.   **(3 marks)**

181 An entity's working capital financing policy is to finance working capital using short-term financing to fund all the fluctuating current assets as well as some of the permanent part of the current assets.

The above policy is an example of:

A   an aggressive policy

B   a conservative policy

C   a short-term policy

D   a moderate policy

182 BE has been offering 60-day payment terms to its customers, but now wants to improve its cash flow. BE is proposing to offer a 1.5% discount for payment within 20 days.

Assume a 365-day year and an invoice value of $1,000.

What is the effective annual interest rate that BE will incur for this action?   **(4 marks)**

183 The trade receivables ledger account for customer C shows the following entries:

		Debits	Credits
		$	$
Balance brought forward		0	
10 June X6	Invoice 201	345	
19 June X6	Invoice 225	520	
27 June X6	Invoice 241	150	
3 July X6	Receipt 1009 – Inv 201		200
10 July X6	Invoice 311	233	
4 August X6	Receipt 1122 – Inv 225		520
6 August X6	Invoice 392	197	
18 August X6	Invoice 420	231	
30 August X6	Receipt 1310 -- Inv 311		233
7 September X6	Invoice 556	319	
21 September X6	Receipt 1501 – Inv 392		197
30 September X6	Balance	845	

Prepare an aged analysis showing the outstanding balance on a monthly basis for customer C at 30 September 20X6.   **(4 marks)**

184 DR has the following balances under current assets and current liabilities:

Current assets	$
Inventory	50,000
Trade receivables	70,000
Bank	10,000

Current liabilities	$
Trade payables	88,000
Interest payable	7,000

DR's quick ratio is

A   0.80 : 1

B   0.84 : 1

C   0.91 : 1

D   1.37 : 1

185 SK sells bathroom fittings throughout the country in which it operates. In order to obtain the best price, it has decided to purchase all its annual demand of 10,000 shower units from a single supplier. RR has offered to provide the required number of showers each year under an exclusive long-term contract.

Demand for shower units is at a constant rate all year. The cost to SK of holding one shower unit in inventory for one year is $4 plus 3% of the purchase price.

RR is located only a few miles from the SK main showroom. It has offered to supply each shower unit at $400 with a transport charge of $200 per delivery. It has guaranteed such a regular and prompt delivery service that SK believes it will not be necessary to hold any safety inventory (that is, buffer inventory) if it uses RR as its supplier.

Using the economic order quantity model (EOQ model), calculate the optimal order size, assuming that RR is chosen as the sole supplier of shower units for SK.   **(3 marks)**

186 Which of the following would be LEAST likely to arise from the introduction of a Just-in-Time inventory ordering system?

A   Lower inventory holding costs

B   Less risk of inventory shortages

C   More frequent deliveries

D   Increased dependence on suppliers

187 Which of the following is LEAST relevant to the simple economic order quantity (EOQ) model for inventory?

A   Safety stock

B   Annual demand

C   Holding costs

D   Order costs

188   PB uses 2,500 units of component X per year. Its production director has calculated that the cost of placing and processing a purchase order for component X is $185, and the cost of holding one unit of component X for a year is $25.

What is the economic order quantity (EOQ) for component X and, assuming a 52-week year, what is the average frequency at which purchase orders should be placed?

	EOQ	*Frequency of orders*
A	136 units	3 weeks
B	136 units	6 weeks
C	192 units	4 weeks
D	192 units	5 weeks

189   Calculate the economic order quantity (EOQ) for the following item of inventory:

- quantity required per year 32,000 items
- order costs are $15 per order
- inventory holding costs are estimated at 3% of inventory value per year
- each unit currently costs $40.

190   The economic order quantity formula includes the cost of placing an order. However, the Management Accountant is unsure which of the following items would usually be included in 'cost of placing an order':

(i)   administrative costs

(ii)   postage

(iii)   quality control cost

(iv)   unit cost of products

(v)   storekeeper's salary.

Which THREE of the above would be regarded as part of the cost of placing an order?

A   (i), (ii) and (iii) only

B   (i), (iv) and (v) only

C   (ii), (iii) and (iv) only

D   (i), (ii) and (v) only

191   DS uses the Economic Order Quantity (EOQ) model. Demand for DS's product is 95,000 units per annum. Demand is evenly distributed throughout the year. The cost of placing an order is $15 and the cost of holding a unit of inventory for a year is $3.

How many orders should DS make in a year?   **(3 marks)**

192   A bond with a coupon rate of 7% is redeemable in eight years' time for $100. Its current purchase price is $82. What is the percentage yield to maturity?   **(4 marks)**

193 CX purchased $10,000 of unquoted bonds when they were issued by Z. CX now wishes to sell the bonds to B. The bonds have a coupon rate of 7% and will repay their face value at the end of five years. Similar bonds have a yield to maturity of 10%.

Calculate the current market price for the bonds. **(3 marks)**

194 A bond has a current market price of $83. It will repay its face value of $100 in 7 years' time and has a coupon rate of 4%.

If the bond is purchased at $83 and held, what is its yield to maturity?

(4 marks)

195 DK is considering investing in government bonds. The current price of a $100 bond with 10 years to maturity is $88. The bonds have a coupon rate of 6% and repay face value of $100 at the end of the 10 years.

Calculate the yield to maturity. **(4 marks)**

Section 2

SECTION B-TYPE QUESTIONS

COST ACCOUNTING SYSTEMS

196 MARGINAL COST PROFIT AND CASH FLOW

Briefly discuss the assertion that marginal costing profits are a better indicator of cash flow than absorption costing profits. **(5 marks)**

197 BACKFLUSH ACCOUNTING (SEP 10 EXAM)

Explain why a backflush cost accounting system may be considered more appropriate than a traditional cost accounting system, in a company that operates a just-in-time production and purchasing system.

(5 marks)

198 ACTIVITY BASED COSTING

The following information relates to the budget for the year ahead.

Production overhead cost budget

	£
Machinery costs	285,000
Set-up costs	235,000
Purchasing costs	300,000
Total production overheads	820,000

The following table shows the total budgeted activities of the company (it manufactures many different types of products) and the details relating to the manufacture of two product lines: S and T.

Data	Total	Product S	Product T
Machine hours	95,000	2 per unit	1 per unit
Number of production runs	235	20	5
Purchase orders	5,000	100	100
Production quantities of S & T		5,000 units	20,000 units

Calculate, using activity based costing, the production overhead costs that would be attributed to one unit of Product S and one unit of Product T. **(5 marks)**

199   OVER ABSORPTION (NOV 09 EXAM)

A new company, which manufactures only one type of product, had the following budget for its first year of business:

Production and sales   2,000 units

	$
Revenue	100,000
Variable production costs	30,000
Variable selling and administration costs	6,000
Fixed production overheads	40,000
Fixed selling and administration costs	10,000
Profit	14,000

The actual results for the year showed that 1,800 units were produced but only 1,700 units were sold. These were sold at the budgeted selling price. The fixed production overheads were $39,000. All of the other costs behaved as expected.

Calculate:

(i)   the under or over absorbed fixed production overheads

(ii)   the actual profit for the year using absorption costing

(iii)   the actual profit for the year using marginal costing

(5 marks)

200   IMPROVING THE THROUGHPUT ACCOUNTING RATIO

Management considers that the throughput accounting (TA) ratio for product C in relation to the labour-intensive packing process is unacceptably low. Explain three actions that could be considered to improve the TA ratio. **(5 marks)**

201   ABC AND PROFITABILITY

Explain the circumstances in which the use of activity based costing is likely to result in more meaningful information about product costs and profitability. **(5 marks)**

202   MANUFACTURING RESOURCE PLANNING SYSTEM (MAY 07 EXAM)

Briefly explain the role of a Manufacturing Resource Planning System in supporting a standard costing system. **(5 marks)**

203   JUST IN TIME (MAY 07 EXAM)

Briefly explain the main differences between the traditional manufacturing environment and a just-in-time manufacturing environment. **(5 marks)**

204 THROUGHPUT ACCOUNTING (NOV 08 EXAM)

Two of the products that are manufactured by a company use the same machines. The products (P1 and P2) are manufactured using two machines (M1 and M2). During the next period the time available on the machines are 126 hours for M1 and 195 hours for M2.

The company uses throughput accounting. Unit details of the two products are:

	P1	P2
	$	$
Selling price	36.00	39.00
Materials	14.20	16.75
Labour	6.00	7.50
Variable production overheads	1.00	1.25
Fixed production overheads	2.00	2.50
Profit	12.80	11.00

Any mix of output can be sold at the above prices and there is unlimited demand for each of the products.

The machine time needed to make one unit of the products is:

	P1	P2
M1	0.35 hours	0.40 hours
M2	0.60 hours	0.65 hours

(a) (i) Calculate the maximum production that is possible from each machine for each of the two products and state the bottleneck.

(ii) Calculate the throughput accounting ratio for each product.

(5 marks)

(b) Identify, using a throughput approach, the production plan for the next period that would result in the most profitable use of the machines. (All workings must be shown). **(5 marks)**

(Total: 10 marks)

205 MRP AND ABB (MAY 10 EXAM)

A medium-sized manufacturing company, which operates in the electronics industry, has employed a firm of consultants to carry out a review of the company's planning and control systems. The company presently uses a traditional incremental budgeting system and the inventory management system is based on economic order quantities (EOQ) and reorder levels. The company's normal production patterns have changed significantly over the previous few years as a result of increasing demand for customised products. This has resulted in shorter production runs and difficulties with production and resource planning.

The consultants have recommended the implementation of activity based budgeting and a manufacturing resource planning system to improve planning and resource management.

(a) Explain how a manufacturing resource planning system would improve the planning of purchases and production for the company. **(5 marks)**

(b) Explain the benefits for the company that could occur following the introduction of an activity based budgeting system. **(5 marks)**

206 TOTAL QUALITY MANAGEMENT (MAY 08 EXAM)

Describe THREE key features that are present in any organisation that is successfully focused on Total Quality Management (TQM). **(5 marks)**

207 MARGINAL AND ABSORPTION COSTING (MAY 06 EXAM)

A manufacturing company uses a standard costing system. Extracts from the budget for April are shown below:

Sales	1,400	units
Production	2,000	units
	$	
Direct costs	15	per unit
Variable overhead	4	per unit

The budgeted fixed production overhead costs for April were $12,800.

The budgeted profit using marginal costing for April was $5,700.

(i) Calculate the budgeted profit for April using absorption costing. **(3 marks)**

(ii) Briefly explain two situations where marginal costing is more useful to management than absorption costing. **(2 marks)**

(Total: 5 marks)

208 MARGINAL COSTING AND THROUGHPUT ACCOUNTING (MAY 06 EXAM)

Compare and contrast marginal costing and throughput accounting. **(5 marks)**

STANDARD COSTING

209 FIXED OVERHEAD VOLUME VARIANCE

Explain the meaning of the fixed production overhead volume variance and discuss briefly its usefulness to management. **(5 marks)**

210 LABOUR VARIANCES (NOV 05 EXAM)

A management consulting company had budgeted the staff requirements for a particular job as follows:

	$
40 hours of senior consultant at $100 per hour	4,000
60 hours of junior consultant at $60 per hour	3,600
Budgeted staff cost for job	7,600

The actual hours recorded were:

	$
50 hours of senior consultant at $100 per hour	5,000
55 hours of junior consultant at $60 per hour	3,300
Actual staff cost for job	8,300

The junior consultant reported that for 10 hours of the 55 hours recorded there was no work that she could do.

Calculate the following variances:

- idle time variance

- labour mix variance

- labour efficiency variance. **(5 marks)**

211 PLANNING AND OPERATING VARIANCES (MAY 07 EXAM)

A company uses variance analysis to monitor the performance of the team of workers which assembles Product M. Details of the budgeted and actual performance of the team for last period were as follows:

	Budget	Actual
Output of product M	600 units	680 units
Wage rate	$30 per hour	$32 per hour
Labour hours	900 hours	1,070 hours

It has now been established that the standard wage rate should have been $31.20 per hour.

(i) Calculate the labour rate planning variance and calculate the operational labour efficiency variance.

(ii) Explain the major benefit of analysing variances into planning and operational components. **(5 marks)**

212 STANDARD COSTING AND THE NEW MANAGEMENT ACCOUNTING

A company has adopted TQM and JIT in its recently automated manufacturing plant. Explain how the company's standard costing system will need to be adapted in the new environment. **(5 marks)**

213 RITZER'S MCDONALDIZATION MODEL

Explain the four dimensions in Ritzer's McDonaldization model, as applied to standard costing for services. **(5 marks)**

214 DIAGNOSTIC RELATED GROUPS

Explain how the use of diagnostic related groups enables standard costing to be applied in the healthcare industry. **(5 marks)**

215 MIX AND YIELD VARIANCES

Explain the meaning of the materials mix and yield variances and discuss briefly any limitations in their usefulness. **(5 marks)**

216 LABOUR RATE VARIANCE

State FIVE possible causes of an adverse labour rate variance. **(5 marks)**

217 INVESTIGATION OF VARIANCES (NOV 05 EXAM)

An analysis of past output has shown that batches have a mean weight of 90 kg and that the weights conform to the normal distribution with a standard deviation of 10 kg. The company has a policy to investigate variances that fall outside the range that includes 95% of outcomes. In September one sample batch weighed 110 kg.

(a) Calculate whether the material usage variance for this batch should be investigated according to the company policy described above. **(3 marks)**

(b) Discuss two other important factors that should be taken into account when deciding whether to investigate this variance. **(2 marks)**
(Total: 5 marks)

218 INVESTIGATION OF VARIANCES (2) (MAY 07 EXAM)

Briefly explain three factors that should be considered before deciding to investigate a variance. **(5 marks)**

219 BENCHMARKING

Explain benchmarking and how it can be used to improve an organisation's performance. **(5 marks)**

220 HOSPITAL CARE (MAY 06 EXAM)

The standard cost schedule for hospital care for a minor surgical procedure is shown below.

Standard cost of hospital care for a minor surgical procedure

Staff: patient ratio is 0.75:1

	$
Nursing costs: 2 days × 0.75 × $320 per day	480
Space and food costs: 2 days × $175 per day	350
Drugs and specific materials	115
Hospital overheads: 2 days × $110 per day	220
Total standard cost	**1,165**

The actual data for the hospital care for one patient having the minor surgical procedure showed that the patient stayed in hospital for three days. The cost of the drugs and specific materials for this patient was $320. There were 0.9 nurses per patient on duty during the time that the patient was in hospital. The daily rates for nursing pay, space and food, and hospital overheads were as expected.

Prepare a statement that reconciles the standard cost with the actual costs of hospital care for this patient. The statement should contain FIVE variances that will give useful information to the manager who is reviewing the cost of hospital care for minor surgical procedures. **(5 marks)**

221 C PLC (MAY 06 EXAM)

C plc uses a just-in-time (JIT) purchasing and production process to manufacture Product P. Data for the output of Product P, and the material usage and material price variances for February, March and April are shown below:

Month	Output (units)	Material usage variance		Material price variance	
February	11,000	$15,970	Adverse	$12,300	Favourable
March	5,100	$5,950	Adverse	$4,500	Favourable
April	9,100	$8,400	Adverse	$6,200	Favourable

The standard material cost per unit of Product P is $12.

Prepare a sketch (not on graph paper) of a percentage variance chart for material usage and for material price for Product P for the three-month period. (***Note:*** Your workings must show the co-ordinates of the points that would be plotted if the chart were drawn accurately.) **(5 marks)**

222 MODERN BUSINESS ENVIRONMENT (MAY 06 & MAY 07 EXAM)

Briefly discuss THREE reasons why standard costing may not be appropriate in a modern business environment. **(5 marks)**

BUDGETING

223 ZERO BASED BUDGETING (ZBB) (SEP 10 EXAM)

XY, a not-for-profit charity organisation which is funded by public donations, is concerned that it is not making the best use of its available funds. It has carried out a review of its budgeting system and is considering replacing the current system with a zero-based budgeting system.

Explain the potential advantages AND disadvantages for the charity of a zero-based budgeting system..   **(5 marks)**

224 PRODUCTION COST BUDGET (MAY 10 EXAM)

The production budgets for quarters 1 and 2 for a manufacturing company are as follows:

	Quarter 1	Quarter 2
Production (Units)	15,000	20,000
Budgeted production costs	$	$
Direct materials	180,000	240,000
Production labour	155,000	195,000
Production overheads	210,000	240,000

The cost structure, which is expected to continue unchanged in quarter 3, is as follows:

(i)   The variable cost elements are linear and vary in direct proportion to volume.

(ii)   There is a bulk purchase discount of 5% on materials if orders exceed $250,000 per quarter. The discount will apply to the purchase of all materials in that quarter.

(iii)   The company operates a JIT system for material purchases.

(iv)   Fixed production overheads will increase by $20,000 per quarter at production output levels in excess of 22,000 units in a quarter.

The budgeted production volume for quarter 3 is 23,000 units.

Prepare the production cost budget for quarter 3.   **(5 marks)**

225 J LIMITED (NOV 05 EXAM)

J Limited has recently been taken over by a much larger company. For many years the budgets in J have been set by adding an inflation adjustment to the previous year's budget. The new owners of J are insisting on a 'zero-based' approach when the next budget is set, as they believe many of the indirect costs in J are much higher than in other companies under their control.

(a)   Explain the main features of 'zero-based budgeting'.   **(2 marks)**

(b)   Discuss the problems that might arise when implementing this approach in J Limited.
                                                                                (3 marks)

                                                                        (Total: 5 marks)

226 ZBB (MAY 09 EXAM)

(a)   Explain how "zero based budgeting" can overcome the problems that are associated with "incremental budgeting".   **(5 marks)**

(b)   A management consulting company had set the budget for the staff requirements for a particular job as follows:

	£
50 hours of senior consultant at £120 per hour	6,000
90 hours of junior consultant at £80 per hour	7,200
Budgeted staff cost for job	13,200

The actual hours recorded were:

	£
60 hours of senior consultant at £130 per hour	7,800
90 hours of junior consultant at £75 per hour	6,750
Actual staff cost for job	14,550

The junior consultant reported that for 10 hours of the 90 hours he recorded there was no work that he could do.

(i)   Calculate the following variances:

- Idle time variance
- Labour mix variance   **(3 marks)**

(ii)   Explain the worth, or otherwise, of this company calculating the labour mix variance in this situation.   **(2 marks)**

(Total for sub-question (b) = 5 marks)

(c)   Explain the importance to management, for planning and control purposes, of the differing definitions of "variable" costs offered by traditional costing methods and activity based costing.   **(5 marks)**

(d)   A company budgeted to produce 400 units of a product in a period. The standard cost card of the product showed that the standard cost of the material used to manufacture each unit of the product was 6 kg costing £12 per kg.

The actual results for the period were that 380 units were produced from 2,500 kg of material which had cost £29,000.

It has now been realised that the standard material content per unit should have been 6.75 kg.

Calculate

- the materials usage planning variance
- the operational materials price variance
- the operational materials usage variance   **(5 marks)**

227   QR (SEP 10 EXAM)

QR uses an activity based budgeting (ABB) system to budget product costs. It manufactures two products, product Q and product R. The budget details for these two products for the forthcoming period are as follows:

	Product Q	Product R
Budgeted production (units)	80,000	120,000
Number of machine set ups per batch	4	2
Batch size (units)	5,000	4,000

The total budgeted cost of setting up the machines is $74,400.

Required:

(i)   **Calculate** the budgeted machine set up cost per unit of product Q.   **(3 marks)**

(ii)   **State** TWO potential benefits of using an activity based budgeting system.   **(2 marks)**

(Total: 5 marks)

228   MCDONALDIZATION AND BUDGETS (NOV 05 EXAM)

UV Limited is a catering company that provides meals for large events. It has a range of standard meals at fixed prices. It also provides meals to meet the exact requirements of a customer and prices for this service are negotiated individually with each customer.

Discuss how a 'McDonaldization' approach to service delivery would impact on budget preparation and control within UV Limited.   **(5 marks)**

229   ST PLC (NOV 05 EXAM)

ST plc is a medium-sized engineering company using advanced technology. It has just implemented an integrated enterprise resource planning (ERP) system in place of an old manufacturing resource planning (MRP) system.

Discuss the changes that are likely to be seen after the implementation of the ERP system in:

(a)   the budget-setting process; and

(b)   the budgetary control process.   **(5 marks)**

230 QBQ (NOV 07 EXAM)

The following data are given for sub-questions 216 (a) and 216 (b) below.

QBQ produces one type of product. Details of the budgeted sales and production are given below.

Selling price and costs per unit

	$
Selling price	40
Material FX: 1.5kg @ $6 per kg	9
Conversion costs (variable)	8
Fixed production overheads	15

The fixed production overhead absorption rate is based on annual production overheads of $720,000 and budgeted annual output of 48,000 units. The fixed overheads will be incurred evenly throughout the year.

The company also incurs fixed costs for administration of $200,000 per year.

Budgeted sales

Quarter	Units
1	10,000
2	12,000
3	14,000
4	12,000

Inventory

It has been decided that inventory levels are to be reduced. Details are as follows:

Finished goods: 5,500 units are currently held but it has been decided that the closing inventories for Quarters 1, 2 and 3 will be 45%, 40% and 35% of the following quarter's sales respectively.

Raw materials: 4,500 kg are currently held but it has been decided that the closing inventories for Quarters 1 and 2 will be 25% and 20% of the following quarter's production requirements respectively.

Required:

(a)   Prepare a materials purchase budget for Quarter 1.   **(5 marks)**

(b)   In Quarter 3 the opening and closing inventories of finished goods will be 5,600 units and 4,200 units respectively. QBQ adjusts for any under- or over-absorption of overheads at the end of each quarter.

Assume that production and sales volumes were as budgeted and that inventory levels were as planned. Also assume that all costs and revenues were as budgeted.

(i)   Calculate using marginal costing the profit for Quarter 3.

(ii)   Calculate using absorption costing the profit for Quarter 3.

(iii)   Explain the difference, if any, in the profits you have calculated.   **(5 marks)**

(c)   Briefly explain three reasons why budgetary planning and control might be inappropriate in a rapidly changing business environment.   **(5 marks)**

(d)   Briefly explain Just-in-Time (JIT) and two major requirements for the successful operation of a JIT system.   **(5 marks)**

(e)   A nursing home uses incremental budgeting. The previous period's budget is adjusted by reference to a set of indices. It is adjusted firstly for 'volume changes' and then for changes in the cost of resources. The indices are referenced to the previous period's budget by using that budget as the base index number of 100. The index numbers to be used to prepare Period 3's budget from that of Period 2 are as follows:

	Index
Patient days costs	90
House-keeping costs	106
Nursing costs	105
Administration costs	104

The budget for Period 2 was:	$
House-keeping costs (all variable)	125,000
Nursing costs (see below)	324,000
Administration costs (all fixed)	100,000

Nursing costs are semi-variable. The nursing costs for Period 2 were adjusted from the total nursing costs of $280,000 for Period 1 by using a patient days index of 125 and a nursing costs index of 108.

Prepare the budget for Period 3.   **(5 marks)**

(Total: 25 marks)

231   TIME SERIES IN FORECASTING

Describe the strengths and weaknesses of using time series analysis to prepare forecasts.   **(5 marks)**

232   X PLC (NOV 06 EXAM)

The following scenario is given for sub-questions (a) to (d).

X plc manufactures specialist insulating products that are used in both residential and commercial buildings. One of the products, Product W, is made using two different raw materials and two types of labour. The company operates a standard absorption costing system and is now preparing its budgets for the next four quarters. The following information has been identified for Product W:

Sales

| Selling price | $220 per unit |

Sales demand

Quarter 1	2,250 units
Quarter 2	2,050 units
Quarter 3	1,650 units
Quarter 4	2,050 units
Quarter 5	1,250 units
Quarter 6	2,050 units

Costs

Materials

A	5 kgs per unit @ $4 per kg
B	3 kgs per unit @ $7 per kg

Labour

Skilled	4 hours per unit @ $15 per hour
Semi-skilled	6 hours per unit @ $9 per hour
Annual overheads	$280,000
	40% of these overheads are fixed and the remainder varies with total labour hours. Fixed overheads are absorbed on a unit basis.

Inventory holding policy

Closing inventory of finished goods	30% of the following quarter's sales demand
Closing inventory of materials	45% of the following quarter's materials usage

The management team is concerned that X plc has recently faced increasing competition in the marketplace for Product W. As a consequence there have been issues concerning the availability and costs of the specialised materials and employees needed to manufacture Product W, and there is concern that these might cause problems in the current budget-setting process.

(a) Prepare the following budgets for each quarter for X plc:

    (i) Production budget in units

    (ii) Raw material purchases budget in kgs and value for Material B.   **(5 marks)**

(b) X plc has just been informed that Material A may be in short supply during the year for which it is preparing budgets. Discuss the impact this will have on budget preparation and other areas of X plc.   **(5 marks)**

(c) X plc currently uses incremental budgeting. Explain how Zero-Based Budgeting could overcome the problems that might be faced as a result of the continued use of the current system.   **(5 marks)**

(d) Briefly explain how linear regression analysis can be used to forecast sales and briefly discuss whether it would be a suitable method for X plc to use.   **(5 marks)**

(Total: 20 marks)

RISK AND DECISION MAKING

233   INDEPENDENT CINEMA (NOV 09 EXAM)

The management of an independent cinema is considering whether or not to hire a movie to show in its cinema for one week. If the management decides to hire the movie it will be screened 32 times during the week. The cost of hiring the movie for the week is $256,000. The cinema's accountant has been asked to evaluate the financial effects of the decision to hire the movie and has made the following estimates:

Customers

The number of customers watching the movie at each screening is uncertain but has been estimated as follows:

500 customers	40% probability
700 customers	35% probability
350 customers	25% probability

The entrance price for each screening of the movie is $6 per customer.

Customer contribution from sale of refreshments

The average contribution per customer earned from the sale of refreshments is also uncertain but has been estimated as follows:

$10 customers	50% probability
$12 customers	20% probability
$8 customers	30% probability

The cinema's accountant has already started to produce a two-way data table. This table is shown below where "$" represents the net average contribution from each screening and "pr" represents the probability of that combination of customers and refreshment contribution.

Refreshment contributions	Number of customers					
	700		500		350	
	$	pr	$	pr	$	pr
$12	a	0.070	1,000	0.08	(1,700)	0.050
$10	3,200	0.175	0	b	(2,400)	0.125
$8	1,800	0.105	(1,000)	0.12	c	0.075

Unfortunately, the cinema's accountant has been called away before he could complete the table or prepare any notes to interpret it for tomorrow's management meeting.

Required

(a)   Calculate the values to be inserted in the table at the points marked a, b, and c.

(3 marks)

(b)   Explain how the values in the data table can be used by the management of the cinema and recommend whether or not the movie should be hired.

(7 marks)

(Total: 10 marks)

234   MUTUALLY EXCLUSIVE

A company is considering which of two mutually exclusive projects it should undertake.

The finance director thinks that the project with the higher NPV should be chosen whereas the managing director thinks that the one with the higher IRR should be undertaken especially as both projects have the same initial outlay and length of life.

The company anticipates a cost of capital of 10% and the net after tax cash flows of the projects are as follows (cash flows are in $000):

Year	Project X	Project Y
0	− 200	− 200
1	35	218
2	80	10
3	90	10
4	75	4
5	20	3
NPV at 10%	29.14	18.52
IRR	16.1%	18.8%

Required:

Recommend, with reasons, which project you would undertake (if either) and explain the inconsistency in ranking of the two projects in view of the remarks of the directors.

(5 marks)

235   H COMPANY

H Company is considering purchasing a new machine to alleviate a bottleneck in its production facilities. At present it uses an old machine which can process 200 units of Product P per hour. H could replace it with machine AB, which is product-specific and can produce 500 units an hour. Machine AB costs $500,000. If it is installed, two members of staff will have to attend a short training course which will cost the company a total of $5,000. Removing the old machine and preparing the area for machine AB will cost $20,000.

The company expects demand for P to be 12,000 units per week for another three years. After this, early in the fourth year, the new machine would be scrapped and sold for $50,000. The existing machine will have no scrap value. Each P earns a contribution of $1.40. The company works a 40-hour week for 48 weeks in the year. H Company normally expects a payback within two years and its after-tax cost of capital is 10% per annum. The company pays corporation tax at 30% and receives writing-down allowances of 25%, reducing balance. Corporation tax is payable quarterly, in the seventh and tenth months of the year in which the profit is earned, and in the first and fourth months of the following year.

Required:

(a)   Prepare detailed calculations that show the tax relief and contribution received from the new machine.   **(5 marks)**

(b)   Calculate the NPV of the new machine and state whether the management of H Company should proceed with the purchase.   **(5 marks)**

(Total: 10 marks)

236 UNIVERSITY (SEP 10 EXAM)

A university is trying to decide whether or not to advertise a new post-graduate degree programme. The number of students starting the programme is dependent on economic conditions. If conditions are poor it is expected that the programme will attract 40 students without advertising. There is a 60% chance that economic conditions will be poor. If economic conditions are good it is expected that the programme will attract only 20 students without advertising. There is a 40% chance that economic conditions will be good.

If the programme is advertised and economic conditions are poor, there is a 65% chance that the advertising will stimulate further demand and student numbers will increase to 50. If economic conditions are good there is a 25% chance the advertising will stimulate further demand and numbers will increase to 25 students.

The cost of advertising the programme will be $15,000.The profit expected, before deducting the cost of advertising, at different levels of student numbers are as follows:

Number of students	Profit $
15	(10,000)
20	15,000
25	40,000
30	65,000
35	90,000
40	115,000
45	140,000
50	165,000

Demonstrate, using a decision tree, whether the programme should be advertised.

(5 marks)

237 HYPERMARKET

A hypermarket now delivers to a significant number of customers that place their orders via the internet and this requires a fleet of delivery vehicles that is under the control of local management. The cost of the fleet is now significant and management is trying to determine the optimal replacement policy for the vehicle fleet. The total purchase price of the fleet is $220,000.

The running costs for each year and the scrap values of the fleet at the end of each year are:

	Year 1 $000	Year 2 $000	Year 3 $000	Year 4 $000	Year 5 $000
Running costs	110	132	154	165	176
Scrap value	121	88	66	55	25

The hypermarket's cost of capital is 12% per annum. Ignore tax and inflation.

Required:

(a)   Calculate the overall net present value (NPV) of each replacement option.   **(5 marks)**

(b)   Determine how often the hypermarket should replace its fleet of delivery vehicles from a financial perspective.   **(5 marks)**

(Total: 10 marks)

238 A COMPANY (MAY 05 EXAM)

A company is considering the replacement of its delivery vehicle. It has chosen the vehicle that it will acquire but it now needs to decide whether the vehicle should be purchased or leased.

The cost of the vehicle is $15,000. If the company purchases the vehicle it will be entitled to claim tax depreciation at the rate of 25% per year on a reducing balance basis. The vehicle is expected to have a trade-in value of $5,000 at the end of three years.

If the company leases the vehicle, it will make an initial payment of $1,250 plus annual payments of $4,992 at the end of each of three years. The full value of each lease payment will be an allowable cost in the computation of the company's taxable profits of the year in which the payments are made.

The company pays corporation tax at the rate of 30% of its profits.

50% of the company's corporation tax is payable in the year in which profits are made and 50% in the following year. Assume that the company has sufficient profits to obtain tax relief on its acquisition of the vehicle in accordance with the information provided above.

The company's after-tax cost of capital is 15% per year.

Note: Tax depreciation is not a cash cost but is allowed as a deduction in the calculation of taxable profits.

Required:

(a)   Calculate the NPV of buying the new machine.   **(5 marks)**

(b)   Calculate the NPV of leasing the new machine, and state whether the company should lease or buy the machine from a financial point of view.   **(5 marks)**

(Total: 10 marks)

239 CANAL BOATS (MAY 07 EXAM)

A company operates a fleet of three canal boats that provide cruises for tourists around the canals of a city. The company seeks your advice as to whether it is better to replace its boats every year, every two years or every three years. The company has provided the following data:

	$
Annual sales revenue from operating each boat	800,000
Purchase cost of each boat	400,000

Operating costs, which include maintenance, servicing, and similar costs are paid at the end of each year. Operating costs and end of year trade-in values vary depending on the age of the boat and are as follows for each year of the boat's life:

Year	Operating costs	Trade-in values
	$	$
1	300,000	240,000
2	400,000	150,000
3	600,000	80,000

These costs do not include depreciation or any other fixed costs of providing the tourist service. These other fixed costs are a constant $100,000 per year regardless of the age of the boat.

The company uses an 8% cost of capital for its investment decisions.

Required:

(a) Produce calculations to determine the optimum replacement cycle of the boats and state clearly your recommendations. Ignore taxation. **(5 marks)**

The same company is also considering investing in one of three marketing campaigns to increase its profitability. All three marketing campaigns have a life of five years, require the same initial investment and have no residual value. The company has already evaluated the marketing campaigns taking into consideration the range of possible outcomes that could result from the investment. A summary of the calculations is shown below:

Marketing campaign	J	K	L
Expected net present value	$400,000	$800,000	$400,000
Standard deviation of net present value	$35,000	$105,000	$105,000

Required:

(b) (i) Explain the meaning of the data shown above.

(ii) Briefly explain how the data may be used by the company when choosing between alternative investments. **(5 marks)**

(Total: 10 marks)

240 SENSITIVITY ANALYSIS (MAY 06 EXAM)

A manager is evaluating a three-year project which has the following relevant pre-tax operating cashflows:

Year	1	2	3
	$000	$000	$000
Sales revenue	4,200	4,900	5,300
Costs	2,850	3,100	4,150

The project requires an investment of $2m at the start of year 1 and has no residual value.

The company pays corporation tax on its net relevant operating cash flows at the rate of 20%. Corporation tax is payable in the same year as the net relevant pre-tax operating cash flows arise. There is no tax depreciation available on the investment.

The manager has discounted the net relevant post-tax operating cash flows using the company's post-tax cost of capital of 7% and this results in a post-tax net present value of the project of $1.018m.

Required:

(a) Briefly explain sensitivity analysis and how the manager may use it in the evaluation of this project. **(5 marks)**

(b) Calculate the sensitivity of the project to independent changes in:

(i) the selling price;

(ii) the cost of capital. **(5 marks)**

(Total: 10 marks)

241 EVENTS MANAGEMENT (MAY 10 EXAM)

An events management company is trying to decide whether or not to advertise an outdoor concert. The sale of tickets is dependent on the weather. If the weather is poor it is expected that 5,000 tickets will be sold without advertising. There is a 70% chance that the weather will be poor. If the weather is good it is expected that 10,000 tickets will be sold without advertising. There is a 30% chance that the weather will be good.

If the concert is advertised and the weather is poor, there is a 60% chance that the advertising will stimulate further demand and ticket sales will increase to 7,000. If the weather is good there is a 25% chance the advertising will stimulate demand and ticket sales will increase to 13,000.

The profit expected, before deducting the cost of advertising, at different levels of ticket sales are as follows:

Number of tickets sold	Profit $
5,000	(20,000)
6,000	(5,000)
7,000	35,000
8,000	55,000
9,000	70,000
10,000	90,000
11,000	115,000
12,000	130,000
13,000	150,000

The cost of advertising the concert will be $15,000.

Required:

Demonstrate, using a decision tree, whether the concert should be advertised.

(5 marks)

MANAGING SHORT-TERM FINANCE

242 AM (MAY 05 EXAM)

AM is a trading entity operating in a country where there is no sales tax. Purchases are on credit, with 70% paid in the month following the date of purchase and 30% paid in the month after that.

Sales are partly on credit and partly for cash. Customers who receive credit are given 30 days to pay. On average 60% pay within 30 days, 30% pay between 30 and 60 days and 5% pay between 60 and 90 days. The balance is written off as irrecoverable. Other overheads, including salaries, are paid within the month incurred.

AM plans to purchase new equipment at the end of June 20X5, the expected cost of which is $250,000. The equipment will be purchased on 30 days' credit, payable at the end of July.

The cash balance on 1 May 20X5 is $96,000.

The actual/budgeted balances for the six months to July 20X5 were:

All figures $000	Actual			Budgeted		
	Feb	Mar	Apr	May	Jun	Jul
Credit sales	100	100	110	110	120	120
Cash sales	30	30	35	35	40	40
Credit purchases	45	50	50	55	55	60
Other overhead expense	40	40	40	50	50	50

Required:

Prepare a monthly cash budget for the period May to July 20X5 and assess the likelihood of AM being able to pay for the equipment when it falls due. (Round all figures to the nearest $000.) **(5 marks)**

243 HL (MAY 09 EXAM)

HL has been trading profitably, but has recently been accused of overtrading.

Required:

(i) Define the meaning of overtrading, and explain what is likely to happen if HL is overtrading. **(3 marks)**

(ii) Identify actions that HL could take to correct the problems of overtrading. **(2 marks)**

(Total: 5 marks)

244 DISCOUNTS (MAY 07 EXAM)

DN currently has an overdraft on which it pays interest at 10% per year. DN has been offered credit terms from one of its suppliers, whereby it can either claim a cash discount of 2% if payment is made within 10 days of the date of the invoice or pay on normal credit terms within 40 days of the date of the invoice. Assume a 365-day year and an invoice value of $100.

Required:

Explain to DN, with reasons and supporting calculations, whether it should pay the supplier early and take advantage of the discount offered. **(5 marks)**

245 SCL

SCL is a wholesale supplier of building materials. It is experiencing severe short-term cash flow difficulties. Sales invoices are about $2 million per month. The usual credit period extended to customers is 60 days, but the average period being taken is 90 days. The overdraft rate is 9% per annum.

A factoring company has offered a full factoring agreement without recourse on a permanent basis. The factor will charge a fee of 2.5% on total invoicing and will provide an immediate advance of 80% of invoiced amounts at an annual interest rate of 10%. Settlement of the remaining 20% will be after 60 days. SCL should avoid $300,000 a year in the administration costs of running the receivables ledger if the factoring arrangement is taken up.

Required:

Calculate the annual net cost, in cash terms, of the proposed factoring agreement assuming that there are 360 days in a year. State any other assumptions you have made. (Ignore taxation.)   **(5 marks)**

246 HX (MAY 09 EXAM)

HX is suffering from a constantly increasing level of outstanding balances on trade receivables. The outstanding balance has doubled in 12 months. HX's customers all pay by cheque.

HX is considering offering a discount to its customers in an effort to improve cash flow and reduce the trade receivables outstanding balance.

HX normally offers 30 day payment terms, but its customers take an average of 60 days to pay. To improve its cash flow HX is considering offering a 2·5% discount for payment within 14 days.

Required:

(i)   Calculate the effective interest rate of the 2·5% discount offered to its customers by HX for early payment. Assume a 365 day year.   **(3 marks)**

(ii)   Identify other methods that HX could use to reduce its level of outstanding trade receivables.   **(2 marks)**

(Total: 5 marks)

247 BILLS OF EXCHANGE (MAY 09 EXAM)

Bills of exchange are sometimes used for export transactions.

A bill of exchange with a face value of $1,000 has 91 days to maturity. The discount yield required by an investor, HG, is 7%. Assume a 365 day year.

Required:

(i)   Identify THREE ways in which an accepted bill of exchange can be used by the holder.   **(3 marks)**

(ii)   Calculate the maximum price HG should be willing to pay for the bill.   **(2 marks)**

(Total: 5 marks)

248 AGED RECEIVABLES ANALYSIS (MAY 10 EXAM)

The trade receivable ledger account for customer J from 1 January to 30 April 2010 shows the following:

All figures in $			Debit	Credit	Balance
01-Jan-2010	Balance b/fwd				125
10-Jan-2010	Invoice No. 234		181		306
12-Jan-2010	Invoice No. 263		92		398
18-Jan-2010	Invoice No. 297		287		685
23-Jan-2010	Receipt No. 85	(Balance b/fwd + Inv No.263)		217	468
09-Feb-2010	Invoice No. 328		294		762
13-Feb-2010	Credit Note No.167	(Inv No. 234)		63	699
05-Mar-2010	Invoice No. 365		135		834
15-Mar-2010	Invoice No. 379		232		1,066
18-Mar-2010	Receipt No. 102	(Inv No. 297)		287	779
25-Mar-2010	Invoice No. 391		71		850
01-Apr-2010	Receipt No. 126	(Inv No. 328)		294	556
24-Apr-2010	Invoice No. 438		145		701

(i)   Prepare an age analysis of trade receivables, for customer J, at 30 April 2010 showing the outstanding balance analysed by month.   **(3 marks)**

(ii)   State two benefits of preparing an age analysis of trade receivables.

(2 marks)

(Total: 5 marks)

249 PRINCIPLES OF SHORT-TERM INVESTMENT

You are working as assistant to the Treasurer of GIL, a company that currently has a large cash surplus of about $250 million. The directors of GIL have not yet decided what to do with this money. They might use it to finance a takeover, or they might use it to pay a special dividend to the shareholders at the end of the year. The board have decided to defer a decision, and expect to hold the cash for at least another nine months, possibly longer.

The money is currently held in a bank deposit account, but the return is quite low, and the directors are hoping that the money can be invested elsewhere to earn more money. One director believes that GIL should invest in Treasury bills, and another has argued that corporate bonds would be more appropriate. In order to provide a focus for a board discussion, they have asked you to prepare a memo.

Required:

Prepare a brief memo setting out the principles that are applied when deciding how to invest large but short-term cash surpluses, and suggest how investing in Treasury bills or investing in corporate bonds would relate to these principles.   **(5 marks)**

250   JE (NOV 09 EXAM)

The following is an extract from JE's financial statements for the years ended 30 September 2008 and 2009.

	As at September X8	As at September X9
Balance Sheet extracts	$000	$000
Trade receivables	250	390
Inventories	160	200
Bank and cash equivalents	90	10
Trade payables	300	500
Bank overdraft	0	100

Income Statement extracts		
Revenue (all credit sales)	2,250	3,150
Cost of sales*	1,910	2,800
Gross Profit	340	350

*there are no purchases for cash

Required:

Calculate five relevant working capital and efficiency ratios for JE for the two years ended 30 September 2008 and 2009.

(5 marks)

251   INVENTORY LEVELS (MAY 10 EXAM)

A company, which uses the EOQ inventory management model, purchases 64,000 units of raw materials per year. The purchase price of the raw material is $10 per unit. The cost of holding one unit in inventory is $1·20 per year. The cost of reordering and taking delivery is $150 per order regardless of the size of the order.

Assuming that usage is predictable and spread evenly throughout the year and that ordering and delivery are simultaneous, calculate for the raw material:

(i)   The total annual cost of holding and ordering inventory.   **(3 marks)**

Past experience has shown that the supplier of the raw material can be unreliable and that the delivery period can be between one week and three weeks. If the company wants to hold enough raw material to ensure that it never runs out, calculate for the raw material:

(ii)   The lowest inventory level at which raw material should be reordered.

(2 marks)

(Total: 5 marks)

252 SHORT TERM FUNDING (MAY 07 EXAM)

DF, a sports and fitness training equipment wholesaler, has prepared its forecast cash flow for the next six months and has calculated that it will need $2 million additional short-term finance in three months' time.

DF has an annual gross revenue of $240 million and achieves a gross margin of 50%. It currently has the following outstanding working capital balances:

- $16 million trade payables

- $20 million trade receivables

- $5 million bank overdraft.

DF forecasts that it will be able to repay half the $2 million within three months and the balance within a further three months.

Required:

Advise DF of possible sources of funding available to it. **(5 marks)**

253 SHORT TERM INVESTMENT (NOV 07 EXAM)

ES estimates from its cash flow forecast that it will have $120,000 to invest for 12 months.

ES is considering the following investments:

(i) Purchase of fixed term bonds issued by a 'blue chip' entity quoted on the local stock exchange. The bonds have a maturity date in 12 months' time and pay 12.5% interest on face value. The bonds will be redeemed at face value in 12 months' time. ES will incur commission costs on purchasing the bonds of 1% of cost. The bonds are currently trading at $102 per $100

(ii) An internet bank is offering a deposit account that pays interest on a monthly basis at 0.8% per month.

Required:

Identify which is the most appropriate investment for the year, giving your reasons. **(5 marks)**

254 BH (NOV 05 EXAM)

BH purchased a bond with a face value of $1,000 on 1 June 20X3 for $850. The bond has a coupon rate of 7%. BH intends holding the bond to its maturity on 31 May 20X8 when it will receive its face value.

Required:

(a) Explain the difference between the coupon rate of a security and its yield to maturity. **(2 marks)**

(b) Calculate the bond's yield to maturity. **(3 marks)**

(Total: 5 marks)

255   RISK AND YIELD (NOV 06 EXAM)

DH raised cash through an equity share issue to pay for a new factory it planned to construct. However, the factory contract has been delayed and payments are not expected to be required for three or four months. DH is going to invest its surplus funds until they are required.

One of the directors of DH has identified three possible investment opportunities:

(i)   Treasury bills issued by the central bank of DH's country. They could be purchased on 1 December 20X6 for a period of 91 days. The likely purchase price is $990 per $1,000.

(ii)   Equities quoted on DH's local stock exchange. The stock exchange has had a good record in recent months with the equity index increasing in value for 14 consecutive months. The director recommends that DH invests in three large multinational entities, each paying an annual dividend that provides an annual yield of 10% on the current share price.

(iii) DH's bank would pay 3.5% per year on money placed in a deposit account with 30 days' notice.

Required:

As Assistant Management Accountant, you have been asked to prepare notes on the risk and effective yield of each of the above investment opportunities for use by the Management Accountant at the next board meeting.   **(5 marks)**

256   EOQ (SEP 10 EXAM)

BB manufactures a range of electronic products. The supplier of component Y has informed BB that it will offer a quantity discount of 1.0% if BB places an order of 10,000 components or more at any one time.

Details of component Y are as follows:

Cost per component before discount $2.00

Annual purchases 150,000 components

Ordering costs $360 per order

Holding costs $3.00 per component per annum

Required:

(i)   **Calculate** the total annual cost of holding and ordering inventory of component Y using the economic order quantity and ignoring the quantity discount.   **(2 marks)**

(ii)   **Calculate** whether there is a financial benefit to BB from increasing the order size to 10,000 components in order to qualify for the 1.0% quantity discount.

(3 marks)

(Total: 5 marks)

257 CASH FORECAST (NOV 08 EXAM)

GN is a retailer, selling directly to the public for cash payment and to other entities on credit. GN is preparing a cash forecast for the first three months of 20X9. Credit customers are given 30 days to pay. Credit sales are expected to be six times the value of direct sales to the public.

GN's estimate of sales for the first three months of 20X9 is as follows:

Month	January	February	March
	$000	$000	$000
Sales value	400	400	500

Actual and estimated sales for the last three months of 20X8 are:

Month	October (actual)	November (estimate)	December (estimate)
	$000	$000	$000
Sales value	396	428	550

From past experience, GN expects 10% of credit customers to pay in the same month as the sale is made, a further 25% to pay in the month after the sale, and 63% in the month after that. The outstanding balance is expected to be written off. **(5 marks)**

SECTION C-TYPE QUESTIONS

COST ACCOUNTING SYSTEMS

258 HENSAU

Hensau has a single production process for which the following costs have been estimated for the period ending 31 December 20X1.

	$
Material receipt and inspection cost	15,600
Power cost	19,500
Material handling cost	13,650

Three products − X, Y and Z − are produced by workers, who perform a number of operations on material blanks using hand-held electrically powered drills. The workers have a wage rate of $4 per hour.

The following budgeted information has been obtained for the period ending 31 December 20X1.

	Product X	Product Y	Product Z
Production quantity (units)	2,000	1,500	800
Batches of material	10	5	16
Data per product unit			
Direct material (square metres)	4	6	3
Direct material ($)	5	3	6
Direct labour (minutes)	24	40	60
Number of power drill operations	6	3	2

Overhead costs for material receipt and inspection, process power and material handling are presently each absorbed by product units using rates per direct labour hour.

An activity-based costing investigation has revealed that the cost drivers for the overhead costs are as follows.

Material receipt and inspection	number of batches of material
Process power	number of power drill operations
Material handling	quantity of material (square metres) handled

Required:

Prepare a summary which shows the budgeted product cost per unit for each of the products X, Y and Z for the period ending 31 December 20X1, detailing the unit costs for each cost element:

(a)   using the existing method for the absorption of overhead costs, and   **(6 marks)**

(b)   using an approach which recognises the cost drivers revealed in the activity-based costing investigation.   **(14 marks)**

(c)   Comment on the results of your calculations and evaluate the benefits to the business of using activity based costing.   **(10 marks)**

                                                                                   (Total: 30 marks)

259   BRUNTI

The following budgeted information relates to Brunti for the forthcoming period:

	Products		
	XYI	*YZT*	*ABW*
	(000)	*(000)*	*(000)*
Sales and production (units)	50	40	30
	$	$	$
Selling price (per unit)	45	95	73
Prime cost (per unit)	32	84	65
	Hours	*Hours*	*Hours*
Machine department (machine hours per unit)	2	5	4
Assembly department (direct labour hours per unit)	7	3	2

Overheads allocated and apportioned to production departments were as follows:

Machine department $504,000

Assembly department $437,000

You ascertain that the above overheads could be re-analysed into 'cost pools' as follows:

Cost pool	$000	Cost driver	Quantity for the period
Machining services	357	Machine hours	420,000
Assembly services	318	Direct labour hours	530,000
Set-up costs	26	Set-ups	520
Order processing	156	Customer orders	32,000
Purchasing	84	Suppliers' orders	11,200
	941		

You have also been provided with the following estimates for the budget period:

	Products		
	XYI	*YZT*	*ABW*
Number of set-ups	120	200	200
Customer orders	8,000	8,000	16,000
Suppliers' orders	3,000	4,000	4,200

Required:

Prepare and present budgeted profit statements using:

(a)   conventional absorption costing; and   **(6 marks)**

(b)   activity based costing.   **(12 marks)**

(c)   Comment on these results.   **(6 marks)**

                                                                                          (Total: 24 marks)

(d)   Actual results for the period are now available as follows:

Cost pool	$000	Cost driver	Quantity for the period
Machining services	385	Machine hours	402,000
Assembly services	302	Direct labour hours	535,000
Set-up costs	30	Set-ups	560
Order processing	154	Customer orders	32,050
Purchasing	78	Suppliers' orders	11,150
	949		

	Products		
	XYI	*YZT*	*ABW*
Units produced	48,000	35,000	32,000
Number of set-ups	140	220	200
Customer orders	7,850	8,100	16,100
Suppliers' orders	2,950	4,100	4,100

Calculate the total over or under absorption of set-up costs, order processing costs and purchasing costs.   **(6 marks)**

                                                                                          (Total: 30 marks)

260   RJ (MAY 2007 EXAM)

RJ produces and sells two high performance motor cars: Car X and Car Y. The company operates a standard absorption costing system. The company's budgeted operating statement for the year ending 30 June 2008 and supporting information is given below:

Operating statement year ending 30 June 2008

	Car X	Car Y	Total
	$000	$000	$000
Sales	52,500	105,000	157,500
Production cost of sales	40,000	82,250	122,250
Gross profit	12,500	22,750	35,250
Administration costs			
Variable	6,300	12,600	18,900
Fixed	7,000	9,000	16,000
Profit/(loss)	(800)	1,150	350

The production cost of sales for each car was calculated using the following values:

	Car X		Car Y	
	Units	$000	Units	$000
Opening inventory	200	8,000	250	11,750
Production	1,100	44,000	1,600	75,200
Closing inventory	300	12,000	100	4,700
Cost of sales	1,000	40,000	1,750	82,250

Production costs

The production costs are made up of direct materials, direct labour, and fixed production overhead. The fixed production overhead is general production overhead (it is not product specific). The total budgeted fixed production overhead is $35,000,000 and is absorbed using a machine hour rate. It takes 200 machine hours to produce one Car X and 300 machine hours to produce one Car Y.

Administration costs

The fixed administration costs include the costs of specific marketing campaigns: $2,000,000 for Car X and $4,000,000 for Car Y.

Required:

(a) Produce the budgeted operating statement in a marginal costing format. **(7 marks)**

(b) Reconcile the total budgeted absorption costing profit with the total budgeted marginal costing profit as shown in the statement you produced in part (a).
(5 marks)

The company is considering changing to an activity based costing system. The company has analysed the budgeted fixed production overheads and found that the costs for various activities are as follows:

	$000
Machining costs	7,000
Set up costs	12,000
Quality inspections	7,020
Stores receiving	3,480
Stores issues	5,500
	35,000

The analysis also revealed the following information:

	Car X	Car Y
Budgeted production (number of cars)	1,100	1,600
Cars per production run	10	40
Inspections per production run	20	80
Number of component deliveries during the year	492	900
Number of issues from stores	4,000	7,000

Required:

(c) Calculate the budgeted production cost of one Car X and one Car Y using the activity based costing information provided above. **(10 marks)**

(d) Prepare a report to the Production Director of RJ which explains the potential benefits of using activity based budgeting for performance evaluation. **(8 marks)**

(Total: 30 marks)

261 PHARMACEUTICAL DRUGS (MAY 05 EXAM)

F plc supplies pharmaceutical drugs to drug stores. Although the company makes a satisfactory return, the directors are concerned that some orders are profitable and others are not. The management has decided to investigate a new budgeting system using activity-based costing principles to ensure that all orders they accept are making a profit.

Each customer order is charged as follows. Customers are charged the list price of the drugs ordered plus a charge for selling and distribution costs (overheads). A profit margin is also added, but that does not form part of this analysis.

Currently F plc uses a simple absorption rate to absorb these overheads. The rate is calculated based on the budgeted annual selling and distribution costs and the budgeted annual total list price of the drugs ordered.

An analysis of customers has revealed that many customers place frequent small orders with each order requesting a variety of drugs. The management of F plc has examined more carefully the nature of its selling and distribution costs, and the following data have been prepared for the budget for next year:

Total list price of drugs supplied	$8m	
Number of customer orders	8,000	
Selling and distribution costs	*$000*	Cost driver
Invoice processing	280	See Note 2
Packing	220	Size of package – see Note 3
Delivery	180	Number of deliveries – see Note 4
Other overheads	200	Number of orders
	———	
Total overheads	880	
	———	

Notes:

(1) Each order will be shipped in one package and will result in one delivery to the customer and one invoice (an order never results in more than one delivery).

(2) Each invoice has a different line for each drug ordered. There are 28,000 invoice lines each year. It is estimated that 25% of invoice processing costs are related to the number of invoices, and 75% are related to the number of invoice lines.

(3) Packing costs are $32 for a large package, and $25 for a small package.

(4) The delivery vehicles are always filled to capacity for each journey. The delivery vehicles can carry either 6 large packages or 12 small packages (or appropriate combinations of large and small packages). It is estimated that there will be 1,000 delivery journeys each year, and the total delivery mileage that is specific to particular customers is estimated at 350,000 miles each year. $40,000 of delivery costs are related to loading the delivery vehicles, and the remainder of these costs are related to specific delivery distance to customers.

The management has asked for two typical orders to be costed using next year's budget data, using the current method, and the proposed activity-based costing approach. Details of two typical orders are shown below:

	Order A	Order B
Lines on invoice	2	8
Package size	Small	Large
Specific delivery distance	8 miles	40 miles
List price of drugs supplied	$1,200	$900

Required:

(a) Calculate the charge for selling and distribution overheads for Order A and Order B using:

   (i) the current system; and   (5 marks)

   (ii) the activity-based costing approach.   (15 marks)

(b) Write a report to the management of F plc in which you:

   (i) assess the strengths and weaknesses of the proposed activity-based costing approach for F plc; and   (5 marks)

   (ii) recommend actions that the management of F plc might consider in the light of the data produced using the activity-based costing approach.   (5 marks)

(Total: 30 marks)

262 RETAIL COMPANY (NOV 09 EXAM) *Walk in the footsteps of a top tutor*

The management team of a retail company has produced the draft income statement and draft balance sheet as shown below.

Budgeted Income Statement for the year ending 31 December 2010

	£
Sales revenue	3,900,000
Cost of sales	2,600,000
Gross profit	1,300,000
Selling and administration costs	860,000
Operating profit	440,000

Budgeted Balance Sheet as at 31 December 2010

	£	£
Non-current assets		
Land	200,000	
Buildings	1,500,000	
Plant and machinery	1,250,000	
Accumulated depreciation	(910,000)	
		2,040,000
Current assets		
Inventory	182,280	
Receivables	501,000	
Cash	289,300	
		972,580
Current liabilities		
Payables (for goods for resale)		(428,980)
Total assets less current liabilities		2,583,600
Shareholders' funds		
Share capital	380,000	
Retained earnings	2,203,600	
		2,583,600

(a) The team now thinks that its forecasts may have been too optimistic and would like to assess the impact of several independent changes (that would occur on 1 January 2010) on the draft budget statements:

(i) increase inventory to £200,000;

(ii) increase receivables days to 60 days;

(iii) reduce selling prices by 5%.

Required:

Identify the effect and then calculate the result of each of the *independent* changes on the items shown in the table below. Reproduce the table in your answer book and insert the figures that would appear for the items in the revised draft income statements and draft balance sheets as a result of the independent changes (i), (ii) and (iii). **(11 marks)**

	(i)	(ii)	(iii)
Operating profit			
Inventory			
Receivables			
Cash			
Payables			

The team is considering a proposal from a manufacturer who has offered to become the sole supplier to the company. The supplier would reduce the unit cost of sales by 20% in return for an annual fee of £600,000. Currently the cost of sales is wholly variable and 40% of the selling and administration costs vary with sales revenue.

Required:

(b)   (i)   Calculate the current break even point (in £000).

(ii)   Calculate the break even point in (£000) if the supplier's offer is accepted.

(iii)   Discuss the advantages and disadvantages of this offer to the retail company.

(10 marks)

(c)   Explain why the Beyond Budgeting model may be more appropriate than traditional budgeting in an organisation that has adopted Total Quality Management.   (9 marks)

(Total: 30 marks)

STANDARD COSTING

263   PRODUCT MANAGER (NOV 09 EXAM)   *Walk in the footsteps of a top tutor*

A company manufactures many different products. Each product has a Product Manager. The company's management information system produces cost reports for each of the products that are made.

An analysis of previous reports has revealed the following information for Product X:

Units produced	Average variable cost per unit	Total product-specific costs	Head office costs
	$	$000	$000
5,000	160	500	300
10,000	150	500	600
15,000	140	800	900
20,000	140	800	1,200
25,000	155	1,100	1,500
30,000	170	1,100	1,800

Required:

(a)   Explain, for each of the three costs in the above table, possible reasons for the cost/volume relationships.   (6 marks)

Budgeted and actual information for Product Y for the previous period was as follows:

	Budget	*Actual*
Output	80,000 units	76,000 units
Direct materials	480,000 kg	430,000 kg
Direct labour	200,000 hours	196,000 hours
	$	$
Direct materials	960,000	924,500
Direct labour	1,600,000	1,626,800
Fixed production overheads	640,000	590,000

The company uses standard absorption costing.

Required:

(b) **Produce a statement that reconciles the standard and actual total costs for the previous period's output and shows the variances in as much detail as possible.**

(11 marks)

(c) **It has now been realised that the standard price of the direct materials used to manufacture Product Y in the previous period should have been $2.10 per kg.**

(i) **Calculate the direct materials planning variance.**

(ii) **Calculate the operational direct materials price and usage variances.**

(4 marks)

(Total: 21 marks)

264 DL HOSPITAL TRUST

You have been appointed as the management accountant of the DL Hospital Trust, a newly-formed organisation with specific responsibility for providing hospital services to its local community. The hospital trust is divided into a number of specialist units: one of these, unit H, specialises in the provision of a particular surgical operation.

Although the trust does not have profit maximisation as its objective, it is concerned to control its costs and to provide a value-for-money service. To achieve this, it engages teams of specialist staff on a sub-contract basis and pays them an hourly rate based upon the direct hours attributable to the surgical operation being carried out. Surgical team fees (i.e. labour costs) are collected and attributed to each surgical operation, whereas overhead costs are collected and attributed to surgical operations using absorption rates. These absorption rates are based on the surgical team fees. For the year ended 31 December 20X3, these rates were:

Variable overhead	62.5% of surgical team fees; and
Fixed overhead	87.5% of surgical team fees.

Each surgical operation is expected to take ten hours to complete, and the total fees of the team for each operation are expected to be $2,000. The budget for the year ended 31 December 20X3 indicated that a total of 20 such surgical operations were expected to be performed each month, and that the overhead costs were expected to accrue evenly throughout the year. During November 20X3 there were 22 operations of this type completed. These took a total of 235 hours and the total surgical team fees amounted to $44,400.

Overhead costs incurred in unit H in November 20X3 amounted to:

Variable overhead $28,650

Fixed overhead $36,950

Required:

(a)   Prepare a statement which reconciles the original budget cost and the actual cost for this type of operation within unit H for the month of November 20X3, showing the analysis of variances in as much detail as possible from the information given.

(18 marks)

(b)   Distinguish between the use of budgetary control and standard costing as a means of cost control in service-based organisations.

Explain clearly the arguments in favour of using BOTH of these methods simultaneously.   **(6 marks)**

(c)   The DL Hospital Trust has been preparing its budgets for 20X4, and the finance director has questioned the appropriateness of using surgical team fees as the basis of attributing overhead costs to operations.

Write a brief report to her explaining the arguments for and against the use of this method.   **(6 marks)**

(Total: 30 marks)

265   FX (MAY 08 EXAM)

The newly-appointed Managing Director of FX has received the variance report for Month 6, which is shown below:

Month 6 Variance Report

Output and Sales for Month 6. Budget: 1,000 units. Actual: 1,200 units.

	£	£	£
Budgeted contribution			90,000
Budgeted fixed costs			70,000
Budgeted profit			**20,000**
Volume variance			18,000
Expected profit on actual sales			38,000
Sales price variance			12,000
Production variances	*Favourable*	*Adverse*	
Materials price		6,300	
Materials usage		6,000	
Labour rate	5,040		
Labour efficiency		2,400	
Variable overhead expenditure	–	–	
Variable overhead efficiency		1,200	
Fixed overhead		4,000	
	5,040	19,900	14,860
Actual profit			**11,140**

Background information (not seen by the Managing Director)

The report did not include any other information. Details relating to the company and the product that it makes are given below:

FX produces one type of product. It operates a standard marginal costing system.

The standard unit cost and price of the product is as follows:

	£	£
Selling price		250
Direct material (5 kg at £20)	100	
Direct labour (4 hours at £10)	40	
Variable overheads (4 hours at £5)	20	160
		___
Contribution		90

The variable overhead absorption rate is based on direct labour hours.

The company has budgeted fixed overheads of £70,000 per month.

Budgeted sales and production levels are 1,000 units per month.

Month 6

The company has just completed Month 6 of its operations. Extracts from its records show:

1   1,200 units were produced and sold.

2   The actual direct materials purchased and used was 6,300 kg costing £132,300

3   The actual direct labour hours worked were 5,040 hours.

Required:

(a)   **Prepare a report for the Managing Director of FX that explains and interprets the Month 6 variance report. The Managing Director has recently joined the company and has very little previous financial experience.**   **(17 marks)**

The Managing Director was concerned about the Material Price variance and its cause. He discovered that a shortage of materials had caused the market price to rise to £23 per kg.

Required:

(b)   **In view of this additional information, calculate for Direct Materials:**
   - **the total variance;**
   - **the planning variance;**
   - **the two operational variances.**   **(7 marks)**

(c)   **Discuss the advantages and disadvantages of reporting planning and operational variances. Your answer should refer, where appropriate, to the variances you calculated in (b) above.**   **(6 marks)**

(Total: 30 marks)

266   WC (NOV 07 EXAM)

WC is a company that installs kitchens and bathrooms for customers who are renovating their houses. The installations are either pre-designed 'off-the-shelf' packages or highly customised designs for specific jobs.

The company operates with three divisions: Kitchens, Bathrooms and Central Services. The Kitchens and Bathrooms divisions are profit centres but the Central Services division is a cost centre.   The costs of the Central Services division, which are thought to be predominantly fixed, include those incurred by the design, administration and finance departments. The Central Services costs are charged to the other divisions based on the budgeted Central Services costs and the budgeted number of jobs to be undertaken by the other two divisions.

The budgeting and reporting system of WC is not very sophisticated and does not provide much detail for the Directors of the company.

The budgeted details for last year were:

	Kitchens	Bathrooms
Number of jobs	4,000	2,000
	$	$
Average price per job	10,000	7,000
Average direct costs per job	5,500	3,000
Central Services recharge per job	2,500	2,500
Average profit per job	2,000	1,500

The actual results were as follows:

	Kitchens	Bathrooms
Number of jobs	2,600	2,500
	$	$
Average price per job	13,000	6,100
Average direct costs per job	8,000	2,700
Central Services recharge per job	2,500	2,500
Average profit per job	2,500	900

The actual costs for the Central Services division were $17.5 million.

Required:

(a)   Calculate the budgeted and actual profits for each of the profit centres and for the whole company for the year.   **(4 marks)**

(b)   Calculate the sales price variances and the sales mix profit and sales quantity profit variances.   **(6 marks)**

(c)   Prepare a statement that reconciles the budgeted and actual profits and shows appropriate variances in as much detail as possible.   **(10 marks)**

(d)   Using the statement that you prepared in part (c) above, discuss the performance of the company for the year.   **(5 marks)**

                                                                                                                    (Total: 25 marks)

267 RG (SEP 10 EXAM)

FX Corporation produces a single product RG. The company operates a standard absorption costing system and a just-in-time purchasing system.

Standard production cost details per unit of product RG are:

	$
Materials (5 kg at $20 per kg)	100
Labour (4 hours at $10 per hr)	40
Variable overheads (4 hours at $5 per hr)	20
Fixed overheads (4 hours at $12.50 per hr)	50
	210

Fixed and variable overheads are absorbed on the basis of labour hours.

Budget data for product RG for July are detailed below:

Production and sales	1,400 units
Selling price	$250 per unit
Fixed overheads	$70,000

Actual data for product RG for July are as follows:

Production and sales	1,600 units
Selling price	$240 per unit
Direct materials	7,300 kg costing $153,300
Direct labour	5,080 hours at $9 per hour
Variable overheads	$25,400
Fixed overheads	$74,000

Required:

(a)   **Produce a statement that reconciles the budgeted and actual gross profit for product RG for July showing the variances in as much detail as possible.   (13 marks)**

(b)   The following details have been extracted from the company's accounting records for August.

	Budget	Actual
Output of RG	800 units	890 units
Materials	4,000kg	4,375kg
Cost per kg	$20.00	$21.60

It has now been realised that the standard cost per kg of the material should have been $20.90. Calculate the following materials variances for August:

(i)   **The total materials cost variance.**

(ii)   **The planning variance for materials price.**

(iii)   **The operational variances for materials price and materials usage.   (6 marks)**

(c)   **Discuss THREE advantages of using a standard costing system that identifies both planning and operational variances.   (6 marks)**

(Total: 25 marks)

268 WESTERN EUROPE (MAY 10 EXAM)

A company manufactures a range of industrial cleaning products from its automated factory in Western Europe. The company has recently introduced a just-in-time system for raw material purchases.

The company uses a standard absorption costing system for planning and control purposes although this system is now under review.

The following budget data relate to the production of one of its major products CP1 for April. The product is manufactured by mixing two raw materials ETH1 and RXY2.

	Quantity	Cost/kg	Cost
Raw material input			
ETH1	0.30kg	$18.00	$5.40
RXY2	0.70kg	$6.00	$4.20
Raw material cost per kg of input			$9.60
Yield			96%
Raw materials cost per kg of output			$10.00
Fixed production overheads per kg of output			$4.00
Total standard cost per kg of output			$14.00

Budget data for product CP1 for the period is detailed below:

- Sales – 72,000kg
- Production – 70,000kg
- Opening inventory – 2,000kg of CP1 (valued at $28,000)
- Selling price per kg – $20.00
- Fixed production overheads – $280,000

The fixed production overhead absorption rate is based on the budgeted number of kilograms produced.

Actual data for product CP1 for the period was as follows:

- Sales – 71,000kg
- Production – 69,000kg
- Selling price per kg – $20.30
- Fixed production overheads incurred – $278,000
- Cost per kg of ETH1 – $18.10
- Cost per kg of RXY2 – $5.80
- Input of ETH1 – 22,100kg
- Input of RXY2 – 47,900kg

Required:

(a) Produce a statement that reconciles the budgeted and actual profit for CP1 for April showing the variances in as much detail as possible. **(19 marks)**

(b) Discuss three reasons why the use of a standard costing system is considered inappropriate in a company that operates in an advanced manufacturing technology environment. **(6 marks)**

(Total: 25 marks)

269 FA AND FB (NOV 08 EXAM) *Walk in the footsteps of a top tutor*

A company manufactures two types of fertilizer (FA and FB). The company uses a standard costing system for planning and control purposes. Standards are set annually but budgets and variance reports are prepared each period.

Chemicals

Three chemicals (C1, C2 and C3) are used to make the fertilizers. C2 and C3 can be input directly to the manufacturing process but C1 has to be treated before it can be used. The treatment results in a loss of 30% of the chemicals treated. There are no further losses in the manufacturing process.

Details of the standards for the chemicals are as follows:

	C1	C2	C3
Price per kg	$8	$15	$12
Treatment loss	30%		
Content of finished product:			
per unit of FA	0.20kg	0.15kg	Nil
per unit of FB	0.20kg	Nil	0.25kg

Inventory Policies

Chemicals: end of period holdings must be equal to 50% of the following period's requirements.

Treated C1 is used immediately. There are never any inventories of treated C1 at the start or end of any period.

Fertilizers: no finished products are to be held.

Period 1 Output and sales

	Budget	Actual
FA	40,000 units	38,000 units
FB	24,000 units	25,000 units

Periods 2 and 3 Sales budgets

	Period 2	Period 3
FA	40,000 units	44,000 units
FB	24,000 units	33,000 units

Required:

(a) During Period 1, the quantity of C1 used was 17,740 kg. Calculate for Period 1 for C1:

    (i) the materials usage variance for the whole process

    (ii) the treatment loss percentage **(6 marks)**

(b) In Period 1, the company purchased and used 6,450 kg of C3. The cost of this purchase was $94,000. It has now been realised that the standard price of C3 should have been $14.50 per kg for Period 1.

    (i) Calculate the planning variance, and the operational price and usage variances for C3 for Period 1. **(7 marks)**

    (ii) Explain two problems associated with the reporting of planning variances. **(3 marks)**

(c) Prepare the Purchases Budget for C2 for Period 2. **(5 marks)**

(d) 'Variance analysis presents results after the actual events have taken place and therefore it is of little use to management for planning and control purposes, particularly in a modern manufacturing environment'.

    Discuss the above statement. **(9 marks)**

(Total: 30 marks)

270 SATELLITE NAVIGATION SYSTEMS (MAY 05 EXAM)

S Limited installs complex satellite navigation systems in cars, at a very large national depot. The standard cost of an installation is shown below. The budgeted volume is 1,000 units installed each month. The operations manager is responsible for three departments, namely: purchasing, fitting and quality control. S Limited purchases navigation systems and other equipment from different suppliers, and most items are imported. The fitting of different systems takes differing amounts of time, but the differences are not more than 25% from the average, so a standard labour time is applied.

Standard cost of installation of one navigation system

	$	Quantity	Price ($)
Materials	400	1 unit	400
Labour	320	20 hours	16
Variable overheads	140	20 hours	7
Fixed overheads	300	20 hours	15
Total standard cost	1,160		

The Operations Department has gathered the following information over the last few months. There are significant difficulties in retaining skilled staff. Many have left for similar but better paid jobs and as a result there is a high labour turnover. Exchange rates have moved and commentators have argued this will make exports cheaper, but S Limited has no exports and has not benefited. Some of the fitters have complained that one large batch of systems did not have the correct adapters and would not fit certain cars, but this was not apparent until fitting was attempted. Rent, rates, insurance and computing facilities have risen in price noticeably.

The financial results for September to December are shown below.

Operating statement for S Limited for September to December

	September $	October $	November $	December $	4 months $
Standard cost of actual output	1,276,000	1,276,000	1,102,000	1,044,000	4,698,000
Variances materials					
Price	5,505 F	3,354 F	9,520 A	10,340 A	11,001 A
Usage	400 A	7,200 A	800 A	16,000 A	24,400 A
Labour rate	4,200 A	5,500 A	23,100 A	24,000 A	56,800 A
Efficiency	16,000 F	0	32,000 A	32,000 A	48,000 A

	September $	October $	November $	December $	4 months $
Variable overheads					
Expenditure	7,000 A	2,000 A	2,000 F	0	7,000 A
Efficiency	7,000 F	0	14,000 A	14,000 A	21,000 A
Fixed overheads					
Expenditure	5,000 A	10,000 A	20,000 A	20,000 A	55,000 A
Volume	30,000 F	30,000 F	15,000 A	30,000 A	15,000 F
Actual costs	1,234,095	1,267,346	1,214,420	1,190,340	4,906,201

A = adverse variance   F = favourable variance

Required:

(a) Prepare a report to the operations manager of S Limited commenting on the performance of the company for the four months to 31 December. State probable causes for the key issues you have included in your report and state the further information that would be helpful in assessing the performance of the company.

(15 marks)

(b) Prepare a percentage variance chart for material usage and material price for the four-month period. Explain how this could be used to decide whether or not to investigate the variances.

(10 marks)

(Total: 25 marks)

271   X LTD (NOV 06 EXAM)

X Ltd uses an automated manufacturing process to produce an industrial chemical, Product P.

X Ltd operates a standard marginal costing system. The standard cost data for Product P is as follows:

Standard cost per unit of Product P

Materials

A	10 kgs	@ $15 per kilo	$150
B	8 kgs	@ $8 per kilo	$64
C	5 kgs	@ $4 per kilo	$20
	23 kgs		

Total standard marginal cost	$234
Budgeted fixed production overheads	$350,000

In order to arrive at the budgeted selling price for Product P the company adds 80% mark-up to the standard marginal cost. The company budgeted to produce and sell 5,000 units of Product P in the period. There were no budgeted inventories of Product P.

The actual results for the period were as follows:

Actual production and sales		5,450 units
Actual sales price		$445 per unit
Material usage and cost		
A	43,000 kgs	$688,000
B	37,000 kgs	$277,500
C	23,500 kgs	$99,875
	103,500 kgs	
Fixed production overheads		$385,000

Required:

(a)   Prepare an operating statement which reconciles the budgeted profit to the actual profit for the period. (The statement should include the material mix and material yield variances.)   **(12 marks)**

(b)   The Production Manager of X Ltd is new to the job and has very little experience of management information. Write a brief report to the Production Manager of X Ltd that:

(i)   interprets the material price, mix and yield variances;

(ii)   discusses the merits, or otherwise, of calculating the materials mix and yield variances for X Ltd.   **(8 marks)**

(Total: 20 marks)

BUDGETING

272   RF LTD (MAY 07 EXAM)   *Walk in the footsteps of a top tutor*

RF Ltd is a new company which plans to manufacture a specialist electrical component. The company founders will invest $16,250 on the first day of operations, that is, Month 1. They will also transfer fixed capital assets to the company.

The following information is available:

Sales

The forecast sales for the first four months are as follows:

Month	Number of components
1	1,500
2	1,750
3	2,000
4	2,100

The selling price has been set at $10 per component in the first four months.

Sales receipts

Time of payment	% of customers
Month of sale	20*
One month later	45
Two months later	25
Three months later	5

The balance represents anticipated bad debts.

*A 2% discount is given to customers for payment received in the month of sale.

Production

There will be no opening inventory of finished goods in Month 1 but after that it will be policy for the closing inventory to be equal to 20% of the following month's forecast sales.

Variable production cost

The variable production cost is expected to be $6.40 per component.

	$
Direct materials	1.90
Direct wages	3.30
Variable production overheads	1.20
Total variable cost	6.40

Notes:

Direct materials: 100% of the materials required for production will be purchased in the month of production. No inventory of materials will be held. Direct materials will be paid for in the month following purchase.

Direct wages will be paid in the month in which production occurs.

Variable production overheads: 60% will be paid in the month in which production occurs and the remainder will be paid one month later.

Fixed overhead costs

Fixed overhead costs are estimated at $75,000 per annum and are expected to be incurred in equal amounts each month. 60% of the fixed overhead costs will be paid in the month in which they are incurred and 30% in the following month. The balance represents depreciation of fixed assets.

Calculations are to be made to the nearest $1.

Ignore VAT and Tax.

Required:

(a)   **Prepare a cash budget for each of the first three months and in total.**   **(15 marks)**

(b)   **There is some uncertainty about the direct material cost. It is thought that the direct material cost per component could range between $1.50 and $2.20.**

   Calculate the budgeted total net cash flow for the three month period if the cost of the direct material is:

   (i) $1.50 per component; or

   (ii) $2.20 per component.   **(6 marks)**

(c)   **Using your answers to part *(a)* and *(b)* above, prepare a report to the management of RF Ltd that discusses the benefits or otherwise of performing 'what if' analysis when preparing cash budgets.**   **(9 marks)**

(Total: 30 marks)

273   PMF

PMF is a long-established public transport operator that provides a commuter transit link between an airport and the centre of a large city.

The following data has been taken from the sales records of PMF for the last two years:

Quarter	Number of passengers carried	
	Year 1	Year 2
1	15,620	34,100
2	15,640	29,920
3	16,950	29,550
4	34,840	56,680

The trend equation for the number of passengers carried has been found to be

$$x = 10,000 + 4,200q$$

Where	x	=	number of passengers carried per quarter
and	q	=	time period (year 1 quarter 1: $q = 1$)
			(year 1 quarter 2: $q = 2$)
			(year 2 quarter 1: $q = 5$)

Based on data collected over the last two years, PMF has found that its quarterly costs have the following relationships with the number of passengers carried:

Cost item	Relationship
Premises costs	$y = 260{,}000$
Premises staff	$y = 65{,}000 + 0.5x$
Power	$y = 13{,}000 + 4x$
Transit staff	$y = 32{,}000 + 3x$
Other	$y = 9{,}100 + x$
where	y = the cost per quarter (\$),
and	x = number of passengers per quarter.

Required:

(a) Using the trend equation for the number of passengers carried and the multiplicative (proportional) time series model, determine the expected number of passengers to be carried in the third quarter of year 3. **(8 marks)**

(b) Explain why you think that the equation for the transit staff cost is in the form y = 32,000 + 3x. **(4 marks)**

(c) Using your answer to part (a) and the cost relationships equations, calculate for each cost item and in total, the costs expected to be incurred in the third quarter of year 3. **(4 marks)**

(d) Explain why there may be differences between the actual data for the third quarter of year 3 and the values you have predicted. **(10 marks)**

(e) Explain the difference between the multiplicative and additive models for producing seasonally adjusted data and why the multiplicative model may be more appropriate for PMF. **(4 marks)**

(Total: 30 marks)

274 Q (MAY 08 EXAM)

Q, a new company, is being established to manufacture and sell an electronic tracking device: the Trackit. The owners are excited about the future profits that the business will generate. They have forecast that sales will grow to 2,600 Trackits per month within five months and will be at that level for the remainder of the first year.

The owners will invest a total of $250,000 in cash on the first day of operations (that is the first day of Month 1). They will also transfer non-current assets into the company.

Extracts from the company's business plan are shown below.

Sales

The forecast sales for the first five months are:

Month	Trackits (units)
1	1,000
2	1,500
3	2,000
4	2,400
5	2,600

The selling price has been set at $140 per Trackit.

Sales receipts

Sales will be mainly through large retail outlets. The pattern for the receipt of payment is expected to be as follows:

Time of payment	% of sales value
Immediately	15*
One month later	25
Two months later	40
Three months later	15

The balance represents anticipated bad debts.

*A 4% discount will be given for immediate payment.

Production

The budget production volumes in units are:

Month 1	Month 2	Month 3	Month 4
1,450	1,650	2,120	2,460

Variable production cost

The budgeted variable production cost is $90 per unit, comprising:

	$
Direct materials	60
Direct wages	10
Variable production overheads	20
Total variable cost	90

Direct materials: Payment for purchases will be made in the month following receipt. There will be no opening inventory of materials in Month 1. It will be company policy to hold inventory at the end of each month equal to 20% at of the following month's production requirements. The direct materials cost includes the cost of an essential component that will be bought in from a specialist manufacturer.

Direct wages will be paid in the month in which the production occurs.

Variable production overheads: 65% will be paid in the month in which production occurs and the remainder will be paid one month later.

Fixed overhead costs

Fixed overheads are estimated at $840,000 per annum and are expected to be incurred in equal amounts each month. 60% of the fixed overhead costs will be paid in the month in which they are incurred and 15% in the following month. The balance represents depreciation of non-current assets.

Ignore VAT and Tax.

Required:

(a) Prepare a cash budget for each of the first three months and for that three-month period in total. **(14 marks)**

(b) There is some uncertainty about the cost of the specialist component (this is included in the direct material cost). It is thought that the cost of the component could range between $32 and $50 per Trackit. It is currently included in the cost estimates at $40 per Trackit.

Calculate the budgeted total net cash flow for the three-month period in total if the cost of the component was:

(i) $32

(ii) $50 **(6 marks)**

(c) Prepare a report for the owners of Q that offers advice about the profitability of their business and the situation revealed by the extracts from the business plan and your answers to (a) and (b) above. **(10 marks)**

(Total: 30 marks)

275 THIRTEEN WEEKS (MAY 09 EXAM)

A company manufactures and sells a single product. Next year's budgeted profit (based on absorption costing) on the projected sales of 810,000 units is £1,611,000. In view of this figure the company is thinking of investing in new machinery at some time in the forthcoming year.

The company is preparing its cash budget for next year. The company divides the year into four periods, each of thirteen weeks. Sales and production will occur at even rates within each period. Details are as follows:

Sales budget (810,000 units)

The selling price is £30 per unit. All sales will be on credit and payment will be received five weeks after the date of sale. It is expected that 2% of all sales will become bad debts. The budgeted sales units are:

Period	1	2	3	4
Sales (units)	150,000	200,000	180,000	280,000

The product incurs variable selling costs of £1.60 per unit. These are paid in the period in which they are incurred.

Production budget (860,000 units)

Period	1	2	3	4
Production (units)	210,000	210,000	220,000	220,000

Production cost per unit	£	Notes
Raw materials	9.50	Purchased on credit. Paid for four weeks after purchase.
Production wages	8.20	Paid one week in arrears. These are variable costs.
Production expenses	7.00	See below.
	24.70	

Raw material inventory

The company wishes to increase inventory to six weeks of forward production by the end of Period 1 and then to seven weeks by the end of Period 2. Purchases will occur evenly throughout the periods.

Production expenses

The production expenses of £7·00 per unit are detailed below:

	£	Notes
Variable expenses	1.10	Paid in the period incurred
Depreciation	2.70	This is an annual fixed cost that is absorbed on a per unit basis by the budgeted production of 860,000 units
Fixed expenses	3.20	Absorbed on a per unit basis based on the annual production of 860,000 units. Paid in two equal instalments at the beginning of periods 1 and 3.

Long term borrowing

The company has a long term loan. The balance on this loan at the start of the year will be £10m. Interest on this loan is charged at 9% per annum on the amount outstanding at the start of the year and is to be paid in two equal instalments at the end of period 2 and at the end of period 4. The loan is "interest only": there are no capital repayments due.

Opening balances

	£
Raw materials inventory	710,000 (all purchased at the current price)
Trade receivables (net of bad debts)	2,430,000
Bank and cash	76,000
Trade payables	612,000
Unpaid wages	130,000
Loan	10,000,000

Required:

(a)   Calculate, in units, the budgeted break even point and margin of safety for the next year. **(6 marks)**

(b)   It is now thought that the price of raw materials could range from £7.50 to £11.50 for each unit produce. Produce a diagram that shows the sensitivity of the budgeted profit to changes in the price of the raw materials. **(4 marks)**

(c)   Prepare, showing all cash flows, a cash budget for period 1 and a cash budget for period 2 (assume the price of raw materials is £9.50 for each unit produced).

(14 marks)

(d)   Explain three areas from your cash budget which would cause problems for the company's management team. **(6 marks)**

(Total: 30 marks)

FINANCIAL INFORMATION FOR LONG-TERM DECISION MAKING

276   REGIONAL AIRPORT (MAY 10 EXAM) *Walk in the footsteps of a top tutor*

A small regional airport is modernising its facilities in anticipation of significant growth in the number of passengers using the airport. It is expected that the number of passengers will increase by 10% per annum as a result of a "low cost" airline opening new routes to and from the airport.

At present, the airport has only one food outlet selling sandwiches and other cold food and drinks. To improve the facilities available to customers, the management of the airport is considering opening a restaurant selling a range of hot food and drinks. The cost of fitting out the new restaurant, which will have to be fully refurbished after four years, is estimated to be $350,000. These assets are expected to have a residual value of $30,000 at the end of four years.

A firm of consultants carried out an extensive study in relation to this project at a cost of $30,000. The key findings from their report, regarding expected revenue and contribution from the restaurant, are as follows:

- Average revenue: $9·00 per customer
- Average variable cost: $5·00 per customer
- Demand in year 1: 500 customers per day

Future demand for the restaurant is expected to rise in line with passenger numbers.

The airport operates for 360 days per year.

Other relevant information from the consultants' report is listed below:

1   **Staffing of the new restaurant:**

- Number of employees (Years 1 and 2): 4
- Numbers employees (Years 3 and 4): 5
- Average salary per employee: $20,000 per annum

2 Overheads

- The annual budgeted fixed overhead of the airport which will be apportioned to the restaurant is $80,000.
- The annual overheads apportioned to the cold food outlet will be $30,000.
- The airport's overheads are expected to increase by the following annual amounts as a direct result of the opening of the restaurant:

  - Electricity: $40,000
  - Advertising: $20,000
  - Audit: $10,000

3 Cold food outlet

The average contribution from the sale of cold food is $2.50 per customer. If the restaurant is not opened it is expected that the cold food outlet will sell to 1,200 customers per day in the coming year and in subsequent years the customer numbers will rise in line with passenger numbers.

If the restaurant is opened, the consultants expect sales from the existing cold food outlet to initially reduce by 40% in year 1 and then to increase in line with passenger numbers.

The airport's Financial Director has provided the following taxation information:

- Tax depreciation: 25% reducing balance per annum.
- The first year's tax depreciation allowance is used against the first year's net cash inflows.
- Taxation rate: 30% of taxable profits. Half of the tax is payable in the year in which it arises, the balance is paid the following year.
- Any taxable losses resulting from this investment can be set against profits made by the airport company's other business activities since the airport company is profitable.
- The airport company uses a post-tax cost of capital of 8% per annum to evaluate projects of this type. Ignore inflation.

Required:

(a) Calculate the net present value (NPV) of the restaurant project. **(16 marks)**

(b) The Managing Director of a company has been presented with the details of three potential investment projects. He has very little experience of project appraisal and has asked you for help.

The project details are given below:

	Project A	Project B	Project C
Expected NPV	$150,000	$180,000	$180,000
Standard Deviation of Expected NPV	$10,000	$50,000	$30,000
IRR	12%	12%	10%

The three projects will require the same level of initial investment. The projects are mutually exclusive and therefore the Managing Director can only choose one of them.

Required:

Interpret the information for the Managing Director (your answer should include an explanation of the factors he should consider when deciding which project to undertake). **(9 marks)**

(Total: 25 marks)

277 GYMNASIUM (SEP 10 EXAM)

The management of a hotel is considering expanding its facilities by providing a gymnasium and spa for the use of guests. It is expected that the additional facilities will result in an increase in the occupancy rate of the hotel and in the rates that can be charged for each room.

The cost of refurbishing the space, which is currently used as a library for guests, and installing the spa is estimated to be $100,000. The cost of the gymnasium equipment is expected to be $50,000. The gymnasium and spa will need to be refurbished and the equipment replaced every four years. The equipment will be sold for $15,000 cash at the end of year 4. This amount includes the effect of inflation.

The hotel's accountants have produced a feasibility report at a cost of $10,000. The key findings from their report, regarding occupancy rates and room rates are as follows:

Current occupancy rate: 80%

Number of rooms available: 40

Current average room rate per night: $250

Occupancy rates, following the opening of the gymnasium and spa, are expected to rise to 82% and the average room rate by 5%, excluding the effect of inflation.

The hotel is open for 360 days per year.

Other relevant information from the accountants' report is listed below:

1   **Staffing of the gymnasium and spa**

Number of employees : 4

Average salary per employee: $30,000 per annum

2   **Overheads**

The current budgeted overhead absorption rate for the hotel is $80 per square metre per annum. The area required for the gymnasium and spa is 400 square metres.

The hotel's overheads are expected to increase by $42,000 directly as a result of opening the gymnasium and spa.

3   **Inflation**

Inflation is expected to be at a rate of 4% per annum and will apply to sales revenue, overhead costs and staff costs. The rate of 4% will apply from Year 2 to each of the subsequent years of the project.

4   **Taxation**

The hotel's accountants have provided the following taxation information:

Tax depreciation available on all costs of refurbishing, installation and equipment: 25% reducing balance per annum.

Taxation rate: 30% of taxable profits. Half of the tax is payable in the year in which it arises, the balance is paid the following year.

Any losses resulting from this investment can be set against taxable profits made by the company's other business activities.

The company uses a post-tax money cost of capital of 12% per annum to evaluate projects of this type.

Required:

(a)   Calculate the net present value (NPV) of the gymnasium and spa project. **(16 marks)**

(b)   Calculate the post-tax money cost of capital at which the hotel would be indifferent to accepting / rejecting the project.   **(4 marks)**

(c)   Discuss an alternative method for the treatment of inflation that would result in the same NPV.

Your answer should consider the potential difficulties in using this method when taxation is involved in the project appraisal.   **(5 marks)**

(Total: 25 marks)

278   SQ (NOV 07 EXAM)   *Walk in the footsteps of a top tutor*

SQ manufactures and sells a range of products. Details for one of the products, product Q, are shown below.

Existing production facility

The present production facility can continue to be used to produce up to 120,000 units of product Q each year. It is estimated that the facility can be used for a further five years but annual maintenance costs will rise substantially. An analysis of the latest costs is set out below:

	$ per unit
Direct materials	50
Direct labour	30
Variable production overhead	25
Fixed production overhead*	20
Variable selling and distribution overhead**	10

* The fixed production overhead costs are absorbed into product costs using an absorption rate which is 25% of prime cost. These fixed overhead costs are mainly central production facility costs that are not specific to any particular product or activity and would continue to be incurred regardless of the production method used by SQ. However, they also include facility maintenance costs (see above). In addition, SQ incurs annual fixed non-production costs of $24 million.

** These are selling and distribution costs which are not affected by the production method that is used for the product.

Proposed new production facility

The company is considering an investment of $4 million in a new production facility for product Q. The new facility is to be operational from 1 January 2008. It will have a life of five years and at the end of its life it will have a residual value of $0.4 million. It is expected that the facility will have significant benefits. Firstly it will increase SQ's production capacity for product Q by 30%, secondly it will reduce product Q's direct labour and variable production overhead costs by 20% per unit, and finally the savings in annual maintenance costs will be as follows:

Year	$000
2008	70
2009	80
2010	80
2011	110
2012	130

You have also obtained the following further information:

Demand

Currently SQ produces 120,000 units of product Q each year and these sell for $150 per unit. There is significant demand for the product and SQ estimates that it could sell more units if it had the capacity to produce them. If the selling price remains unchanged, customer demand for 2008 and future years is estimated to be as shown in the following table:

Year	Customer demand (units)
2008	130,000
2009	140,000
2010	147,000
2011	154,000
2012	162,000

Cost structure

No changes are expected to either cost structure or to cost levels other than those referred to above.

Taxation

SQ pays corporation tax at the rate of 30% of its taxable profits. Half of this tax is payable in the year in which the profit is earned and the other half is payable one year later. If the investment in the new production facility goes ahead on 1 January 2008 (the first day of SQ's accounting year), it will qualify for tax depreciation at the rate of 25% per annum on a reducing balance basis.

Cost of capital

SQ's after-tax cost of capital is 12% per annum.

Required:

(a) (i)   Calculate the Net Present Value (NPV) of the investment in the new facility.
(14 marks)

(ii)   Explain two other factors that SQ should consider before making its decision.
(4 marks)

(b)   A company is thinking of investing in a new project. The details are as follows:

Investment	$15,000
Time span	3 years
Annual cash inflows	$30,000
Annual cash outflows	$22,500
Cost of capital	10%
NPV @ 10%	$3,652.50

The project does not have a residual value. Ignore taxation.

(i)   **Calculate the Internal Rate of Return (IRR) of the investment proposal.**
                                                                    (3 marks)

(ii)   **Calculate the sensitivity of the investment to changes in the annual cash inflows.**
                                                                    (4 marks)

                                                                    (Total: 25 marks)

279 FRANTISEK COMPANY

Frantisek Company is a mechanical engineering company specialising in the manufacture of brass valves using general-purpose lathes. Frantisek Company's cost of money is 12%.

A number of lathes have reached the end of their useful lives and Frantisek Company's managing director has asked you to advise on replacement strategy after giving you the following information:

'It may be that we will still be making brass valves in 20 years' time. However, I forecast that our markets will adopt new technology in five to ten years' time, at which point our production facility would abruptly become redundant.'

The costs associated with the purchase and maintenance of two alternative models of lathe are as follows:

	Useful life	Purchase price	Maintenance cost per year		
			Years 1–5	Years 6–10	Years 11–15
		$	$	$	$
Model A	15 years	60,000	2,000	2,800	3,900
Model B	10 years	45,000	3,100	5,300	–

The residual value of a lathe drops by one-third of its purchase price during the first year of its ownership and thereafter declines by 4% of purchase price (model A) and 6% of purchase price (model B) per year;

New model B lathes can be rented on the following terms:

- annual rentals (including maintenance costs) paid in advance of $10,200 (first year), $10,250 (subsequent four years) and $10,995 (final five years); the lathes are returned to the hirer at the end of ten years;

- the rental may be terminated at any time on payment of a penalty – this would be $10,000, declining by $1,000 per year with each year of the rental agreement completed.

Required:

(a)   Advise which of the options (purchase A, purchase B, rent B) is most economic assuming that valve production is to continue for at least 20 years.

Advise which of the options is most economic assuming that valve production is to continue for only five years.   (12 marks)

(b)   Draw a diagram in order to illustrate fully the sensitivity of the three options to the time at which valve production ceases between years 5 and 10; in particular, the diagram should show the number of years' production required in order to make buying and renting a model B lathe equally viable.   (9 marks)

(c)   Explain the non-financial factors that might be relevant to decision making in this case.   (4 marks)

                                                                           (Total: 25 marks)

280   INVESTMENT APPRAISAL WITH TAX

Wilbur Frump is an author who makes his living by writing novels. All rights connected with his novels are vested in Frump Art and Literature Company (FAL), a company owned by the Frump family. Frump is currently planning to start work on his new novel (entitled *Buy My Love a Gun*). He expects to start work on 1 January 20X5 and to complete the novel on 31 August 20X5 in time for publication on 31 October 20X5.

On the basis of experience with previous books, Frump forecasts that sales of *Buy My Love a Gun* will be as follows:

Year to 31 October 20X6	100,000 copies
Year to 31 October 20X7	140,000 copies
Year to 31 October 20X8	200,000 copies
Year to 31 October 20X9	80,000 copies

There is a possibility that sales could continue up to 31 October 20Y2. Two publishing companies have offered to publish *Buy My Love a Gun,* on the following terms:

- Publisher A:

    –   an initial payment of $180,000 ($80,000 payable when writing starts and $100,000 payable when it finishes) to be treated as an interest-free advance on royalties;

    –   royalties (40p per copy sold) are payable at six monthly intervals starting 30 April 20X6; no royalties will be paid to FAL until the advance is repaid.

- Publisher B:

    –   an initial payment (at the date writing starts) of $90,000 to be treated as an interest-bearing advance on royalties;

    –   10% is added to the advance outstanding on 31 December each year as interest;

    –   royalties (50p per copy sold) are payable at six-monthly intervals starting 30 April 20X6;

    –   50% of royalties payable will be withheld by the publisher as repayments of the advance.

FAL pays corporation tax at the rate of 30% and its financial year ends on 31 December. You may assume that tax for any year is paid in two instalments, the first on the last day of the year in which the tax is due, and the second on the last day of the following year.

The company's cost of capital is 16%

Required:

(a) **Advise FAL's management which of the two offers it should accept. Your advice should be supported by a full financial analysis allowing for the precise dates on which payments are received. Assume that there will be no sales of the book after 20X9 and that the tax authorities will treat any advance as a loan to FAL. (18 marks)**

(b) **Advise FAL's management on the minimum sales (average copies per year) for the years 20Y0 to 20Y2 that would be required to justify changing the advice you gave in answer to (a). (7 marks)**

(Total: 25 marks)

281 RESTAURANT (NOV 08 EXAM)

A restaurant company is considering further investment in order to increase its seating capacity. The company prepares its accounts to 31 December each year and, if accepted, the proposed investment would be made on 1 January 20X9 and will become operational immediately.

Based on the actual results for the year to date, the latest forecast income statement for the company for the year to 31 December 20X8 is as follows:

	£000	£000
Food sales	180	
Drink sales	150	330
Food costs	125	
Drink costs	70	
Staff costs	55	
Other costs *	45	295
	---	---
Profit		35
		---

*These other costs include rent, light & heat, power and administration overheads. 30% of these costs vary in proportion to the value of sales and the remainder are fixed costs.

The proposed investment

At present the restaurant is not able to exploit the growing demand from customers because it does not have sufficient seating capacity. The restaurant is considering the investment of £40,000 on 1 January 20X9. It is expected that this will increase the seating capacity of the restaurant by 30% compared to the present level. The lease of the current business premises ends at the end of 20Y2. At that time the £40,000 investment will have no residual value. Of this total investment, £30,000 will qualify for 100% tax depreciation in 20X9 and the remainder will qualify for 20% tax depreciation per year, commencing in 20X9, calculated on a reducing balance basis. Any balancing tax charge will be made or allowance will be available at the end of 20Y2.

Sales

It is expected that the additional sales of food and drink will be proportional to the seating capacity increase and that the mix of food sales and drink sales will not change.

Costs

It is expected that apart from the effects of inflation (see below):

Food costs and drink costs will continue to be the same percentages of food sales and drink sales as they are in the forecast income statement shown above.

Staff costs are step costs and are expected to increase by 20% from their forecast value for 20X8 if there is any capacity increase.

The variable element of other costs is expected to increase in proportion to the capacity increase; the fixed cost element is expected to increase by £10,000 if there is any capacity increase.

Inflation

Cost inflation is predicted to be 4% per annum for each of the years 20X9 to 20Y2 whereas selling prices are only expected to increase by 3% per annum during the same period.

Taxation

The company pays tax on its profits at 20%. This is payable one year after the profit is earned.

Cost of capital

The company's post tax money cost of capital for evaluating this investment is 8% per annum.

Required:

(a) **Prepare calculations to show whether the investment is worthwhile assuming that the 30% increase in seating capacity is fully utilised and recommend whether the investment should proceed.** **(14 marks)**

(b) **Calculate and interpret the Internal Rate of Return (IRR) of the proposed investment.** **(6 marks)**

(c) **Calculate the sensitivity of your recommendation to changes in the percentage capacity utilisation.** **(5 marks)**

(Total: 25 marks)

282 CAF COMPANY

CAF Company is a large multinational organisation that manufactures a range of highly engineered products/components for the aircraft and vehicle industries. The directors are considering the future of one of the company's factories in the UK which manufactures product A. Product A is coming to the end of its life but another two years' production is planned. This is expected to produce a net cash inflow of $3 million next year and $2.3 million in the product's final year.

Product AA

CAF Company has already decided to replace product A with product AA which will be ready to go into production in two years' time. Product AA is expected to have a life of eight years. It could be made either at the UK factory under consideration or in an Eastern European factory owned by CAF Company. The UK factory is located closer to the markets and therefore if product AA is made in Eastern Europe, the company will incur extra transport costs of $10 per unit. Production costs will be the same in both countries. Product AA will require additional equipment and staff will need training; this will cost $6 million at either location. 200,000 units of product AA will be made each year and each unit will generate a net cash inflow of $25 before extra transport costs. If product AA is made in the UK, the factory will be closed and sold at the end of the product's life.

Product X

Now, however, the directors are considering a further possibility: product X could be produced at the UK factory and product AA at the Eastern European factory. Product X must be introduced in one year's time and will remain in production for three years. If it is introduced, the manufacture of product A will have to cease a year earlier than planned. If this happened, output of product A would be increased by 12.5% to maximum capacity next year, its last year, to build inventory prior to the product's withdrawal. The existing staff would be transferred to product X.

The equipment needed to make product X would cost $4 million. 50,000 units of product X would be made in its first year; after that, production would rise to 75,000 units a year. Product X would earn a net cash flow of $70 per unit. After three years' production of product X, the UK factory would be closed and sold. (Product AA would not be transferred back to the factory in the UK at that stage; production would continue at the Eastern European site.)

Sale of factory

It is expected that the UK factory could be sold for $5.5 million at any time between the beginning of year 2 and the end of year 10. If the factory is sold, CAF Company will make redundancy payments of $2 million and the sale of equipment will raise $350,000.

CAF Company's cost of capital is 5% each year.

Required:

(a) Prepare calculations that show which of the three options is financially the best.

(15 marks)

(b) The directors of CAF Company are unsure whether their estimates are correct. Calculate and discuss the sensitivity of your choice of option in (a) to:

(i) changes in transport costs; (3 marks)

(ii) changes in the selling price of the factory. (3 marks)

(c) Briefly discuss the business issues that should be considered before relocating to another country. (4 marks)

(Total: 25 marks)

283   PK GLASS COMPANY

W Company is a division of PK Glass Company. W Company produces commercial window glass. The glass is fragile and must be packaged very carefully. The packaging is done internally in W Company's packaging department by an automated packaging machine. The estimated annual cost, based on the current costs of the packaging department, is as follows:

	$000
Prime cost	700
Departmental overhead	
Supervisors' salaries	70
Rent	50
Depreciation of machinery	190
Maintenance of machinery	100
Allocation of general overhead	140
	1,250

Although the machinery is only two years old, it has become unreliable and costly to maintain. The machinery cost $1 million and had an estimated useful life of five years, after which it could be sold as scrap for $50,000. If the machinery was scrapped today it would generate $70,000.

In order to reduce packaging costs, the management team of W Company is considering two alternatives from two external companies (X Packaging Company and Y Company).

Alternative 1 – Closure of the packaging department

X Packaging Company has offered to undertake all of the packaging for a fixed fee of $950,000 per annum for the next three years. If W Company accepts this offer, its packaging department would be closed down.

Details relating to the closure are:

Buildings

The buildings currently used by W Company's packaging department would be used by another department in W Company that currently pays rent of $60,000 per annum for accommodation.

Direct labour

30% of the estimate for prime cost is direct labour. Redundancy payments of 10% of the annual wages will be paid.

Direct materials

The packaging materials currently held in inventory have a book value of $100,000 and a scrap value of $20,000. The current replacement cost of the materials is $125,000.

Supervisors

The supervisors would be redeployed in another department within W Company.

Alternative 2 – Sub-contract the maintenance

Y Company has offered to maintain the machinery for a fixed fee of $80,000 per annum for the next three years.

Taxation

W Company incurs 30% tax on corporate profits. Tax allowances on the cost of the packaging machine are 25% per annum on a reducing balance basis. At the end of the machine's life, a balancing charge or allowance will arise equal to the difference between the scrap proceeds and the tax written-down value. Corporation tax is payable 50% in the year in which the profit is earned and 50% in the following year.

The company's after-tax cost of capital is 12%.

Required:

(a) Determine which of the alternatives is the best one from a financial point of view. (You should show all calculations and state any assumptions that you have made.)

(19 marks)

(b) Briefly discuss any other issues that might affect the recommendation you have made in your answer to part (a).

(6 marks)

(Total: 25 marks)

284 H (MAY 08 EXAM)

H is a well-established manufacturer of household products. It produces its accounts to 31 December each year.

The machinery that is currently being used to manufacture one of H's products will have to be scrapped on 31 December 20X8, because H can no longer obtain a safety certificate for it. H is considering investing $500,000 in new machinery on 1 January 20X9 in order to continue manufacturing this product. If the project does not go ahead, H will no longer be able to manufacture the product.

The new machinery will have sufficient production capacity to meet the expected sales demand levels for the next five years. It will have a life of five years, and at the end of that time it will be sold for $100,000. It will qualify for tax depreciation at the rate of 20% per annum on a reducing balance basis.

Sales revenues and production costs for the current year, which ends on 31 December 20X8, are predicted to be as follows:

	$000
Sales revenue	540
Production costs	
Variable production costs	240
Fixed overhead *	120
	360
Fixed non-production costs	80
Profit before tax	100

* Fixed production overhead cost includes $20,000 for depreciation of the existing machinery.

Sales

The following table of index numbers (20X8 = 100) shows the predicted levels of sales volume.

	20X9	20Y0	20Y1	20Y2	20Y3
Sales volume	103	105	109	107	110

Assume there are no changes in the selling price other than those caused by selling price inflation, which is expected to be 4% per year.

Costs

Production costs are not expected to change as a result of investing in the new machinery, but production cost inflation is expected to be 5% per year. Non-production cost inflation is expected to be 3% per year.

Taxation

H is liable to pay tax on its profits at the rate of 30%. Half of this is payable in the year in which the profit is earned and the remainder is payable in the following year.

H has a post tax money cost of capital of 14% per annum.

Required:

(a)   Calculate the Net Present Value (NPV) of the project (to the nearest $000).

(15 marks)

(b)   Calculate the post tax money cost of capital at which H would be indifferent to accepting/rejecting the project.   (4 marks)

(c)   Explain your treatment of inflation in your solution to part (a) above and describe an alternative method that would have provided the same NPV.   (6 marks)
(Total: 25 marks)

285   PRINTING COMPANY (MAY 05 EXAM)

A printing company is considering investing in new equipment which has a capital cost of $3 million. The machine qualifies for tax depreciation at the rate of 25% per year on a reducing balance basis and has an expected life of five years. The residual value of the machine is expected to be $300,000 at the end of five years.

An existing machine would be sold immediately for $400,000 if the new machine were to be bought. This existing machine has a tax written down value of $250,000.

The existing machine generates annual revenues of $4 million and earns a contribution of 40% of sales. The new machine would reduce unit variable costs to 80% of their former value and increase output capacity by 20%. There is sufficient sales demand at the existing prices to make full use of this additional capacity.

The printing company pays corporation tax on its profits at the rate of 30%, with half of the tax being payable in the year in which the profit is earned and half in the following year.

The company's after tax cost of capital is 14% per year.

Required:

(a) Evaluate the proposed purchase of the new printing machine from a financial perspective using appropriate calculations, and advise the company as to whether the investment is worthwhile. **(15 marks)**

(b) Explain sensitivity analysis and prepare calculations to show the sensitivity of the decision to independent changes in each of the following:

    (i)   annual contribution;

    (ii)   rate of corporation tax on profits. **(10 marks)**

(Total: 25 marks)

286 HOTEL GROUP (NOV 09 EXAM)

A hotel group is considering the purchase of a new hotel on 1 January 20X0, the first day of its next financial year. The building will cost $650,000 and the equipment and other furnishings are expected to cost $250,000, also at the start of 20X0. The equipment and other furnishings will qualify for tax depreciation at the rate of 20% per annum on a reducing balance basis. No tax depreciation is available on the cost of the building. The building will be sold at the end of 20X4 for $650,000 and the equipment will be sold for $100,000 at the same time.

Guest revenue

The hotel is expected to open to guests on 1 July 20X0 and guest revenue for the remainder of 20X0 is expected to be $130,000. The number of guests in future calendar years is expected to increase in accordance with the following index (20X0 = 100):

20X1	180
20X2	190
20X3	210
20X4	220

Guest related costs

Variable guest related costs, which vary in direct proportion to the number of guests, are expected to be $20,000 in 20X0. In addition, there are annual guest related fixed costs which are expected to be $40,000 in 20X0. These fixed costs are not affected by the number of guests or by the opening dates of the hotel.

Other fixed costs

In addition to the guest related costs identified above, the hotel expects to incur other fixed costs of $25,000 per year, at 20X0 prices.

Inflation

The hotel group expects that cost inflation (applying to all types of cost) will be in accordance with the following index (20X0 = 100):

20X1	104
20X2	105
20X3	107
20X4	110

The group has decided that it will increase its prices to guests and these will increase in accordance with the following index (20X0 = 100):

20X1	100
20X2	102
20X3	104
20X4	107

Taxation

The hotel will be liable to Corporation Tax on its profits at the rate of 30%, payable in two equal instalments; one in the year in which the profits are earned and one in the following year.

Cost of capital

The hotel group's post tax money cost of capital is 8% per annum.

Required:

(a)   **Calculate the net present value of the cash flows arising from the investment and recommend to the hotel group whether or not to proceed with the purchase of the hotel.** **(14 marks)**

(b)   **Calculate the sensitivity of the investment to a change in the value of "other fixed costs".** **(6 marks)**

(Total: 20 marks)

287   X COMPANY

All of the 100 accountants employed by X Company are offered the opportunity to attend six training courses per year. Each course lasts for several days and requires the delegates to travel to a specially selected hotel for the training. The current costs incurred for each course are:

Delegate costs:

	$ per delegate per course
Travel	200
Accommodation, food and drink	670
	870

It is expected that the current delegate costs will increase by 5% per annum.

Course costs:

	$ per course
Room hire	1,500
Trainers	6,000
Course material	2,000
Equipment hire	1,500
Course administration	750
	11,750

It is expected that the current course costs will increase by 2.5% per annum.

The Human Resources Director of X Company is concerned at the level of costs that these courses incur and has recently read an article about the use of the Internet for the delivery of training courses (e-learning). She decided to hire an external consultant at a cost of $5,000 to advise the company on how to implement an e-learning solution.

The consultant prepared a report which detailed the costs of implementing and running and e-learning solution:

	Notes	$
Computer hardware	(1)	1,500,000
Software licences	(2)	35,000 per annum
Technical Manager	(3)	30,000 per annum
Camera and sound crew	(4)	4,000 per course
Trainers and course material	(5)	2,000 per course
Broadband connection	(6)	300 per delegate per annum

Notes:

(1) The computer hardware will be depreciated on a straight-line basis over five years. The scrap value at the end of the five years is expected to be $50,000.

(2) The company would sign a software licence agreement which fixes the annual software licence fee for five years. This fee is payable in advance.

(3) An employee working in the IT Department currently earning $20,000 per annum will be promoted to Technical Manager for this project. This employee's position will be replaced. The salary of the Technical Manger is expected to increase by 6% per annum.

(4) The company supplying the camera and sound crew for recording the courses for Internet delivery has agreed to hold its current level of pricing for the first two years but then it will increase costs by 6% per annum. All courses will be recorded in the first quarter of the year of delivery.

(5) The trainers will charge a fixed fee of $2,000 per course for the delivery and course material in the first year and expect to increase this by 6% per annum thereafter. The preparation of the course material and the recording of the trainers delivering the courses will take place in the first quarter of the year of delivery.

(6) All of the accountants utilising the training courses will be offered $300 towards broadband costs which will allow them to access the courses from home. They will claim this expense annually in arrears. Broadband costs are expected to decrease by 5% per annum after the first year as it becomes more widely used by Internet users.

(7) X Company uses a 14% cost of capital to appraise projects of this nature.

Ignore taxation.

Required:

As the Management Accountant for X Company:

(a) Prepare a financial evaluation of the options available to the company and advise the directors on the best course of action to take, from a purely financial point of view. (Your answer should state any assumptions you have made.)   **(16 marks)**

(b) (i) Using the annual equivalent technique, calculate the breakeven number of delegates per annum taking each of the six e-learning courses that is required to justify the implementation of the e-learning solution.

(Note that you should assume that the number of delegates taking the e-learning courses will be the same in each of the five years.)   **(6 marks)**

(ii) Comment on the implications of the breakeven number you have calculated in your answer to (b) (i).   **(3 marks)**

(Total: 25 marks)

288   JK (NOV 06 EXAM)

JK plc prepares its accounts to 31 December each year. It is considering investing in a new computer-controlled production facility on 1 January 20X7 at a cost of $50m. This will enable JK plc to produce a new product which it expects to be able to sell for four years. At the end of this time it has been agreed to sell the new production facility for $1m cash.

Sales of the product during the year ended 31 December 20X7 and the next three years are expected to be as follows:

Year ended 31 December	20X7	20X8	20X9	20Y0
Sales units (000)	100	105	110	108

Selling price, unit variable cost and fixed overhead costs (excluding depreciation) are expected to be as follows during the year ended 31 December 20X7:

	$
Selling price per unit	1,200
Variable production cost per unit	750
Variable selling and distribution cost per unit	100
Fixed production cost for the year	4,000,000
Fixed selling and distribution cost for the year	2,000,000
Fixed administration cost for the year	1,000,000

The following rates of annual inflation are expected for each of the years 20X8 – 20Y0:

	%
Selling prices	5
Production costs	8
Selling and distribution costs	6
Administration costs	5

The company pays taxation on its profits at the rate of 30%, with half of this being payable in the year in which the profit is earned and the remainder being payable in the following year. Investments of this type qualify for tax depreciation at the rate of 25% per annum on a reducing balance basis.

The Board of Directors of JK plc has agreed to use a 12% post-tax discount rate to evaluate this investment.

Required:

(a) Advise JK plc whether the investment is financially worthwhile.   (17 marks)

(b) Calculate the Internal Rate of Return of the investment.   (3 marks)

(c) Define and contrast (i) the real rate of return and (ii) the money rate of return, and explain how they would be used when calculating the net present value of a project's cash flows.   (5 marks)

(Total: 25 marks)

THE TREATMENT OF UNCERTAINTY IN DECISION MAKING

289   A BANK (MAY 08 EXAM)

A bank is reviewing the bank account it offers to its business customers and the charges it makes for routine transactions (for example paying into the account, writing cheques, making electronic payments and transfers). Currently, the bank's charges to its business customers are £0.60 per routine transaction. The bank pays interest to the customer at 0.1% per year on any balance in the account.

According to the bank's records, there are currently one million business customers. Each customer makes one thousand routine transactions each year; 45% of business customers maintain an average balance of £2,000 in their account. The accounts of the other 55% of business customers are overdrawn with an average overdraft balance of £4,000. Interest on overdrawn accounts is charged at 20% per year.

In addition, the bank has a number of savings account customers which, together with the bank's business customers, result in a balance of net funds that are invested by the bank and yield an annual return by 3% per year.

The bank is concerned about a growing tendency for its competitors to provide routine transactions free of charge to their business customers. As a result the bank is considering two account options:

Account Option One

An account that charges the business customer a fixed fee of £10 per month, with no further charges for any routine transactions. Interest would be paid to the business customer at 0.5% per year on any balances in the account. The bank expects that if it adopts this charging structure, it will increase the number of business customers by 5% from its present level.

Account Option Two

An account that does not charge the customer for any routine transactions, but pays no interest on any balances in the account. The bank expects that if it adopts this charging structure, this will increase the number of business customers by 10% from its present level. The bank does not expect the profile of new business customers to be different from existing business customers in terms of the balances in their accounts or the number of routine transactions they make. Interest will continue to be charged at 20% per year on overdrawn accounts. The bank does not expect that either of these options will result in any changes to its existing staffing or other resources.

The bank also expects that if it takes no action and continues with its existing bank account that the number of business customers will fall by 20%.

Required:

(a) **Recommend which course of action the bank should take by preparing calculations to show the annual profits from:**

   (i) **continuing with the existing bank account**

   (ii) **each of the two account options described above.** **(12 marks)**

The bank is also reviewing its policy with regard to small loans. Currently, the bank charges an arrangement fee of £500 per loan and interest on the average loan balance. The profit the bank makes on the interest it charges is 5% of the average loan balance. The bank's records show that there are 200,000 small loans in issue at any one time. The average loan balance is £5,000.

Market research undertaken by the bank has shown that if it were to carry out an advertising campaign that specifically targeted the small loans market, the number of loans would increase, though the amount of the increase is uncertain. It is predicted that the advertising campaign may increase the number of loans in issue at any one time to 250,000, 280,000 or 300,000.

Furthermore, it is believed that the advertising campaign would increase the value of the loans. The amount of the increase is uncertain, but it is believed that the average loan balance may increase to £7,500; or that they may increase by £9,000; or that they may increase by £10,000.

The expected total cost of the advertising campaign and the associated administrative costs are £112 million.

Required:

(b) **(i)** **Prepare a two-way data table that shows profit that would be earned by the bank for each of the NINE possible outcomes that are expected to arise as a result of the advertising campaign.** **(8 marks)**

   (ii) **State any other factors the bank should consider before making its decision and advise the bank on whether or not it should carry out the advertising campaign.** **(5 marks)**

(Total: 25 marks)

290   TICKET AGENT

A ticket agent has an arrangement with a concert hall that holds concerts on 60 nights a year whereby he receives discounts as follows per concert:

For purchase of	He receives a discount of
200 tickets	20%
300 tickets	25%
400 tickets	30%
500 tickets or more	40%

Purchases must be in full hundreds. The average price per ticket is $3.

He must decide in advance each year the number of tickets he will purchase. If he has any tickets unsold by the afternoon of the concert he must return them to the box office. If the box office sells any of these he receives 60% of their price.

His sales records over a few years show that for a concert with extremely popular artistes he can be confident of selling 500 tickets, for one with less known artistes 350 tickets, and for one with relatively unknown artistes 200 tickets.

His records show that 10% of the tickets he returns are sold by the box office.

His administration costs incurred in selling tickets are the same per concert irrespective of the popularity of the artistes.

There are two possible scenarios in which his sales records can be viewed:

Scenario 1:   that, on average, he can expect concerts with lesser known artistes.

Scenario 2:   that the frequency of concerts will be:

	%
with popular artistes	45
with lesser known artistes	30
with unknown artistes	25
	——
	100

Required:

(a)   Calculate separately for each of Scenarios 1 and 2:

- the expected demand for tickets per concert;
- the level of his purchases of tickets per concert that will give him the largest profit over a long period of time;
- the profit per concert that this level of purchases of tickets will yield.

(15 marks)

(b)   Calculate for Scenario 2 only the maximum sum per annum that the ticket agent should pay to a concert specialist for 100% correct predictions as to the likely success of each concert.

(10 marks)

(Total: 25 marks)

291   THE RS GROUP

The RS Group owns a large store in Ludborough. The store is old-fashioned and profits are declining. Management is considering what to do – there appear to be three possibilities:

(1)   Shut down and sell the site for $15m.

(2)   Continue as before with profits declining at 10% per annum.

(3)   Upgrade the store.

The Group has had similar problems in the past and experience suggests that when stores are upgraded, 60% achieve good results and 40% poor results. Because of the doubts, management is considering whether to contract a leading market research company to carry out consumer research in Ludborough for $1m. It has been fortunate in obtaining details of the track record of the research company, as follows:

		Actual outcome	
		Good	*Poor*
Attitude predicted by research:	*Positive*	0.85*	0.10
	Negative	0.15	0.90

*This means that when the results were good the research had predicted this 85% of the time.

If the research indicates a positive attitude, management will consider de-luxe upgrading which will generate more profit but will cost $12m, as compared with standard upgrading costing $6m. If the research indicates a negative attitude, then management will consider standard upgrading compared with shutting down and selling the site.

The time scale for the analysis is 10 years and the following estimates of returns have been made:

With de-luxe upgrading:

Good results	$40m total present value
Poor results	$20m total present value

With standard upgrading:

Good results	$25m total present value
Poor results	$10m total present value

If operations continue as before, returns next year will be $2m in present value terms but this will fall by 10% per annum.

Required:

(a)   **to analyse the above position and to present your results using a decision tree;**

  Notes:

  (1)   **No discounting is necessary for this question as the values are already expressed in present-day terms.**

  (2)   **Your workings must be shown.**   **(16 marks)**

(b)   **to recommend what decisions should be taken;**   **(3 marks)**

(c)   **to comment about the basis of your analysis.**   **(6 marks)**

                                                                                    (Total: 25 marks)

292 EHI COMPANY

Enterprise Health International Company (EHI) is a commercial healthcare organisation that undertakes the development and marketing of new treatments. EHI is based in the United Kingdom and receives patients from around the world. One possible new treatment is under review. The demand for this treatment is very uncertain.

Preliminary research has indicated that the treatment can be developed but there are two alternative approaches to its design. The details of these alternatives are:

- a low technology route using existing surgical treatment and drugs; this involves a development cost of $800,000 and a variable cost of $40,000 per treatment. This route will take one year to develop, with the development cost being paid for one year from now;

- a high technology route using new surgical treatment, drugs and equipment; this involves a development cost of $6,300,000 and a variable cost of $18,000 per treatment. This route will take three years to develop, with development costs being paid for in three equal annual instalments, the first of which is one year from now.

EHI's managers are uncertain which of the two development alternatives to follow. They are considering an offer from a firm of strategic consultants to advise on the annual level of demand for treatments. For the purpose of appraising this offer it may be assumed that two levels of annual demand for treatments are possible – weak (30 treatments and 0.4 probability) and strong (65 treatments and 0.6 probability). It may be assumed that the consultants have a 92% chance of correctly forecasting each level of demand.

EHI appraises projects using cash flows over a period of ten years from now and a 10% annual discount rate. It is forecast that the selling price of each treatment will be $43,000.

Required:

(a) Calculate the minimum number of treatments demanded annually to make:

   (i)   the low technology route viable;

   (ii) the high technology route viable; and

   (iii) calculate the number of treatments demanded annually to make the low- and high-technology routes equally viable. **(9 marks)**

(b) Draw a diagram to illustrate the relative sensitivity of the two alternative routes to the number of treatments demanded annually. **(7 marks)**

(c) Advise EHI's managers on the maximum amount they should pay for the forecast of the annual demand for treatments. In preparing your advice, you are advised to use decision-tree analysis. **(9 marks)**

(Total: 25 marks)

293 H PRINTING (MAY 07 EXAM)

H, a printing company, uses traditional absorption costing to report its monthly profits.

It is seeking to increase its business by winning work from new customers. It now has the opportunity to prepare a quotation for a large organisation that currently requires a new catalogue of its services.

A technical report on the resource requirements for the catalogues has been completed at a cost of $1,000 and its details are summarised below:

Production period

It is expected that the total time required to print and despatch the catalogue will be one week.

Material A

10,000 sheets of special printing paper will be required. This is a paper that is in regular use by H and the company has 3,400 sheets in inventory. These originally cost $1.40 per sheet but the current market price is $1.50 per sheet. The resale price of the sheets held in inventory is $1.20 per sheet.

Material B

This is a special ink that H will need to purchase at a cost of $8 per litre. 200 litres will be required for this catalogue but the supplier has a minimum order size of 250 litres. H does not foresee any other use for this ink, but will hold the surplus in inventory. H's inventory policy is to review slow moving items regularly. The cost of any inventory item that has not been used for more than six months is accounted for as an expense of the period in which that review occurs.

Direct labour

Sufficient people are already employed by H to print the catalogue, but some of the printing will require overtime working due to the availability of a particular machine that is used on other work.

The employees are normally paid $8 per hour, the order will require 150 hours of work and 50 of these hours will be in excess of the employees' normal working week. A rate of $10 per hour is paid for these overtime hours. Employees are paid using an hourly rate with a guaranteed minimum wage for their normal working week.

Supervision

An existing supervisor will take responsibility for the catalogue in addition to her existing duties. She is not currently fully employed and receives a salary of $500 per week.

Machinery

Two different types of machine will be required:

Machine A will print the catalogues. This is expected to take 20 hours of machine time. The running cost of machine A is $5 per hour. There is currently 30 hours of unused time on machine A per week that is being sold to other printers for $12 per hour.

Machine B will be used to cut and bind the catalogues. This machine is being used to full capacity in the normal working week and this is why there is a need to work overtime. The catalogue will require 25 machine hours and these have a running cost of $4 per hour.

Despatch

There will be a delivery cost of $400 to transport the catalogues to the customer.

Fixed overhead costs

H uses a traditional absorption costing system to attribute fixed overhead costs to its work. The absorption rate that it uses is $20 per direct labour hour.

Profit mark-up

H applies a 30% mark-up to its costs to determine its selling prices.

Required:

(a)   In order to assist the management of H in preparing its quotation, prepare a schedule showing the relevant costs for the production of the catalogues. State clearly your reason for including or excluding each value that has been provided in the above scenario.   **(15 marks)**

(b)   Explain how the use of relevant costs as the basis of setting a selling price may be appropriate for short-term pricing decisions but may be inappropriate for long-term pricing decisions. Your answer should also discuss the conflict between reporting profitability within a traditional absorption costing system and the use of relevant cost based pricing.   **(10 marks)**

(Total: 25 marks)

294   D RESCUE (MAY 07 EXAM)

D provides a motorist rescue service to its members. At present all members pay a basic fee of $100 per year but D is considering the introduction of different fees for members depending on the data they provide when joining the service. The number of members, and therefore the fee income of D, is uncertain but the following estimates have been made:

Number of members	Probability
20,000	0.3
30,000	0.5
40,000	0.2

Required:

(a)   Calculate the expected annual fee income of D.   **(2 marks)**

The operating costs to be incurred by D have been analysed between call-out costs and administration costs. These operating costs have been assumed to vary in relation to the number of members and consequently the average costs per member for next year are expected to be:

Call-out cost per member for the year $50
Administration cost per member for the year $10

Each of these operating costs may vary by plus or minus 20%. There is equal probability of these costs being as expected, 20% higher, or 20% lower. In addition D expects to incur annual fixed costs of $1,100,000.

Required:

(b)   Using expected values, calculate the breakeven number of members.   **(3 marks)**

(c)   Prepare a two-way data table that shows the nine possible profit values.   **(6 marks)**

(d)   Explain the meaning of table that you have produced in (c) above and, by including appropriate probability values, how it may be used by management.   **(4 marks)**

Now that you have presented your calculations and explanations to the Management Team of D they have questioned the validity of the assumption that costs are caused by and therefore vary in relation to the number of members. They referred to the activities that are performed by the company:

- processing applications for membership;

- operating the call centre that deals with logging and scheduling rescues;

- providing patrol vehicles and mechanics for breakdown assistance;

- recording details of the time taken to respond to members' rescues;

- recording details of the costs incurred in carrying out each rescue.

The Management Team collectively agreed that your assumption that operating costs are driven by the number of members was too simplistic and that in future the Administration department should request the following information from members:

- member's date of birth;

- member's address;

- number of years the member has been a qualified driver;

- age of vehicle;

- make and model of vehicle;

- average annual mileage.

Required:

(e) **Explain how and why the collection of this data from members might improve the information that would be available to the Management Team.** **(10 marks)**

(Total: 25 marks)

295 MP ORGANISATION (NOV 05 EXAM)

The MP Organisation is an independent film production company. It has a number of potential films that it is considering producing, one of which is the subject of a management meeting next week. The film which has been code named CA45 is a thriller based on a novel by a well-respected author.

The script has already been written at a cost of $10,000 and preliminary discussions have been held with the lead actors. The MP Organisation has incurred travel and other incidental costs of $4,000 to date.

The following additional costs have been estimated in order to produce the film:

	$000
Production director's fee	100
Set design	10
Costumes and wardrobe	20
Actors' fees	50
Musician / Songwriter for soundtrack	5
Camera and equipment hire	20
Actors' travel and accommodation costs	10

	$000
Other production costs	5

Production of the film is estimated to take 16 weeks, and all of the above costs would be incurred during this period, though there is some uncertainty about the accuracy of these cost estimates. These cost values are those most likely to be incurred. With the exception of the payment to the production director which is a fixed fee, the other costs could be up to 10% higher or lower than the values estimated.

In addition there will be advertising, promotion and marketing costs of $15,000 immediately, $10,000 in each of years 1 and 2, and then $5,000 during each of the next three years. These figures are not subject to any uncertainty.

The film is expected to have a life of five years. During the first three years the film will be sold to cinemas through distributors and MP will receive 25% of the gross revenues. The film will be sold as a DVD for the remaining two years and MP will receive 100% of these revenues. The expected gross revenues are as follows:

Year	Source	Gross revenue	MP's share
1	Cinema	$400,000	25%
2	Cinema	$600,000	25%
3	Cinema	$450,000	25%
4	DVD	$50,000	100%
5	DVD	$30,000	100%

However it is thought that the gross revenues could vary by as much as 20% higher or lower than those stated, depending on the popularity of the film. The initial level of popularity will continue for all five years.

The MP Organisation evaluates new films using a cost of capital of 15% per year.

Required:

(a) **Prepare calculations for each combination of the most likely, optimistic and pessimistic cost and revenue values to evaluate whether or not the MP Organisation should continue with the production of the film. Discuss your analysis and make a recommendation to MP.** **(15 marks)**

(b) **Prepare notes for the management meeting that explain how probabilities can be used:**

(i) **to calculate the expected NPV; and**

(ii) **in a simulation model to evaluate the risk of a long-term decision. (10 marks)**

(Total: 25 marks)

296 HEALTH CLINIC (MAY 06 EXAM)

A health clinic is reviewing its plans for the next three years. It is a not-for-profit organisation but it has a financial responsibility to manage its costs and to ensure that it provides a value for money service to its clients. The health clinic uses the net present value technique to appraise the financial viability of delivering the service, but it also considers other non-financial factors before making any final decisions.

The present facilities, which incur an annual total cost of $300,000, are only sufficient to meet a low level of service provision, so the manager is considering investing in facilities to meet potential higher levels of demand. For the purpose of evaluating this decision the possible levels of demand for the health clinic's services have been simplified to high, medium or low.

The possible demand for the services in the first year and the level of demand that could follow that specific level in the next years, and their expected probabilities, are as follows:

Year 1	Probability	Years 2 and 3	Probability
Low	30%	Low	40%
		Medium	60%
		High	0%
Medium	50%	Low	30%
		Medium	40%
		High	30%
High	20%	Low	0%
		Medium	30%
		High	70%

The level of demand will be the same in years 2 and 3.

The manager is considering two alternative investments in facilities:

Facility A has the capacity to meet the low and medium levels of demand and requires an investment at the start of year 1 of $500,000. Thereafter it incurs annual fixed costs of $100,000 and annual variable costs depending on the level of operation. These annual variable costs are expected to be $150,000 at the low level of operation and $250,000 at the medium level of operation.

Facility B has the capacity to meet all levels of demand and requires an investment at the start of year 1 of $800,000. Thereafter it incurs annual fixed costs of $200,000 and annual variable costs depending on the level of operation. These annual variable costs are expected to be $100,000 at the low level of operation, $150,000 at the medium level of operation and $200,000 at the high level of operation.

Neither of these alternative investments has any residual value at the end of year 3.

If the facilities of the health clinic are insufficient to meet the level of service demand that occurs, the clinic must obtain additional facilities on a yearly contract basis at the following annual costs:

Level of service provision available internally	Level of service provision demanded	Annual cost of additional facilities
Low	Medium	$100,000
Low	High	$250,000
Medium	High	$150,000

These additional facilities are not under the direct control of the health clinic manager.

Note: All monetary values used throughout the question have been stated in terms of their present value. No further discounting is required.

Required:

(a) Prepare a decision tree to illustrate the investment decision that needs to be made by the manager of the health clinic. (Numerical values are NOT required.) (6 marks)

(b) Advise the manager of the health clinic which investment decision should be undertaken on financial grounds. (15 marks)

(c) Briefly discuss any non-financial factors that the manager should consider before making her final investment decision. (4 marks)

(Total: 25 marks)

297 THEATRE (NOV 06 EXAM)

A theatre has a seating capacity of 500 people and is considering engaging MS and her orchestra for a concert for one night only. The fee that would be charged by MS would be $10,000. If the theatre engages MS, then this sum is payable regardless of the size of the theatre audience.

Based on past experience of events of this type, the price of the theatre ticket would be $25 per person. The size of the audience for this event is uncertain, but based on past experience it is expected to be as follows:

	Probability
300 people	50%
400 people	30%
500 people	20%

In addition to the sale of the theatre tickets, it can be expected that members of the audience will also purchase confectionery both prior to the performance and during the interval. The contribution that this would yield to the theatre is unclear, but has been estimated as follows:

Contribution from confectionery sales	Probability
Contribution of $3 per person	30%
Contribution of $5 per person	50%
Contribution of $10 per person	20%

Required:

(a) Using expected values as the basis of your decision, advise the theatre management whether it is financially worthwhile to engage MS for the concert.
(5 marks)

(b) Prepare a two-way data table to show the profit values that could occur from deciding to engage MS for the concert. (5 marks)

(c) Explain, using the probabilities provided and your answer to (b) above, how the two-way data table can be used by the theatre management to evaluate the financial risks of the concert, including the probability of making a profit. (9 marks)

(d) Calculate the maximum price that the theatre management should agree to pay for perfect information relating to the size of the audience and the level of contribution from confectionery sales. (6 marks)

(Total: 25 marks)

MANAGING SHORT TERM FINANCE

298   MERTON INC

The following financial information relates to Merton Inc, a supplier of photographic equipment and film services to the film industry.

Income statements for years ended 30 April

	20X6	20X5	20X4
	$m	$m	$m
Sales revenue	160.0	145.0	132.0
Cost of sales	120.0	105.3	95.7
	40.0	39.7	36.3
Operating expenses	30.0	26.0	23.5
Operating profit	10.0	13.7	12.8
Interest	3.6	3.3	3.3
Profit before tax	6.4	10.4	9.5
Taxation	1.9	3.1	2.8
Profit after tax	4.5	7.3	6.7
Dividends	1.5	1.7	1.6
Net change in equity (retained profits)	3.0	5.6	5.1
Share price at 30 April	$2.70	$5.11	$4.69

Statements of financial position (Balance sheets) as at 30 April

	20X6		20X5	
	$m	$m	$m	$m
Non-current assets		45		35
Current assets				
Inventory	36		32	
Receivables	41		24	
Cash	1		16	
		78		72
		123		107
Equity and liabilities				
Ord shares (50¢ par)	10		10	
Reserves	50		47	
Total equity		60		57

Non-current liabilities			
10% loan stock 20X8	13	13	
8% loan stock 20Y3	25	25	
	38		38
Current liabilities			
Trade payables	17	11	
Overdraft	8	1	
	25		12
Total equity and liabilities	123		107

Notes: All sales are on credit. Merton currently pays interest on its overdraft at an annual rate of 4%, although this rate is variable.

The Finance Director decided when taking up his appointment that substantial improvement was needed in the area of working capital management and asked the factoring subsidiary of a major bank to provide a quotation for non-recourse factoring. The factor has indicated that it would require an annual fee of 0.5% of sales. It would advance Merton Inc 80% of the face value of sales at an interest rate 1% above the current overdraft rate. It expects the average time taken by receivables to pay to fall immediately to 75 days, with a reduction to no more than the average for the sector within two years.

The Finance Director has also been assured that irrecoverable debts, currently standing at $500,000 per year, would fall by 80%. Savings in current administration costs of Merton Inc of $100,000 per year would be achieved as a result of factoring.

The Finance Director has collected the following average data for the media sector:

Inventory days	100 days
Receivables days	60 days
Payables days	50 days
Current ratio	3.5
Quick ratio	2.5

Required

(a) Using appropriate ratios and financial analysis, comment on the view of the Finance Director that substantial improvement is needed in the area of working capital management of Merton Inc;   **(15 marks)**

(b) Determine whether the factoring company's offer can be recommended on financial grounds. Assume a working year of 365 days and base your analysis on financial information for 20X6.   **(10 marks)**

(Total: 25 marks)

299 FLG CO *Walk in the footsteps of a top tutor*

FLG Co has annual credit sales of $4.2 million and cost of sales of $1·89 million. Current assets consist of inventory and accounts receivable. Current liabilities consist of accounts payable and an overdraft with an average interest rate of 7% per year. The company gives two months' credit to its customers and is allowed, on average, one month's credit by trade suppliers. It has an operating cycle of three months.

Other relevant information:

Current ratio of FLG Co   1.4

Cost of long-term finance of FLG Co   11%

Required:

(a)   **Discuss the key factors which determine the level of investment in current assets.**
                                                                (6 marks)

(b)   **Discuss the ways in which factoring and invoice discounting can assist in the management of accounts receivable.**   **(6 marks)**

(c)   **Calculate the size of the overdraft of FLG Co, the net working capital of the company and the total cost of financing its current assets.**   **(6 marks)**

(d)   FLG Co wishes to minimise its inventory costs. Annual demand for a raw material costing $12 per unit is 60,000 units per year. Inventory management costs for this raw material are as follows:

Ordering cost: $6 per order

Holding cost: $0.5 per unit per year

The supplier of this raw material has offered a bulk purchase discount of 1% for orders of 10,000 units or more. If bulk purchase orders are made regularly, it is expected that annual holding cost for this raw material will increase to $2 per unit per year.

Required:

(i)   **Calculate the total cost of inventory for the raw material when using the economic order quantity.**   **(4 marks)**

(ii) **Determine whether accepting the discount offered by the supplier will minimise the total cost of inventory for the raw material.**   **(3 marks)**

                                                        (Total: 25 marks)

300 PKA CO *Walk in the footsteps of a top tutor*

PKA Co is a European company that sells goods solely within Europe. The recently-appointed financial manager of PKA Co has been investigating the working capital management of the company and has gathered the following information:

Inventory management

The current policy is to order 100,000 units when the inventory level falls to 35,000 units. Forecast demand to meet production requirements during the next year is 625,000 units. The cost of placing and processing an order is €250, while the cost of holding a unit in stores is €0.50 per unit per year. Both costs are expected to be constant during the next year. Orders are received two weeks after being placed with the supplier. You should assume a 50-week year and that demand is constant throughout the year.

Accounts receivable management

Domestic customers are allowed 30 days' credit, but the financial statements of PKA Co show that the average accounts receivable period in the last financial year was 75 days. The financial manager also noted that bad debts as a percentage of sales, which are all on credit, increased in the last financial year from 5% to 8%.

Accounts payable management

PKA Co has used a foreign supplier for the first time and must pay $250,000 to the supplier in six months' time. The financial manager is concerned that the cost of these supplies may rise in euro terms and has decided to hedge the currency risk of this account payable. The following information has been provided by the company's bank:

Spot rate ($ per €):   1.998 ± 0.002

Six months forward rate ($ per €):   1.979 ± 0.004

Money market rates available to PKA Co:

	Borrowing	Deposit
One year euro interest rates:	6.1%	5.4%
One year dollar interest rates:	4.0%	3.5%

Assume that it is now 1 December and that PKA Co has no surplus cash at the present time.

Required:

(a) Identify the objectives of working capital management and discuss the conflict that may arise between them.   **(3 marks)**

(b) Calculate the cost of the current ordering policy and determine the saving that could be made by using the economic order quantity model.   **(7 marks)**

(c) Discuss ways in which PKA Co could improve the management of domestic accounts receivable.   **(7 marks)**

(Total: 17 marks)

301 FRANTIC CO (PART I)

Frantic Co is a specialist car manufacturer and is a member of a group of companies that provides a range of automobile products and services. It is currently facing difficulties in the management of its working capital and the financial controller of Frantic Co is to investigate the situation with a view to optimising supplier payments and customer discounts to ease projected cash flow problems.

Payables

Payables arise only for engine purchases. Engine suppliers have offered an early settlement discount of 1.5% if invoices are settled within one month of delivery. If the settlement discount is not taken, normal payment terms of two months from delivery apply.

Receivables

The cars are sold at $42,500 each and unit sales are equal to the units produced in each month. 50% of the cars are made to order and payment is on a 'cash on delivery' basis. The remaining cars are sold to specialist retailers who take two months' credit. Frantic is considering offering the specialist retailers a 2% discount for payments made within one month of sale. It is expected that 75% of the retailers would take up the offer.

The company uses its bank overdraft rate of 15% as its discount rate.

Required:

(a)   Calculate:

(i)   if it is beneficial for Frantic to change from a two month payment period to a one month payment period for payables   **(3 marks)**

(ii)   if it is beneficial for Frantic to implement the 2% discount for receivables.
                                                                                          (2 marks)

(b)   Write a report to the Managing Director which identifies:

–   how cash flow problems can arise

–   the methods available for easing cash shortages

–   the techniques, besides cash budgeting, that could be used to monitor and manage cash resources

–   the benefits of centralising cash management in a treasury department for group companies.   **(20 marks)**

In all your answers clearly state any assumptions you make.   **(Total: 25 marks)**

302 FRANTIC CO (PART II)

Frantic Co is a specialist car manufacturer and is a member of a group of companies that provides a range of automobile products and services. It is currently facing difficulties in the management of its working capital and the financial controller of Frantic Co is to investigate the situation with a view to optimising supplier payments, inventory ordering and receivables discounts to ease projected cash flow problems.

Payables

Payables arise only for engine purchases. Engine suppliers have offered an early settlement discount of 1.5% if invoices are settled within one month of delivery. Frantic has decided to accept its suppliers offer.

Inventory

Frantic has a budgeted production of 800 cars for the year. The most expensive bought-in components for the cars are engines. Other components are either made in-house or are minor items which are bought-in but which do not require special inventory management. Engine purchase prices are subject to quantity discounts according to the following schedule:

Order quantity	Order quantity
0–49 units	0%
50249 units	2%
above 249 units	3%

Other details are:

Engine price (before discounts):	$1,300
Inventory holding costs per annum (as a percentage of engine costs):	22%
Delivery costs per order:	$1,200

There is zero lead-time on engine orders.

Receivables

The cars are sold at $42,500 each and unit sales are equal to the units produced in each month. 50% of the cars are made to order and payment is on a 'cash on delivery' basis. The remaining cars are sold to specialist retailers who take two months' credit.

Other factors

A budget forecast is to be prepared for a six-month period. Other variable costs (including the other components) represent 65% of sales value and are payable immediately. Fixed costs are $18,000 per month for the first three months, rising to $22,000 per month thereafter. The first instalment of $3.2 million for a major re-tooling operation will be paid in month three of the budget forecast.

Assume that the opening bank overdraft is $25,000 and that there are payables outstanding to the value of $97,500 which will be paid in the first month of the budget plan. It is expected that receivables payments of $1,062,500 will be received in each of the first two months.

The company uses its bank overdraft rate of 15% as its discount rate. Assume one month comprises 30 days, that no opening inventory of engines is held and that production is evenly spread throughout the year.

Required:

(a)   Calculate the optimal ordering policy for engines   **(7 marks)**

(b)   On the basis of your answer to part (a), and the information given above, prepare the cash budget for Frantic for each of the next six months.   **(18 marks)**

In all your answers clearly state any assumptions you make.   **(Total: 25 marks)**

303 JACK GEEP

141

Jack Geep will set up a new business as a sole trader on 1 January 20X8 making decorative glassware. Jack is in the process of planning the initial cash flows of the business. He estimates that there will not be any sales demand in January 20X8 so production in that month will be used to build up inventories to satisfy the expected demand in February 20X8. Thereafter it is intended to schedule production in order to build up sufficient finished goods inventory at the end of each month to satisfy demand during the following month. Production will, however, need to be 5% higher than sales due to expected defects that will have to be scrapped. Defects are only discovered after the goods have been completed. The company will not hold inventories of raw materials or work in progress.

As the business is new, demand is uncertain, but Jack has estimated three possible levels of demand in 20X8 as follows:

	High demand	Medium demand	Low demand
	$	$	$
February	22,000	20,000	19,000
March	26,000	24,000	23,000
April	30,000	28,000	27,000
May	29,000	27,000	26,000
June	35,000	33,000	32,000

Demand for July 20X8 onwards is expected to be the same as June 20X8. The probability of each level of demand occurring each month is as follows:

High 0.05; Medium 0.85; Low 0.10.

It is expected that 10% of the total sales value will be cash sales, mainly being retail customers making small purchases. The remaining 90% of sales will be made on two months' credit. A 2.5% discount will, however, be offered to credit customers settling within one month. It is estimated that customers, representing half of credit sales by value, will take advantage of the discount while the remainder will take the full two months to pay.

Variable production costs (excluding costs of rejects) per $1,000 of sales are as follows:

	$
Labour	300
Materials	200
Variable overhead	100

Labour is paid in the month in which labour costs are incurred. Materials are paid one month in arrears and variable overheads are paid two months in arrears. Fixed production and administration overheads, excluding depreciation, are $7,000 per month and are payable in the same month as the expenditure is incurred.

Jack employed a firm of consultants to give him initial business advice. Their fee of $12,000 will be paid in February 20X8. Smelting machinery will be purchased on 1 January 20X8 for $200,000 payable in February 20X8. Further machinery will be purchased for$50,000 in March 20X8 payable in April 20X8. This machinery is highly specialized and will have a low net realisable value after purchase.

Jack has redundancy money from his previous employment and savings totalling $150,000, which he intends to pay into his bank account on 1 January 20X8 as the initial capital of the business. He realises that this will be insufficient for his business plans, so he is intending to approach his bank for finance in the form of both a fixed term loan and an overdraft. The only asset Jack has is his house that is valued at $200,000, but he has an outstanding mortgage of $80,000 on this property.

The consultants advising Jack have recommended that rather than accumulating sufficient inventory to satisfy the following month's demand he should not maintain any inventory levels but merely produce sufficient in each month to meet the expected demand for that month.

Jack's production manager objected: 'I need to set up my production schedule based on the expected average demand for the month. I will reduce production in the month if it seems demand is low. However, there is no way production can be increased during the month to accommodate demand if it happens to be at the higher level that month. As a result, under this new system, there would be no inventory to fall back on and the extra sales, when monthly demand is high, would be lost, as customers require immediate delivery.' In respect of this, an assessment of the impact of the introduction of just-in-time inventory management on cash flows has been made that showed the following:

	January	February	March	April	May	June
Net cash flow ($)	143,000	(223,279)	(7,587)	(50,667)	1,843	1,704
Month-end balance ($)	143,000	(80,279)	(87,866)	(138,533)	(136,690)	(134,986)

Required:

(a) Prepare a monthly cash budget for Jack Geep's business for the six month period ending 30 June 20X8. Calculations should be made on the basis of the expected values of sales. The cash budget should show the net cash inflow or outflow in each month and the cumulative cash surplus or deficit at the end of each month.

For this purpose ignore bank finance and the suggested use of just-in-time inventory management. **(17 marks)**

(b) Evaluate the impact for Jack Geep of introducing just-in-time inventory management. This should include an assessment of the wider implications of just-in-time inventory management in the particular circumstances of Jack Geep's business. **(8 marks)**

(Total: 25 marks)

304 ANJO

Extracts from the recent financial statements of Anjo Inc are as follows:

Income statements

	20X6	20X5
	$000	$000
Sales revenue	15,600	11,100
Cost of sales	9,300	6,600
Gross profit	6,300	4,500
Administration expenses	1,000	750
Profit before interest and tax	5,300	3,750
Interest	100	15
Profit before tax	5,200	3,735

Statements of financial position (Balance sheets)

		20X6		20X5
	$000	$000	$000	$000
Non-current assets		5,750		5,400
Current assets				
Inventory	3,000		1,300	
Receivables	3,800		1,850	
Cash	120		900	
		6,920		4,050
Total assets		8,800		7,700
Total equity		4,930		5,950
Current liabilities				
Trade payables	2,870		1,600	
Overdraft	1,000		150	
		3,870		1,750
Total equity and liabilities		8,800		7,700

All sales were on credit. Anjo Inc has no long-term debt. Credit purchases in each year were 95% of cost of sales. Anjo Inc pays interest on its overdraft at an annual rate of 8%. Sector averages:

Inventory days:	90 days
Receivables days:	60 days
Payables days:	80 days

Required:

(a) Calculate the following ratios for each year and comment on your findings.

    (i)   Inventory days

    (ii)   Receivables days

    (iii) Payables days   **(6 marks)**

(b) Calculate the length of the cash operating cycle (working capital cycle) for each year and explain its significance.   **(4 marks)**

(c) Discuss the relationship between working capital management and business solvency, and explain the factors that influence the optimum cash level for a business.   **(7 marks)**

(d) A factor has offered to take over sales ledger administration and debt collection for an annual fee of 0.5% of credit sales. A condition of the offer is that the factor will advance Anjo Inc 80% of the face value of its receivables at an interest rate 1% above the current overdraft rate. The factor claims that it would reduce outstanding receivables by 30% and reduce administration expenses by 2% per year if its offer were accepted.

Evaluate whether the factor's offer is financially acceptable, basing your answer on the financial information relating to 20X6.   **(8 marks)**

                                                        (Total: 25 marks)

305 BLIN

Blin is a company listed on a European stock exchange, with a market capitalisation of €6m, which manufactures household cleaning chemicals. The company has expanded sales quite significantly over the last year and has been following an aggressive approach to working capital financing. As a result, Blin has come to rely heavily on overdraft finance for its short-term needs. On the advice of its finance director, the company intends to take out a long-term bank loan, part of which would be used to repay its overdraft.

Required:

(a) Discuss the factors that will influence the rate of interest charged on the new bank loan, making reference in your answer to the yield curve.   **(9 marks)**

(b) Explain and discuss the approaches that Blin could adopt regarding the relative proportions of long- and short-term finance to meet its working capital needs, and comment on the proposed repayment of the overdraft.   **(9 marks)**

(c) Explain the meaning of the term 'cash operating cycle' and discuss its significance in determining the level of investment in working capital. Your answer should refer to the working capital needs of different business sectors.   **(7 marks)**

                                                         (Total: 25 marks)

306 PNP PLC

The following financial information relates to PNP plc, a UK-based firm, for the year just ended.

	£000
Sales revenue	5,242.0
Variable cost of sales	3,145.0
Inventory	603.0
Receivables	744.5
Payables	574.5

Segmental analysis of receivables

	Balance	Average payment period	Discount	Irrecoverable
Class 1	£200,000	30 days	1.0%	None
Class 2	£252,000	60 days	Nil	£12,600
Class 3	£110,000	75 days	Nil	£11,000
Overseas	£182,500	90 days	Nil	£21,900
	£744,500			£45,500

The receivables balances given are before taking account of irrecoverable debts. All sales are on credit. Production and sales take place evenly throughout the year. Current sales for each class of receivables are in proportion to their relative year-end balances before irrecoverable debts. The overseas receivables arise from regular export sales by PNP to the USA. The current spot rate is $1.7348/£ and the three-month forward rate is $1.7367/£.

It has been proposed that the discount for early payment be increased from 1.0% to 1.5% for settlement within 30 days. It is expected that this will lead to 50% of existing Class 2 receivables becoming Class 1 receivables, as well as attracting new business worth £500,000 in turnover. The new business would be divided equally between Class 1 and Class 2 receivables. Fixed costs would not increase as a result of introducing the discount or by attracting new business. PNP finances receivables from an overdraft at an annual interest rate of 8%.

Required:

(a) Calculate the net benefit or cost of increasing the discount for early payment and comment on the acceptability of the proposal. **(9 marks)**

(b) Calculate the current cash operating cycle and the revised cash operating cycle caused by increasing the discount for early payment. **(4 marks)**

(c) Identify and explain the key elements of a receivables management system suitable for PNP plc. **(10 marks)**

(Total: 23 marks)

Section 4

ANSWERS TO SECTION A-TYPE QUESTIONS

COST ACCOUNTING SYSTEMS

1 B

	$
Marginal costing profit	45,000
Less: fixed cost included in opening inventory (28,000 – 16,000)	(12,000)
Plus: fixed cost included in closing inventory (36,400 – 20,800)	15,600
Absorption costing profit	48,600

Alternative approach

Increase in inventory using marginal costing	$4,800
Increase in inventory using absorption costing	$8,400
Difference = fixed overhead absorbed in inventory	$3,600

Inventory is increasing so absorption costing profit is higher than marginal costing profit by the amount of fixed overhead absorbed.

Absorption costing profit = $45,000 + $3,600 = $48,600

2 B

The opening inventory was 400 units and the closing inventory was 900 units, therefore inventory has increased.

If production is greater than sales then absorption costing will show the higher profit.

Difference in profit: = Change in inventory × Fixed production cost per unit

= (900 – 400) × $29,500/5,000 units = $2,950

3 A

OAR = $330,000/220,000 = $1.50 per unit

	$
Overhead absorbed (200,000 units × $1.50)	300,000
Actual overhead	260,000
Over absorbed	40,000

4   C

$$\text{Return per minute} = \frac{\text{Selling price - material cost}}{\text{Time on bottleneck resource}}$$

$$= \frac{50 - 16}{8}$$

$$= \text{€}4.25$$

Return per hour $= \text{€}4.25 \times 60 \qquad = \text{€}255$

5   (a)

	Product S	*Product T*

Throughput of process X per day

$13.5 \text{ hrs} \times \dfrac{60}{5} = 162.00 \qquad\qquad 13.5 \text{ hrs} \times \dfrac{60}{7.5} = 108.00$

(Production time: 15 − 1.5 = 13.5 hours)

Throughput of process Y per day

$14 \text{ hrs} \times \dfrac{60}{18} = 46.67 \qquad\qquad 14 \text{ hrs} \times \dfrac{60}{12} = 70.00$

(Production time: 15 − 1 = 14 hours)

Process Y is the bottleneck process because it limits the production of both products to figures that are less than sales demand.

(b)   Throughput contribution per hour of product S: $\dfrac{(\$95.00 - 20.00)}{18} \times 60 = \$250.00$

Throughput contribution per hour of product T: $\dfrac{(\$85.00 - 20.00)}{12} \times 60 = \$325.00$

The optimum production plan to maximise throughput contribution per day is to produce 70 units of product T.

6   A

This is the CIMA *Official Terminology* definition of a bottleneck. With a throughput accounting approach, the aim should be to reduce or remove bottlenecks, so as to increase throughput.

7

Return per factory hour = $\dfrac{\$12-\$5}{0.75\text{hrs}}$ = $9.333

Cost per factory hour = $144,000/12,000 = $12

TA ratio = 9.3333/12 = 0.778

A profitable product should have a ratio greater than 1. This product is making a loss as cost per hour is exceeding throughput per hour.

8   B

Using marginal costing inventory is valued at the variable production cost per unit

	$
Direct materials	20,000
Direct labour	6,300
Variable production overhead	4,700
Total variable cost	31,000

Inventory value = 400 units × 31,000/4,000 = $3,100

9   D

Using throughput accounting inventory is valued at material cost

Inventory value = 20,000/4,000 × 400 units = $2,000

10   B

The inventory will be valued at production cost, to be more precise at variable production cost.

Cost per unit = $\dfrac{\$40,000+\$12,600+\$9,400}{2,000\text{units}}$ = $31 per unit

No. of units in closing inventory = 2,000 – 1,750 = 250 units.

Therefore value of closing inventory = 250 units × $31 = $7,750.

11   A

Under throughput accounting, finished goods will be valued at direct material cost.

Cost per unit = $\dfrac{\$40,000}{2,000\text{units}}$ = $20 per unit

No. of units in closing inventory = 2,000 – 1,750 = 250 units.

Therefore value of closing inventory = 250 units × $20 = $5,000

12

	Z1	Z2
	Maximum production	*Maximum production*
Department 1	480 min/12 min = 40 units	480 min/16 min = 30 units
Department 2	840 min/20 min = 42 units	840 min/15 min = 56 units

Department 1 is the problem for both products. We can make 42 units of Z1 as far as Department 2 is concerned, but Department 1 is only able to process 40 units. Similarly for Z2, Department 2 can deal with 56 units, but Department 1 can only cope with 30. In both cases Department 1 is the bottleneck.

13

	Z1	Z2
	$	$
Selling price	50	65
Variable cost	26.80	30.40
Contribution	23.20	34.60
No. of bottleneck min per unit	12	16
Contribution per min	1.93	2.16
Priority	2nd	1st

The optimum plan is to concentrate on Z2. We will make the maximum, which is 30 units (from Question 31).

Contribution = 30 units × $34.60 per unit = $1,038.

14

	Z1	Z2
	$	$
Selling price	50	65
Direct material	10	15
Throughput	40	50
No. of bottleneck min per unit	12	16
Throughput per min	3.33	3.13
Priority	1st	2nd

The optimum plan is to concentrate on Z1. We will make the maximum, which is 40 units.

Throughput = 40 units × $40 per unit = $1,600.

15

(a)   **Absorption costing**

Value of closing inventory =$(13,500 + 11,800 + 32,400) × 200/2,000 = $5,770

	$	$
Sales (1,800 × $45)		81,000
Cost of production	57,700	
Less closing inventory	5,770	
Cost of sales		51,930
Gross profit		29,070
Non-production overhead		21,900
Profit		7,170

(b)   **Marginal costing**

Value of closing inventory = $(13,500 + 11,800) × 200/2,000 = $2,530

	$	$
Sales		81,000
Variable cost of production	25,300	
Less closing inventory	2,530	
Cost of sales		22,770
Contribution		58,230
Fixed overhead		54,300
Profit		3,930

(c)   **Throughput accounting**

Value of closing inventory = $13,500 × 200/2,000 = $1,350

	$	$
Sales		81,000
Material costs	13,500	
Less closing inventory	1,350	
Cost of sales		12,150
Throughput		68,850
Operating expenses		66,100
Net profit		2,750

16   B

$$\text{Breakeven sales revenue} = \frac{\text{fixed costs}}{\text{C/S ratio}}$$

$$800,000 = \frac{\$320,000}{\text{C/S ratio}}$$

$$\text{C/S ratio} = \frac{\$320,000}{\$800,000} = 40\%$$

Sales revenue required to achieve a target profit of $50,000

$$= \frac{\$320,000 + 50,000}{40\%} = \underline{\$925,000}$$

17   B

Activity	Classification
(i)	Facility-sustaining
(ii)	Facility-sustaining
(iii)	Product-sustaining
(iv)	Product-sustaining
(v)	Facility-sustaining

18   A

$$\text{Cost driver rate} = \frac{\text{Budgeted cost of orders}}{\text{Budgeted number of orders}} = \frac{\$110,010}{2,895} = \$38 \text{ for each order}$$

	$
Cost recovered: 210 orders × $38	7,980
Actual costs incurred	7,650
Over-recovery of costs for four-week period	330

19   D

Statement (i) provides a definition of a cost driver. Cost drivers for long-term variable overhead costs will be the volume of a particular activity to which the cost driver relates, so Statement (ii) is correct. Statement (iii) is also correct. In traditional absorption costing, standard high-volume products receive a higher amount of overhead costs than with ABC. ABC allows for the unusually high costs of support activities for low-volume products (such as relatively higher set-up costs, order processing costs and so on).

20

(a)

Budgeted number of batches:		
Product D (100,000/100)	=	1,000
Product R (100,000/50)	=	2,000
Product P (50,000/25)	=	2,000
		5,000

(b)

Budgeted machine set-ups:		
Product D (1,000 × 3)	=	3,000
Product R (2,000 × 4)	=	8,000
Product P (2,000 × 6)	=	12,000
		23,000

(c)

Budgeted number of purchase orders:		
Product D (1,000 × 2)	=	2,000
Product R (2,000 × 1)	=	2,000
Product P (2,000 × 1)	=	2,000
		6,000

(d)

Budgeted processing minutes:		
Product D (100,000 × 2)	=	200,000
Product R (100,000 × 3)	=	300,000
Product P (50,000 × 3)	=	150,000
		650,000 minutes

21

Budgeted cost per set-up:

$$= \frac{\$150,000}{23,000} = \$6.52$$

$$\text{Budgeted unit cost of R: } = \frac{\$6.52 \times 4}{50} = \$0.52$$

Budgeted cost per order:

$$= \frac{\$70,000}{6,000} = \$11.67$$

Budgeted unit cost of R: $= \dfrac{\$11.67 \times 1}{50} = \$0.23$

Budgeted processing cost per minute:

$$= \frac{\$80,000}{650,000} = \$0.12 \quad \text{Budgeted unit cost of R} = \$0.12 \times 3 = \$0.36$$

Total budgeted unit cost of R is:

		$	
Set-up costs	=	0.52	
Purchasing costs	=	0.23	
Processing costs	=	0.36	
Total cost	=	1.11	per unit

22   ABC

Costs could be higher under ABC if:

* a product is produced in small batches

* there is production complexity not represented in direct labour hours.

Management may choose to increase batch sizes and/or increase selling prices in order to cover the extra product costs.

23   D

Statements A, B and C are incorrect. JIT makes an organisation more vulnerable to disruptions in the supply chain, because there are no buffer inventories as protection against a breakdown in supply. JIT is easier to implement when an organisation operates within a narrow geographical area, and close to its suppliers. (At Toyota, where JIT originated, manufacturing operations were initially carried out within a 50 kilometre radius.) With little or no inventories, the risk of inventory obsolescence should not exist.

Statement D is correct. When demand is difficult to predict, it becomes more difficult to operate a demand-driven operation.

24   A

Instead of building up product costs sequentially from start to finish of production, backflush accounting calculates product costs retrospectively, at the end of each accounting period, when goods are completed or sold.

25   C

Item (ii) is not an aspect of JIT. There will be more small production runs and so more time spent on machine set-up. Total machine set up time will therefore rise rather than decline if JIT is introduced. Producing only in response to demand, and organising work into work cells, with each cell producing an entire product or job (and so reducing material movements), are characteristic features of JIT.

26   A

	$
Actual overhead incurred	481,250
Less under-absorbed overhead	19,250
Overhead absorbed	462,000

Overhead absorbed = Actual standard hours charged × OAR

So OAR = overhead absorbed/actual standard hours charged = $462,000/38,500 = $12

OAR = Budgeted overheads/budgeted labour hours

So budgeted overheads = OAR × budgeted labour hours = $12 × 38,000 = $456,000

27   D

Training should prevent future failure costs. Reworking costs are an internal failure cost.

28   A

	$000	$000
Sales revenue		820
Variable cost of sales		
Opening inventory	0	
Variable production costs	300	
	300	
Less c1osing inventory	45	
		255
		565
Variable selling costs		105
Contribution		460
Fixed costs		
Production	180	
Selling	110	
		290
Profit		170

Working

The closing inventory is valued at cost. As it is a marginal costing system the inventory is valued at variable cost, i.e. $300,000/1,000 units = $300 per unit. The closing inventory is 150 units, therefore the closing inventory value is $300/unit × 150 units = $45,000.

29   A

These are the official CIMA definitions for MRP and ERP respectively.

30   A

Option (i) is true.

Option (ii) is false. Flexible manufacturing systems may not be simple and may have a substantial degree of automation.

Option (iii) is false. EDI is most often used to allow communication with outside businesses, with customers and suppliers.

31   B

Definition 1 is of an MRP1 system and definition 2 is of throughput accounting.

32   A

(i) is correct .An FMS is a highly automated, complex, computerised production system so (ii) is incorrect. JIT purchases inventory as required so (iii) is incorrect.

33   C

Option A may lead to over-absorption but this will depend on the extent to which actual overhead costs differ from budget. Option B describes under-absorption. Option D refers to budgeted overheads, which are used to calculate the OAR but otherwise not used in the calculation of under-/over-absorption.

34   B

(i) and (ii) are the correct definitions. An MRP system is a computer system for production, planning, purchasing and inventory control. It does not integrate all aspects of a business.

35   B

OAR = $500,000/2,000 = $250 per unit

Inventory has fallen by 300 units in the period.

Absorption costing profit will be 300 × $250 = $75,000 lower than marginal costing profit as some fixed overhead from previous periods will be brought forward to be matched against sales in the period using absorption costing. In marginal costing only the fixed overhead incurred in the period will be included in the profit statement.

36

	A	B	C
	$	$	$
Selling price	200	150	150
Direct materials	41	20	30
Throughput	159	130	120
Machine P – minutes per unit	12	10	7
Return per factory minute	159/12	130/10	120/7
	13.25	13	17.14
Return per factory hour × 60 minutes	**$795**	**$780**	**$1,028**

Note: Product C return per factory hour = $1,029 with no rounding

37

	Assembly	Finishing	Stores	Maintenance	Total
Budgeted overhead	100,000	150,000	50,000	40,000	340,000
Reapportion maintenance	16,000	18,000	6,000	(40,000)	–
			56,000		
Reapportion stores	33,600	22,400	(56,000)		–
Total overhead	149,600	190,400			340,000

OAR for assembly department = $149,600/100,000 = $1.496 per unit

	$
Overhead absorbed 120,000 × 1.496	179,520
Overhead incurred	180,000
Under-absorption	480

STANDARD COSTING

38   C

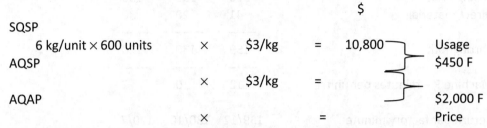

                                                              $
SQSP
        6 kg/unit × 600 units   × $3/kg   =   10,800 ⎤ Usage
AQSP   ⎬ $450 F
                                     × $3/kg   =   ⎦
AQAP $2,000 F
                                     ×   =   Price

This is a 'backwards' question. Given some information including the variances, we then
have to work backwards to find some missing numbers – here, the number of kg purchased.

                                                              $
SQSP
        6 kg/unit × 600 units   × $3/kg   =   10,800 ⎤ Usage
AQSP   ⎬ $450 F
        3,450 kg^Bal 2   × $3/kg   =   10,350^Bal 1 ⎦
AQAP $2,000 F
                                     ×   =   Price

The question can also be answered as follows:

	Kg	
600 units should use (× 6 kg)	3,600	
Usage variance in kg ($450(F)/3)	150	(F)
Therefore 600 units did use	3,450	

Given no change in stock levels, usage quantity = purchase quantity.

39   D

Direct labour variance

                                                              $
AHSR
        24,000 hrs   × $15/hr   =   360,000 ⎤
AHAR   ⎬ $24,000 F
                                                        =   336,000 ⎦ Rate

40   A

Variable overhead variance

                                                              $
SHSR
        2 hrs/unit × 11,000 units   × $6/hr   =   132,000 ⎤ Efficiency
AHSR   ⎬ $12,000 A
        24,000 hrs   × $6/hr   =   144,000 ⎦

41   C

Option A is an ideal standard, option B is an attainable standard and option D is a current
standard.

42 **D**

	$
Budget overhead	2,500,000
Actual overhead	2,010,000
Expenditure variance	490,000 F

43 **C**

OAR = $2,500,000/500,000 = $5 per unit

Budgeted volume	500,000 units
Actual volume	440,000 units
	60,000 units
× OAR per unit	× $5
Volume variance	$300,000 A

44 **A**

	$
Expected cost = ($800 + $0.0002 × 4,100²) × 1.03	4,287
Actual cost	5,000
	713A

45 **C**

This is the CIMA definition.

46 **B**

Absorption rate = $\dfrac{\$170,000}{42,500}$ = $4/unit

	Units	
Budgeted output	42,500	
Actual output	40,000	
Volume variance in units	2,500	(A)
Standard fixed overhead cost/unit	× $4	
Fixed overhead volume variance in $	$10,000	(A)

47   C

Labour variances

				$		
SHSR						
10 hrs/unit × 6,200 units	×	$9.50/hr	=	589,000	⎤	Efficiency
AHSR					⎬	$8,455 A
62,890 hrs	×	$9.50/hr	=	597,455	⎭	
AHAR						$1,043 F
			=	596,412		Rate

The variances could also be calculated as follows:

Rate variance:

	$	
62,890 hours should cost (× $9.50)	597,455	
They did cost	596,412	
	————	
Labour rate variance	1,043	(F)
	————	

Efficiency variance:

	Hours	
6,200 units should take (× 10)	62,000	
They did take	62,890	
	————	
Efficiency variance in hours	890	(A)
	————	

Efficiency variance in $ = 890 hours (A) × $9.50 per hour = $8,455 Adverse.

48   B

Inventories are valued at standard prices, so the material price variance must be calculated by reference to the quantity purchased.

Price variance

	Kgs
Actual quantity used	13,050
Reduction in stock	500
	————
Quantity purchased	12,550 kgs
	————

Material variances

				$		
SQSP						
6 kg/unit × 2,192 units	×	$6.75/kg	=	88,776	⎤	Usage
AQSP					⎬	$688.50 F
13,050 kg	×	$6.75/kg	=	88,087.50	⎦	

For a usage variance the quantity must be the quantity used.

$

AQSP

    12,550 kg   × $6.75/kg =   84,712.50

AQAP

                                             $11,812.50 A

                                   =   72,900   Price

As the price variance is calculated at the time of *purchase* then the quantity must be the quantity *purchased* and we had to use the more complicated format than the usual 3-line format.

	$
12,550 kgs should cost ($6.75/kg)	84,712.50
They did cost	72,900.00
Price variance	$11,812.50 (F)

Usage variance	kgs
2,192 finished units should use (× 6)	13,152
They did use	13,050
Usage variance in kgs	102 kgs (F)

Usage variance in $ = 102 kgs (F) × $6.75/kg (standard price) = $688.50 (F)

49   B

Labour variance

$

SHSR

    0.75 hrs/unit × 11,000 units × $20/hr   =   165,000   Efficiency

AHSR $5,000 F

        8,000 hrs   × $20/hr   =   160,000

The variances could be calculated as follows:

	Hours	
11,000 units should take (× 0.75 hr)	8,250	
did take	8,000	
Efficiency variance in hours	250	Favourable
Standard rate per hour	× $20	
Efficiency variance in $	$5,000	Favourable

50   C

Variable overhead variance

$

AHSR

    8,000 hrs   × $15/hr =   120,000 ⎫

AHAR   ⎬ $12,000 A

                   =   132,000 ⎭   Expenditure

The variance could also be calculated as follows:

	$	
8,000 hours should cost (×$15)	120,000	
did cost	132,000	
	———	
Expenditure variance	12,000	Adverse
	———	

51   A

The operational labour efficiency variance uses the revised standard time of 12 minutes.

SHSR

          $

$\frac{12}{60}$ × 370 × $10/hr =   740 ⎫

AHSR   ⎬   Efficiency $60 A

   80 hrs × $10/hr =   800 ⎭

52   A

The fixed overhead volume variance is the difference between budgeted and actual production volume multiplied by the standard absorption rate per unit. This is the same as the difference between budgeted value of fixed overheads (budgeted volume × standard absorption rate per unit) and standard fixed overheads absorbed by actual production (actual volume × standard absorption rate per unit).

53   C

OAR = $1,500,000/300,000 = $5 per unit

Fixed production overhead variance is the level of over/under absorption. An adverse variance means that overhead is under absorbed.

	$
Overhead absorbed	
Actual output × $5	?
Actual overhead	1,950,000
	———
Under absorbed	150,000

Working backwards, Overhead absorbed = 1,950,000 − 150,000 = 1,800,000 and actual output = 1,800,000/5 = 360,000 units

54   D

Sales price variance

		$
Std selling price	500	
Actual selling price	465	
Sales price variance	35	(A)
× Actual no of units sold	× 642	
	22,470	

55   C

Sales volume contribution variance

		Units
Budgeted quantity sold	600	
Actual quantity sold	642	
Sales volume variance in units	42	(F)
× Std contribution per unit (25% × $500)	× $125	
	$5,250	(F)

56

	Actual mix Litres	Standard mix Litres	Difference Litres		Price $	Variance $	
X	984	885.6	98.4	(A)	2.50	246.0	(A)
Y	1,230	1,328.4	98.4	(F)	3.00	295.2	(F)
Totals	2,214	2,214.0	nil			49.2	(F)

57

Expected output $= \dfrac{2,214}{30} = 73.8$ units

Actual output   = 72.0 units

Shortfall   = 1.8 units

1.8 units × $84/unit   = $151.2 (A)

An alternative would be only 73 complete units of output were expected, thus the shortfall would be 1 unit. The variance would be 1.0 × $84 per unit = $84 adverse.

58 Weighted average standard price per litre = $26/10 = $2.60

	Actual usage Litres		Standard mix Litres	Mix variance Litres		Rate $	Mix variance $	
Material C	200	(6/10)	180	20	(A)	(3 – 2.60)	8	(A)
Material D	75	(3/10)	90	15		(1 – 2.60)	24	
					(F)			(A)
Material E	25	(1/10)	30	5	(F)	(5 – 2.60)	12	(F)
	300		300	Nil			20	(A)

The variance for material C is adverse because actual usage was greater than standard, for a material costing more than the weighted average cost.

The variance for material D is adverse because actual usage was less than standard, for a material costing less than the weighted average cost.

The variance for material E is favourable because actual usage was less than standard, for a material costing more than the weighted average cost.

59

	Litres	
Standard usage for actual output of X2	280	
Actual usage	300	
Yield variance in litres	20	(A)
× weighted average standard price per litre	× $2.60	
Yield variance in $	$52	(A)

60 There are two methods of calculating mix and yield variances – one is the individual unit price method and the other is the weighted average price method. The two methods give different mix variances for individual materials, but give the same total mix variance. We are only asked for the total mix variance and so either method can be used. We have shown both methods. Most people would prefer the first.

(a) **Individual material price method**

Mix variance	Material D Litres	Material E Litres	Material F Litres	Total Litres
Actual input	4,300	3,600	2,100	10,000
Actual input in std proportions 4:3.5:2.5	4,000	3,500	2,500	⇐10,000
Difference in quantity	300 A	100 A	400 F	
× Std price	× $9	× $5	× $2	
Mix variance	$2,700 A	$500 A	$800 F	$2,400 A

Weighted average price method

Weighted average standard price per litre = $\dfrac{\$58.50}{4.0+3.5+2.5\,\text{litres}}$ = $5.85 per litre

Mix variance

	Material D	Material E	Material F	Total
	Litres	Litres	Litres	Litres
Actual input	4,300	3,600	2,100	10,000
Actual input in std proportions 4:3.5:2.5	4,000	3,500	2,500	⇐ 10,000
Difference in quantity	300	100	− 400	
× Difference in price (weighted av.std price − Ind. Material std price)				
× (5.85 − 9)	× − 3.15			
× 5.85 − 5)		× 0.85		
× (5.85 − 2)			3.85	
Mix variance	$945 A	$85 F	$1,540 A	$2,400 A

(b) **Yield variance**

This is calculated in exactly the same way under both methods.

Std cost per litre of output = $\dfrac{\$58.50}{9\,\text{litres}}$ = $6.50/litre

	Litres
Std yield	
10,000 × 90%	9,000
Actual yield	9,100
	100 F
× Std cost per litre of output	× 6.50
Yield variance	$650 F

61 C

Event (i) is more likely to result in a favourable usage variance therefore it is not correct. Event (ii) could cause an adverse usage variance since a lower quality material might lead to higher wastage and a higher level of quality control rejects. Event (iii) could cause an adverse usage variance because lower skilled employees might waste material and quality control rejects might again be higher. Event (iv) would not necessarily cause an adverse usage variance. The usage variance is based on the expected usage for the actual output, not on the budgeted usage for the budgeted output.

62   B

Less experienced employees are likely to take longer than standard to produce a given level of output. The result would be an adverse variable overhead efficiency variance. Option A is more likely to result in a favourable variable overhead efficiency variance because employees are likely to work faster than standard. Option C might also result in a favourable efficiency variance because higher quality material is likely to be easier to process, thus saving time against standard. Option D would result in an adverse variable overhead expenditure variance but would not directly affect the variable overhead efficiency variance.

63

Sales price variance

Budgeted selling price	$10.00
Actual selling price	$9.50

	$0.50	adverse
Actual sales volume (units)	110,000	
	$55,000	adverse

Sales volume profit variance

Budgeted sales volume (units)	100,000
Actual sales volume (units)	110,000

	10,000	favourable
Standard profit per unit ($10 – $8)	$2	
	$20,000	Favourable

64   Unfortunately there are different ways of calculating planning and operational variances and with the way that this question is written the correct answer could be B or D.

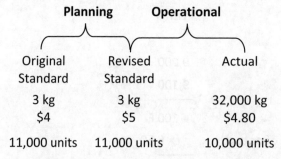

	Planning		Operational	
	Original Standard	Revised Standard	Actual	
	3 kg	3 kg	32,000 kg	
	$4	$5	$4.80	
	11,000 units	11,000 units	10,000 units	

One way is to calculate planning variances as the difference between the original standard and revised standard.

Planning price variance = ($4 – $5) × 3 kg × 11,000 units = $33,000 A

The correct answer is D using the first method.

Alternatively the variance could be calculated on the actual number of units:

Planning price variance = ($4 – $5) × 3 kg × 10,000 units = $30,000 A

The correct answer is B using the second method.

65   **D (SEE NEXT ANSWER)**

66   **B**

Material variance

						$
SQSP						
	3 kg/unit × 10,000 units	×	$5/kg	=	150,000	Usage
AQSP						$10,000 A
	32,000 kg	×	$5/kg	=	160,000	
AQAP						$6,400 F
	32,000 kg	×	$4.80/kg	=	153,600	Price

The standards here are the revised standards.

67   **B**

Mix variance

Liquid	Standard mix	Actual mix	Mix variance	Standard price	Mix variance
	ltr			$	$
X	2,250	2,200	50 F	16	800 F
Y	2,700	2,750	50 A	25	1,250 A
	4,950 l	4,950 l			450 A

68   Mix variance = $500 Favourable

	Actual mix (kg)	Actual quantity/ Standard mix (kg)	Difference (kg)	Standard price (£)	Mix variance (£)
P	1,030	1,000	30A	75	2,250 A
Q	560	600	40F	100	4,000 F
R	410	400	10A	125	1,250 A
	2,000	2,000			500 F

69   Yield variance = $11,306 Favourable

2,000 kgs should produce 2,000/100 × 90	1,800 kg of output	
did produce	1,910 kg of output	
Difference	110 F	
Value at standard cost per kg ($9,250/90)	$11,306 F	

70   Idle hours = 61,500 − 56,000 = 5,500

Standard rate per hour = $540,000/60,000 = $9

Idle time variance = 5,500 × $9 = $49,500 Adverse

71

14,650 units should take	60,000/15,000 = 4 hours per unit	58,600 hours
Did take		56,000 hours
		————
Difference		2,600 hours F
Value at standard rate per hour ($9)		$23,400 F

72 **B**

8,200 × ($31 − $26) = $41,000 F

73 **A**

OAR = $34,800/8,700 = $4 per unit

Standard profit per unit = $26 − $10 − $4 = $12

Volume variance = (8,700 − 8,200) × $12 = $6,000 A

74 **A**

(8,700 − 8,200) × $4 = $2,000 A

75 **C**

Production volume ratio = standard hours produced/budgeted capacity = 95 %

So budgeted hours > standard hours

76 Material price planning variance

Original standard price	$4.10
Revised standard price	$4.50
	———
	.40 A × 11,200 units = $4,480 A

(b) Operational material usage variance

1,600 units should use (× 7)	11,200 kg
did use	12,000 kg
	———
	800 kg A

Valued at revised standard price ($4.50) $3,600 A

77

11,500 units should use 5 hours each	57,500 hours
Did use	?
Variance in hours	
Value at $12 per hour	
Labour efficiency variance	$30,000 A

Working backwards:

The variance in hours = $30,000/12 = 2,500 A

The actual hours used are 57,500 + 2,500 = 60,000

60,000 hours should cost (× $12)	720,000
Did cost	?
Labour rate variance	45,000 A

Working backwards:

The actual labour cost = $765,000

so the actual rate paid per hour = $765,000/60,000 = $12.75.

BUDGETING

78   C

The budget communicates to individual managers what is expected of them in the forthcoming budget period and how much expenditure they can incur in meeting their targets. Thus communication (i) is a purpose of budgeting. An agreed budget provides authorisation for individual managers to incur expenditure in undertaking the activities in their own budget centre. Therefore authorisation (ii) is a purpose of budgeting. Although an organisation might have an objective of maximising sales and might set a budget to enable them to achieve this objective, the maximisation of sales is not in itself a purpose of budgeting. Therefore (iii) is not correct. Individual budget targets are set within the framework of the plan for the organisation as a whole and in this way a budget provides a means of coordinating the efforts of everyone within the organisation. Therefore (iv) is correct.

79   D

80

	E	F	G	Total
Budgeted number of batches to be produced:	75,000/200	120,000/60	60,000/30	
	= 375	= 2,000	= 2,000	
Machine set-ups per batch:	5	3	9	
Total machine set-ups	1,875	6,000	18,000	25,875

So budgeted cost per set-up: $180,000/25,875 = $6.96 per set-up

Therefore the budgeted machine set-up cost per unit of F produced is:

($6.96 × 3)/60 = $0.35 per unit or $6.96 × 6,000/120,000 = $0.35 per unit

81   D

See workings in next answer.

82   D

In the year ended October 20X3 total variable costs were $850,000 × 60% = $510,000. These can be analysed as follows:

	People	Packages (kg)	Total
Variable costs 50:50	$255,000	$255,000	$510,000
Units in year	4,420	30,500	–
Cost per unit	$57.69	$8.36	–
Adjusted cost (× 1.02)	$58.84	$8.53	–
Activity for period to 31 January 20X4	1,150	8,100	–
Total related costs	$67,666	$69,093	$136,759

83   D

Production overhead:

	Units		$
High	800	(× 1.75)	1,400
Low	500	(× 2.50)	1,250
	300		150

Variable cost = $150/300 = $0.50

Fixed cost = $1,400 – (800 × $0.50) = $1,000

Other overhead:

	Units		$
High	800	(× 0.625)	500
Low	500	(× 1.00)	500

This is a wholly fixed cost.

Variable cost per unit:

	$
Direct material	2.00
Direct labour	1.50
Variable production overhead	0.50
	4.00

Period fixed cost:

	$
Fixed production overhead	1,000
Other overhead	500
	1,500

84   C

Note that the material usage figure is not required.

	Units
Sales	30,000
Add closing inventory (3,500 × 1.35)	4,725
Less opening inventory	(3,500)
Production	31,225

85   C

At output of 6,000 units, overhead = 6,000 × $3.20 = $19,200

At output of 10,000 units, overhead = 10,000 × $3.00 = $30,000

$\cdot$ Variable overhead / unit = $\dfrac{\$30,000 - \$19,200}{10,000 - 6,000}$ = $2.70

Fixed overhead = $19,200 – (6,000 × $2.70) = $3,000

At activity of 7,350 units, budgeted production overhead = $3,000 + (7,350 × $2.70) = $22,845

86   B

A zero based budgeting system begins each budget from scratch every time. All expenditure on the activity must be justified from zero and the method of carrying out each activity must be re-evaluated as if it were being carried out for the first time.

87   Orders = [100,000 + (30 × 240)] × 1.08 = 115,776

Overhead cost = $10,000 + (£0.25 × 115,776) = $38,944

Answer is $39,000

88   D

Quarter	Value of x		Trend units			Forecast sales units
1	25	y = (26×25) + 8,850	9,500	×85%	=	8,075.0
2	26	y = (26×26) + 8,850	9,526	×95%	=	9,049.7
3	27	y = (26×27) + 8,850	9,552	×105%	=	10,029.6
4	28	y = (26×28) + 8,850	9,578	×115%	=	11,014.7
						38,169.0

Difference between Q1 and Q4 budgeted sales = 11,014.7 – 8,075.0 = 2,939.7 units

89 D

Since no inventories are held, budgeted production will be equal to budgeted sales.

Budgeted production each quarter = 38,169/4 = 9,542.25 units

90 D

Trend	=	$9.72 + (5.816 \times 23)$
	=	143.488
Seasonal factor	+	6.5
		———
Forecast		149.988
		———

To the nearest whole unit, the forecast number of units to be sold is 150.

91 C

Probability of rainy summer	=	$1.0 - 0.4 = 0.6$
Expected value of sales volume	=	$(80,000 \times 0.4) + (120,000 \times 0.6)$
	=	104,000 units

92 D

It is known that there is a stepped fixed cost of $10,000 above 35,000 units. Removing the stepped fixed cost at 40,000 units leaves $184,000.

(i)   Variable cost per unit = $\dfrac{\$184,000 - \$143,500}{40,000 - 25,000} = \$2.70$

(ii)

	At 25,000 units
Total cost	143,500
Total variable cost $2.70 \times 25,000$	67,500
	———
Fixed cost	76,000
	———

Therefore fixed cost at 36,000 units = $76,000 + $10,000 = $86,000

93 C

Budgetary slack is also called budget bias. Budget holders may sometimes try to obtain a budget that is easier to achieve. They may do this either by bidding for expenditure in excess of what they actually need or, in the case of sales budgets, by deliberately setting easy revenue targets.

94   C

	Machine hours	$
High	12,212	39,477
Low	8,480	31,080
Change	3,732	8,397

Variable cost per machine hour $\quad= \quad$ \$8,397/3,732

$\quad\quad\quad\quad\quad\quad\quad\quad\quad\quad\quad\quad\quad= \quad$ \$2.25

Fixed cost = \$39,477 − (12,212 × \$2.25) $\quad=\quad$ \$12,000

Budget cost allowance for 9,340 machine hours:

	$
Fixed cost	12,000
Variable cost (9,340 × \$2.25) $\quad=$	21,015
	33,015

95   We have been given the trend equation. We need to plug in the value for x so that we can find y.

X is the time period reference number and for the first quarter of year 1 is 1. The time period reference number for the third quarter of year 7 is 27. (Just keep adding 1 to the time period reference number for each new quarter, thus quarter 2, year 1, x = 2; quarter 3, year 1, x = 3; quarter 4, year 1, x = 4; quarter 1, year 2, x = 5, etc.)

$\quad\quad$ y = 25,000 + 6,500 × 27 = 200,500 units

This is the trend we now need to multiply by the seasonal variation for quarter 3:

Forecast = 200,500 × 150/100 = 300,750 units.

96

	January units	February units	March units
Production budget			
Sales	4,000	5,000	6,000
Add closing inventory	1,500	1,800	
	5,500	6,800	
Less opening inventory	1,200	1,500	
Production	4,300	5,300	

Materials budget

Production (units)	4,300	5,300
× No. of units of material per unit of product	× 1 unit	× 1 unit
Usage quantity (units)	4,300	5,300
Add closing inventory	1,325	
	5,625	
Less op inventory	1,075	
Purchase quantity (units)	4,550	
× purchase price	× $8	
Purchase cost (£)	36,400	

The purchase cost of materials in January is $36,400. This will be paid in February.

97

$$\text{OAR} = \frac{\text{Budgeted overheads}}{\text{Budgeted level of activity}}$$

$$= \frac{\$22,000 + \$34,000 + \$32,000}{8,000 \text{ hours}} = \$11 \text{ per direct labour hour}$$

$$\text{Labour rate} = \frac{\$128,000}{8,000 \text{ hours}} = \$16 \text{ per direct labour hour}$$

	$
Direct materials	21.50
Direct labour	4.80
Overheads	3.30
	29.60

98

	$
Direct material	21.50
Direct labour	4.80
Overheads	
Set-up costs	16.67
Quality testing costs	11.33
Other overhead costs	1.20
	55.50

$$\text{Set-up costs} = \frac{\$22,000}{88 \text{ set-ups}} = \$250 \text{ per set-up}$$

Charge to Product Z = $250 per set-up × 2 set-ups per batch ÷ 30 units per batch = $16.67

Quality testing costs = $\dfrac{\$34,000}{40\,\text{tests}}$ = $850 per test

Tests are performed every 75 units, therefore charge per unit = $850/75 = $11.33

Other overhead costs = $\dfrac{\$32,000}{8,000\,\text{hours}}$ = $4 per direct labour hour

Charge to product Z = $4 × 0.3 hours = $1.20

99 C

The P/V line will move down as profit will be lower at all units of sales. The gradient represents the C/S ratio and this will be unchanged.

100 C

High Low Method	*Activity*	$	
	6,500	33,000	
	4,500	29,000	
Difference	2,000	4,000	
So the variable cost	= $4,000/2,000	= $2 per unit	
Substitute into either activity	6,500	33,000	Total cost
	6,500 × $2	13,000	Variable cost
	Difference	$20,000	Fixed cost

The estimated production cost for 5,750 units = 5,750 × $2 + $20,000 = $31,500

101 D

The index values should add to 400 as there are four seasons.

80 + 80 + 110 + ? = 400

so ? = 130

102

Forecast sales volume for June, July and August is:

Month		Cumulative sales (units)		Monthly sales (units)
June		1,500		1,500
July	$1,500 \times 2^{0.6}$	2,274	2,274 − 1,500	774
August	$1,500 \times 3^{0.6}$	2,900	2,900 − 2,274	626

103

	Sales	
		$
Month 4	$108,000 × 20%	21,600
Month 3	$120,000 × 80% × 40% × 0.985	37,824
Month 2	$105,000 × 80% × 30%	25,200

104 Purchases are sold at cost plus 25% so cost of sales is 100/125= 0.8 × Sales

Closing inventory = 0.5 × Following month's cost of sales

Closing inventory = Opening inventory of the following month

Month	Sales	Cost of sales	Opening inventory	Closing inventory	Purchase	Paid
July	100	80	40	36	76	
August	90	72	36	50	86	**76**
September	125	100	50	56	106	**86**
October	140	112	56			**106**

105 $10M × 0.15 + $20M × 0.1 + ?M = $5.5M + $1M

$3.5m + ?m = $6.5m   so ? = $3m

Revenue needed to ensure a profit of $2m = 3/0.25 = $12m

106 D

This is the definition of a master budget.

107

	W	X	Y	Total
Number of purchase requisitions	1,200	1,800	2,000	5,000
Number of set-ups	240	260	300	800
	W	X	Y	Total
	$	$	$	$
Receiving/inspecting quality assurance (W1)	336,000	504,000	560,000	1,400,000
Production scheduling/machine set-up (W2)	360,000	390,000	450,000	1,200,000
Total overhead cost	696,000	894,000	1,010,000	2,600,000
Units produced and sold	10,000	15,000	18,000	
Overhead cost per unit	69.60	59.60	56.11	

Selling price	200	183	175
Direct material	50	40	35
Direct labour	30	35	30
Overhead cost per unit	69.60	59.60	56.11
Profit per unit	50.40	48.40	53.89

Workings

(W1) 1,200/5,000 × 1,400,000 = 336,000

      1,800/5,000 × 1,400,000 = 504,000

      2,000/5,000 × 1,400,000 = 560,000

(W2) 240/800 × 1,200,000 = 360,000

      260/800 × 1,200,000 = 390,000

      300/800 × 1,200,000 = 450,000

108 B

Average time for first	1 unit	=	7 hours	
Average time for first	2 units	=	0.9 × 7	= 6.3 hours
Average time for first	4 units	=	0.92 × 7	= 5.67 hours
Average time for first	8 units	=	0.93 × 7	= 5.103 hours
			Hours	
Total time for first 4 units =		4 × 5.67 =	22.680	
Total time for first 8 units =		8 × 5.103 =	40.824	
. Total time for units 5 to 8 =			18.144	

109 As output doubles, cumulative time per unit reduces by 75%.

Units	Average time / unit (minutes)	Total time (minutes)
1	12.00	12.00
2	12.00 × 75% = 9.00	9.00 × 2 = 18.00
4	9.00 × 75% = 6.75	6.75 × 4 = 27.00

Total time = 27 minutes

110

Units	Cumulative average time	Total time
1	3	3
2		
4	2.091675	8.3667

The learning curve model states that the cumulative average time taken falls by the learning rate each time output doubles. Therefore:

$3 \times r \times r = 2.091675$

$r^2 = 2.091675/3 = 0.835$

The learning rate is 83.5%

111

	Cumulative average time		Total time
For first 7 units y = 6 × 7 $^{-0.415}$ =	2.676	× 7 =	18.72982
For first 6 units y = 6 × 6 $^{-0.415}$ =	2.8525	× 6 =	17.11472
			_____
Time for 7th assignment			1.6151

Answer 1.62 hours to nearest 0.01 hours

 Key answer tips

The question requires an answer to the nearest 0.01 hours. Do not round your workings too early as this will introduce an error. It is preferable to leave full figures in your calculator as far as possible when carrying out the workings.

---

112 B

Time taken for 5 units:

Y	=	ax – b
Y	=	21 × 5 – 0.3219
	=	21 × 0.595664277
	=	12.52 minutes

Time taken for 6 units:

Y	=	ax – b
Y	=	21 × 6 – 0.3219
	=	21 × 0.561711237
	=	11.80 minutes

	Minutes
Total time taken for 6 units at 11.80 minutes =	70.80
Total time taken for 5 units at 12.51 minutes =	62.55
	_____
Therefore time taken for 6th unit	8.25
	_____

FINANCIAL INFORMATION FOR LONG-TERM DECISION MAKING

113 A

Annual contribution	= annual cash profit + annual cash fixed costs
	= $450,000 + $190,000 = $640,000
Contribution / unit	= $220 − $55 = $165
∴ Units sold pa	= $640,000 ÷ $165 = 3,879 units.

The NPV of the project can fall by $127,600 before it becomes zero.

The NPV of total annual revenue is expected to be $3,879 \times \$220 \times 4.623 = \$3,945,175$.

For this to fall by $127,600, it must suffer a decrease of:

$$\frac{127,600}{3,945,175} \times 100\% = 3.2\%$$

114 C

	$	Tax saved at 25%	Yr 1	Yr 2	Yr 3
Cost of asset	80,000				
Year 1 writing down allowance (20%)	16,000	4,000	2,000	2,000	
Balance	64,000				
Year 2 writing down allowance (20%)	12,800	3,200		1,600	1,600
				3,600	

Cash flows in the second year

	$
Tax relief on asset	3,600
Cash inflow	25,000
Tax due – year 1 cash flow $25,000 × 25% × 0.5	(3,125)
Tax due – year 2 cash flow $25,000 × 25% × 0.5	(3,125)
	22,350
Discount factor, year 2 at 5%	0.907
Present value of cash flows in Year 2	$20,271

115 A

Annual cost of capital: 10%. Inflation rate: 4%

Real rate: $(1.10/1.04) - 1 = 0.0577$

Year 1 discount rate:	$1/1.0577$	0.945
Year 2 discount rate:	$1/(1.0577^2)$	0.894
Year 3 discount rate:	$1/(1.0577^3)$	0.845
Year 4 discount rate:	$1/(1.0577^4)$	0.799
		———
		3.483
		———

Annual inflow years 1–4: $6,000 \times \$12 = \$72,000$

			Discount rate	$
Year 0	Investment	$250,000	0	250,000
Year 1–4	Inflow	$72,000	3.483	250,776
				———
	NPV			$776 i.e. $800
				———

Alternatively, you can reach the same solution (with some differences possibly for rounding error) by inflating all the cash flows at 4% to their 'out-turn' amount, and discounting these inflated cash flows at the money cost of capital, 10%. The cash flows would be ($72,000 × 1.04) $74,880 in year 1, $77,875 in year 2, $80,990 in year 3 and $84,230 in year 4.

116 C

The annual cash inflows over four years of $72,000 per annum will pay back the $250,000 investment in $250,000/$72,000 = 3.5 years. By looking at the cumulative present value table we can see that, over a four-year period, the rate that gives a discount factor of 3.5 over four years is between 5% (when the rate is 3.546) and 6% (when the rate is 3.465). To get to an approximate rate:

Rate at 5%	3.546
Rate at 6%	3.465
	———
	0.081
	———

This means that each 0.1% between 5% and 6% is worth 0.081/10 = 0.0081 discount rate.

Rate at 5%	3.546
Rate at x%	3.500
	———
	0.046
	———

The number of 0.1 percentage points to add to 5% is 0.046/0.0081 = 5.7

Therefore the discount rate x that gives a nil NPV after three years is 5.57.

Formula for discount rate where there is inflation: $[(1+r)/(1+I)]-1=$ discount rate

$[(1 + r)/(1.06)] - 1 = 0.0557$

$r= (1.0557 \times 1.06) - 1$

Real cost of capital
$= 0.119$, i.e. 11.9%.

The answer is C, allowing for rounding errors in the calculations.

117 B

Year	Cash inflow/(outflow)	Discount factor @ 8%	Present value $
0	(60,000)	1.000	(60,000)
1	23,350	0.926	21,622
2	29,100	0.857	24,939
3	27,800	0.794	22,073
Net present value			8,634

Workings

Cash flows

Flow $	Probability	$
Year 1		
35,000	0.25	8,750
20,000	0.55	11,000
18,000	0.20	3,600
Expected value		23,350
Year 2		
40,000	0.25	10,000
26,000	0.55	14,300
24,000	0.20	4,800
Expected value		29,100
Year 3		
32,000	0.25	8,000
28,000	0.55	15,400
22,000	0.20	4,400
Expected value		27,800

118 A

Annual cost of capital: 8%

Inflation rate: 3%

Real rate: $(1.08/1.03) - 1 = 0.0485$

Year 1 discount rate:	1/1.0485	0.954
Year 2 discount rate:	$1/(1.0485^2)$	0.910
Year 3 discount rate:	$1/(1.0485^3)$	0.868
		2.732

Annual inflow years 1–3: $4,000 \times \$5 = \$20,000$

		Discount rate		$
Year 0	Investment	$50,000	0	50,000
Year 1–3	Inflow	$20,000	2.732	54,640
	NPV			4,640 i.e. $4,500

Alternatively, you can reach the same solution (with some differences possibly for rounding error) by inflating all the cash flows at 3% to their 'out-turn' amount, and discounting these inflated cash flows at the money cost of capital, 8%. The cash flows would be (20,000 × 1.03) $20,600 in year 1, $21,218 in year 2 and $21,855 in year 3.

119 C

The annual cash inflows over three years of $20,000 per annum will pay back the $50,000 investment in $50,000/$20,000 = 2.5 years. By looking at the cumulative present value table we can see that, over a three-year period, the rate that gives a discount factor of 2.5 over three years is between 9% (when the rate is 2.531) and 10% (when the rate is 2.487). To get to an approximate rate:

Rate at 9%	2.531
Rate at 10%	2.487
	0.044

This means that each 0.1% between 9% and 10% is worth 0.044/10 = 0.0044 discount rate.

Rate at 9%	2.531
Rate at x%	2.500
	0.031

The number of 0.1 percentage points to add to 9% is 0.031/0.0044 = 7

Therefore, the discount rate x that gives a nil NPV after three years is 9.7%.

Formula for discount rate where there is inflation: $[1 + r)/(1 + I)] - 1 = $ discount rate

$(1 + r)/(1.04) - 1 = 0.097$

$r = (1.097 \times 1.04) - 1$

Real cost of capital $= 0.141$ i.e. 14%

120 A

The present value of expected sales revenue is as follows:

Year	Item	Cash flow	Discount factor at 10%	PV
		$		$
1	Sales revenue	40,000	0.909	36,360
2	Sales revenue	40,000	0.826	33,040
3	Sales revenue	24,000	0.751	18,024
NPV				87,424

The NPV is $3,190, so the maximum reduction in sales price that can occur without the project ceasing to be viable is (3,190/87,424) = 0.036 = 3.6%.

121 B

The present value of the annual net cash flows, ignoring the machine cost and residual value, is: $(19,998 + 18,172 + 7,510) = $45,680.

If the machine costs $X, the net cost of the machine, in present value terms and allowing for the residual value at the end of year 3, is:

$X - (0.751 \times 20\%$ of X)

$= X - 0.1502X$

$= 0.8498X$.

If 0.8498X exceeds $45,680, the project will not be viable. The maximum amount the machine can cost without the project ceasing to be viable is therefore $45,680/0.8498 = $53,754, say $54,000.

122 C

Sensitivity = NPV of project / PV of figures which vary = $320,000 / $630,000 = 51%

123

Year	Cash	15%	PV
	$		$
0	(75,000)		(75,000)
1 – 5	25,000	3.352	83,800
			8,800

Try 20%

Year	Cash	20%	PV
	$		$
0	(75,000)		(75,000)
1 – 5	25,000	2.991	74,775
			(225)

$$\text{IRR} = 15\% + \frac{8,800}{(8,800 + 225)} \times 5\%$$

$$\text{IRR} = 15\% + \frac{8,800}{9,025} \times 5\%$$

$$\text{IRR} = 19.88\%$$

124 PV of labour cost

$$= \$20,000 \times 3.352$$

$$= \$67,040$$

∴ Allowable change

$$= \frac{8,800}{67,040} \times 100$$

$$= 13.13\%$$

125 1.11/1.X6 = 1.0472

Real rate = 4.72%

126 Annuity factor

$$= \frac{1 - (1 + r)^{-n}}{r}$$

$$= \frac{1 - (1.0472)^{-10}}{0.0472}$$

$$= 7.8278$$

NPV = 40,000 × 7.8278 – 300,000 = $13,112

127

Year	Discount factor	Increase in costs ($000)	Present value ($000)	Savings ($000)	Present value ($000)
1	0.833	16	13.328	150	124.95
2	0.694	20	13.880	160	111.04
3	0.579	24	13.896	170	98.43
4	0.482	30	14.460	180	86.76
			55.564		421.18

PV of costs increase by $55,564.

NPV falls to $22,900 − $55,564 = − $32,664

∴ PV of savings must rise by $32,664

or $\dfrac{32,664}{421,180} \times 100 = 7.8\%$

128

Year	Cash ($000)	17% discount factor	Present value ($000)
0	(400)	1.000	(400.00)
1	210	0.855	179.55
2	240	0.731	175.44
3	320	0.624	199.68
			154.67

Maximum PV of advertising expenditure = $154,670.

Annualise by dividing by annuity factor for years 0 to 2 = 1 + 0.855 + 0.731 = 2.586.

Therefore, maximum cash = $154,670 ÷ 2.586 = $59,811, or $60,000 (rounded to the nearest $000).

129 NPV = $0

Let $x be annual rent.

Annuity factor for year 5 at 17% is 3.199.

∴ $x × 3.199 = 27,200

∴ $x = 8,502

130   Contribution per annum   = $320,000 + $160,000

                                    = $480,000

           Contribution per unit   = $180 – $60

                                    = $120 per unit

           ∴ Level of activity   = $\dfrac{\$480,000}{\$120}$ = 4,000 units

NPV can fall by $244,170.

Converted to annual cash equivalent:

                                    = $\dfrac{\$244,170}{3.791}$ = $64,408 per annum

∴ Unit selling price can fall by up to:

$\dfrac{\$64,408}{4,000\text{units}}$ = $16.10 per unit

As a percentage: $\dfrac{\$16.10}{\$180} \times 100$ =   8.9%

131   (1 + real rate)   = $\dfrac{(1 + \text{money rate})}{(1 + \text{inflation rate})}$

           = $\dfrac{1.07}{1.04}$

           =   1.0288

∴ Real rate = 2.88% per annum.

Discounting money cash flow at the money rate.

Money cash flow		Discount factor at 7%	Present value
Yr 0	(500,000)	1	(500,000)
Yr 1	130,000 × 1.04 = 135,200	0.935	126,412
Yr 2	130,000 × 1.04^2 = 140,608	0.873	122,751
Yr 3	130,000 × 1.04^3 = 146,232	0.816	119,325
Yr 4	130,000 × 1.04^4 = 152,082	0.763	116,039
	Net present value		(15,473)

Alternatively, discounting real cash flow at the real rate

		Discount factor at 7%	Present value
Yr 0	(500,000)	1	(500,000)
Yr 1–4	130,000	3.7278 (W1)	484,612
	Net present value		(15,387)

Annuity factor for a discount rate of 2.88% for four years is calculated using the formula $(1 - (1 + 0.0288)^4)/0.0288$

132 Capital allowance in Year 2:

Year	Written down value	Capital allowance	Tax saving	Cash timing
1	$75,000	$25,000	$7,500	$3,750
2	$56,250	$18,750	$5,625	$3,750 + $2,812.50
				$2,812.50

Year	Capital allowance benefit	Annual cash inflow	Corporation tax	Net cash	Discount factor	Present value
2	$6,562.50	$20,000	$(6,000)	$20,562.50	0.857	$17,622

133 C

Profitability index = NPV per $ invested = $140,500 / $500,000 = 0.28

134 1.11/1.X6 = 1.0472

Real rate = 4.72%

$$\frac{1-(1+r)^{-n}}{r}$$

Annuity factor = $\dfrac{1-(1.0472)^{-10}}{0.0472}$

= 7.8278

NPV = 40,000 × 7.8278 − 300,000 = $13,112

135 The internal rate of return of the project is:

$$10\% + \frac{\$12,304}{(\$12,304 + \$3,216)} \times (15 - 10)\% \ = 14\%$$

136 B

$50,000 × 3.605 = $180,250

This would need to fall by $160,000 to make the project non-viable, a fall of

160,000/180,250 = 88.8%

137 34%

ARR	= Average annual profit / Average investment value

Cash flows received over project lifetime = $(80,000 + 90,000 + 100,000 + 60,000 + 40,000)

= $370,000

No residual value, so depreciation over lifetime of project = full investment cost = $200,000

Lifetime profit	= $370,000 – $200,000 = $170,000
Average annual profit	= $170,000 / 5 = $34,000
Average capital invested	= $200,000 / 2
ARR = 34,000 / 100,000	= 34%

138 26%

NPV at 10% = $87,980. Discounting the cash flows using a higher discount rate, say 20% gives:

Year	Cash flow $	DF	PV $
0	(200,000)	1.000	(200,000)
1	80,000	0.833	66,640
2	90,000	0.694	62,460
3	100,000	0.579	57,900
4	60,000	0.482	28,920
5	40,000	0.402	16,080
			32,000

Using the formula:

$$IRR \approx A + (B - A)\frac{N_A}{N_A - N_B}$$

Where	A	=	lower discount rate	(10%)
	B	=	higher discount rate	(20%)
	N_A	=	NPV at rate A (87,980)	
	N_B	=	NPV at rate B (32,000)	

IRR (%) = 20 + (10 × 87,980/55,980) = 26%

139

Year	$000	$000
0	(400)	(400)
1	100	(300)
2	120	(180)
3	140	(40)
4	120	80

Payback period = 3 years + 40/120ths of year 4 = **3.33 years or 3 years 4 months**

140 Discounted cash flows are:

Year	$000	Present value $000	Cumulative present value $000
0	(450 × 1)	(450)	(450)
1	130 × 0.909	118.17	(331.83)
2	130 × 0.826	107.38	(224.45)
3	130 × 0.751	97.63	(126.82)
4	130 × 0.683	88.79	(38.03)
5	130 × 0.621	80.73	42.70

Discounted payback occurs in year 5 and can be estimated as:

4 years plus 38.03 / 80.73 of year five = 4.47 years

141 NPV at 10% is given as $48,000 in the question. Since the NPV is positive the IRR must be higher.

Try discounting at 20%

Year	Cash flow $000	Discount factor	Present value $000
0	(350)	1.000	(350)
1	50	0.833	42
2	110	0.694	76
3	130	0.579	75
4	150	0.482	72
5	100	0.402	40
NPV			(45)

IRR = 10% + [48/(48 + 45) × (20 − 10)%] = **15% (approx)**

142 C

Investment	J $000	K $000	L $000	M $000	N $000
Initial investment	400	350	450	500	600
Net present value (NPV)	125	105	140	160	190
Profitability index (NPV per $ invested)	0.3125	0.30	0.3111	0.32	0.3166
Ranking	3	4		1	2

J would be chosen before L and, as they are mutually exclusive, L can be disregarded.

The optimum investment plan is $500,000 in M and the remaining $500,000 in N.

143 Depreciation is not a cash flow so needs to be added back to profit to calculate cash flows.

Depreciation on straight line basis = ($400,000 − $50,000)/5 = $70,000 per year

Year	Profit ($)	Cash flow ($)	Cumulative cash flow ($)
0		(400,000)	(400,000)
1	175,000	245,000	(155,000)
2	225,000	295,000	140,000

Payback period = 1 + 145 / 295 years = 1.5 years to nearest 0.1 years

144 The present value of a $1 perpetuity is 1/r.

The present value of the rental income is $80,000/0.08 = $1,000,000

The NPV of the investment is $1,000,000 − $850,000 = $150,000

THE TREATMENT OF UNCERTAINTY IN DECISION MAKING

145 **B**

Project	EV $000	Workings
L	500	(500 × 0.2) + (470 × 0.5) + (550 × 0.3)
M	526	(400 × 0.2) + (550 × 0.5) + (570 × 0.3)
N	432.5	(450 × 0.2) + (400 × 0.5) + (475 × 0.3)
O	398	etc
P	497.5	

∴ Project M will maximise expected cash.

146 **D**

If market condition is forecast as Poor, then Project P should be chosen as this project yields the highest cash flow under a poor market.

However, if the market condition is forecast as Good or Excellent, then Project M should be chosen as M will yield the highest cash.

In summary:

Market condition	Selected project	Cash (x) $000	Probability (p)	px
Poor	P	600	0.20	120
Good	M	550	0.50	275
Excellent	M	570	0.30	171
			1.00	566

Expected return with perfect information	$566,000
Expected return without (answer to 1.2)	$526,000
∴ Value of information	$40,000

147   A probability tree may be used:

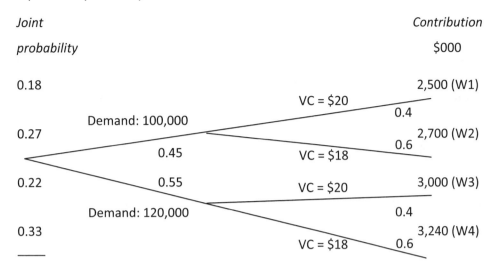

Joint	*Contribution*
probability	$000
0.18	2,500 (W1)
0.27	2,700 (W2)
0.22	3,000 (W3)
0.33	3,240 (W4)
1.00	

Existing contributon:

($50 – $21) × 90,000 units = 2,610 ($000)

Contribution is greater than this in (W2), (W3) and (W4) above.

∴ The probability of the profit being higher is:

0.27 + 0.22 + 0.33 =   0.82

Workings

(W1)   ($45 – $20) × 100,000 units

(W2)   ($45 – $18) × 100,000 units

(W3)   ($45 – $20) × 120,000 units

(W4)   ($45 – $18) × 120,000 units

148   Expected demand:

(100,000 × 0.45) + (120,000 × 0.55)	111,000 units
Expected variable cost:	
($20 × 0.40) + ($18 × 0.60)	$18.80
Contribution per unit:	
$45 – $18.50	$26.20
Expected contribution:	
111,000 × $26.20	$2,908,200
Less fixed costs	($1,200,000)
Expected profit	$1,708,200

149 Produce a payoff table:

Demand	Probability	Supply		
		100	200	300
100 units	0.25	$400	$0 (W1)	($400) (W2)
200 units	0.40	$400	$800	$400 (W3)
300 units	0.35	$400	$800	$1,200

Workings

(W1) $100 \times \$8 - 200 \times \$4$ = $0

(W2) $100 \times \$8 - 300 \times \$4$ = ($400)

(W3) $200 \times \$8 - 300 \times \$4$ = $400

Expected profits:

If supply 100 units, EVs = $400

If supply 200 units, EV = $0 × 0.25 + $800 × 0.4 + $800 × 0.35 = $600

If supply 300 units, EV = ($400) × 0.25 + $400 × 0.4 + $1,200 × 0.35 = $480

∴ Profit is maximised by supplying 200 units.

150 To generate a contribution greater than $20,000 it is necessary to earn a unit contribution greater than $20. Consider each of the feasible combinations:

Selling price $	Variable cost $	Contribution per unit $	Probability
50	20	30	0.45 × 0.55 = 0.2475
60	20	40	0.25 × 0.55 = 0.1375
60	30	30	0.25 × 0.25 = 0.0625
		Answer =	**0.4475**

Answer = 44.75%

151 **D**

Expected selling price	$	Expected cost	$
$20 × 0.25	5	$8 × 0.2	1.6
$25 × 0.4	10	$10 × 0.5	5
330 × 0.35	10.5	$12 × 0.3	3.6
	25.5		10.2

Expected unit contribution = $25.50 − $10.20 = $15.30 × 1,000 = $15,300

152 C

Monthly contribution will exceed $13,500 if unit contribution exceeds $13.50. This will be the case for the following combinations:

Sales price	Variable cost	Probability	Joint probability
$25	$8	0.4×0.2	0.08
$25	$10	0.4×0.2	0.20
$30	($8)		
$30	($10)	0.35×1	0.35
$30	($12)		
Total			0.63

153 Contribution table

		Daily demand		
		10	11	12
	10 (W1)	500	500	500
Batches baked	11 (W2)	480	550	550
	12 (W3)	460	530	600

Workings

(W1) If 10 batches are baked they will all be sold earning a contribution of $500

(W2) If 11 batches are baked and 10 are sold this earns a contribution of $10 \times 50 - 20 = 480$

(W3) If 12 batches are baked and 10 are sold contribution = $10 \times 50 - 40 = 460$

A regret table can now be produced which shows the shortfall from the maximum contribution that could be earned at each demand level. So, if demand is 12 batches, the maximum contribution is $600. If only 10 batches are baked, the contribution earned is $500, a regret of $100.

Regret table		Daily demand			
		10	11	12	Max. Regret
	10	0	50	100	100
Batches baked	11	20	0	50	50
	12	40	20	0	40

So to minimise the maximum regret bake 12 batches.

The following combinations of selling price and variable cost per unit yield a contribution of more than $20 per unit:

Selling price	Variable cost	Contribution	Probability
$50	$20	$30	$0.45 \times 0.55 = 0.2475$
$60	$30	$30	$0.25 \times 0.25 + 0.0625$
$60	$20	$40	$0.25 \times 0.55 + 0.1375$
			0.4475

Answer = 44.75%

MANAGING SHORT TERM FINANCE

154   C

Businesses that regularly fail to pay their suppliers on time may find it difficult to obtain future credit.

155   D

A conservative working capital policy is one which only uses short-term financing for part of the fluctuating current assets..

156   The answer is $755,760.

		Cash received
		$
April sales	20% × $780,000	156,000
March sales	80% × 0.98 × $770,000 × 60%	362,208
February sales	80% × 0.98 × $760,000 × 30%	178,752
January sales	80% × 0.98 × $750,000 × 10%	58,800
		———
		755,760
		———

157   B

The current ratio is all current assets including inventory divided by current liabilities, while the acid test is the current asset figure *less inventory* divided by current liabilities. These can only be equal if a firm carries no inventory.

158   The answer is $4,800.

	Current assets	Current liabilities
	$	$
Credit purchase:		
Inventory	+ 18,000	
Trade payables		+ 18,000
Credit sale:		
Trade receivables	+ 24,000	
Inventory (24,000 × 100/125)	− 19,200	

Working capital will increase by $4,800, as a result of the credit sale.

159 The answer is $252,000.

	$
Budgeted sales	240,000
Expected decrease in receivables	12,000
	252,000

The reduction in receivables means that the company will expect to receive more cash next month than the total of its credit sales for the month. Changes in inventory levels have no effect on expected cash receipts.

160 The answer is 44.24 days.

Receivables

	$		$
B/f	68,000	Returns	2,500
Sales	250,000	Cash	252,100
		Irrecoverable debts	
		$(68,000 \times 0.05)$	3,400
		C/f	60,000
	318,000		318,000

Receivable days = $60/495 \times 365$ = 44.24 days

(**Note:** That the estimated sales cover a period of only six months, so the annual sales figure is $495,000 $(2 \times 250,000 - 2,500.)$

161 B

Turnover cycle		Days
Inventory	$(8/30) \times 365$	97.3
Trade receivables	$(4/40) \times 365$	36.5
Trade payables	$(3/15) \times 365$	(73.0)
Cash conversion cycle		60.8

Note: The annual cost of purchases would be useful for measuring the inventory turnover period for raw materials. Since the question does not state whether inventory is mainly raw materials, work-in-progress or finished goods, it is probably appropriate to use the annual cost of sales to measure the average inventory turnover time. However, it is reasonable to assume that most trade payables relate to purchases of raw materials, and the annual purchases figure has been used to calculate the payment cycle for trade payables.

162 C

Average receivables = ($10 million + $12 million)/2 = $11 million

Average trade-related receivables = 90% × $11 million = $9.9 million

Annual sales on credit = $95 million

Average collection period = (9.9 million/95 million) × 365 days = 38 days

163 B

	$
Balance b/fwd	22,000
Credit sales	290,510
	312,510
Less: Balance c/fwd ($290,510 × 49/365)	(39,000)
Receipts	273,510

164 B

	$
Purchases on credit	360,000
Increase in trade payables	15,000
Therefore payments to suppliers	345,000

165 C

($82,000 − 12,250) × 97% = $67,657

166 The answer is $345,589.

	$
Owed to credit suppliers at 1 November 2006	42,000
Cost of goods sold	350,000
Less: Opening inventory reflected in cost of goods sold	(56,000)
Add: Closing inventory deducted from cost of goods sold	
60/365 × 350,000	57,534
Less: Amounts owed to credit suppliers at 31 October 2007	
50/365 × 350,000	(47,945)
Amount paid to credit suppliers during the year to 31 October 2007	345,589

167 The answer is 88.4 days.

Trade receivable days = 290/2,400 × 365 = 44.1 days

Inventory days (assuming that inventories are finished goods)

$$= 360/1,400 × 365 = 93.9 \text{ days}$$

Trade payable days = 190/1,400 × 365 = 49.6 days

Working capital cycle = Inventory days + Receivable days − Payable days

$$= 93.9 + 44.1 − 49.6 = 88.4 \text{ days}$$

168   The answer is $19,800.

Sales in	Total sales	Cash sales	Credit sales	Received in May	
	$	$	$		$
April	20,000	8,000	12,000	(97% × 12,000)	11,640
May	20,400	8,160	12,240		8,160
					————
					19,800
					————

169   **B**

Overtrading is associated with fast-growing companies that have insufficient long-term capital, and rely on short-term liabilities to finance their growth. The finance is largely provided by suppliers (trade payables) and a bank overdraft. As a result, there is an increasing bank overdraft (higher borrowing) and very low or even negative working capital. A typical overtrading enterprise is experiencing rapid growth and rising sales. Although it should be profitable, its problem will be a shortage of cash and liquidity. Cash balances will be not be rising, since the overdraft is increasing.

170   **D**

An aged analysis for trade payables is an analysis of unpaid invoices from suppliers according to the length of time since the issue of the invoice. It is not a list (therefore answer A and answer B are incorrect), but a table. A spreadsheet might be used to construct the analysis. The analysis can be used to decide which suppliers should be paid, and how much.

An aged analysis for trade receivables is similar, except that it relates to unpaid invoices sent to credit customers. This analysis is used to decide which customers to 'chase' for payment.

171   **C**

The equivalent annual return offered by supplier P is:

$(100/99)^{12} - 1 = 12.82\%$

This is below the minimum required rate of return of 12.85% and should not be accepted.

The equivalent annual return offered by supplier Q is:

$(100/98)^{12/2} - 1 = 12.89\%$

This is just above the minimum required rate of return of 12.85% and therefore should be accepted.

172   The answer is 27.86%.

Annual rate of interest $= (100/98)^{(365/30 - 0)} - 1$

$= 0.2786$ or 27.86%

173   The three main services provided by a without recourse factor are:

- sales ledger administration/debt collection
- credit insurance (which is the without recourse element of the service)
- factor finance (providing short-term finance against the security of the unpaid invoices).

174   C

Invoice discounting is a method of obtaining short-term funds. Specific invoices are 'sold' to a finance organisation, typically a factor, which provides finance up to a proportion (about 70%) of the value of the invoice. The invoice discounter is repaid with interest out of the money from the invoice payment, when it is eventually paid.

175   D

If $1 million is invested for one year at 7%, the value of the investment will be $1,000,000 × 1.07 = $1,070,000 after one year.

If $1 million is invested for three months at 6.5% per year and then for nine months at 7.5% per year, this means that the interest for the first three months will be 6.5% × 3/12 = 1.625%, and the interest for the next nine months will be 7.5% × 9/12 = 5.625%. The value of the investment after one year will therefore be:

$1,000,000 × 1.01625 × 1.05625 = $1,073,414.

This is $3,414 more than the income that would be obtained by investing at 7% for the full year. However, there is a risk that interest rates will not rise during the first three months, and XYZ will not be able to invest at 7.5% for the nine months, but only at a lower rate.

176   A

The customer cannot be asked for immediate payment once a bill of exchange has been accepted.

177   C

The instrument is a bill of exchange drawn on the bank. This is often called a bank bill (as distinct from a commercial bill, which is a bill drawn on a non-bank company). A bill drawn on a bank under a short-term financing arrangement is also known as an acceptance credit.

178   A

Forfaiting is a method of obtaining medium-term export finance, involving the issue of promissory notes by the importer/buyer, which the exporter is able to sell to a forfaiting bank at a discount to obtain finance. Promissory notes are promises to pay a specified amount of money at a specified future date. The importer's promissory notes have settlement dates spread over a number of years, often the expected useful economic life of the imported items. The importer is therefore able to pay for the imported goods over a period of several years, whilst the exporter can obtain immediate payment by selling the promissory notes.

179 Forms of short-term finance generally available to small entities include:

- trade credit
- bank overdraft
- term loan
- factoring
- hire purchase or leasing.

180 The answer is 40.4%.

AL offers 1.5% interest for 16 days

(100/98.5) (365/16) − 1 =

(1.015) 22.813 − 1 = 40.4%

181 A

Working capital financing involves deciding the mix of long-term and short-term debt. An aggressive policy involves using short-term finance to fund all the fluctuating current assets, as well as some of the permanent part of the current assets. So answer A is correct. A conservative policy is where all of the permanent assets (i.e. non-current assets and the permanent part of current assets) are financed by long-term funding. Short-term financing is only used for part of the fluctuating current assets. So answer B is incorrect. A moderate policy matches short-term finance to the fluctuating current assets and long-term finance to the permanent part of current assets plus non-current assets. So answer D is also incorrect.

182 The answer is 14.8%.

Annual cost = $(100/98.5)^{(365/(60-20))} - 1$

$= (100/98.5)^{9.125} - 1$

$= 14.8\%$

183

	$
June debts: 345 + 520 + 150 − 200 − 520	295
July debts: 233 − 233	0
Augusts debts: 197 + 231 − 197	231
September debts: 319	319
	845

184 B

(70,000 + 10,000) : (88,000 + 7,000)

80,000 : 95,000

0.84 : 1

185 The answer is 500 units.

$$\text{Optimal order quantity} = \sqrt{\frac{2 \times 200 \times 10{,}000}{[4 + (3\% \times 400)]}}$$

= 500 units

186 B

With JIT purchasing, the objective is to receive deliveries exactly at the time required, so that the ideal inventory level is always 0. Therefore inventory holding costs should be lower. There will be an increased dependence on suppliers to deliver exactly on time, but there will be a risk (probably an increased risk) of inventory shortages due to failure by suppliers to deliver on time. However, since purchases will be made to meet demand requirements, there are likely to be much more frequent deliveries.

187 A

The simple EOQ model formula is:

$$\text{EOQ} = \sqrt{\frac{2cd}{h}}$$

where d = annual demand

h = cost of holding one unit for one year

c = cost of placing order

188 C

$$\text{EOQ} = \sqrt{\frac{2C_oD}{C_h}} = \sqrt{\frac{2 \times \$185 \times 2{,}500}{\$25}}$$

$$= \sqrt{37{,}000}$$

$$= 192 \text{ units}$$

Each week $\dfrac{2{,}500}{52}$ = 48 units are required.

Therefore each order of 192 units will last $\dfrac{192}{48}$ = 4 weeks.

189 The answer is $895.

$$\sqrt{\frac{2 \times \$15 \times 32{,}000}{\$1.2}} = \sqrt{800{,}000} = 894.43 \text{ units}$$

190 A

The cost of placing an order under the EOQ formula includes administrative costs, postage and quality control costs.

191 The answer is 98

$$Q = \sqrt{\frac{2C_oD}{C_h}}$$

$$\sqrt{\frac{2 \times 15 \times 95,000}{3}} = 974.68$$

$95,000/975 = 97.4$.

192 The answer is 10.5%.

The yield to maturity must be more than the coupon rate of 7% as the purchase price of the bond is less than maturity value. Using the maths tables to compute the present values of the sums receivable under the bond, the maturity value can be calculated as follows:

$t = 8; r = 10$

$(7 \times 5.335) + (100 \times 0.467) = 37.345 + 46.7 = \$84.045$

$t = 8; r = 11$

$(7 \times 5.146) + (100 \times 0.434) = 36.022 + 43.4 + \$79.422$

By interpolation:

$10\% + ((84.045 - 82.0)/(84.045 - 79.422)) = 10\% + (2.045/4.623) = 10.44\%$

193 The answer is $8,863.7.

$\$700 \times$ (Annuity factor for $t = 5; r = 10$) + $10,000 \times$ (Discount factor $t = 5; r = 10$) =

$$(\$700 \times 3.791) + (10,000 \times 0.621) = 2,653.7 + 6,210 = \$8,863.7$$

194 The answer is 7.2%

Using $t = 7$ and $r = 6$ and 8, from tables

(4×5.582) and $(100 \times 0.665) = 22.328 + 66.5 = 88.828$

(4×5.206) and $(100 \times 0.583) = 20.824 + 58.3 = 79.124$

$$6 + \left\{\frac{88.828 - 83.00}{88.828 - 79.124}\right\} \times 2 = 6 + \left\{\frac{5.828}{9.704} \times 2\right\}$$

$6 + 1.20 = 7.20\%$

195 The answer is 7.77%.

Interest = $0.06 \times 100 = 6$ pa for 10 years

Gain on redemption = $100 - 88 = 12$

The yield to maturity is effectively the internal rate of return of the bond, which is found by trial and error. Let us assume a discount rate of 8% for the first calculation:

Time	Cash flow	Discount factor @ 8%	Discounted cash flow
	$		$
T_0	(88)	1	(88)
$T_1 - T_{10}$	6	6.710	40.26
T_{10}	100	0.463	46.3
			(1.44)

As this gives an NPV close to zero, use 7% for our next calculation:

Time	Cash flow	Discount factor @ 7%	Discounted cash flow
	$		$
T_0	(88)	1	(88)
$T_1 - T_{10}$	6	7.024	42.14
T_{10}	100	0.508	50.8
			4.94

Change in NPV between 7% and 8% is 6.38 (4.94 + 1.44) so, to get an NPV of zero, rate needs to be:

$8\% - 1.44/6.38 = 8 - 0.23 = 7.77\%$

Section 5

ANSWERS TO SECTION B-TYPE QUESTIONS

COST ACCOUNTING SYSTEMS

196   MARGINAL COST PROFIT AND CASH FLOW

Marginal costing systems differ from absorption costing systems in the way that they treat fixed production overheads. In a marginal costing system the fixed production overheads are charged against the sales revenue in the period that they are incurred.

In contrast an absorption costing system will attribute some of the fixed production overheads to any units held in inventory and thus some fixed production overheads will be carried forward in inventory to future periods. These overheads will not be charged in calculating the profit in the month they are incurred, but in the month when the inventory is sold i.e. the charging of the fixed overheads against profit does not reflect the actual cash flow.

Thus marginal costing profits will provide a better indication of cash flow than will absorption costing profits, since more of the costs actually incurred will be charged against the sales revenue for the period. However there will still be a discrepancy between marginal costing profits and cash flow because of factors such as credit sales and purchases and the treatment of capital expenditure in profit calculations.

197   BACKFLUSH ACCOUNTING (SEP 10 EXAM)

In a traditional accounting system, inventory is a key item. Therefore detailed inventory records are kept and costs (for items such as labour, materials and overheads) are tracked at each stage of production and charged to inventory. This is done so that the cost of using inventory is accurately recorded in the income statement and that closing inventory is properly valued on the balance sheet.

Just-In-Time (JIT) control systems hold negligible levels of inventory and therefore the traditional costing system is less important. Companies who employ JIT are more likely to use backflush accounting. Instead of charging costs to inventory at each stage of production, backflush accounting values closing inventory (if there is any) at standard cost and the balance of costs are deemed to be production costs that get charged to the income statement.

This is a much simpler and quicker method, though it is less accurate than the traditional system. However, because inventory levels are very low, accuracy becomes much less important.

198 ACTIVITY BASED COSTING

Overhead recovery rates:

Cost	Total Cost	Cost driver	Recovery rate
	£		£
Machinery cost	285,000	Machine hours	3 / hour
Set-up costs	235,000	Production runs	1000/ run
Purchasing costs	300,000	Purchase orders	60 / order

Allocation to each product:

Product S

Cost	Calculation	£
Machinery cost	2 per unit × £3 / hour	6.00
Set-up costs	(20 runs × £1000/run) / 5,000 units	4.00
Purchasing costs	(100 orders × £60 / order) / 5,000 units	0.12
		£10.12

Product T

Cost	Calculation	£
Machinery cost	1per unit × £3/ hour	3.00
Set-up costs	(5 runs × £1000/run) / 20,000 units	0.25
Purchasing costs	(100 orders × £60 / order) / 20,000 units	0.30
		£3.55

199 OVER ABSORPTION (NOV 09 EXAM)

(i) **Under/over absorption**

		$
Absorbed overheads	(1,800 units x $20/unit*)	36,000
Actual overheads		39,000
Under absorption		3,000

*Overhead absorption rate = Budgeted fixed prod'n overheads / budgeted production

= $40,000 / 2,000 units

= $20 / unit

(ii) **Absorption costing profit**

Standard profit per unit	=	$24,000 / 2,000 units	=	$12 per unit
Number of units sold			=	1,700
Standard profit on actual sales	=	$12 x 1,700	=	$20,400
Fixed selling costs	=		=	$10,000
Under absorption			=	$3,000
Absorption costing profit	=	20,400 – 10,000 – 3,000	=	$7,400

(iii) **Marginal costing profit**

Standard contribution per unit	= $64,000 / 2,000 units	=	$32 per unit
Number of units sold		=	1,700
Total contribution	= $32 x 1,700	=	$54,400
Total fixed overheads	= $39,000 + $10,000	=	$49.000
Marginal costing profit		=	$5,400

200 IMPROVING THE THROUGHPUT ACCOUNTING RATIO

$$\text{TA ratio} = \frac{\text{throughput per hour of bottleneck resource}}{\text{operating expenses per hour of bottleneck resource}}$$

Three actions that could be considered to improve the TA ratio are as follows:

(i) Increase the selling price of the product. This would improve the throughput per hour in the packing process, i.e. the numerator in the calculation and the TA ratio would increase.

(ii) Reduce the operating expenses in the packing process. This would reduce the denominator in the ratio calculation.

(iii) Improve the productivity of the employees engaged in the packing process, thus reducing the time taken to pack each unit of product C. Throughput per packing hour would increase, but the operating expenses per packing hour would remain unchanged. Therefore the TA ratio would increase.

201 ABC AND PROFITABILITY

Activity based costing (ABC) could provide more meaningful information about product costs and profitability in the following circumstances.

(i) Where indirect costs are high relative to direct costs. The cost of direct materials, for example, can usually be attributed to cost units relatively easily. The attribution of overhead costs tends to be more problematic. Traditionally, overhead costs have been attributed to cost units by fairly arbitrary methods such as absorption costing on the basis of direct labour hours. The introduction of new technology has typically resulted in a reduction in labour cost and an increase in overhead cost and labour hours may no longer be an appropriate absorption basis. An ABC approach should lead to more accurate costings of products and departments by considering the processes that actually cause overhead costs to be incurred.

(ii) Where products or services are complex. By identifying the activities that consume resources and the cost drivers for each activity, the costs incurred can be traced more accurately to products and services according to the number of cost drivers that they generate.

(iii) Where some products or services are produced in large numbers but others are produced in small numbers. Products and services incur overhead costs because of the activities that go into producing them. These activities are not necessarily related to the volumes that are produced. An ABC system recognises that direct labour hours and machine hours are not the drivers of cost in many modern business environments.

(iv) Where products or services are tailored to customer specifications. An ABC system is more likely to trace accurately the costs incurred on each specific customer order. The result will be more accurate cost determination which will help in decisions such as pricing.

202 MANUFACTURING RESOURCE PLANNING SYSTEM (MAY 07 EXAM)

A manufacturing resource planning system contains details of all of the inputs into production, including raw materials, components, labour and machine capacity, and coordinates these to provide an optimal production and purchasing plan.

In order to ensure that a manufacturing resource planning system operates effectively it is essential to have:

- A master production schedule, which specifies both the timing and quantity demanded of each product.

- A bill of materials file for each sub-assembly, component and part, containing details of the number of items on hand, scheduled receipts and items allocated to released orders but not yet drawn from inventories.

- A master parts file containing planned lead times of all items to be purchased and sub-assemblies and components to be produced internally.

- A master labour and machine capacity file which specifies both the timing and quantity demanded to achieve planned production levels.

- Details of inputs can then be used in a standard costing system to set parameters for materials, labour and overhead capacity. These will then be used to measure performance through variance analysis.

203 JUST-IN-TIME (MAY 07 EXAM)

Just-in-time (JIT) is a system whose objective is to produce or procure products or components as they are required by a customer or for use, rather than for inventory. It is a philosophy which aims to eliminate all waste and non value adding activities in an organisation. The main differences between JIT and a traditional manufacturing environment are:

- JIT is a 'pull system' which responds to demand, in contrast to a 'push system' in a traditional manufacturing environment, in which inventories act as buffers between the different elements of the system, such as purchasing, production and sales.

- The main focus in a traditional manufacturing environment is on maximising output and minimising costs. In a JIT environment it may be more cost effective to allow resources to stand idle than to produce goods for inventory.

- In a traditional manufacturing environment labour are organised into specialist roles and performance is measured against pre determined standards. In a JIT environment labour are multi skilled and carry out routine maintenance tasks as well as working on products. They are empowered to find methods of cost reduction.

- Companies using JIT are likely to have long term contracts with few, carefully chosen suppliers, whereas traditional producers will seek the cheapest quote from several suppliers for raw materials.

204 THROUGHPUT ACCOUNTING

(a) **Bottleneck**

(i) Maximum possible production from each machine:

		M1	M2
Hours available		126	195
Hours taken per unit			
	P1	0.35	0.60
	P2	0.40	0.65
Maximum level of production (units)			
	P1	360	325
	or		
	P2	315	300

Machine M2 is the bottleneck. Machine M1 can produce a greater total of either product, but the process is restricted because machine M2 can produce 35 fewer units of P1 or 15 fewer units of P2.

(ii) Throughput accounting ratio

$$\frac{\text{Throughput per hour on Machine M2}}{\text{Operating expenses per hour on Machine M2}}$$

		P1	P2
Sales price		36.00	39.00
Direct materials		(14.20)	(16.75)
Throughput		21.80	22.25
Hours in bottleneck	(M2)	0.60	0.65
Throughput per hour		36.33	34.23
Operating expenses		9.00	11.25
Hours in bottleneck	(M2)	0.60	0.65
Operating expenses per hour		15.00	17.30
Throughput accounting ratio		= 36.33	= 34.23
		15.00	17.30
		= 2.42	**= 1.98**

(b) **Throughput accounting**

Product P1 has the highest throughput per hour and should therefore take priority in the production plan. As many units as possible of P1 should be made on machine M2. This means that 325 units of product P1 should be manufactured. This will give a total throughput of (325 × £21.80 =) £7,085. Total profit would be (325 × £12.80 =) £3,510 (assuming that the fixed production overheads of product P2 could be avoided.

205   MRP AND ABB (MAY 10 EXAM)

(a)   **Manufacturing Resource Planning (MRP)**

MRP is a computerised planning system for materials. It determines the quantity and timing of the finished goods demanded and uses this to determine the requirements for raw materials etc. at each prior stage of production. It would therefore replace the existing EOQ system for ordering materials which relies on constant and predictable demand. The MRP system can cope with varying demand and take account of the changes in the company's environment.

An MRP system is very flexible and can account for sudden changes in demand. It can also cope better with bespoke/customised products and create a production and ordering system for each 'job'.

It should also reduce inventory levels as it would not order items that were not needed. However, in this particular instance it would appear that the biggest benefit would be in improved inventory levels – the purchasing department would know exactly what type and quantity of materials would be required and when it would be required. This should remove the difficulties that currently being experienced.

(b)   **Activity Based Budgeting (ABB)**

ABB is defined as 'a method of budgeting based on an activity framework and utilising cost driver data in the budget-setting and variance feedback processes' (CIMA Official Terminology). This means that cost drivers would be identified for each activity and a cost per unit of activity in each cost pool would be used as a charge to products.

The company in question are likely to experiencing a rise in overheads due to a change in their production methods (for example, there might be more machine running costs or greater supervision etc.). ABB would give better detail on the make-up and causes of these overheads which would allow better cost control and planning.

The existing incremental system is likely to simply build on past deficiencies and not consider the changes in the company's environment and its production methods. It will also potentially have a poor identification of the nature and cause of overheads. ABB should eradicate both of these problems.

206   TOTAL QUALITY MANAGEMENT (MAY 08 EXAM)

Three elements that are present in any business that is successfully focused on a TQM programme are:

*   **Customer focus**. Quality is examined from a customer perspective and the system is aimed at meeting customer needs and expectations.
*   **Continuous improvement**. The 'kaizen' system aims to make lots of small improvements over time that add up to overall large improvements.
*   **Getting things right first time**. TQM aims for zero defects and zero waste. It recognises that it costs less to prevent problems than it does to rectify mistakes afterwards.

207 MARGINAL AND ABSORPTION COSTING (MAY 06 EXAM)

(i)   OAR = $12,800/2,000 = $6.40 per unit

Inventory is budgeted to increase and therefore absorption costing profit will be higher than marginal costing profit.

Absorption costing profit = 5,700 + (600 × $6.40) = $9,540

(ii)   Marginal costing is useful for:

- decision making because variable and fixed costs are separated. Often fixed costs are not relevant to a decision and so can be ignored;

- flexible budgeting as costs must be identified as fixed or variable to calculate the flexed budget allowance.

208 MARGINAL COSTING AND THROUGHPUT ACCOUNTING (MAY 06 EXAM)

The underlying methodology is the same except that throughput accounting (TA) assumes that direct materials are the only 'variable' cost and that labour is a fixed cost.

TA is based on the ideas of the 'Theory of Constraints' and seeks to maximise profits by maximising throughput by identifying and, where possible, removing bottlenecks.

Maximising throughput on a bottleneck is similar to the marginal costing (MC) idea of maximising contribution per unit of scarce resource.

TA controls production costs through a series of ratios that focus on throughput per bottleneck resource.

MC is used in many aspects of decision making such as pricing and breakeven analysis.

STANDARD COSTING

209 FIXED OVERHEAD VOLUME VARIANCE

The fixed production overhead volume variance is reported in a standard absorption costing system. It arises due to the use of a predetermined overhead absorption rate based on budgeted costs and activity levels.

The standard absorption rate is designed so that, if the actual costs and activity levels are exactly the same as budgeted, then there will be no fixed production overhead variances. In practice of course this is rarely the case and any difference between the actual and budgeted production volume results in a fixed production overhead volume variance.

The fixed production overhead volume variance is the difference in output volume multiplied by the absorption rate per unit of output. It represents the under- or over-absorbed fixed production overhead due to a change in production volume from the budgeted level. If the volume of output is higher than budgeted, the variance is favourable (over-absorbed overhead). If the volume of output is lower than budgeted, the variance is adverse (under-absorbed overhead).

If the variance is adverse, then it is necessary to investigate why output was lower than budgeted. This is not necessarily a bad thing, if output were deliberately reduced because sales volume was lower than expected. In this case the cause of the sales shortfall would need to be investigated, rather than questioning the shortfall in production. If production had proceeded as budgeted, then this would have reduced the volume variance but this would not necessarily be the correct action for the organisation as a whole, if as a result the units remained unsold in inventory.

Similarly, if the variance is favourable this is not necessarily a good thing. If the output were sold, then the increase in production was worthwhile. However, simply increasing output in order to produce a favourable overhead volume variance would not be the correct action, if the extra units cannot be sold.

In conclusion it is not the fixed production overhead volume variance itself which provides useful information for management but the reason why the production volume differed from that budgeted and the consequential effects of that volume difference.

210 LABOUR VARIANCES (NOV 05 EXAM)

Labour variance – senior consultant

				$	
SHSR					
40 hours	×	$100/hr	=	4,000	Efficiency
AHSR					$1,000 A
50 hours	×	$100/hr	=	5,000	

Labour variance – junior consultant

				$	
SHSR					
60 hours	×	$60/hr	=	3,600	Efficiency
AHSR					$900 F
45 hours	×	$60/hr	=	2,700	

The efficiency variance looks at whether people **work** fast or slow and looks at hours **worked.**

The total efficiency variance was thus $1,000 A + $900 F = $100 A.

Idle time variance

The idle time variance is the difference between the actual hours worked and the actual hours paid for, then multiplied by the standard labour rate per hour.

Idle time variance = 10 hours × $60 per hour = $600 A

Mix variance

	Senior consultant hrs	Junior consultant hrs	Total hrs
Actual hours	50	45	95
Actual hours in std proportions			
4:6	38	57	⇐ 95
Difference in hours	12 A	12 F	
× Std rate	× 100	× 60	
Mix variance	$1,200 A	$720 F	$480 A

The mix and yield variances are sub-divisions of the efficiency variance and thus focus on hours worked. (Note: the mix variance was calculated using the individual unit prices; the weighted average method could also have been used.)

211 PLANNING AND OPERATING VARIANCES (MAY 07 EXAM)

(i)   Budgeted wage rate = $30 per hour

Revised wage rate = $31.20 per hour

Standard hours for actual output = 680 × 900/600 = 1,020

Planning labour rate variance = standard hours for actual output × difference in wage rate = 1,020 × $1.20 = $1,224 Adverse

Operational labour efficiency variance

680 units should take	1,020 hours
did take	1,070 hours
	—————
	50 A
Value at revised rate per hour	$31.20
Operational labour efficiency variance	**$1,560 Adverse**

Tutorial note

Planning variance

The original labour rate variance is:

1,070 hours	*should cost $30 per hour*	*$32,100*
	did cost $32 per hour	*$34,240*
		—————
		$2,140 A

It may be tempting to split this variance into a planning variance (1,070 × $1.20 = $1,284 A) and an operational variance (1,070 × $0.80 = $856 A). This approach ignores part of the effect of the revision to the wage rate; the part that impacts on the calculation of the efficiency variance. The original labour efficiency variance is 50 hours Adverse × $30 = $1,500 A. By revising the wage rate the operational efficiency variance increases to $1,560 A. There is a 'planning effect' of $60 F to reconcile back to the original variance. The net planning effect is $1,284 A − $60 F = $1,224 A. This is all caused by the revision to the wage rate and is therefore a planning labour rate variance.

(ii)   The major benefit of analysing the variances into planning and operational components is that the revised standard should provide a realistic standard against which to measure performance. Any variances should then be a result of operational management efficiencies and inefficiencies and not faulty planning.

212 STANDARD COSTING AND THE NEW MANAGEMENT ACCOUNTING

The company's standard costing system will need to be adapted in a number of ways in the new environment.

(i) Cost reduction v cost control

TQM enforces a management policy of continuous improvement and hence is focused on cost reduction. However, traditional standard costing is concerned with cost control where performance standards often remain constant for the life cycle of a product. In order to use standard costing successfully in a TQM environment it would be necessary to continually review and tighten the standards each period.

(ii) Management responsibility

Under standard costing individual responsibility for reported variances is encouraged. With TQM and JIT it is necessary to focus on group responsibility for performance. For standard costing to work in a TQM and JIT environment it would be necessary for each team of employees to bear group responsibility for variances.

(iii) Demand based manufacturing

JIT manufacturing only allows production to occur if the demand for the final product exists. In contrast, standard costing can encourage managers to produce for inventory. For example a favourable fixed overhead volume variance will result if output is increased, regardless of whether a demand exists. The standard costing variances reported would need to be adapted to reflect the demand based manufacturing of JIT.

(iv) Direct material variances

Both TQM and JIT encourage long-term relationships with suppliers, who are expected to deliver on time at the right quality. In return for the high level of service demanded, a fair price will be agreed. Thus material price and material usage variances will no longer be necessary.

(v) Direct labour efficiency variance

It will be important to ensure that workers do not focus on faster production, in order to minimise the efficiency variance, at the expense of the quality of output.

(vi) Historical versus future information

Standard costing is concerned with reviewing actual costs after the period has ended. JIT and TQM both focus on how improvements can be made in the future. Management will need to develop strategies to achieve better results in the future.

213 RITZER'S MCDONALDIZATION MODEL

The four dimensions to the McDonaldization model described by Ritzer are efficiency, calculability, control and predictability.

(i) **Efficiency**

The optimum means must be chosen to achieve a given end, so that consumers are able to get the service they want more rapidly and with less effort.

(ii) **Calculability**

Each service unit must be identical and the input must be measurable. Non-human technologies should be used as much as possible in order to standardise operations and the service output.

(iii) **Control**

There should be effective control over both employees and customers. Again, the use of non-human technologies in the provision of the service assists in the achievement of control.

(iv) **Predictability**

Customers and employees should know exactly what service will be provided, wherever in the world it is being provided. Predictability helps the service to be standardised so that standard costing can be used as a means of control.

214 DIAGNOSTIC RELATED GROUPS

Diagnostic related groups (DRGs) are a means of classifying patients according to certain characteristics such as their age, diagnosis and required treatment. Once a patient is classified into a certain group it is possible to determine a standard cost for their treatment and care. The standard cost will be based upon estimates of the standard consumption of hospital resources required and the expected length of stay.

This standard then provides a control measure against which the actual cost of the patient's treatment and care can be monitored. Therefore control by comparison can be achieved in the same way that product standard costs are used for control purposes.

The system was originally developed in the USA where the DRG classification provides a basis for determining the maximum payment that will be received by the hospital from a medical insurance company. This provides a direct incentive for hospital management to keep costs below the maximum payment that will be received from the insurance company.

215 MIX AND YIELD VARIANCES

When two or more materials are mixed together it may be possible to analyse further any recorded materials usage variance. The further analysis would subdivide the total usage variance into its component parts of materials mix variance and materials yield variance.

The materials mix variance is the change in standard cost caused by mixing the materials in a different proportion to standard. For example, if proportionately more of a cheaper material is used in the mix then a favourable mix variance will result.

The materials yield variance is the change in standard cost caused by using a different amount of material in total than the standard expected for the output achieved.

There are a number of limitations in the usefulness of material mix and yield variances.

(i)   Mix and yield variances can only provide useful control information where the mix of materials is within the control of management, and where the information about total yield is more useful than usage variances for the individual materials calculated separately.

(ii)   It is often found that the mix and yield variances are interdependent, and that one variance cannot be assessed without also considering the other. For example an adverse yield variance might be explained by the fact that the mix had a larger than expected proportion of cheaper material (favourable mix variance).

(iii)   If management is able to achieve a cheaper mix of materials without affecting the yield then the standard becomes obsolete. The cheaper mix should become the new standard mix.

(iv)   Control measures to achieve a favourable mix variance are likely to affect the quality of the output. Analysing mix and yield variances for control purposes does not take account of quality issues.

216 LABOUR RATE VARIANCE

Possible causes of an adverse labour rate variance include the following:

(i)   The standard labour rate per hour may have been set too low.

(ii)   Employees may have been of a higher grade than standard, with a consequent increase in the hourly rate paid.

(iii)   There may have been an unexpected increase in the prevailing market rate of pay for employees with appropriate skills.

(iv)   Where bonuses are included as a part of direct labour costs, increased bonus payments may have been made, above the standard level expected.

(v)   There may have been a change in the composition of the work force, which resulted in an increase in the average rate of pay.

217 INVESTIGATION OF VARIANCES (NOV 05 EXAM)

(a)   From the normal distribution tables, 95% of outcomes lie within 1.96 standard deviations of the mean.

1.96 standard deviations $\times$ 10 kg = 19.6 kg

90 kg $\pm$ 19.6 kg = a range between 70.4 kg and 109.6 kg

The actual weight of the sample batch was 110 kg, which falls outside the 95% control limits and the variance should thus be investigated.

(b)   Four factors are listed below. Only two were asked for.

The cost of investigating the variance and correcting it

If the financial value of the variance is minor and/or the cost of investigating and correcting the variance is substantial, then the variance should not be investigated. The benefit from the control action must exceed the cost of the investigation.

The trend of the variance

If the variance is below 1.96 standard deviations, but has been showing a worsening of performance for a number of months, then it may be decided to investigate the variance now rather than wait for it to actually hit the control limit.

The controllability of the variance

If the variance cannot be controlled (cannot be fixed), then there may be no point in incurring the cost of investigating it.

The reliability of the standards

If the standard is not set on a reliable basis in the first place, then any variance from the standard is also unreliable and any variances falling outside the 95% control limits might not actually need investigating, or indeed some variances falling within the 95% limits should be investigated.

218 INVESTIGATION OF VARIANCES (2) (MAY 07 EXAM)

Three factors that should be considered before deciding to investigate a variance are:

- The benefit should exceed the cost. This may depend on the importance (materiality) of the variance in the business and whether the cost can be controlled

- Trend. Actual costs will be expected to fluctuate around the standard from period due to it being a long run average. If there appears to be a trend of a variance steadily worsening this maybe an indication that the cost is out of control.

- Interrelationships. Some variances may be caused by the same factor. For example, purchasing cheaper material may lead to a favourable material price variance, an adverse material usage variance and an adverse labour efficiency variance. The net impact may be considered before deciding whether action is necessary.

219 BENCHMARKING

Benchmarking is the practice of identifying an external organisation whose performance can be used as a comparator or benchmark for the organisation's own performance. The principle is that, by a close analysis of and comparison with other practices and processes, changes and adjustments can be made to those processes that will improve overall performance.

Four main types of benchmarking can be identified.

- *Internal benchmarking* involves comparisons with another department or division within the same company.

- *Competitive benchmarking* involves comparisons with the most successful competitors in the same field.

- *Functional benchmarking* is carried out by comparing the performance of a business function, for example the finance department, with the performance of the finance function in an organisation of similar size but which is not a direct competitor.

- *Strategic benchmarking* is a form of competitive benchmarking aimed at reaching decisions for strategic action and organisational change.

Benchmarking might help to improve overall performance by:

- providing managers with a warning about the need for change;
- enabling learning from others in order to improve performance;
- gaining a competitive edge (in the private sector);
- improving services (in the public sector).

220   HOSPITAL CARE (MAY 06 EXAM)

	$	$
Standard cost for 2-day procedure		1,165
Length of stay variances		
Nursing costs: 1 day × 0.75 × $320 per day	240 A	
Space and food costs: 1 day × $175 per day	175 A	
Hospital overheads	110 A	525 A
Standard cost for 3-day stay		1,690
Drug and specific cost variances		205 A
Nursing staffing variance: 3 days × $320 × (0.9 − 0.75)		144 A
Actual cost		2,039

221   C PLC (MAY 06 EXAM)

		Feb	March	April
1	Std material cost of output ($)	132,000	61,200	109,200
2	Usage variance ($)	15,970	5,950	8,400
3	Std cost of actual purchases ($)	147,970	67,150	117,600
4	Price variance ($)	12,300	4,500	6,200
	Usage % variance (2/1)	12.1%	9.7%	7.7%
	Price % variance (4/3)	8.3%	6.7%	5.3%

Percentage variance chart for February to April

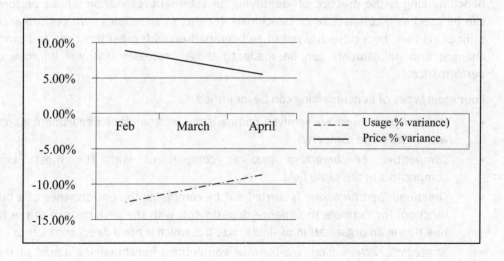

222 MODERN BUSINESS ENVIRONMENT (MAY 06 & MAY 07 EXAM)

Standard costing may not be appropriate in a modern business environment because:

- it is most appropriate for large volumes of similar products. In the modern environment products tend to be customised and produced in smaller batches;
- it is normally based on attainable working conditions. The modern environment emphasises continuous improvement and zero defects;
- it focuses on maximising the utilisation of capacity and minimising cost. In the modern environment breaks in production may be preferred to match production to demand and higher quality higher price inputs may be preferred such as highly skilled staff.

BUDGETING

223 ZERO BASED BUDGETING (ZBB) (SEP 10 EXAM)

ZBB starts each budget with the assumption that the function does not exist and that cost is zero. It ignores any past performance or budgets. It has the following advantages:

- All costs must be justified. Therefore if an activity cannot be justified it will not be performed. In this way it will force the charity to examine whether their activities are worthwhile.
- It should lead to improved resource utilisation by, for example, determining the best use of charity staff. This should assist managers in determining where discretionary expenditure gets allocated.

But the system also has some disadvantages:

- It is a complicated system. For a charity who's managers might lack financial expertise this may prove too difficult to implement.
- The charity's activities are unlikely to change drastically from year to year and therefore simpler systems such as incremental budgeting may be more appropriate.
- Donators may not be happy that too much time is spent on budgeting rather than on charitable activities.

224 PRODUCTION COST BUDGET (MAY 10 EXAM)

Production cost budget		*Quarter 3*
Production (units)		23,000
		$
Direct materials	(W1)	262,200
Production labour	(W2)	219,000
Production overheads	(W3)	278,000
		————
Total budgeted production cost		759,200
		————

(W1) Materials

Cost per unit = ($180,000 / 15,000) = $12/unit.

Budgeted cost = 23,000 x $12 = $276,000.

This would qualify for the 5% discount so the actual cost would be $276,000 x 95% = $262,200.

(W2) **Labour**

Increase in cost in first two quarters = $195,000 - $155,000 = $40,000.

Increase in production in first two quarters = 5,000 units.

Variable cost per unit = $40,000 / 5,000 units = $8 per unit.

Fixed costs = $195,000 – ($8 x 20,000) = $35,000.

Budgeted cost for 23,000 units = $35,000 + (23,000 x $8) = $219,000.

(W3) **Production overheads**

Increase in cost in first two quarters = $240,000 - $210,000 = $30,000.

Increase in production in first two quarters = 5,000 units.

Variable cost per unit = $30,000 / 5,000 units = $6 per unit.

Fixed costs = $240,000 – ($6 x 20,000) = $120,000.

Budgeted cost for 23,000 units = $120,000 + (23,000 x $6) + $20,000 = $278,000.

225 J LIMITED (NOV 05 EXAM)

(i) With zero-based budgeting (ZBB), nothing is taken for granted. The budget is started from scratch. This can be contrasted with incremental budgeting where the starting point is last year's budget or actual results and then possibly a percentage is added on to account for inflation, or any expected changes in the level of activity. With ZBB each manager sets out what he or she wishes to accomplish over the forthcoming period.

For each activity that they wish to undertake, they look at alternative methods of achieving the objective, and look at providing the service at different levels.

Each activity is put into what is known as a decision package and the costs and benefits are estimated. The activity will only go ahead if the benefits exceed the costs. Also, once all the packages have been evaluated, they can be ranked against each other and the company resources can be allocated to the best packages.

ZBB is usually used in service organisations and is particularly common in local government, where ZBB acts as a control to improve efficiency in the absence of competitive markets.

ZBB can be used to decide whether an activity is better carried out internally or whether it should be sub-contracted/outsourced.

(ii) A ZBB approach will definitely be more expensive and will be more time-consuming. The benefit from a better budget must exceed the extra cost.

The managers of J Limited may not have the skill or inclination to undertake the more time-consuming, laborious ZBB exercise. The staff may have to be persuaded as to the value of the exercise. This may be expensive in terms of senior management's time as they have to coax the staff of J Limited into taking on the culture change necessary for implementing a ZBB approach.

The ZBB exercise may need to be implemented with the aid of external consultants. This will, of course, be expensive and will also make things more complicated as now the consultants will have to be managed.

ZBB involves 're-inventing the wheel', where each year worthwhile activities are evaluated from scratch to see whether the benefit exceeds the cost.

226   ZBB (MAY 09 EXAM)

(a)   **Zero Based Budgeting**

Incremental budgeting is a method of budgeting that starts with the current year's budget and adjusts this for known changes. The main problems associated with it are that:

- it can lead to inaccurate allocation of resources;

- managers may build in slack to make achieving targets easier.

Zero-Based Budgeting is a method of budgeting that requires all costs to be specifically justified by the benefits expected. Costs are built up from a zero base and ranked against other activities competing for limited resources. This should eliminate slack and lead to an optimal allocation of resources.

(b)   **Labour variances**

(i)   **Idle time variance**

The idle time variance is the difference between the actual hours worked and the actual hours paid for, then multiplied by the standard labour rate per hour.

Idle time variance = 10 hours × $80 per hour = $800 A

Mix variance

	Senior consultant hrs	Junior consultant hrs	Total hrs
Actual hours *worked*	60	80	140
Actual hours in std proportions 50:90	50	90	⇐ 140
Difference in hours	10 A	10 F	
× Std rate	× 120	× 80	
Mix variance	$1,200 A	$800 F	$400 A

The mix variance was calculated using the individual unit prices; the weighted average method could also have been used.

(ii)   **Benefits of the labour mix variance**

One of the key factors that can determine the performance of a professional practice is the manner in which the work of senior staff is integrated with that of their juniors. In this scenario it will be important to discover that the senior consultants worked for ten extra hours than expected which cost the company $400. This could also explain the ten hours of idle time experienced by the junior staff – which gave a further cost of $800.

(c) **Variable costs**

Variable costs are defined as 'a cost which varies with a measure of activity'.

Under traditional costing methods a short-term view of variable costs is taken. This means that any cost that varies directly with changes in this year's production would be included as a variable cost and removed from overheads. However, for planning and control purposes, any costs that fall outside this definition are treated as a fixed cost and these are often apportioned between products on an arbitrary basis. This makes it more difficult to price products, gauge their profitability and to control costs due to a lack of understanding of their underlying cause.

However, in the longer term, all costs are variable. By identifying activities that use up resources that give rise to costs, ABC can provide useful information about product profitability, for controlling overhead costs over the longer term. Since costs are allocated to products on the basis of resource-consuming activities, ABC provides useful information about the economic cost of products, and which products are more profitable than others.

Traditional costing does not do this because there is no relationship between the overhead costs allocated to products and the consumption of overhead resources.

(d) **Variances**

    (i) **Material usage planning variance**

		£
Original planned cost	400 units x 6 kgs x £12/kg	28,800
Revised planned cost	400 units x 6.75kgs x £12/kg	32,400
Planning Variance		3,600 A

    (ii) **Operational materials price variance**

		£
Actually spent on materials cost		29,000
2500kgs should have cost	x £12/kg	30,000
Price Variance		1,000 F

    (iii) **Operational materials usage variance**

380units should use	x 6.75 kgs	2,565 kgs
Actually used		2,500 kgs
Favourable Usage Variance		65 kgs
Standard price		£12 /kg
Material usage variance		£780 Fav

227   QR (SEP 10 EXAM)

Production cost budget

	Product Q	Product R
Number of batches produced	16	30
Number of machine set ups / batch	4	2
Total number of set ups	64	60

Overhead recovery rate = $\dfrac{\text{Total overheads}}{\text{Total number of set ups}}$

Overhead recovery rate = $\dfrac{\$74,400}{124}$

Overhead recovery rate = $600 / set up

Total charge to Product Q = $600 x 64 set ups = $38,400

Cost per unit of Product Q = $38,400 / 80,000 units = $0.48

Activity based budgeting can have the following advantages:

- It draws attention to overheads (which may be a large proportion of total costs) and should therefore improve cost control.

- The allocation of overheads between products can be improved which should, for example, improve product pricing.

228   MCDONALDIZATION AND BUDGETS (NOV 05 EXAM)

The concept of McDonaldization comes from the successes of the fast food company. The term was defined by George Ritzer (1996) as 'the process by which the principles of the fast-food restaurant are coming to dominate more and more sectors of American society, as well as the rest of the world'. Ritzer identified four dimensions to McDonaldization which are critical to the success of the model:

(1)   Efficiency

(2)   Calculability

(3)   Control

(4)   Predictability.

Management should be able to set accurate budgets for what it takes, in terms of materials and time, to provide standard items to customers and it should be very cheap to provide that information.

Owing to the supposed lack of variation the actual costs should be very close to the budgeted costs and thus any variances will be an indication of good or bad operational performance.

For UV Limited the provision of standard meals for large events does conform to the characteristics of McDonaldization and it should be very possible to flex the budgeted costs in accordance with the number of meals provided in order to predict costs accurately and then set prices which will guarantee a profit. These prices could then be used for a published price list.

UV Limited also provides meals to meet the exact requirements of a customer and prices are negotiated individually with each customer. This type of service does not have the characteristics of McDonaldization and the budgeting for this type of service will have to be different.

229   ST PLC (NOV 05 EXAM)

(a)   An enterprise resource system is a powerful computer system that integrates information from all parts of the organisation. It is an extension of the MRP philosophy, but provides more integration between different parts of the organisation. The implementation of the ERP system can affect the budget-setting process for ST plc in the following ways:

  - The ERP system integrates the entire business and the financial effects of changing the operational plans can be quickly calculated, reducing the time taken for the budget-setting process.

  - Once the operational plans have been created they can be easily amended, thus sensitivity analysis is facilitated and also budgets can be flexed more accurately.

  - It has been argued by some that the budget-setting process almost disappears, because an effective ERP system will produce the budget figures as a natural consequence of the planning process.

(b)   An ERP system causes more significant changes in terms of the budgetary control process.

  - The actual data can be entered into the system and compared with the budget and all sorts of management reports/budgetary control statements can be produced within a very small timescale, leading to improved control and more rapid responses.

  - The role of the accountant is reduced as much of the output from the system is produced automatically and can be delivered to the operational managers without the intervention of the management accountant.

  - Less resources are needed to operate the budgetary control system (on the other hand the ERP system may require a considerable amount of resources to implement).

230   QBQ (NOV 07 EXAM)

(a)   *Tutorial note:* First produce a production budget and a materials usage budget. Then adjust for changes in raw material inventories to arrive at a material purchase budget. The budget for Quarter 1 is required but this often requires production figures for the next period to arrive at a closing inventory value. Leave space to add additional workings if required.

Quarter	1	2
Sales (units)	10,000	12,000
Add closing inventory (finished goods)		
45% × 12,000	5,400	
40% × 14,000		5,600
Less opening inventory (finished goods)	(5,500)	(5,400)
Production budget (units)	9,900	12,200
Material usage budget (× 1.5kg)	14,850	18,300
Add closing inventory (raw materials) 25% × 18,300	4,575	
Less opening inventory (raw materials)	(4,500)	
Materials purchase budget (kg)	14,925	
Materials purchase budget ($) (× $6)	$89,550	

(b) **Quarter 3**

Sales units	14,000 units
Opening inventory	5,600 units
Closing inventory	4,200 units

So production is 14,000 – 5,600 + 4,200 = 12,600 units

(i) Using marginal costing, production and inventory are valued at the variable production cost per unit = 9 + 8 = $17 per unit

	$
Sales (14,000 × 40)	560,000
Variable cost of sales (14,000 × $17)	238,000
	—————
Contribution	322,000
Less fixed costs	
Production ($720,000/4)	(180,000)
Administration ($200,000/4)	(50,000)
	—————
Profit	92,000

(ii) Using absorption costing production and inventory are valued at the full production cost = 17 + 15 = $32.

In addition profit must be adjusted for any over/under absorption of overhead. Overhead is absorbed by $15 for each unit of production.

Overhead absorbed (12,600 × $15)	189,000
Overhead incurred	180,000
	—————
Over-absorption	9,000

	$
Sales (14,000 × 40)	560,000
Cost of sales (14,000 × $32)	448,000
	—————
	112,000
Administration cost	(50,000)
	—————
Add overabsorption	9,000
	—————
Profit	71,000

(iii) The profit calculated using marginal costing is greater than the profit calculated using absorption costing by $21,000. This is due to inventory decreasing by 1,400 units. Using absorption costing, each unit of inventory includes $15 of fixed overhead which is carried forward to a future period to be matched against sales. This is a total of 1,400 × $15 = $21,000. Using marginal costing fixed overhead is treated as a period cost and charged against sales for the current period.

(c)   Budgetary planning and control might be inappropriate in a rapidly changing business environment because;

- Budgets may provide static targets which stifle innovation. Managers' attention may be focused on achieving the budget targets rather than responding to opportunities which may arise.

- Budgets may become quickly out of date and therefore be misleading for control purposes. Rolling budgets may allow targets to be updated more regularly but are time consuming. Constantly changing targets may be confusing and demotivating for managers if they feel that the 'goal posts' are constantly moving.

- It may be difficult to incorporate cost reduction in a budget. As long as budget targets are achieved there is no incentive for managers to continually seek methods of improving efficiency and removing any non-value added activities. In a rapidly changing business environment these may be the key to success.

(d)   The objective of JIT is to remove all non value added activities from the production system. This includes reducing inventory to as close to zero as possible. Raw materials are ordered only when they are required for production and products are only produced when demanded by a customer. Production systems are arranged in an optimal layout to reduce material movements. Labour are multi skilled to allow production or routine maintenance to be carried out and high quality material is important to prevent wastage and rejects.

To be successful there must be:

- High quality suppliers willing to deliver material as required. Suppliers must be located nearby to achieve short lead times.

- Predictable demand patterns. Uneven demand would make it very difficult to operate with low inventories.

- Sophisticated real time ordering systems to link customers with the production facility and to be able to order materials when required.

(e)   Administration costs = $100,000 \times \dfrac{104}{100}$ = $104,000

House-keeping costs = $125,000 \times \dfrac{90}{100} \times \dfrac{106}{100}$ = $119,250

The nursing costs are more of a problem, because they are semi-variable. We will need to use the high/low method to break the cost into its fixed and variable elements. Before we do that we will need to strip out the effects of inflation, i.e. we will need to deflate the period 2 figures to period 1 prices (we could, alternatively, inflate the period 1 figures to period 2 prices).

$324,000 \times \dfrac{100}{108}$ = $300,000 in period 1 prices

Variable costs $= \dfrac{\$300,000 - \$280,000}{125 - 100}$

                    = $800 per index point (in period 1 prices)

	High level	OR	Low level
	$		$
Semi-variable cost	300,000		280,000
Variable part			
$800 × 125	100,000		
$800 × 100			80,000
	———		———
Fixed cost	200,000		200,000
	———		———

	Period 1		Period 2		Period 3
	$		$		$
Variable cost	$80{,}000 \times \dfrac{125}{100} \times \dfrac{108}{100}$		$108{,}000 \times \dfrac{90}{100} \times \dfrac{105}{100}$		102,060
Fixed cost	$200{,}000 \times \dfrac{108}{100}$		$216{,}000 \times \dfrac{105}{100}$		226,800
	———		———		———
	280,000		324,000		328,860
	———		———		———

Period 3 Budget	$
House-keeping	119,250
Nursing	328,860
Administration	104,000
	———
	552,110
	———

231   TIME SERIES IN FORECASTING

The strengths of time series analysis as a basis for forecasting are that:

* forecasts are based on clearly understood assumptions;
* trend lines can be reviewed after each successive time period to assess the reliability of the forecasts;
* forecasting accuracy can be improved with experience.

The limitations of the technique stem from the following assumptions that are made in its application. These assumptions may not be valid:

* that past events are a reliable guide to what will happen in the future;
* that there is a straight line trend;
* that seasonal variations are constant, either in absolute values if the additive model is used, or as a proportion of the trend line value in a multiplicative model.

232 X PLC (NOV 06 EXAM)

(a) **Tutorial note:** The budget for the next four quarters is required. However, closing stock values are determined by the following quarter's sales demand and material usage, so the budget for Q5 will also be prepared.

Units	Q1	Q2	Q3	Q4	Q5
Sales demand	2,250	2,050	1,650	2,050	1,250
Add closing inventory (W1)	615	495	615	375	616
Less opening inventory (W2)	(675)	(615)	(495)	(615)	(375)
Production budget	2,190	1,930	1,770	1,810	1,490
Raw material usage (× 3kg)	6,570	5,790	5,310	5,430	4,470
Closing inventory (W3)	2,605.5	2,389.5	2,443.5	2,011.5	
Opening inventory (W4)	(2,956.5)	(2,605.5)	(2,389.5)	(2,443.5)	
Purchases budget for B in kgs	6,219	5,574	5,364	4,998	
Purchases budget for B in $	43,533	39,018	37,548	34,986	

Total purchases budget for material B for Quarters 1–4 = $155,085

Workings

(W1) Q1 0.3 × 2,050

(W2) The opening inventory for any quarter is the same as the closing inventory of the previous quarter. The opening inventory for Q1 is 0.3 × 2,250 = 675

(W3) Q1 0.45 × 5,790

(W4) The opening inventory for any quarter is the same as the closing inventory of the previous quarter. The opening inventory for Q1 is 0.45 × 6,570 = 2,956.5

(b) If Material A is in short supply then this becomes the principal budget factor. This will affect budget preparation because the first step in the budgetary process will be to determine the optimum mix of products according to their contribution per kg of Material A. The optimum production plan can then be determined and the sales budget can be derived from the production plan. It may be necessary to revise the policy for holding inventory whilst Material A is in short supply.

Once the production plan has been determined then Material B, labour and overhead budgets can be derived. The limit on the level of production may mean that there is spare capacity in the factory and the fixed overhead absorption rate will increase. This will increase the cost per unit of products and lower profitability. In addition lower production levels may mean that there are spare labour resources. This could mean that output of products which do not use Material A could be increased.

In the long term, if the supply of Material A continues to be limited, X plc may wish to seek alternative sources of supply, change product design or produce alternative products.

(c)   Incremental budgeting is a method of budgeting that starts with the current year's budget and adjusts this for known changes. The main problems associated with it are that:

- it can lead to inaccurate allocation of resources;

- managers may build in slack to make achieving targets easier.

Zero-Based Budgeting is a method of budgeting that requires all costs to be specifically justified by the benefits expected. Costs are built up from a zero base and ranked against other activities competing for limited resources. This should eliminate slack and lead to an optimal allocation of resources.

(d)   Linear regression analysis can be used to forecast sales when it can be assumed that there is a linear relationship between sales and time. Sales data can be plotted on a scattergraph and a line of best fit fitted by eye for forecasting purposes. Regression analysis is a statistical technique that calculates the line of best fit using formulae given for a and b in the straight line equation:

$y = a + bx$

where y = sales and x = time

Once the formula has been established, this can be used to forecast sales at any future time.

It can be seen that sales of Product W do not appear to have a linear trend over time. Linear regression analysis will therefore not be a suitable method for X plc to use for forecasting.

RISK AND DECISION MAKING

233   INDEPENDENT CINEMA (NOV 09 EXAM)

(a)

a

700 customers and an average refreshment contribution of $10 each

Average contribution per sitting

		$
Entrance price	$6 x 700 people	4,200
Refreshments	$12 x 700 people	8,400
Cost per screening	$256,000 / 32 screenings	(8,000)
		———
a		4,600
		———

b

Probability of 500 customers (40%) paying $10 each (50%) = 40% x 50% = 0.20

c

350 customers and an average refreshment contribution of $8 each

Average contribution per sitting

		$
Entrance price	$6 x 350 people	2,100
Refreshments	$8 x 350 people	2,800
Cost per screening	$256,000 / 32 screenings	(8,000)
c		(3,100)

(b)   The data in the table show management the range of nine possible outcomes that might occur on average. They show that in a 'best case scenario' (i.e. where there are 700 customers who spend an average of $12 each on refreshments) profit could be as high as $4,600 per screening. The 'worst case scenario' (i.e. where attendance is only 350 customers and they spend only $8 each on refreshment) will result in a loss of $3,100 per screening. In all likelihood the reality is going to be somewhere between these points. In fact the highest combined probability is when 500 customers spend an average of $10 each (a probability of 20% overall). This results in a break even position (i.e. a profit of $0).

But the overall expected value of the movie hire is =

$(0.070 \times 4,600) + (0.175 \times 3,200) + (0.105 \times 1,800) + (0.08 \times 1,000) - (0.12 \times 1,000) - (0.050 \times 1,700) - (0.125 \times 2,400) - (0.075 \times 3,100) =$

= $413.50

Therefore, overall the hire should proceed and the company can expect to make ($413.50 x 32 screenings) $13,232 over the week.

234   MUTUALLY EXCLUSIVE

Project X when discounted at the cost of capital 10% has the highest NPV. Therefore project X should be accepted in preference to project Y. However project Y has a higher IRR than project X. When a conflict arises between the NPV and IRR criteria select the project with the highest NPV. It can be shown that under perfect information the shareholders should gain the value of the NPV of the project if the project is undertaken, therefore it is in the interest of the shareholders that the NPV criteria should be used. From an opportunity point of view the value of accepting X rather than Y is equal to the difference of their NPVs i.e. 29.14 – 18.52 = $10,620.

Project Y's cash flows occur mainly in year 1 while most of X's come in the years 2 to 4. This is the reason for Y's higher IRR, because the IRR calculation assumes that any monies reinvested during the life of the project are reinvested at the project's IRR rather than at the company's cost of capital (the latter being the assumption of the NPV calculation). The same decision would be made if a payback criteria were used, for the same reason. If the company were uncertain of obtaining the later cashflows then, because of the risk factor, they might prefer project Y.

235 H COMPANY

(a) Investment: $500,000 + $20,000 = $520,000

Scrap   = $50,000

Total capital allowance:$470,000

Capital allowance schedule (W1)

Year	Written down value	Capital allowance	Tax saving	Cash	Timing	Net cash saving
1	390,000	130,000	39,000	19,500		19,500
2	292,500	97,500	29,250	19,500	+ 14,625	34,125
3	219,375	73,125	21,938	14,625	+ 10,969	25,594
4 scrap	$50,000	169,375	50,813	10,969	+ 25,407	36,376
		470,000		25,406		25,406

Contribution

Current production	200 × 40 hr =	8,000 units pw
New capacity	500 × 40 hr =	20,000 units pw
Demand		12,000 units pu
∴ Increase in production and sales	4,000 units pw	
		× $1.40
∴ Increase in contribution		$5,600
		× 48 week
Increase PER ANNUM		$268,800

(b) **Net present value calculation ($000)**

Year	Capital	Training	Cont'n	Corporation tax on cont'n	Corporation tax on training	Tax relief (W1)	Net cash	10% discount factor	PV
0	(520)	(5)					(525)		(525)
1			268.8	(40.32)	0.75	19.50	248.73	0.909	226.10
2			268.8	(80.64)	0.75	34.13	223.04	0.826	184.23
3			268.8	(80.64)		25.59	213.75	0.751	160.53
4	50			(40.32)		36.38	46.06	0.683	31.46
5						25.41	25.41	0.621	15.78
									93.1

Net present value: $93,100

Payback period = 2¼ years, 2 years 3 months – slightly outside normal payback.

Despite the project exceeding the normal payback period of two years, the project should be accepted. There is a predicted NPV of $93,100. A good return on the investment.

236 UNIVERSITY (SEP 10 EXAM)

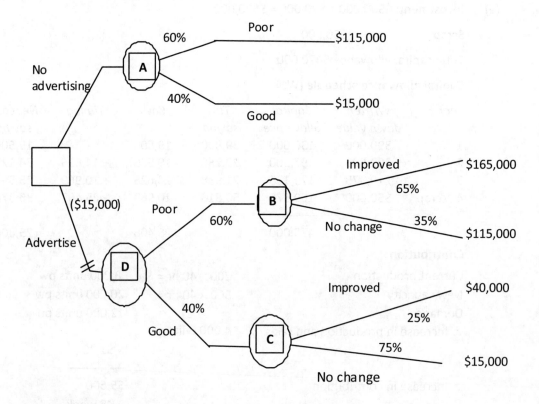

Key

=	☐	Decision point
=	○	Outcome point

Expected values

A	= (0.6 x 115,000) + (0.4 x 15,000)	=	$75,000
B	= (0.65 X 165,000) + (0.35 X 115,000)	=	$147,500
C	= (0.25 x 40,000) + (0.75 x 15,000)	=	$21,250
D	= (0.6 x 147,500) + (0.4 x 21,250)	=	$97,000

Advertising would have an overall expected value of (97,000 – 15,000) $82,000, compared to an expected value of $75,000 without advertising. It would therefore be better to advertise the programme as the university can expect to be $7,000 better off.

237 HYPERMARKET

(a) **Overall NPV**

Replacement at the end of the first year:

($220,000 × 1.00) + (($110,000 – $121,000) × 0.893) = $210,177

Replacement at the end of the second year:

($220,000 × 1.00) + ($110,000 × 0.893) + (($132,000 – $88,000) × 0.797) = $353,298

Replacement at the end of the third year:

($220,000 × 1.00) + ($110,000 × 0.893) + ($132,000 × 0.797) + (($154,000 – $66,000) × 0.712) = $486,090

Replacement at the end of the fourth year:

($220,000 × 1.00) + ($110,000 × 0.893) + ($132,000 × 0.797) + ($154,000 × 0.712) + (($165,000 – $55,000) × 0.636)) = $603,042

Replacement at the end of the fifth year:

($220,000 × 1.00) + ($110,000 × 0.893) + ($132,000 × 0.797) + ($154,000 × 0.712) + ($165,000 × 0.636) + (($176,000 – $25,000) × 0.567)) = $723,639

(b)   **Annual equivalent cost**

1 year annualised equivalent cost = $\dfrac{\$210,177}{0.893}$ = $235,361

2 year annualised equivalent cost = $\dfrac{\$353,298}{1.69}$ = $209,052

3 year annualised equivalent cost = $\dfrac{\$486,090}{2.402}$ = $202,369

4 year annualised equivalent cost = $\dfrac{\$603,042}{3,037}$ = $198,565

5 year annualised equivalent cost = $\dfrac{\$723,639}{3.605}$ = $200,732

The fleet should be replaced at the end of four years.

238   A COMPANY (MAY 05 EXAM)

Key answer tips

Remember to include the tax relief for the initial lease payments.

(a)   **Purchase option**

Year	Capital	Tax benefit (W1)	Net cash	15% factors	Present values
	$	$	$		$
0	(15,000)		(15,000)		(15,000)
1		563	563	0.870	490
2		984	984	0.756	744
3	5,000	938	5,938	0.658	3,907
4		515	515	0.572	295
					(9,564)

Capital Allowance Schedule (W1)

Year	WDV	Tax saving	Cash timing	Total cash
	$	$	$	$
	15,000			
1	(3,750)	1,125	563	563
	11,250			
2	(2,813)	844	562 + 422	984
	8,437			
3	(3,437)	1,031	422 + 516	938
	5,000			
			515	515

(b) **Lease option**

Year	Lease	Tax benefit	Net cash	15% factors	Present values
	$	$	$		$
0	(1,250)	188	(1,062)		(1,062)
1	(4,992)	936	(4,056)	0.870	(3,529)
2	(4,992)	1,498	(3,494)	0.756	(2,641)
3	(4,992)	1,498	(3,494)	0.658	(2,299)
4		749	749	0.572	428
					(9,102)

Tax benefits

30% of $1,250 = $375 (half in year 0 and half in year 1)

30% of $4,992 = $1,498 for years 1 to 3. The tax saving will be phased into years 1/2, 2/3 and 3/4.

The cheapest option is to LEASE the machine.

239 CANAL BOATS (MAY 07 EXAM)

(a) As the three options are of different durations, in order to compare them it is necessary to compare the annualised equivalent cash flows. The annual sales revenue and fixed costs are the same for each option and are therefore not relevant to the decision. Depreciation is also irrelevant because it is not a cash cost.

One-year cycle

Year	0	1
Purchase cost	$400,000	
Operating costs		$300,000
Trade-in value		($240,000)
Cash flow	$400,000	$60,000
Discount factor	1.000	0.926
Present value	$400,000	$55,560

Net present value of cost = $455,560.

Annualised equivalent cost = $455,560 / 0.926 = $491,965

Two-year cycle

Year	0	1	2
Purchase cost	$400,000		
Operating costs		$300,000	$400,000
Trade-in value			($150,000)
	——	——	——
Cash flow	$400,000	$300,000	$250,000
Discount factor	1.000	0.926	0.857
	——	——	——
Present value	$400,000	$277,800	$214,250

Net present value of cost = $892,050

Annualised equivalent cost = $455,560 / (0.926 + 0.857) = $500,308

Three-year cycle

Year	0	1	2	3
Purchase cost	$400,000			
Operating costs		$300,000	$400,000	$600,000
Trade in value				($80,000)
	——	——	——	——
Cash flow	$400,000	$300,000	$400,000	$520,000
Discount factor	1.000	0.926	0.857	0.794
	——	——	——	——
Present value	$400,000	$277,800	$342,800	$412,880

Net present value of cost = $1,433,480

Annualised equivalent cost = $1,433,480 / (0.926 + 0.857 + 0.794) = $556,259

The one-year cycle gives the lowest annualised cost, so this should be chosen.

(b) (i) The net present value of a project is the sum of the present values of the future cash flows which have been discounted at a rate which takes account of the time value of money.

The expected net present value takes into account the uncertainty or risk associated with the campaigns by weighting each possible outcome by its probability and finding the sum of the results.

The expected value alone gives no indication of the range of possible outcomes. The standard deviation provides a measure of the spread of the possible outcomes; a higher standard deviation indicates a wide range of possible outcomes and therefore a higher level of risk.

(ii) The company needs to assess the expected outcome of the different campaigns alongside the level of risk in order to decide which campaign to go ahead with. Campaigns J and L have the same expected outcome but L has a higher standard deviation, indicating a higher risk. Campaign J is therefore preferable to campaign L. Campaign K has the same level of risk as L but a higher expected value. K is therefore preferable to L. Campaign K has a higher expected value than J but also has a higher standard deviation and is therefore more risky. The choice between J and K will depend on the risk appetite of the company and how risk averse it is.

240 SENSITIVITY ANALYSIS (MAY 06 EXAM)

(a) Sensitivity analysis identifies the most critical elements of a decision by measuring the extent to which each individual element must change before it causes the decision maker to change their decision. The lower the percentage change the greater is the sensitivity and managers will need to focus their attention on the most sensitive elements.

The manager may use this technique to identify whether sales revenue, costs, rate of taxation, or cost of capital is the element which will be the most likely to affect the successful outcome of the project.

(b) (i) The NPV of sales revenue must reduce by $1.018m before the manager's decision changes. The post-tax present value of sales revenue is:

Year		
1	$4.2m × 80% × 0.935 =	$ 3.142m
2	$4.9m × 80% × 0.873 =	$ 3.422m
3	$5.3m × 80% × 0.816 =	$ 3.460m
		$10.024m

The % change required (i.e. sensitivity) = $1.018m / $10.024m = 10%

(ii) The sensitivity of the cost of capital is found by determining the discount % that causes the NPV to equal zero (i.e. the IRR). At a discount rate of 7% the NPV is $1,018m. The IRR is higher so try discounting at 20%.

Year		
1	($4.2m – $2.85m) × 0.8 × 0.833 =	$0.900m
2	($4.9m – $3.10m) × 0.8 × 0.694 =	$0.999m
3	($5.3m – $4.15m) × 0.8 × 0.579 =	$0.533m
		$2.432m
Less initial investment		$2.000m
NPV		$0.432m

IRR = 7% + [1.018/(1.018–0.432) × (20–7)%] = 29.6%

The % change required is 22.6 / 7 = 323%

241 EVENTS MANAGEMENT (MAY 10 EXAM)

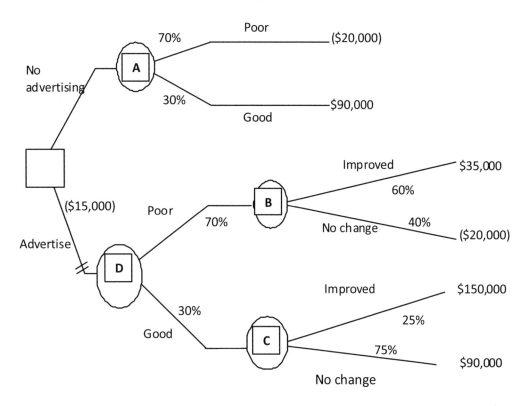

Key

☐ = Decision point

◯ = Outcome point

Expected values

A	= (0.7 x -20,000) + (0.3 x 90,000)	= $13,000
B	= (0.6 X 35,000) + (0.4 X -20,000)	= $13,000
C	= (0.25 x 150,000) + (0 .75 x 90,000)	= $105,000
D	= (0.7 x 13,000) + (0.3 x 105,00)	= $40,600

Advertising would have an overall expected value of (40,600 – 15,000) $25,600, compared to an expected value of $13,000 without advertising. It would therefore be better to advertise the concert.

MANAGING SHORT TERM FINANCE

242   AM (MAY 05 EXAM)

	May $000	June $000	July $000
Cash sales	35	40	40
Receipts from credit sales (W1)	101	104	111
Total receipts	136	144	151
Payments for purchases (W2)	50	54	55
Expenses paid	50	50	50
Equipment			250
Total payments	100	104	355
Net cash	36	40	(204)
Balance b/f	96	132	172
Balance c/f	132	172	(32)

Based on the above figures, AM will not be able to pay for the equipment when it falls due.

Workings

(W1) **Credit sales – receipts**

	Total $000	May $000	June $000	July $000
February	100	5		
March	100	30	5	
April	110	66	33	6
May	110		66	33
June	120			72
Totals		101	104	111

(W2) **Credit purchases – payments**

	Total $000	May $000	June $000	July $000
March	50	15		
April	50	35	15	
May	55		39	16
June	55			39
Totals		50	54	55

243 HL

Overtrading means a company it growing too quickly without the long term finance to support its growth. This will result in rapid increase in turnover, high levels of inventory, receivables, payables, little increase in share capital and long term loans and problems with liquidity when short term funding is used to support the growth.

The actions HL could take to correct the problem could be:

- Inject more long term capital into the business by issuing more share capital or raising long term loans;
- Cut back on trading and be more selective of who they sell to;
- Reduce the working capital cycle to improve liquidity, i.e. chase receivables to collect cash faster, reduce inventory levels and delay payables within reasonable levels.

244 DISCOUNTS (MAY 07 EXAM)

Taking the discount is equivalent to receiving interest at a rate of 27.86%. Therefore if DN needs to increase its overdraft to make the payment, it is beneficial to do so as long as the interest rate charged is less than 27.86%.

Alternatively, it would be beneficial for DN to use any surplus cash in its current account or cash in any short-term investments yielding less than 27.86%,.

Workings

If DN pays $98 on day 10 instead of day 40, it will need to borrow $98 for 30 days. The effective annual interest rate is:

$$\frac{365}{30} = 12.1667\%$$

$$1 + r = \left\{ \frac{100}{98} \right\}^{12.1667}$$

$$1 + r = 1.2786$$

$$r = 0.2786 \text{ or } 27.86\%$$

245 SCL

Annual sales $2 million $\times$ 12 = £24 million.

			$
Factor's annual fee	(2.5% × $24 million)		(600,000)
Saving in administration costs			300,000
		$	
Current average receivables	($24 million × 90/360)	6,000,000	
Receivables with the factor	(0.20 × $24m × 60/360)	800,000	
Reduction in average receivables		5,200,000	
Savings in interest at 9%			468,000
Factor finance interest	((0.80 × $24m × 60/360 × 10%)		(320,000)
Net annual cost			(152,000)

246   HX (MAY 09 EXAM)

The customers are required to pay in 30 days but currently take 60 days.

If the discount is introduced they will pay in 14 days, currently saving 46 days.

If we estimate an invoice to be worth £1,000 we can either wait 60 days and get $1,000 or wait 14 days and get $975 ($1,000 less discount 2.5%).

The effective interest cost would be:

(1000/975) to power of 365/46 less 1 = 22.2%

The question doesn't ask you to comment on this figure but it means that if this happened over and over again throughout the year it would cost us 22.2% to get less money faster, we would compare this to the bank overdraft rate to see if this was worthwhile.

Other methods to reduce the level of receivables could be:

- Factoring/invoice discounting;
- Better credit control training to chase debts as soon as they are overdue;
- Charge interest on overdue accounts.

247   BILLS OF EXCHANGE (MAY 09 EXAM)

Three ways to use a bill of exchange are:

- Hold the bill of exchange until maturity and collect the money;
- Transfer the bill of exchange to a bank to gain immediate cash. The bank will discount the bill as this is effectively a loan until the maturity date;
- Transfer the bill of exchange to a supplier as payment of a debt. This again will be at a discount.

When the due date of maturity arises whoever has the bill of exchange will receive payment.

The maximum price that HG should be willing to pay should be:

7% = a year, therefore for 91 days = 91/365 x 7% = 0.017452

The price is calculated by deducting this from 1 = 1 − 0.017452 = 0.982548 x $1,000 (face value) = $982.55

248   AGED RECEIVABLES ANAYLIS (MAY 10 EXAM)

(i)   **Aged debtor analysis**

Outstanding invoices only

	Jan	Feb	Mar	Apr	Total
Invoice no: 234	118				
Invoice no: 365			135		
Invoice no: 379			232		
Invoice no: 391			71		
Invoice no: 438				145	
Totals	118		438	145	701

(ii) **Benefits of an aged debtor analysis**

- This can help determine tactics for trying to collect overdue payments

- It can help collection staff prioritise debtors to prioritise

- It may highlight customers who should no longer be supplied

- It may indicate when cash is likely to come into the business and how much

(choose any two of the above)

249 PRINCIPLES OF SHORT TERM INVESTMENT

To: Board of directors

From: Assistant Treasurer

Date:

Subject: **Short-term investments**

In selecting short-term investments for surplus cash, several criteria or principles should be considered.

Maturity

Many financial instruments are for a fixed maturity (term to settlement). At maturity, there is a payment of principal, possibly with interest, to the investor. Examples of investments with a fixed maturity include bonds, certificates of deposit and bills. A principle of short-term investment is that, to avoid risk, the selected investments should have a maturity that matches the desired term of investment.

Tutorial note

For example, if GIL wishes to invest its cash for nine months, suitable investments would be those maturing in nine months. If investments have a longer maturity than the investment period, they will have to be sold off before maturity, giving rise to a risk of loss due to a fall in the market value of the instrument. If investments have a shorter maturity than the desired term of investment, the money will have to be re-invested when the investments mature, and there is a risk that investment yields might have fallen.

In practice, however, it is often difficult to find suitable investments that match the investment period, or the investment period itself is uncertain. As a consequence, selected investments often have a longer or shorter maturity than the expected investment period.

Return

Investors should seek the best return possible, but only for an acceptable level of risk. Higher yielding investments are often more risky, in the sense that there could be a risk of default or a risk of a fall in the value of the investment.

Security and risk

Investors in short-term investments are often looking for a secure investment. This is an investment that does not have a high risk of default, where it is a debt instrument, or is not exposed to a risk of a fall in market value, where it is a marketable investment.

Liquidity

Investors in short-term investments should prefer liquid investments. A liquid investment is one that can be sold readily at a fair market price, without any risk of significant loss from having to sell at the chosen time. Liquid financial markets are large and active markets, and some investments are more liquid than others.

Building a portfolio to spread the investment risk

The risk of losses or disappointing returns on investments can be reduced by investing in a diversified portfolio of different investments. The principle is that some investments might perform better than expected and others worse, but the overall return on the portfolio is more likely to be close to expectation.

Foreign exchange risk

It might also be added that, although it is possible to invest in foreign currency investments, there will be an exposure to foreign exchange risk (the risk of a fall in investment value and the value of returns due to adverse exchange rate movements).

Treasury bills

Treasury bills are risk-free investments, because they are issued by the government, so that default will not occur. However, yields on Treasury bills are lower than on higher risk investments. In addition, the typical maturity of Treasury bills is 91 days, which means that their maturity is shorter than the planned investment term for the money. The market for Treasury bills, however, is large and liquid.

Corporate bonds

Corporate bonds can be a fairly high-risk investment. The risks arise both from the risk of default by the corporate bond issuer, and also from the risk of movements in the market price of bonds (if there is a rise or fall in general interest rates). To compensate investors for the risk, yields can be relatively high. Most bonds have a long remaining term to maturity, and investing in long-term instruments for the short term means that they will have to be sold to cash in the investment at the end of the investment period. The market for corporate bonds is not particularly liquid, although the bonds of some corporate issuers are more liquid than the bonds of others.

Investing exclusively in Treasury bills or corporate bonds would be inadvisable, because the investment risk would be reduced by building a portfolio of diversified investments – possibly containing some bills and some corporate bonds.

Signed: Assistant Treasurer

250   JE (NOV 09 EXAM)

	20X8		*20X9*
Inventory days	$= \dfrac{160}{1{,}910} \times 365$	$=$	$\dfrac{200}{2{,}800} \times 365$
	$=$ 31 days	$=$	26 days
Receivables days	$= \dfrac{250}{2{,}250} \times 365$	$=$	$\dfrac{390}{3{,}150} \times 365$
	$=$ 41 days	$=$	45 days
Payables days	$= \dfrac{300}{1{,}910} \times 365$	$=$	$\dfrac{500}{2{,}800} \times 365$
	$=$ 57 days	$=$	65 days
Current ratio	$= \dfrac{250 + 160 + 90}{300}$	$=$	$\dfrac{390 + 200 + 10}{500 + 100}$
	$=$ 1.67	$=$	1.00
Quick ratio	$= \dfrac{250 + 90}{300}$	$=$	$\dfrac{390 + 10}{500 + 100}$
	$=$ 1.3	$=$	0.67

251   INVENTORY LEVELS (MAY 10 EXAM)

(i)   **Total annual costs**

$$EOQ = \sqrt{\frac{2C_oD}{C_h}} = \sqrt{\frac{2 \times \$150 \times 64{,}000}{\$1.20}}$$

$$= \sqrt{16{,}000{,}000}$$

$$= \quad 4{,}000 \text{ units}$$

Cost of holding	=	Holding cost per unit x average stock levels (i.e. EOQ/2)
	=	$1.20 x (4,000 / 2)
	=	$2,400
Cost of ordering	=	Cost per order x no. of orders (i.e. demand / EOQ)
	=	$150 x (64,000 / 4,000)
	=	2,400

(Note that at the EOQ, the cost of holding and ordering are equal. So there is technically no need to do a full calculation for the cost of ordering.)

(ii)   **Reorder level**

Average demand per week = 64,000 / 52 = 1,231 units.

Maximum lead time = 3 weeks

Minimum inventory level at which to place an order = 1,231 x 3 = 3,693 units.

252 SHORT TERM FUNDING (MAY 07 EXAM)

DF could obtain short-term finance from any of the following sources:

- by increasing the overdraft

- by taking out a short-term loan

- by taking additional credit from suppliers

  DF currently has trade payable days outstanding of 49 days (16/120 x 365). An increase of $2 million to $18 million would be 55 days (18/120 x 365), This needs to be viewed against the credit period offered by the suppliers. If 60 days' credit is offered, this would be acceptable. If only 45 days is offered, the increase would probably not be acceptable and could cause problems obtaining future credit.

- by improving the receivables collection period:

  DF's trade receivables collection period is currently 30 days (20/240 × 365), which is quite low. So this is unlikely to be a viable option as it would involve reducing the trade receivables collection period to 27 days (18/240 × 365).

- by factoring or invoice discounting. However, this is a long-term solution. It is not suitable for raising a one-off amount.

253 SHORT TERM INVESTMENT (NOV 07 EXAM)

Bonds:	$
Cost, including commission @ 1%	120,000
Cost less commission $120,000 × 100/101 = $118,812	
Value on redemption 118,812 × 100/102	116,482
Interest @ 12.5% on 116,482	14,560
Return	11,042

- Internet bank:

- Interest @ 0.8% per month – so there will be 12 interest periods during the year.

- Value in 12 months' time = $120,000 (1 + 0.008)^{12}$ = $12,041

- The internet bank offers the most appropriate investment based on the return generated. As both investments are relatively low risk, return is an appropriate basis for the decision.

254   BH (NOV 05 EXAM)

(a)   The coupon rate is the interest rate payable on the face (nominal) value of the bond.

The yield to maturity (redemption yield) is the effective yield on a redeemable security, taking into account both the interest yield and any gain or loss due to the fact that it was purchased at a price different to the redemption value.

(b)   The annual interest payable on the bond is $70 ($1,000 × 7%).

There are two ways of calculating the redemption yield on a bond:

(i)   Calculate the internal rate of return of the relevant cash flows, including buying the bond at time zero:

Time		CF	DF@7%	PV	DF@10%	PV
0	(MV)	(850)	1	(850)	1	(850)
1–5	I	70	4.100	287	3.791	265
5	R	1000	0.713	713	0.621	621
				150		36

Yield = IRR ≈ 7 + (10-7)×150/(150-36) = approximately 11%

(ii)   Find the rate that equates the present value of the future receipts with the market value, using trial and error:

Rate   PV of future receipts
7%   (70 × 4.100) + (1,000 × 0.713) = 1,000
10%   (70 × 3.791) + (1,000 × 0.621) = 886
11%   (70 × 3.696) + (1,000 × 0.593) = 852, close enough

255   RISK AND YIELD (NOV 06 EXAM)

Notes on risk and effective yield of potential investments:

Treasury bills

Treasury bills reflect the credit rating of the country, so are generally low risk. However, as the risk is low, the investment is relatively attractive, such that the rate of interest is generally relatively low. In this case a yield of $10 would be earned over three months, which is an effective interest rate of only 1% per quarter.

Yield is achieved through a combination of interest payments and a growth in the value of the bill over time.

Equities

The value of equities can go down as well as up. In this case, the equity index has increased for the last 14 months. However, this cannot be taken as a guarantee of future continued good performance.

The risk associated with a particular share depends upon the risk associated with the market in general and the risk associated with the particular company. In this case, the proposed companies are multinationals, which can result in a lower risk due to diversification.

Due to the higher risk associated with equities, the yield is generally relatively high.

Bank deposit

A bank deposit is an investment in the business of the bank. However, banks are generally very secure, such that it is normally assumed that the investment will be recovered in full.

As with treasury bills, the yield is low to reflect the low risk, so carries a low rate of interest. However, in this case, the company would be required to give 30 days' notice of any withdrawals. This gives the bank more certainty and is reflected in an increased return on the deposit, in the form of an increased interest rate.

256   EOQ (SEP 10 EXAM)

(i)   **Total annual costs**

$$EOQ = \sqrt{\frac{2C_o D}{C_h}} = \sqrt{\frac{2 \times \$360 \times 150,000}{\$3.00}}$$

$$= \sqrt{36,000,000}$$

$$= 6,000 \text{ units}$$

Cost of holding	=	Holding cost per unit x average stock levels (i.e. EOQ/2)
	=	$3.00 x (6,000 / 2)
	=	$9,000

Cost of ordering	=	Cost per order x no. of orders (i.e. demand / EOQ)
	=	$360 x (150,000 / 6,000)
	=	$9,000

(Note that at the EOQ, the cost of holding and ordering are equal. So there is technically no need to do a full calculation for the cost of ordering.)

(ii)   **Bulk discount**

Existing total costs:

		$
Purchase cost	150,000 x $2	300,000
Holding cost		9,000
Order cost		9,000
Total cost		318,000

New total costs

		$
Purchase cost	150,000 x $2 x 99%	297,000
Holding cost	$3 x (10,000/2)	15,000
Order cost	$360 x (150k/10k)	5,400
Total cost		317,400

Benefit of the bulk discount =   318,000 – 317,400   = $600

257   CASH FORECAST (NOV 08 EXAM)

Period	Oct	Nov	Dec	Jan	Feb	Mar
	$000	$000	$000	$000	$000	$000
Total sales	399	427	553	399	399	497
Cash sales (1/7)	57	61	79	57	57	71
Credit sales (6/7)	342	366	474	342	342	426
Receipts:						
10% x current month	34	37	47	34	34	43
25% x previous month		86	92	119	86	86
63% x penultimate month			214	231	299	215
Total credit sales receipts				384	419	344
Cash sales (current month)				57	57	71
Total receipts				**441**	**476**	**415**

Section 6

ANSWERS TO SECTION C-TYPE QUESTIONS

COST ACCOUNTING SYSTEMS

258   HENSAU

Key answer tips

This question tests the treatment of overhead costs under traditional absorption costing and under activity based costing. It is necessary to determine the overhead absorption rates per hour using the budgeted units of each product and their respective direct labour times per unit to identify the budgeted number of hours. For the costs using an activity based approach separate cost driver rates are to be used for each of the three activities.

(a) and (b) **Budgeted costs per unit**

	X		Y		Z	
	(a)	(b)	(a)	(b)	(a)	(b)
	$	$	$	$	$	$
Direct costs						
Materials	5.00	5.00	3.00	3.00	6.00	6.00
Labour	1.60	1.60	2.67	2.67	4.00	4.00
Overheads (W2)						
Materials receipt and inspection W3)	2.40	2.52	4.00	1.68	6.00	10.06
Power (W4)	3.00	6.46	5.00	3.23	7.50	2.15
Material handling (W5)	2.10	2.81	3.50	4.22	5.25	2.11
	14.10	18.39	18.17	14.80	28.75	24.32

Workings

(W1) Direct labour hours

X	$2,000 \times \dfrac{24}{60}$	800
Y	$1,500 \times \dfrac{40}{60}$	1,000
Z	800×1	800
		2,600

(W2) Overhead absorption rates

		Per hour
Materials receipt and inspection	$\dfrac{\$15,600}{2,600}$	$6.00
Power	$\dfrac{\$19,500}{2,600}$	$7.50
Material handling	$\dfrac{\$13,650}{2,600}$	$5.25

(W3) Materials receipt and inspection – ABC approach

Total number of batches	=	31
Cost per batch	=	$\dfrac{\$15,600}{31}$
	=	$503.23

Charged to

		$	$ per unit
X	(× 10)	5,032.30	2.52
Y	(× 5)	2,516.15	1.68
Z	(× 16)	8,051.68	10.06

(W4) Power – ABC approach

Total drill operations	=	12,000 + 4,500 + 1,600
	=	18,100
Cost per operation	=	$\dfrac{\$19,500}{18,100}$
	=	$1.077

Charged to

		$ per unit
X	(× 6)	6.46
Y	(× 3)	3.23
Z	(× 2)	2.15

(W5) **Material handling – ABC approach**

Total quantity handled	=	8,000 + 9,000 + 2,400
	=	19,400 square metres
Cost per square metre	=	$\dfrac{\$13,650}{19,400}$
	=	$0.704

Charged to

		$ per unit
X	(× 4)	2.81
Y	(× 6)	4.22
Z	(× 3)	2.11

(c)

	X	Y	Z
Unit cost using absorption costing	14.10	18.17	28.75
Unit cost using activity based costing	18.39	14.80	24.32
Difference	4.29	(3.37)	(4.43)

Using activity based costing the cost per unit of X increases and the cost per unit of Y and Z decreases. The ABC figures provide a much more accurate figure for the cost of each of the three products. These costs will provide a more sensible basis for production and sales planning and for pricing decisions. If the market will not bear, say, the additional cost of producing a unit of X then the company can take a more informed decision as to whether to continue with its production. Similarly, Hensau now knows that the margin on each unit of Y is higher than it had previously thought and that it might be worth either putting greater effort into selling that, or reducing the selling price in order to get some competitive advantage. It should, however, be borne in mind that this additional information was costly to obtain. If the company cannot rearrange its production and marketing policies then it might be unable to make much use of the new figures.

259 BRUNTI

Key answer tips

This is a basic question on overhead costs. The traditional overhead absorption rates per hour have been provided in the question and these are to be used when preparing the conventional absorption costing profit statement. For the activity based approach cost driver rates must be calculated and applied to the products' activities.

Note that the sales value and prime cost values will be the same in both profit statements. The total profit will be the same in both cases so this should provide a check on your figures.

(a) **Absorption costing**

	XYI	YZT	ABW	Total
Volume (000s)	50	40	30	
	$000	$000	$000	$000
Sales	2,250	3,800	2,190	
Prime cost	(1,600)	(3,360)	(1,950)	
Overheads				
Machinery at $1.20/hr(W1)	(120)	(240)	(144)	
Assembly at $0.825/hr(W2)	(289)	(99)	(49)	
Profit	241	101	47	389

(W1) Hours worked in machine department = 2 × 50,000 + 5 × 40,000 + 4 × 30,000 = 420,000

OAR = $504,000/420,000 = $1.20 per machine hour

(W2) Hours worked in assembly department = 7 × 50,000 + 3 × 40,000 + 2 × 30,000 = 530,000

OAR = $437,000/530,000 = $0.825

(b) **Activity based costing**

	XY1	YZT	ABW	Total
Volume (000s)	50	40	30	
	$000	$000	$000	$000
Sales	2,250	3,800	2,190	
Prime cost	(1,600)	(3,360)	(1,950)	
Overheads (W1)				
Machining @ $0.85/hr	(85)	(170)	(102)	
Assembly @ $0.60/hr	(210)	(72)	(36)	
Setups @ $50/set-up	(6)	(10)	(10)	
Ordering @ $4.875/order	(39)	(39)	(78)	
Purchasing @ $7.50/order	(23)	(30)	(31)	
Profit	287	119	(17)	389

Total = $389,000

Workings

(W1)

Cost pool	Machining	Assembly	Setups	Ordering	Purchasing
$000	357	318	26	156	84
Driver quantity	420,000	530,000	520	32,000	11,200
Rate	$0.85/hr	$0.6/hr	$50/setup	$4.875/order	$7.50/order

(c)   The revised profit statement produced using ABC principles reveals that product ABW is making a loss and that the other two products are more profitable than had appeared to be the case with the conventional absorption costing method.

This is because product ABW is a low volume product and the conventional absorption costing approach, based on hourly rates for overhead, tends to undercharge low volume products and overcharge high volume products with overhead cost.

The data shows that product ABW generates significantly more customer and supplier orders than the other two products. When ordering and purchasing costs are traced to products using the cost drivers identified under the ABC system product ABW absorbs a more realistic share of these costs. Thus its lower profitability is revealed when overhead costs are attributed more accurately to individual products.

(d)   **Set-up costs**

Overhead absorbed 560 × $50	28,000
Overhead incurred	30,000

Under absorption	2,000
Ordering costs	
Overhead absorbed 32,050 × 4.875	156,244
Overhead incurred	154,000

Over absorption	2,244
Purchasing costs	
Overhead absorbed 11,150 × 7.50	83,625
Overhead incurred	78,000

Over absorption	5,625

260   RJ (MAY 07 EXAM)

Key answer tips

In part (a) you will need to calculate the total machine hours in order to determine the overhead recovery rate for absorption costing.

(a)   **Budgeted Operating Statement**

Fixed production overhead = $35,000,000

Budgeted machine hours = $(1,100 \times 200) + (1,600 \times 300) = 700,000$ machine hours

Fixed production overhead absorption rate = $35,000,000/700,000 = $50 per machine hour.

	Car X $ per car	Car Y $ per car
Total production cost per unit		
($44,000,000/1,100)	40,000	
($75,200,000/1,600)		47,000
Fixed overhead absorbed		
(200 × $50)	10,000	
(300 × $50)		15,000
Variable production cost per car	30,000	32,000

Marginal costing operating statement – year ending 30 June 2008

	Car X $000	Car Y $000	Total $000
Sales	52,500	105,000	157,500
Variable production costs			
(1,000 × $30,000)	30,000		
(1,750 × $32,000)		56,000	86,000
Variable administration costs	6,300	12,600	18,900
Contribution	16,200	36,400	52,600
Specific fixed costs			
Marketing	2,000	4,000	6,000
Contribution to general fixed costs	14,200	32,400	46,600
General fixed costs			
Production			35,000
Administration ($16,000 – $6,000)			10,000
Profit			**1,600**

(b) **Reconciliation of Profits**

The difference in the profit figures will be caused by the fixed production overheads that are absorbed into closing inventories. If inventory levels increase, the absorption costing profit will be higher than the profit calculated using marginal costing since a proportion of fixed overhead will be carried forward to be charged against future revenue.

	Car X	Car Y
Change in inventory (units)	+100	−150
Fixed production overhead per car	$10,000	$15,000
Total difference in profits	$1,000,000	$2,250,000

Reconciliation

	$000
Absorption costing profit	350
Car X: inventory impact	(1,000)
Car Y: inventory impact	2,250
Marginal costing profit	1,600

(c) **Budgeted Production Cost**

Activity	Cost Driver		Drivers
Machining costs	Machine hours	From part a)	700,000
Set up costs	No. of production runs	(1,100/10) + (1,600/40)	150
Quality inspections	No. of inspections	(110 × 20) + (40 × 80)	5,400
Stores receiving	No. of deliveries	492 + 900	1,392
Stores issues	No. of issues	4,000 + 7,000	11,000

Activity	$000	Driver	Cost per driver
Machining costs	7,000	700,000	$10 per machine hour
Set up costs	12,000	150	$80,000 per set up
Quality inspections	7,020	5,400	$1,300 per inspection
Stores receiving	3,480	1,392	$2,500 per delivery
Stores issues	5,500	11,000	$500 per issue

	Car X		Car Y	
	Driver	$000	Driver	$000
Machining costs	220,000	2,200	480,000	4,800
Set up costs	110	8,800	40	3,200
Quality inspections	2,200	2,860	3,200	4,160
Stores receiving	492	1,230	900	2,250
Stores issues	4,000	2,000	7,000	3,500
Total overhead		17,090		17,910
Direct costs		33,000		51,200
Total production costs		50,090		69,110
Cars produced		1,100		1,600
Cost per car		**$45,536**		**$43,194**

(d)   **Report**

To: Production Director

From: Management Accountant

Date: 22 May 2007

Subject: Activity Based Budgeting – Performance Evaluation

Introduction

This report presents the potential benefits of adopting an activity based budgeting approach for performance evaluation.

Benefits of activity based budgeting

(1)   **Better understanding of activities which cause costs**

Activity based budgeting provides a clear framework for understanding the link between costs and the level of activity. This would allow us to evaluate performance based on the activity that drives the cost.

The modern business environment has a high proportion of costs that are indirect and the only meaningful way of attributing these costs to individual products is to find the root cause of such costs, that is, what activity is driving these costs. The traditional absorption costing approach collects overhead costs using functional headings which may make many overhead costs appear to be fixed as they are not linked to the volume of output but they may be related to other activities which are variable for a batch or product line.

(2)   **Clearer responsibility for costs**

With an activity based costing approach responsibility for activities and therefore costs can be broken down and assigned accordingly. Individual managers can provide input into the budgeting process and subsequently be held responsible for the variances arising.

(3)   **More detailed analysis of overhead costs**

There is greater transparency with an ABB system due to the level of detail behind the costs. The traditional absorption costing approach combines all of the overheads together using a machine hour basis to calculate an overhead absorption rate and uses this rate to attribute overheads to products. ABB will drill down in much more detail examining the cost and the driver of such costs and calculate a cost driver rate which will be used to assign overheads to products. Therefore ABB has greater transparency than absorption costing and allows for much more detailed information on overhead consumption and so on. This then lends itself to better performance evaluation.

Conclusion

The traditional absorption costing approach to product costing does not enable us to provide a satisfactory explanation for the behaviour of costs. In contrast ABB will provide such details which will allow us to have better cost control, improved performance evaluation and greater manager accountability. If you require any further information please do not hesitate to contact me.

261 PHARMACEUTICAL DRUGS (MAY 05 EXAM)

Key answer tips

Part (a)

Common errors:

- In part (ii) making errors in the calculation of some of the cost driver rates and extending these to the respective orders.

Part (b)

Common errors:

- In part (i), failing to apply the strengths and weaknesses to F plc.

- In part (ii), demonstrating a lack of ideas and/or failing to generate recommended action specific to F plc.

(a) (i) $\text{OAR} = \dfrac{\text{Budgeted overheads}}{\text{Budgeted level of activity}} = \dfrac{\$880{,}000}{\pounds 8m} = 11\%$ of list price

Selling and distribution charge for Order A = 11% of $1,200 = $132

Selling and distribution charge for Order B = 11% of $900 = $99

(ii) Cost driver rates

Invoice processing

Cost per invoice = $\dfrac{25\% \times \$280{,}000}{8{,}000\,\text{invoices}}$ = $8.75 per invoice

Cost per invoice line = $\dfrac{75\% \times \$280{,}000}{28{,}000\,\text{invoice lines}}$ = $7.50 per invoice line

Packing

$32 for large packages and $25 for small packages.

Delivery

Loading costs = $\dfrac{\$40{,}000}{1{,}000\,\text{journeys}}$ = $40 per journey

There are 12 small packages to a lorry and so the loading costs are $40/12 = $3.33 per small package.

There are 6 large packages to a lorry and so the loading costs are $6.67 per large package.

Mileage costs = $\dfrac{\$180{,}00 - \$40{,}000}{350{,}000\,\text{miles}}$ = $0.40 per mile

Other overheads

$$\text{Cost per order} = \frac{\$200,000}{8,000\,\text{orders}} = \$25 \text{ per order}$$

	$	$
Invoice processing	8.75	8.75
$7.20 × 2	15.00	
$7.50 × 8		60.00
Packing	25.00	32.00
Delivery	3.33	6.67
$0.40 × 8	3.20	
$0.40 × 40		16.00
Other overheads	25.00	25.00
	___	___
Charge for selling and distribution	80.28	148.42
	___	___

(b)

Report

To	Management
From	Management Accountant
Date	May 20X5
Subject	Proposed ABC system

(i) **Strengths and weaknesses of proposed system**

The present system is very simple but makes no attempt to link the selling and distribution costs to the factors which cause those costs. The present system simply charges all orders a blanket rate of 11% on list price.

The proposed ABC system is still very simple but makes some effort to determine the cost drivers, i.e. those factors which are most closely related to the way in which the costs of an activity are incurred. For instance, it has been found for the invoice processing costs that the costs are affected by the number of invoices issued, but also by how complicated the invoices are, i.e. how many different lines there are on the invoice.

Charging out the invoice processing costs on the basis of the two cost drivers above will result in more accurate costs and will give more information about the cost structure and the cost drivers in order to improve cost control. Once the cost structure is known, efforts can be made to reduce the volume of activity of the cost driver (e.g. the 28,000 invoice lines) and/or the cost of the cost driver (e.g. the $7.50 per invoice line).

It is argued by ABC supporters that the better costs calculated under ABC can then be used as the basis for fixing selling prices and that these selling prices relate to the true cost of the order and thus will prevent loss-making orders.

F plc can also compare the true costs of the different elements of the system against the costs of outsourcing.

The more accurate costs determined under an ABC system can be used to justify selling prices or selling price increases to customers.

Whilst it is undoubtedly true that ABC gives more accurate costs, it is also true that it will be more expensive to implement and the benefit may not exceed the cost.

The proposed system, here, is still very simple and it is possible that a more detailed analysis would provide further useful information.

ABC attempts to find the cost driver for each type of cost and thus avoid the arbitrariness of absorption costing but, here, some costs are still charged on an arbitrary basis, e.g. the other overheads.

(ii) **Recommendations**

In the light of the ABC information it should be determined whether any orders/customers are loss making and, if so, whether those types of order or customer should be dropped or if the costs can be reduced or the selling prices increased.

The cost per invoice line is very expensive. It should be investigated as to whether this figure can be reduced, perhaps by the purchase of a special software package.

The costs for long distance deliveries are also very high. F plc could consider only accepting orders below a certain maximum distance, or charging a selling price which takes into account the delivery costs of long distance journeys, or outsourcing the deliveries.

The present system for setting selling prices is cost based; whilst this is a simple method of setting selling prices, it does not normally lead to optimum selling prices. The proposed ABC system could be used as the basis for charging selling prices to individual customers. Whilst the proposed system is very simple, it is probably still too complex to be used for charging prices. For instance, if a new customer wants to place a new order, we would need to know how far away they are before we can calculate the cost of the order and thus the price to quote.

262 RETAIL COMPANY (NOV 09 EXAM) *Walk in the footsteps of a top tutor*

Key answer tips

Part (a) of this question is in an unusual format that many students may not have seen before. The key to success will be to read the requirement carefully. Notice that each of the three changes must be dealt with *independently* (for example, the results from part (i) should be ignored when attempting part (ii)). Also, rather than simply stating the effect a number, the revised number must be stated. The final element to be careful with is that the changes take place at the *start* of the accounting year. There will be easy marks for filling in figures that do not change – so make sure you put a figure in every box.

In part (b) of the question, it will be important that you know the break even formulae (a commonly examined area). In this scenario you have to work with the contribution margin (contribution as a % of selling price) rather than the contribution per unit. Part (iii) is the easier part and should be dealt with first (even if you cannot do the calculations).

Part (c) covers an uncommonly examined area and only very well prepared students would score well in this section. This highlights the need for comprehensive syllabus coverage in order to maximise the chance of success in this paper. There are two element – Beyond Budgeting and TQM. There will be marks available for defining each element, so that even if Beyond Budgeting is unfamiliar to you, you should still pick up some marks on TQM (which is regularly examined). Having defined each element, to get full marks you need to link the two elements together and explain why this might be a better relationship than traditional budgeting techniques.

Overall, this is a tricky question where it will be important that you pick out the easy marks available first. There are easy marks for explaining TQM, assessing the proposal, putting figures in the table that don't change etc. Good technique should gain you enough marks to gain a pass. But this needs to be backed up with good syllabus knowledge if you want to gain all the marks.

(a)   **Sensitivity analysis**

	(i)	(ii)	(iii)
Operating profit	440,000	440,000	245,000
Inventory	200,000	182,280	182,280
Receivables	501,000	641,100	475,950
Cash	271,580	149,200	119,350
Payables	428,980	428,980	428,980

Workings:

(i)   **Increase inventory to £200,000**

Assumptions: he change is arrived at from a revaluation of opening *and* closing inventory.

This means that there will be reduction in cash (£17,720) and an increase in closing inventory. All other figures (such as operating profit) will remain unaffected.

(ii)   **Increase receivable days to 60**

Revised receivables can be calculated as follows:

$$= \frac{60}{365} \text{ x Sales revenue}$$

$$= \frac{60}{365} \text{ x } 3,900,000$$

$$= \text{£641, 100}$$

This represents an increase in receivables of £140,100. There would be no impact on sales or operating profit, but cash would reduce by this amount as customers pay later.

(iii) **Reduce selling prices by 5%**

This would have the effect of reducing both sales revenue and receivables by 5%. It would also mean that the cash received from collected sales would also reduce by 5%.

Reduction in sales revenue (and operating profit)	=	5% x 3,900,000	=	£195,000
Reduction in receivables	=	5% x 501,000	=	£25,050
Reduction in cash recovered	=	195,000 – 25,050	=	£169,950

(b) **Break even analysis**

(i) **Break even point**

$$\text{Break even point} = \frac{\text{Fixed costs (W1)}}{\text{Contribution margin (W2)}}$$

$$= \frac{516,000}{24.5\%}$$

$$= £2,106,122$$

Workings

(W1) **Fixed Costs**

= 60% of selling and administration costs

= 60% x 860,000

= 516,000

(W2) **Contribution margin**

Gross profit		=	1,300,000
Variable selling and administration costs	= 40% x 860,000	=	344,000
Contribution		=	£956,000
As a % of sales revenue		=	24.5%

(ii) **Break even point**

$$\text{Break even point} = \frac{\text{Fixed costs (W1)}}{\text{Contribution margin (W2)}}$$

$$= \frac{1,116,000}{37.8\%}$$

$$= £2,952,380$$

Workings

(W1) **Fixed Costs**

= old fixed costs + annual fee

= 516,000 + 600,000

= 1,116,000

(W2) **Contribution margin**

Revised gross profit = 1,300,000 + (20% x 2,600,000)	=	1,820,000
Variable selling and administration costs	=	344,000
Contribution	=	£1,476,000
As a % of sales revenue	=	37.8%

(iii) **Assessment of the proposal**

Advantages

- Dealing with only one supplier will reduce administration and inbound logistics costs. So there may further cost advantages that have not been accounted for.

- The reduction in cost of sales may allow a reduction in selling prices. This might stimulate more sales volume and allow the retailer to become more competitive.

Disadvantages

- The costs outweigh the benefits. The reduction in cost of sales will be £520,000 based on existing (optimistic) forecasts, against an annual fee of £600,000.

- The retailers risk will increase. Because a greater proportion of costs will be fixed the break even point rises by £800,000. This might be more difficult to achieve in the current economic climate.

(c) **Beyond Budgeting**

It has been argued that the budgeting process is limiting and unsuitable for businesses, and better budgeting (for example, by using, say, zero based budgeting) is not an answer to the problem. Instead, budgets should be abandoned.

The argument for abolishing budgets, referred to as **'beyond budgeting'**, is that the modern business environment is constantly changing. Managers need to be flexible and facilitate change. The budgeting system is too rigid. It acts as a barrier to change because managers are expected to conform to budget. The emphasis in budgeting is on minimising costs, not maximising value. Therefore, managers are held back by the budgeting system from achieving the organisation's goals.

Total Quality Management (TQM) has been defined as: 'an integrated and comprehensive system of planning and controlling all business functions so that products or services are produced which meet or exceed customer expectations. TQM is a philosophy of business behaviour, embracing principles such as employee involvement, continuous improvement at all levels and customer focus, as well as being a collection of related techniques aimed at improving quality such as full documentation of activities, clear goal setting and performance measurement from the customer perspective.' (CIMA *Official Terminology*)

Traditional budgets restrict flexibility because individuals feel they are expected to achieve the budget targets. This is a deterrent to continual improvement (and so is inconsistent with TQM). A shift to a 'beyond budgeting' approach would facilitate the flexibility and change needed to support TQM and make it successful. Beyond Budgeting is likely to empower individuals to make the changes needed in a TQM environment and to find more efficient ways to perform tasks. Everyone will be involved in the process – not just the budget setters and budget owners. This will support the 'total' element of TQM.

STANDARD COSTING

263 PRODUCT MANAGER (NOV 09 EXAM) *Walk in the footsteps of a top tutor*

Key answer tips

For students who are comfortable with variances it might be best to skip the unusual part (a) of the question and get straight into the calculations in parts (b) and (c). This is a common scenario type for this paper – the examiner has started with a tricky/unusual part (a), which might knock the confidence of some students (and some might give up completely at that stage). But if (a) has proven to be tough you could leave it out completely and still get full marks in the remaining question parts. This highlights the importance of continuing to tackle each part of a question even when one part proves too difficult.

Part (a) of this question is in an unusual format that many students may not have seen before. It will be important that you don't simply explain the *type* of cost, but focus instead on how it is *behaving* in the scenario. This will mean that you will have to refer to the particular levels of outputs and may have to perform some calculations in order to define the exact relationship between the variables. To score full marks you will also have to discuss the possible *causes* of these relationships.

Part (b) is a much more straightforward variance question. In order to succeed in this requirement you have to begin by calculating the standard cost of materials, labour and overheads for one unit of production using the budgeted information. From that point onwards you then have to work through 6 variances in your usual approach.

Part (c) is an operational variance question for 4 marks. The marks available should provide a hint that there is nothing too complicated expected here. The key to success will be to remember to use the revised standard materials price to calculate the operational variances.

(a)   **Cost behaviour**

Average variable cost per unit

This cost appears to exhibiting features of both economies and diseconomies of scale. As the production increases there is a fall in the average cost which reflects economies of scale that could come from bulk discounts, learning curve effects etc. But when production reached 25,000 units, the average cost rises again and exhibits diseconomies of scale. These can be caused by factors such as the duplication of effort or inertia in the business.

Fixed costs

These costs appear to be stepped in nature. They are fixed at certain levels of production, but they appear to rise by $300,000 after each 10,000 units of production. This could be caused by the need for more space or more supervisors as production increases beyond certain levels.

Head office costs

This cost appears to be related directly at 6% of production. Therefore, as production increases this cost increases in a direct, variable nature.

(b) **Operating statement**

			$
Budgeted production cost (3,200,000 x 76,000/80,000)			3,040,000

Variances:		Fav	Adv		
	Workings	$	$		
Materials price	(W1)	52,000			
Materials usage	(W1)		64,500		
Labour rate	(W2)		48,000		
Labour efficiency	(W2)		58,800		
Overhead expenditure	(W3)	50,000			
Overhead volume	(W3)		32,000		
		102,000	203,300	101,300	A

Actual production cost	3,141,300

(W1) **Material variances**

		$	
SQSP			
	6 kg/unit × 76,000 units × $2/kg	= 912,000	Usage
AQSP			$52,000 F
	430,000 kg × $2/kg	= 860,000	
			$64,500 A
AQAP		=	924,500 Price

(W2) **Labour variances – surgical team fees**

		$	
SHSR			
	2.5 hrs/unit × 76,000 units ×$8/hr	=1,520,000	Efficiency
AHSR			$48,000 A
	196,000 hrs × $8/hr	=1,568,000	
AHAR		=1,626,800	$58,800 A
			Rate

(W3) Fixed overhead expenditure variance

	$
Budgeted Cost	640,000
Actual Cost	590,000
	50,000 F

Fixed overhead volume variance

	Units
Budgeted output	80,000
Actual output	76,000
	4,000 A
× Std fixed overhead cost per unit	× $8
	$32,000 A

The variances can also be calculated in a more traditional manner as follows:

(W1) Material

Rate variance	=	($2/kg x 430,000hrs) – 924,500
	=	$64,500 (A)
Usage variance	=	(6 kgs × 76,000 × $2) – ($2 x 430,000kgs)
	=	$52,000 (F)

(W2) Labour:

Rate variance	=	($8/hr x 196,000hrs) – 1,626,800
	=	$58,800 (A)
Efficiency variance	=	(2.5 hrs × 76,000 × $8) – ($8 x 196,000hrs)
	=	$48,000 (A)

(W3) Fixed overhead:

Expenditure variance	=	$640,000 – 590,000
	=	$50,000 (F)
Volume variance	=	(80,000 – 76,000) × ($640,000 / 80,000)
	=	$32,000 (A)

(c) **Planning variance**

	$	
Materials price planning variance:		
Original planned price	2.00	
Revised price	2.10	
Variance	0.10	A
Actual quantity	430,000	kgs
Direct materials planning variance	$43,000	A

Operational variances

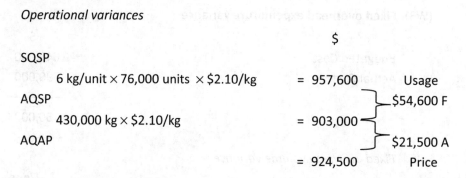

SQSP

    6 kg/unit × 76,000 units × $2.10/kg   = 957,600   Usage

AQSP $54,600 F

    430,000 kg × $2.10/kg   = 903,000

AQAP $21,500 A

                                               = 924,500   Price

264   DL HOSPITAL TRUST

Key answer tips

Be prepared for questions like this which test your understanding of the application of standard costing techniques to non-manufacturing scenarios. This question is set in a service industry. However, although some of the terminology may differ slightly, the basic principles are exactly the same. The starting point is the determination of the measure of activity, which you will use to flex the budget. In this case it is the number of surgical operations. It is a good idea to show the examiner that you are flexible about the terminology you use in different situations – for example, using 'surgical team fees' instead of 'labour' variances. The distinction between budgetary control and standard costing, part (b), is a very common exam question requirement, so make sure you are clear as to the difference. The report in (c) can only be brief for the marks given; you should recognise it as basically the introductory argument for the use of activity based costing instead of traditional labour hour absorption rates.

(a)   **Cost reconciliation statement**

	$	$	$
Budget cost (20 × $5,000) (W1)			100,000
Activity adjustment (100,000 × 2/20)			10,000
			110,000
Cost variances:	Adv.	Fav.	
Surgical team fees:			
Rate variance (W2)		2,600	
Efficiency variance (W2)	3,000		
Variable overhead:			
Expenditure variance (W3)		725	
Efficiency variance (W3)	1,875		
Fixed overhead:			
Expenditure variance (W4)	1,950		
Volume variance (W4)		3,500	
	6,825	6,825	Nil
Actual cost			110,000

(b)   Budgetary control is based on controlling total costs whereas standard costing is based on controlling unit costs.

In service organisations it is common for its activities to be varied and consequently it may be difficult to find a standard measure of activity. It may also be difficult to identify costs with particular activities.

The disadvantage of using only budgetary control is that, whilst it limits expenditure, it does not provide a basis for monitoring the efficiency of expenditure.

In contrast, standard costing provides a basis for monitoring such efficiency without limiting expenditure.

If possible, therefore, both budgetary control and standard costing should be used, though the latter may not be appropriate for some of the organisation's activities.

(c)   **REPORT**

To:	Managing Director
From:	Management Accountant
Date:	XX/XX/XX
Subject:	Overhead absorption

Surgical team fees are representative of the direct labour cost of the DL Hospital Trust. This basis of absorption implies that all of the overhead costs arise due to the surgical team fees cost. Clearly this is likely to be an unjustifiable assumption. However, it does provide an administratively convenient method of attributing overhead costs to surgical operations.

However, management may review the causes of the overhead costs and improve their information provision by attributing costs according to various cost drivers. This would be via an Activity Based Costing system.

Workings

(W1) **Standard cost per operation**

	$
Surgical team fees	
10 hrs × $200/hr	2,000
Variable overhead	
10 hrs × $125/hr	1,250
Fixed overhead	
10 hrs × $175/hr	1,750
	─────
	5,000
	─────

The surgical team fees are $2,000 per operation and each operation takes 10 hours, the fees are therefore $200 per hour.

The variable overheads and the fixed overheads are 62.5% and 87.5% of surgical team fees respectively, so are 62.5% and 87.5% of $200 per hour respectively.

Two answers have been provided for this question. The first method uses a formulaic approach which many people like. The second method is a more traditional approach.

(W2) Labour variances – surgical team fees

$

SHSR

10 hrs/unit × 22 operations × $200/hr =   44,000   Efficiency

AHSR $3,000 A

                    235 hrs   × $200/hr   =   47,000

AHAR   =   44,400 $2,600 F

                                                                                     Rate

(W3) Variable overhead variances

$

SHSR

10 hrs/unit × 22 operations × $125/hr =   27,500   Efficiency

AHSR $1,875 A

                    235 hrs   × $125/hr   =   29,375

AHAR   =   28,650 $725 F

                                                                                     Rate

(W4) Fixed overhead expenditure variance

$

Budgeted Cost 20 operations × $1,750/operation   35,000

Actual Cost   36,950

                                                                        _____

                                                                         1,950 A

Fixed overhead volume variance

                                                                    Operations

Budgeted output   20

Actual output   22

                                                                        ____

                                                                          2 F

× Std fixed overhead cost per unit   × 1,750

                                                                        ____

                                                                      $3,500 F

The variances can also be calculated in a more traditional manner as follows:

(W2) Surgical team fees:

Rate variance	=	$44,400 – ($2,000/10 × 235)
	=	$2,600 (F)
Efficiency variance	=	(235 – (22 × 10)) × $2,000/10
	=	$3,000 (A)

(W3) Variable overhead:

Expenditure variance	=	$28,650 – (235 × ($2,000/10 × 62.5%))
	=	$725 (F)
Efficiency variance	=	(235 – (22 × 10)) × $2,000/10 × 62.5%
	=	$1,875 (A)

(W4) Fixed overhead:

Expenditure variance	=	$36,950 – ($2,000 × 20 × 87.5%)
	=	$1,950 (A)
Volume variance	=	(22 – 20) × ($2,000 × 87.5%)
	=	$3,500 (F)

265 FX (MAY 08 EXAM)

Key answer tips

In part (a) a report was needed which would explain and interpret given variances. The variances were supplied with a standard cost card so effectively you had to work backwards to the actual results. There should have been lots of easy/gettable marks from explaining what a variance told us. For example, explaining that an adverse sales price variance means that the actual selling price was below the standard price, and then trying to consider why this might have happened (e.g. maybe the market has become more competitive). So if you had kept calm there were 8/9 'easy' marks available here without having to do more complicated calculations.

In part (b) there were 1/2 easy marks available for calculating the total and planning variance but this is likely to have been the trickiest part of the question and should have been skipped until you had attempted the final part.

In part (c) a well prepared student should be able to pick up 2/3 of the 6 marks available, but it was important to relate the answers to the scenario.

(a)   **REPORT**

To: The Managing Director of FX

From: Management Accountant

Date:

Subject: Month 6 Variance Report

This report aims to explain and interpret the Month 6 variance report.

Original planned profit

As can be seen from the original standard cost card, the original plan was to sell the product for £250. With a cost per unit of £160 (made up of material, labour and overhead costs), a contribution of £90 was planned for each unit.

FX budgeted to produce and sell 1,000 units so total contribution was expected to be £90,000. Budgeted fixed overheads (which could include items such as rent and insurance) were expected to be £70,000 so that a profit of £20,000 was the company's original target.

As actual profit was only £11,140 there must have been some deviation (or 'variance') away from the original plan. The variance report aims to explain why and where this has occurred.

Variances

There have been a number of deviations away from the original plan and each one is split into a different variance on the variance report.

Volume variance

FX sold 200 units more than was budgeted. So at a contribution of £90 per unit this should have created an extra £18,000 of profit. This is the 'volume variance' so that the expected profit on actual sales of 1,200 units was £38,000. This may have been caused by the fall in selling price (see next variance).

Sales price variance

The sales price variance is negative as it has been deducted from the expected profit – it has had an 'adverse' affect on profit. This tells us that the actual selling price of the product must have been below the original budgeted price of £250.

As 1,200 units were sold and the variance totals £12,000, the reduction in price must have been £10 per unit. So the actual selling price must have been reduced to £240 per unit. Without further investigation we do not know why the price was lowered, it could have been a deliberate marketing strategy or a reaction to similar moves by rivals.

Materials price variance

This is another adverse variance – in order to have an adverse affect on profit the price per kg of material (budgeted to be £20/kg) must have increased. The company spent £132,300 on 6,300kg of material which gives an actual price of £21/kg. This £1/kg increase for the 6,300kg purchased has caused the £6,300 adverse variance. This might have been caused by an uncontrollable change in market price or a switch of supplier.

Materials usage variance

FX originally planned to use 5kg of material on each unit of production. As 1,200 units were produced, 6,000kg should have been used.

6,300kg were actually used which gives an adverse variance of 300kg. At a standard cost of £20/kg, this caused the adverse usage variance of £6,000. This might have been caused by a change in the materials used causing unfamiliarity to staff.

Labour rate variance

A favourable labour rate variance means that there has been a positive effect on profits by a change in the labour rate per hour. £5,040 was saved on the 5,040 hours worked – a saving of £1 per hour.

The budgeted rate per hour was £10 so the company must have paid an average rate of only £9 per hour. Perhaps a lower grade of labour was used – which might also explain the adverse materials usage variance.

Labour efficiency variance

FX budgeted for each unit to take 4 hours of labour. The total expected time for the 1,200 units actually produced would therefore be 4,800 units.

5,040 hours were actually worked, giving 240 extra hours of labour that weren't expected. At a standard cost of £10 per hour this creates a total adverse variance of £2,400. This would be consistent with the use of a lower grade of labour who may take longer to complete the task.

Variable overhead expenditure variance

There was no variance here which means that the planned expenditure on variable overheads per hour (£5) and the actual cost per hour must have been the same.

Variable overhead efficiency variance

Variable overhead efficiency is linked to the labour efficiency variance (and will have an identical cause). Because labour worked 240 hours more than expected, the company's machines, for example, will have had to have been operated for an extra 240 hours – this gives an extra cost to the company.

At a standard cost of £5 per hour for variable overheads, the total extra cost will be £1,200.

Fixed overhead variance

The adverse fixed overhead variance tells us that FX spent £4,000 more than the £70,000 originally budgeted on these costs. More detailed analysis is not possible without a detailed breakdown of the individual elements of the fixed overheads, but this could be caused by extra system costs of monitoring new staff, materials wastage etc.

Overall

The variance report highlights that the main cause of the downturn in profits was the cost overruns – especially on materials. The next step should be to investigate why these variances occurred.

(b) **Direct material variances**

		£
Total variance		
Original Planned expenditure	(1,200 units × £100/unit)	120,000
Actual total expenditure		132,300
		12,300 A

		£
Planning variance		
Original planned expenditure	(1200 units × £100/unit)	120,000
Revised planned expenditure	(1200 units × £23/kg × 5kgs/unit)	138,000
		18,000 A

	£
Operating variances	
Price variance	
Revised budgeted price	23
Actual price	21
Price variance	2 Fav
Materials purchased	6,300 kg
Materials price variance	£12,600 Fav

Usage variance	
1200 units of production should use (× 5 kg)	6,000 kg
They did use	6,300 kg
Usage variance (in kg)	300 kg
Revised standard price	£23/kg
Materials usage variance	£6,900 Adv

(c) **Planning and operating variances**

Planning and operating variances have a number of advantages:

- They allow better prone appraisal against up-to-date standards. FX can focus on the controllable, operational variances when assessing the performance of individual managers.
- The information provided is more useful to management. For FX, management can isolate the impact of the rise in market price.

- Operational staff may be motivated by the system as it will focus on the areas that they can control. For FX, staff responsible for the price of materials would originally have had an adverse variance to explain. When the operational element is removed, they have a favourable variance and may actually be entitled to a bonus.

However there are also some downsides to using planning and operational variances:

- There is a possibility that planning variances are not investigated so that future plans and the planning function overall are not improved.
- Operational managers may argue that a change in circumstances is outside their control and should therefore be deemed to be a planning variance rather than an operational one.

266   WC (NOV 07 EXAM)

Key answer tips

This is a very tough question and it is unlikely that sales mix and quantity variances would be examined again in a long-form section C question. It is included in the exam kit for illustration and completeness.

(a)

Budget	Kitchens	Bathrooms	Total
	$	$	$
Sales	40	14	54
Direct costs	(22)	(6)	(28)
Central services	(10)	(5)	(15)
Budget profit	8	3	11

Actual	Kitchens	Bathrooms	Total
	$	$	$
Sales	33.8	15.25	49.05
Direct costs	(20.8)	(6.75)	(27.55)
Central services	(6.5)	(6.25)	(17.5)
Actual profit	6.5	2.25	4

(b)

	Kitchens	Bathrooms	Total
	$	$	$
Standard selling price	10,000	7,000	
Actual selling price	13,000	6,100	
	3,000 F	900 A	
× Actual no. of units sold	× 2,600	× 2,500	
	7,800,000 F	2,250,000 A	5,550,000 F

Sales mix profit variances

	Actual Sales	Standard Mix of Actual sales	Difference	Value at standard profit	Mix Variance $m
Kitchens	2,600	3,400	800 A	$2,000	1.6 A
Bathrooms	2,500	1,700	800 F	$1,500	1.2 F
	5,100	5,100			0.4 A

Sales quantity profit variances

	Budget Sales	Standard Mix of Actual sales	Quantity Variance	Value at standard profit	Mix Variance $
Kitchens	4,000	3,400	600 A	$2,000	1.20 A
Bathrooms	2,000	1,700	300 A	$1,500	0.45 A
	6,000	5,100			1.65 A

Check

Sales volume variances

Kitchens $\quad\quad$ (4,000 – 2,600) × $2,000 = $2.8m A

Bathrooms $\quad\quad$ (2,000 – 2,500) × $1,500 = $0.75m F $\quad\quad\quad$ Total $2.05m

Sales volume variance $\quad$ = mix variance + quantity variance

$\quad\quad\quad\quad\quad\quad\quad\quad\quad$ = $0.4m A + $1.65m A = $2.05 m

(c)

	F ($m)	A ($m)	$m
Budgeted profit (from part a)			11
Sales mix variance (from part b)			
– kitchens		1.6	
– bathrooms	1.2		
Sales quantity variance (part b)			
– kitchens		1.2	
– bathrooms		0.45	
Sales price variances (part b)			
– kitchens	7.8		
– bathrooms		2.25	
Direct costs (W1)			
– kitchens		6.5	
– bathrooms	0.75		
Central services (W2)			
– volume (kitchens)		3.5	
– volume (bathrooms)	1.25		
– expenditure		2.5	
	11	18	7 A
Actual profit (from part a)			4

Workings

(W1) **Direct cost variances**

Kitchens   2,600 × (5,500 – 8,000) = $6.5m A

Bathrooms 2,500 × (3,000 – 2,700) = $0.75m F

(W2) **Central services volume variances**

Kitchens (4,000 – 2,600) × $2,500 = $3.5m A

Bathrooms (2,500 – 2,000) × $2,500 = $1.25m F

Central services expenditure variance = $15m – $17.5m = $2.5m A

(d)   (Actual profit at $4m is $7m below budgeted profit, a shortfall of 64%). The main causes are as follows:

–   an overall fall in the total volume of sales resulting in a sales quantity variance of $1.65m A. The lower than expected volume has also resulted in central services costs being under absorbed as shown by the volume variances (net impact $2.25A).

–   the sales mix has also switched from more profitable kitchens to less profitable bathrooms and this is reflected in the sales mix variance of $0.4m A.

–   the impact of the lower volume of kitchen sales has been partially offset by the favourable price variance for kitchens. It is possible that a higher proportion of jobs are of the highly customised category rather than the 'off the shelf' packages. This has led to higher average prices being charged but also higher direct costs being incurred. The opposite seems to have occurred with bathrooms.

–   Central services costs have exceeded budget by $2.5m. This may be due to higher costs incurred designing customised jobs.

It would be worth investigating whether the extra price charged for customised designs is covering all of the additional costs incurred. Higher prices may be necessary or better control of costs.

Tutorial note

For part (a): The information given in the question suggests that an OAR of $2,500 per job is used to absorb central services costs. This means that there is under absorbed central services cost of 17.5 – 6.5 – 6.25 = $4.75m. There is no indication that this is charged to profit centres but total costs must be shown to arrive at total profit.

---

267 RG (SEP 2010 EXAM)

Key answer tips

There is approximately one mark per calculation in art (a). Therefore if you get stuck on a particular variance you should leave it out and move on to the next one which may be easier and will be worth the same amount of marks. Part (b) is the trickiest part of the question and you should leave it until last. In part (c) it is important that you *discuss* the advantages (for example, by explaining why they are advantages) rather than simply state them.

(a)   **Operating statement**

Operating statement
April
Product CP1 $

		$	
Budgeted profit	1,400 units x $40 / unit	56,000	
Sales volume variance	(W1)	8,000	Fav
Sales price variance	(W2)	16,000	Adv
		———	
Profit before cost variances		48,000	

Cost variances

		Fav	Adv	
Materials price	(W3)		7,300	
Materials usage	(W4)	14,000		
Labour rate	(W5)	5,080		
Labour efficiency	(W6)	13,200		
Variable overhead rate	(W7)			
Variable overhead efficiency	(W8)	6,600		
Fixed overhead expenditure	(W9)		4,000	
Fixed overhead volume	(W10)	10,000		
		———	———	
		48,880	11,300	37,580
				———
Actual profit	(W11)			85,580
				———

Workings

(W1) Sales volume variance

Actual sales volume		1,600
Budgeted sales volume		1,400
		———
Variance (kgs)		200
Standard profit per unit		$40
		———
Variance ($)		8,000 Fav
		———

(W2) Sales price variance

Actual selling price	240
Budgeted selling price	250
Variance (per kg)	10
Actual sales volume	1,600
Variance ($)	16,000 Adv

(W3) Materials price variance

		$
Standard cost of actual purchases	(7,300 kgs x $20/kg)	146,000
Actual cost of actual purchases		153,300
Variance		7,300 Adv

(W4) Materials usage variance

		kgs
Standard usage for actual production	(5kgs x 1,600)	8,000
Actual usage		7,300
Variance in kgs		700
Standard price		$20/kg
Variance		14,000 Fav

(W5) Labour rate variance

		$
Standard cost of actual hours	(5,080 hrs x $10/hr)	50,800
Actual cost of actual hours	(5,080 hrs x $9/hr)	45,720
Variance		5,080 Fav

(W6) Labour efficiency variance

		hrs
Standard hours for actual production	(4 hrs x 1,600)	6,400
Actual hours		5,080
Variance in hrs		1,320
Standard rate		$10/hr
Variance		13,200 Fav

(W7) Variable overhead rate variance

		$
Standard cost of actual hours	(5,080 hrs x $5/hr)	25,400
Actual cost of actual hours		25,400
Variance		0

(W8) Variable overhead efficiency variance

		hrs	
Standard hours for actual production	(4 hrs x 1,600)	6,400	
Actual hours		5,080	
Variance in hrs		1,320	
Standard rate		$5/hr	
Variance		6,600	Fav

(W9) Fixed overhead expenditure variance

Budgeted overheads – actual overheads = ($50 x 1,400 units) – $74,000 = $4,000 Adv

(W10) Fixed overhead volume variance

Actual sales volume	1,600	
Budgeted sales volume	1,400	
Variance (kgs)	200	Fav
Standard fixed overheads per unit	$50	
Variance ($)	$10,000	Fav

(W11) Actual profit

	$	$
Sales		384,000
Cost of sales:		
Materials	153,300	
Labour	45,720	
Variable overheads	25,400	
Fixed overheads	74,000	
		(298,420)
Actual profit		85,580

(b) Planning and operating variances

(i) Total variance

		$
Standard cost of actual production	(890 units x 5kgs x $20)	89,000
Actual cost of actual production	(4,375 kgs x $21.60)	94,500
		5,500 Adv

(ii) **Planning variance**

		$	
Original planned expenditure	(890 units x 5kgs x $20/kg)	89,000	
Revised planned expenditure	(890 units x 5kgs x $20.90/kg)	93,005	
		4,005	Adv

(iii) **Operating variances**

	$	
Price variance		
Revised budgeted price	20.90	
Actual price	21.60	
Price variance	0.70	Adv
Materials purchased	4,375kgs	
Materials price variance	3,063	Adv

	kgs	
Usage variance		
890 units of production should use 890 x 5kgs	4,450	
They did use	4,375	
Usage variance (in kg)	75	Fav
Revised standard price	$20.90	
Materials usage variance	1,568	Fav

(c) **Benefits of identifying planning variances**

- The use of planning variances is likely to make performance appraisal better. Managers will be appraised against more accurate/fairer operating variances.

- It may reduce the instance of variance investigation. If a variance can be fully attributed to a planning error then no further investigation may be necessary.

- It should allow standard costing to be more acceptable in unstable environments as the target can be adjusted through the use of planning variances.

268 WESTERN EUROPE (MAY 10 EXAM)

Key answer tips

The key to obtaining a good mark in this question is to attempt part (b) first. A well prepared student should be aware of the limitations of standard costing in modern environments and be able to get at least 4 out of 6 in part (b). If you start with part (a) there is a risk that you will run out of time before getting these easier marks which are available in part (b).

In part (a), the mix and yield variances will be the hardest element. It will therefore be important to set up a proforma operating statement and do the other variances first. With a good part (b) and a solid attempt at the other variances, a good student should be able to pick up enough marks to pass the question even if they get no marks at all in the mix and yield calculations.

(a)   **Operating statement**

Operating statement
April
Product CP1

			Fav $	Adv $	$	
Budgeted profit	(W1)				432,000	
Sales volume variance	(W2)				6,000	Adv
Sales price variance	(W3)				21,300	Fav
Profit before cost variances					447,300	
Cost variances						
Materials price						
ETH1	(W4)			2,210		
RXY2	(W4)		9,580			
Materials mix						
ETH1	(W5)			19,800		
RXY2	(W5)		6,600			
Materials yield	(W6)		18,000			
Fixed overhead expenditure	(W7)		2,000			
Fixed overhead volume	(W8)			4,000		
			36,180	26,010	10,170	Fav
Actual profit	(W9)				457,470	

Workings

(W1) **Budgeted profit**

		$
Budgeted sales	(72,000 x $20)	1,440,000
Budgeted production costs	(70,000 x $14)	(980,000)
Opening stock		(28,000)
Budgeted profit		432,000

(W2) **Sales volume variance**

Actual sales volume	71,000	
Budgeted sales volume	(72,000)	
Variance (kgs)	1,000	Adv
Standard profit per unit ($20 - $14)	$6	
Variance ($)	$6,000	Adv

(W3) **Sales price variance**

Actual selling price	20.30	
Budgeted selling price	(20.00)	
Variance (per kg)	0.30	Fav
Actual sales volume	71,000 kgs	
Variance ($)	$21,300	Fav

(W4) **Materials price variance**

		ETH1	RXY2
		$	$
Standard cost of actual purchases	(22,100 x $18.00)	397,800	
	(47,900 x $6.00)		287,400
Actual cost of actual purchases	(22,100 x $18.10)	400,010	
	(47,900 x $5.80)		277,820
Variance		2,210 A	9,580 F

(W5) **Materials mix variance**

	Standard mix	Actual material usage (Kg)	Actual usage at standard mix (Kg)	Mix variance (Kg)	Standard price per kg	Mix variance
ETH1	30%	22,100	21,000	1,100 A	18	19,800 A
RXY2	70%	47,900	49,000	1,100 F	6	6,600 F
Total		70,000	70,000			11,400 A

(W6) **Materials yield variance**

Standard input (69,000 kgs / 96%)	71,875	
Actual input	(70,000)	
Variance (per kg)	1,875	Fav
Standard price per kg of input	$9.60	
Variance ($)	$18,000	Fav

(W7) **Fixed overhead expenditure variance**

Budgeted overheads − actual overheads = $280,000 − $278,000 = $2,000 Fav

(W8) **Fixed overhead volume variance**

Actual sales volume	71,000	
Budgeted sales volume	(72,000)	
Variance (kgs)	1,000	Adv
Standard fixed overheads per kg	$4	
Variance ($)	$4,000	Adv

(W9) **Actual profit**

	$	$
Sales		1,441,300
Cost of sales:		
Opening stock	28,000	
Material – ETH1	400,010	
Material – RXY2	277,820	
Fixed overheads	278,000	
Closing stock	−	983,830
Actual profit		457,470

(b) **Standard costing**

Standard costing might be inappropriate in an advanced manufacturing environment for the following reasons:

- In advanced manufacturing environments, products are often personalised/ bespoke for customer needs and therefore there is no longer one 'standard' set of production inputs. In such systems, cost for resources would still be useful (if standard resources are used, which in itself might not be true), but the usage is likely to become less relevant.

- An advanced manufacturing environment is constantly evolving and changing and therefore standards can quickly become out of date. The standards will therefore be of little use in planning and control – for example, variances would become more common and larger and any investigation is likely to highlight planning errors rather than operational ones.

- Production is highly automated in modern manufacturing environments. This means that overhead costs will increase and labour costs will decrease. Overhead variances will become more important and labour variances will become less important. Normal standard costing overhead variances lack detail and are often poorly related to the actual cause of the variance (as it often assumes that overhead costs are linked to the efficiency of the workforce).

269 FA AND FB (NOV 08 EXAM) *Walk in the footsteps of a top tutor*

Tutors top tips

The question starts with a tough part (a) which may have put some students off (it required the calculation of a usage variance in a process that contained losses).But it was only worth 6 marks and the question got easier from that point.

To some extent it may have been easier to do this question backwards as it gets easier as it goes along and no part relates to previous parts. So start with the discursive elements at the end of the question, then try the (simple) purchases budget, then the discussion on planning variances and you've already attempted 17 of the 30 marks and hopefully built up some marks in case you find the other sections tougher. It may be more difficult to pick up full marks on the other, trickier calculations but if you show a reasonable level of knowledge you should get enough marks overall to pass.

For the variance calculations in part (b) you could start with the usage variances and gain most of the marks. It will be important to use the revised price for materials, but even if the original price is used you will still pick up the majority of the marks and score a high mark in the question overall.

Part (a) is made very tough by the treatment loss percentage and the weaker students who start with part (a) are likely to become disheartened and struggle with the question overall.

(a)   **Chemical C1**

(i)   **Materials usage variance**

63,000 units (combined) of products FA and FB were actually produced. Each product is expected to use 0.2 kg of chemical C1. Therefore the standard quantity should have been 0 .2 kgs for each unit = 12,600 kgs for the finished product.

However, this is after an expected 30% loss in C1 due to the treatment process. So the total C1 used should have been:

$$= \frac{12,600 \, \text{kgs}}{70\%} = 18,000 \text{ kgs}$$

The actual quantity used was 17,740 kgs of C1. This allows us to calculate the total usage variance:

Output of 53,000 units should have used	18,000 kgs	
Actual Quantity used	17,740 kgs	
Variance	260 kgs	Favourable
Standard Price	$8/ kg	
Total usage variance	$2080	Favourable

(ii) **Treatment loss percentage**

Actual quantity used was 17,740 kgs. There were 12,600 kgs of C1 in the finished product. Therefore 5,140 kgs were lost in the treatment of C1. This is 29% of the materials actually used. Alternatively:

Actual quantity used	17,740 kgs
Output of 53,000 units × 0.2kgs per unit	12,600 kgs
Loss	5,140 kgs

$$\% = \frac{5,140\,kgs}{17,740\,kgs} \times 100\% \qquad 29\%$$

(b) (i) **Planning, operational and usage variances**

Planning variance

		$
Original planned expenditure	(25,000 units × 0.25kgs × $12/unit)	75,000
Revised planned expenditure	(25,000 units × 0.25kgs × $14.50/unit)	90,625
		15,625　A

Operating variances

Price variance

		$	
Revised budgeted price		14.50	
Actual price	($94,000 / 6,450kgs)	14.57	
Price variance		0.07	Adv
Materials purchased		6,450	kg
Materials price variance		$475	Fav

Usage variance

25,000 units of production should use	(× 0.25 kg)	6,250	kg
They did use		6,450	kg
Usage variance (in kg)		200	Adv
Revised standard price		$14.50	/kg
Materials usage variance		$2,900	Adv

(ii) **Problems with reporting planning variances**

- There is a possibility that planning variances are not investigated so that future plans and the planning function overall are not improved.

- Operational managers may argue that a change in circumstances is outside their control and should therefore be deemed to be a planning variance rather than an operational one.

(c) **Purchases budget**

Production Units		40,000units
C2 per unit		0 .15kg / unit
Materials Usage		6,000 kgs
Opening Stock	Note 1	(3,000 kgs)
		3,000 kgs
Closing Stock	Note 2	3,300 kgs
Purchases (kgs)		6,300 kgs
Cost / kg		$15 / kg
C2 Purchases Budget		$94,500

Notes:

1 Opening stock   = 50% × 40,000 units × 0.15 kg / unit = 3,000 kgs

2 Closing stock   = 50% × 44,000 units × 0.15 kg / unit = 3,300 kgs

(d)   **Usefulness of variance analysis**

A number of criticisms have been suggested concerning the applicability of standard costing in a modern manufacturing environment. Arguments to support the statement that variance analysis is of little use in modern manufacturing environments are:

1   In modern manufacturing there is an increasing trend away from mass production towards customised and non-standard products. This leads to a greater variability in operating conditions, where constant standards are less useful and measurement against them gives meaningless results.

2   The constant changes that happen in a modern environment (for example, due to shorter product life cycles) would also make it too costly to constantly update and review the standards. It also means that any standard that is used to assess performance will quickly become out of date and its usefulness diminished.

3   The move towards strictly monitored input systems, such as JIT, decreases the variability in input costs, thus rendering variance analysis unnecessary anyway.

4   In modern manufacturing environments direct labour and direct material play a smaller role in the total product cost so that lots of the variances calculated in variance analysis become less useful. Whereas important factors such as quality, customer satisfaction etc. might be ignored.

5   It may now be too late to do anything about the problem. By the cause is discovered for any variance that has been calculated the environment may have moved on so that new problems become more relevant and solving old problems only results in the business falling further behind its rivals.

However, whilst it is true that variance calculation and analysis takes place after the actual events have taken place, variance analysis can still play some role in planning and control – even in a modern manufacturing environment. Examples of this might be:

1   Cost and mix changes from plan will still be relevant in many processing situations. A change in material mix, for example, may continue to warrant investigation to determine whether quality standards and technical specification is being met.

2   If the product mix is relatively stable, performance management may be enhanced by the use of planning and operating variances.

3   Variance trends can be monitored to assess whether a situation is in control or out of control.

4   Even in a TQM environment, budgets will need to be quantified. For example, the level of staff training needs to be planned. Variance analysis can then be focused more on overheads and adapted to techniques such as activity based costing by extending variances to cost drivers.

5   Although variances are calculated after the event has taken place they still provide vital information to managers: they can indicate when a process might need investigation, they can continue to indicate when a process is out of control, and they can be used in feed forward control to improve standard setting and budgeting in the future.

Overall, whilst variance analysis needs to be adapted to modern business environments, it can still play an important role in the planning and control of processes – even after the events have taken place.

270 SATELLITE NAVIGATION SYSTEMS (MAY 05 EXAM)

Key answer tips

Part (a) common errors:

- Demonstrating an inability to link the variances reported to the possible causes, many of which were alluded to in the scenario.

- Not offering in the candidates' discussion many of their own ideas and not developing the report comprehensively.

(a)   **Report**

To   Operations Manager

From   Management Accountant

Date   May 2005

Subject   Performance of S Limited for four months to 31 December

Production and sales

Production and sales were 1,100 units in September and October, 950 units in November and 900 units in December. There has thus been a marked decline over the four-month period. This good performance in the first two months and poor performance in the latter two months may be due to a seasonal variation. If this is the case, it would be good for the budget to reflect the expected seasonal variation, rather than just being a flat 1,000 units per month.

Tutorial note The output was calculated by taking the standard cost of actual output and dividing by the standard cost per system, i.e. $1,276,000/$1,160 = 1,100 units, $1,102,000/$1,160 = 950 units and $1,044,000/$1,160 = 900 units.

Materials

The material price variance was favourable for the first two months, and then very adverse for November and December. This was possibly due to the exchange rate movement if the systems are imported. The effect of the exchange rate variations should be quantified. Any remaining adverse variances may be due to inefficient purchasing by the purchasing manager. It should be investigated as to whether there are alternative suppliers for the systems.

The material usage variance was adverse in every month, but was particularly bad in October and even worse in December. In October the variance was $7,200 A and as the material cost was $400 per unit, this meant that an extra $7,200/$400 = 18 units were used on a production of 1,100 units.   In December, the variance was $16,000/$400 = 40 extra units on production of 900 units. This variance could possibly be due to the large batch of systems which did not have the correct adaptors. The variance needs careful investigation in order to find out where the excess units were used, which systems and which teams of fitters were involved.

Labour

The labour rate variance was adverse in September and October and substantially adverse in November and December. Expressing the variances as percentages, for September the standard labour cost was $320 × 1,100 units = $352,000 and thus the variance was $4,200 A/$352,000 = 1.1% A. In November the variance was $5,500 A/$352,000 = 1.6% A. These minor variances could be explained by more overtime than expected being worked, especially as production was high in the first two months. Then things were much worse in the latter two months, for November the variance was $23,100 A/($320 per unit × 950 units) = 7.6% A and in December the variance was $24,000 A/($320 per unit × 900 units) = 8.3%. These substantial variances are almost certainly due to higher wage rates being offered in order to retain the staff and lower the labour turnover. It would be very useful to have information on the number of staff leaving the business. Overtime is unlikely to be the cause for the variances in November and December as production was lower than budget.

The labour efficiency variance was $16,000 favourable in September ($16,000/$352,000 = 4.5% F), zero in October and $32,000 adverse in November and December ($32,000 A/$320 per unit × 950 units) = 10.5% A, and $32,000 A/$320 per unit × 900 units) = 11.1% A). It would be expected that some of this variance was due to the large batch of systems which did not have the correct adaptors. This problem was not apparent until fitting was attempted, thus involving the fitters in extra work. If this were the case then we would expect the labour efficiency variance to tie up with the material usage variance, but it does not. We are also told that there is a fluctuation of ± 25% in the fitting times, so even the substantial variances for November and December fall within this range and thus might not represent inefficiency, but simply the fitting of a higher proportion of more labour intensive systems. It would be useful to have information on the standard times for different systems and the numbers of the different systems, instead of treating all systems alike. The high labour turnover also means that experienced workers are leaving and that new workers are constantly having to be trained. The efficiency of the new workers would be poor to start off with.

Variable overheads

The variable overhead efficiency variance is based on labour hours and thus simply moves in line with the labour efficiency variance.

The expenditure variance was $7,000 A in September, improved to $2,000 A in October and then $2,000 F in November. It was zero in December. For this variance to have any meaning it must be sub-analysed into its different components in order to determine which ones are being overspent and which ones under spent.

Taking the variable overheads as a whole, the variance gets worse as production levels fall, perhaps indicating that the variable overheads are not entirely variable but may include a fixed element.

Fixed overheads

The fixed overhead volume variance simply reflects the better than expected production in the first two months and the worse than expected production in the latter two months. The fixed overhead volume variance has no significance as it does not represent a cash flow (if we make more or less units than expected then the fixed overheads do not change), but is simply a mathematical device to reconcile budgeted profit with actual profit in an absorption costing system.

The fixed overhead expenditure variance is $5,000 A, $10,000 A, $20,000 A and $20,000 A over the four months and thus shows a worsening pattern, but again in order to understand where things are going wrong we need to sub-analyse the fixed overhead into their different components. We have been told that rent, rates insurance and computing costs have risen in price noticeably; these costs may be regarded as uncontrollable. Managers' attention should be devoted to investigating the controllable costs and reducing any overspend.

Conclusion

Overall the actual cost was 4.4% worse than expected (($4,906,201 − $4,698,000)/ $4,698,000). Whilst this variance might not be regarded as significant, the individual variances in many cases are much bigger and should be investigated. There is a marked decline in performance in November and December. It is important that the individual variances are investigated and their causes understood so that future performance improves.

(b)

	September	October	November	December
	$	$	$	$
Standard cost of actual output	1,276,000	1,276,000	1,102,000	1,044,000
Standard cost per unit	1,160	1,160	1,160	1,160
Actual units of output	1,100	1,100	950	900
Standard material usage (×$400)	440,000	440,000	380,000	360,000
Price % variance	1.25 F	0.76 F	2.51 A	2.87 A
Usage % variance	0.09 A	1.6 A	0.21 A	4.4 A

Percentage variance chart for September to December

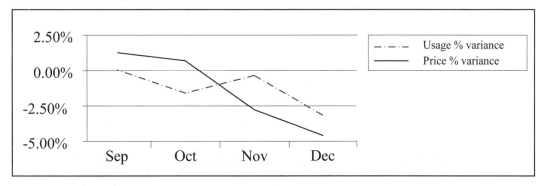

The percentage variance chart can be used to monitor the trend of variances. Significant variances may be identified by setting a control limit. If variances exceed the control limit then action is taken. Alternatively variances which show a worrying trend, such as the material usage variance for S limited, may be investigated before the variance exceeds the control limit.

271   X LTD (NOV 06 EXAM)

Key answer tips

In the real exam, part a) was done well with the most common errors being that students duplicated variances by including the material usage and mix and yield variances, included a fixed overhead volume variance (which is not applicable in a marginal costing environment), used sales price rather than contribution to value the sales volume variance and made errors in showing a variance as favourable or adverse. The main error in part b) was that students gave a general answer rather than describing their answers to part a).

(a)   ***Workings***

    (W1)   Standard price = $234 × 1.8 = $421.20

           Standard profit = $421.20 – $234 = $187.20 per unit

           5,000 × 187.20 – 350,000 = $586,000

    (W2)

Budgeted sales	5,000
Actual sales	5,450
Difference	450 F
× standard profit	$187.20
Sales volume variance	$84,240 F

    (W3)   Sales price variance = ($445 – $421.20) × 5,450 = $129,710 F

    (W4)   Material price variance

		$	$
Material A	43,000 kg should cost (× 15)	645,000	
	did cost	688,000	
			43,000 A
Material B	37,000 kg should cost (× 8)	296,000	
	did cost	277,500	
			18,500 F
Material C	23,500 kg should cost (× 4)	94,000	
	did cost	99,875	
			5,875 A
			30,375 A

(W5)

	Standard mix	Actual material usage (Kg)	Actual usage at standard mix (Kg)	Mix variance (Kg)	Standard price per kg	Mix variance
A	10/23	43,000	45,000	2,000 F	15	30,000 F
B	8/23	37,000	36,000	1,000 A	8	8,000 A
C	5/23	23,500	22,500	1,000 A	4	4,000 A
Total		103,500	103,500			18,000 F

103,500 kg of input should produce   (/23)   4,500 units of product P

did produce   5,450 units of product P

Difference   950 F

Value at standard cost   × $234

Yield variance $222,300

(W6)

	$
Sales revenue	2,425,250
Less material cost	(1,065,375)
Overhead	(385,000)
Actual profit	974,875

Operating statement

	$
Budgeted profit (W1)	586,000
Sales volume variance (W2)	84,240 F
Sales price variance (W3)	129,710 F
Actual sales less standard cost of sales	799,950

Cost variances

	F	A	
Material price (W4)		30,375	
Material mix (W5)	18,000		
Material yield (W5)	222,300		
Fixed production expenditure		35,000	
	240,300	65,375	174,925 F
Actual profit (W6)			974,875

(b)

REPORT

To: Production Manager

From: Management Accountant

Date: November 2006

Subject: Material mix and Yield variances

Introduction

This report explains the meaning of the material price, mix and yield variances included in the operating statement attached. It also explains the merits of calculating mix and yield variances for X Ltd.

Meaning of material price, mix and yield variances for the period

The material price variance measures the impact on profit when the actual price paid for materials is different to standard. This period the total price variance is $30,375 A which has been caused by materials A and C costing more than standard and material B costing less than standard.

The mix variance measures the impact of a change in material mix on profit. This period the mix variance is $18,000 F which has been caused by more of the cheaper materials B and C being used than standard.

The yield variance measures the impact on profit of different output being produced from a given input than standard. This period the yield variance is $222,300 F which has been caused by a much greater level of output being produced than expected from the given input.

It is possible that the higher price paid for material A may have reduced the quantity required in the mix and increased the yield. This may have led to the favourable mix and yield variance.

Merits of mix and yield variances for X Ltd

Mix and yield variances are useful to sub-analyse the material usage variance when material inputs to a product can be varied. X Ltd uses an automated manufacturing process to produce a chemical and it appears that the mix of materials can be varied, so the analysis is appropriate. It is common for mix and yield to be interrelated and, by analysing the variances, an optimal mix can be selected.

BUDGETING

272   RF LTD (MAY 07 EXAM) *Walk in the footsteps of a top tutor*

Tutor's top tips

As with all cash budget questions it is best to have a standardised approach rather than attempting to work through the question on a line-by-line basis. So you should start by setting up a proforma cash budget then put in the easier figures – these are typically the opening balance (in this case it is actually a capital injection in the first month of the business) and the fixed overheads (in this question we actually have to do a working for these but it should still be straightforward).At this stage you will have gained 2/3 marks without having to do anything too challenging.

Next you need to attempt the sales working. The key is to be careful and methodical. Remember that bad debts are not a cash flow and should be ignored. The trick in this calculation is to deal with the discount given in the first month. Lots of students will get this wrong and it is only worth one mark – therefore, if you find it tricky you should leave it out rather than spend lots of time trying to get it right for only one mark (i.e. if you can't deal with it in less than two minutes then it is not worth attempting and it is better for you to move on).

At this stage you should have racked up 7 or 8 marks put of 15. It is not yet enough to pass because if, as is likely, you will find part (b) tough, then you may still have to pick up another 5 or 6 marks to pass the question overall (subject to a reasonable attempt at part (c)). So next we have to deal with the production plan. The key here is to be aware that production = sales –opening stock + closing stock.

If you manage to get the production plan correct then the remaining costs are straightforward. Even if you get it wrong (for example by adding opening stock and deducting closing stock), as long as your technique is fine, you should still get full marks for your workings on materials, labour and variable overhead costs if you base them on your incorrect production but apply the correct technique.

Adding the cash budget up at the end will be worth only around one mark – so keep an eye on the clock. If you have run out of time by now (which is likely) then this is a mark that is not worth spending 5 minutes to acquire.

Part (b) is a much tougher part of the question and it would be advisable to skip it for now and attempt part (c) first. This is mainly 'bookwork' and you should be able to get a good strong mark in order to pass the question overall.

If you have time, return to part (b). This will rely on the production budget in part (a) – but again, you will not be punished if your answer in part (a) was incorrect. Examine how the answer lays out the approach to the question. If you did not get it right this time then you should learn from this for future, similar questions. If you managed to have a go at part (b) then the final marks in the question will be awarded for discussing the results of part (b) in your report in part (c).

(a)   **Cash Budget**

	Month 1 $	Month 2 $	Month 3 $	Total $
Sales receipts (W1)	2,940	10,180	15,545	28,665
Capital	16,250			16,250
Total receipts	19,190	10,180	15,545	44,915
Outflow				
Material purchases (W2)	0	3,515	3,420	6,935
Labour (W3)	6,105	5,940	6,666	18,711
Variable overhead (W4)	1,332	2,184	2,318	5,834
Fixed overhead (W5)	3,750	5,625	5,625	15,000
Total payments	11,187	17,264	18,029	46,480
Net cash flow	8,003	(7,084)	(2,484)	(1,565)
Bal b/fwd	0	8,003	919	0
Bal c/fwd	8,003	919	(1,565)	(1,565)

Workings

(W1) **Sales receipts**

	1	2	3
Sales units	1,500	1,750	2,000
Sales (Units x $10)	15,000	17,500	20,000
Paid in month – 20% x 0.98	2,940	3,430	3,920
45% in the following month		6,750	7,875
25% in 3rd month			3,750
Receipts	2,940	10,180	15,545

(W2) **Production**

	1 units	2 units	3 units	4 units
Required by sales	1,500	1,750	2,000	2,100
Opening inventory		(350)	(400)	
	1,500	1,400	1,600	
Closing inventory (20% × following month's sales)	350	400	420	
Production	1,850	1,800	2,020	
Material price	$1.90	$1.90	$1.90	
Material cost	$3,515	$3,420	$3,838	
Payment		£3,515	$3,420	

(W3) **Labour**

Production units	1,850	1,800	2,020
Rate per unit	$3.30	$3.30	$3.30
Payment	$6,105	$5,940	$6,666

(W4) **Variable Overhead**

Production units	1,850	1,800	2,020
Rate per unit	$1.20	$1.20	$1.20
Variable overhead cost	$2,220	$2,160	$2,424
60% in month	1,332	1,296	1,454
40% in following month		888	864
Payment	1,332	2,184	2,318

(W5) **Fixed overhead**

	6,250	6,250	6,250
60% in month	3,750	3,750	3,750
30% in following month		1,875	1,875
Payment	3,750	5,625	5,625

(b) (i)

	Month 1	*Month 2*	*Month 3*
Production	1,850	1,800	2,020
Material price saving **($1.90 – $1.50)**	$0.40	$0.40	$0.40
Total saving ($)	740	720	808
Received		740	720
Total cash benefit	$1,460		
Current cash flow at $1.90	$(1,565)		
Revised cash flow at $1.50	**$(105)**		

(ii)

	Month 1	*Month 2*	*Month 3*
Production units	1,850	1,800	2,020
Additional cost ($2.20 – $1.90)	$0.30	$0.30	$0.30
Total additional cost ($)	555	540	606
Payment ($)		555	540
Total additional payment	$1,095		
Current cash flow at $1.90	$(1,565)		
Revised cash flow at $2.20	$(2,660)		

(c)   **Report**

To: Management

From: Management Accountant

Date: 22 May 2007

Subject: 'What if' analysis and cash budgets

Introduction

This report evaluates 'what if' analysis in relation to cash budgets.

Benefits of 'what-if' analysis

(1)   It provides an assessment of how responsive the cash flows are to changes in variables.

For example, in preparing the cash budgets it has been identified that there is a degree of uncertainty concerning the direct material cost. The following results have been calculated:

Direct material cost per component	Increase/(decrease) in cash flow	Budgeted cash flow
$2.20	($1,095)	($2,660)
$1.50	$1,460	($105)
$1.90		($1,565)

A 16% increase in material cost to $2.20, results in a negative cash flow of -$2,660. This is a 70% increase in the closing cash negative balance. A 21% decrease in direct material cost to $1.50, results in a revised cash flow of -$105. This is a 93% reduction in the closing cash negative balance. It can be seen that the closing cash balance is sensitive to changes in the price of materials because a small change in price results in a large change in the total cash balance.

(2)   *Directs attention to critical variables*

The sensitivity of each variable can be calculated and the most sensitive variables identified. These can be closely monitored and action taken quickly if they vary from forecast.

(3)   *Assess the risk to the closing cash balance*

'What-if' analysis can be used to assess how likely the expected cash balance is to occur. Managers may decide to take an alternative course of action if the outcome is very risky. For example they may negotiate an overdraft limit if there is a possibility of a cash deficit.

Limitations of 'what-if' analysis

(1)   *Only one variable changes at a time*

'What-if' analysis assesses the impact on the outcome of one variable changing at a time and assumes that each variable is independent. In reality variables are likely to be interdependent.

(2)   *Probabilities of changes unknown*

There is no indication of the likelihood of a key variable changing and therefore the use of 'what if' analysis is limited.

Conclusion

Despite the limitations of 'what-if' analysis it can provide an insight into key variables which can impact on an outcome and give managers a better understanding of the risks involved in a cash budget.

273   PMF

Key answer tips

The trend calculations are very straightforward as you do not have to do any smoothing. The question tests your understanding of why trend analysis is used in forecasting and performance measurement.

(a)   Quarter 3 year 1 = period 3 = Q3

Quarter 3 year 2 = period 7 = Q7

Quarter 3 year 3 = period 11 = Q11

Trend values for quarter 3 of each year: 10,000 + 4,200 Q

The trend value for passenger numbers per quarter (x) can be calculated as fractions.

Year 1 Q3 10,000 + (4,200 × 3) = 22,600

Year 2 Q3 10,000 + (4,200 × 7) = 39,400

To identify the seasonal variation these figures need to be compared with the historical data provided.

	Historical data	*Trend value*	*Q3 Seasonal variation %*
Year 1 Q3	16,950	22,600	75
Year 2 Q3	29,550	39,400	75

Adjust the trend value for Year 3 Q3 (11): ((10,000 + (4,200 × 11)) × 75% = 42,150 passengers to be carried in the third quarter of year 3.

(b)   The transit staff cost item is a semi-variable cost, comprising a fixed element of $32,000 and a variable element of $3 for each passenger. Hence the cost equation is in the form 32,000 + 3x. The reason for this is most likely that transit staff receive a fixed basic salary but are awarded bonuses according to how many passengers are carried as a motivational tool.

(c)   x = 42,150

Cost item	Relationship	Cost
		$
Premises cost	y = 260,000	260,000
Premises staff	y = 65,000 + 0.5x	86,075
Power	y = 13,000 + 4x	181,600
Transit staff	y = 32,000 + 3x	158,450
Other	y = 9,100 + x	51,250
		———
Total costs expected in year 3 Q3		737,375
		———

(d)   It is highly unlikely that the actual data for Year 3 Quarter 3 will be the same as that predicted by the calculations for the following reasons:

- The key variable is the number of passengers predicted. The relationships show that any change in the value of x will have an effect on all the cost items except for the premises costs. While trend value calculations are very useful they are necessarily based on historical data and it is always true that past events are not guaranteed to be replicated. It is therefore possible that the predicted growth in passenger numbers will not happen.

- All the cost relationships apart from premises costs are related to the number of passengers. It may well be that, currently or in the future, other cost drivers might affect the costs. For instance, the number of transit units run on time might be the cost driver for penalties charged by the industry regulator.

- It is also possible that the historical seasonal variation from the trend value of 75% in quarter 3 will also not be replicated. This seasonal variation could have been due to factors that happened in Years 1 and 2 and which might fail to recur in Year 3.

- The derivation of the cost relationships may be flawed, either by particular events that will not be repeated or by failure to include some relationships or the inclusion of others that actually are not true.

- All the cost relationships are linear which, while being a useful approximation for reality, rarely reflect real life. For instance, it may be that once a certain level of passengers is reached there may need to be a step change in the number of staff employed, or the amount of power used as more transit units are run.

- The effect of cost increases unrelated to the number of passengers has not been taken into account. Penalties and staff costs have already been mentioned. Another possibility is that the unit cost of power might change.

(e)   The difference between the multiplicative and additive models is the way in which the seasonal variations are expected to impact on the data. The multiplicative model assumes that the variations will be in the form of fixed proportionate increases/decreases from the basic trend figures.

The additive model assumes that the variations will be absolute.

If, as in this case, the underlying trend is upward, the absolute variations under the additive model will get less and less significant over time. The multiplicative model is thus considered generally more appropriate.

274 Q (MAY 08 EXAM)

Key answer tips

In part (a) I4 marks available for a 3 month cash budget. There were some easier parts to this:

- fixed overheads (the trick will be to ignore depreciation)

- variable overheads (with some payment deferred to second month)

- labour cost (very straight forward)

These therefore should have been attempted first. If you also put in the initial capital investment you should now be close to a pass. You are left with sales and materials but should now only need 2/3 marks to pass so anything that makes sense should get you over the pass mark.

Part (b) would rely on students having a fair attempt at materials in part (a). The key was then to calculate the materials savings/increase rather than re-doing the entire budget. But this was the trickiest part of the question. The key trick was to notice that each Trackit used one and half components so to get the cost per Trackit you had to multiply the cost per component given by 1.5.

For part (c) you should have spotted that this new product makes a positive contribution which would have given you a few marks to discuss. Extra calculations such as first year profit and break even point would also have been useful.

(a) **Cash budget**

Cash Budget

For the first three months

	Month 1 £	Month 2 £	Month 3 £	Total £
Receipts				
Sales (W1)	20,160	65,240	148,820	234,220
Capital Investment	250,000			250,000
Total	270,160	65,240	148,820	484,220
Payments				
Materials (W2)		106,800	104,640	211,240
Wages (W3)	14,500	16,500	21,200	52,200
Var. Overheads (W4)	18,850	31,600	39,110	89,560
Fixed O/Hs (W5)	42,000	52,500	52,500	147,000
Total	75,350	207,400	217,450	500,200
Net inflow/(outflow)	194,810	(142,160)	(68,630)	(15,980)
Balance b/f	0	194,810	52,650	0
Balance C/f	194,810	52,650	(15,980)	(15,980)

Workings

(W1) Sales receipts

		Month 1	Month 2	Month 3
Units		1,000	1,500	2,000
Revenue	(@ $140)	140,000	210,000	280,000
Receipts				
– 0 months	15% × 96%	20,160	30,240	40,320
– 1 month	25%		35,000	52,500
– 2 months	40%			56,000
– 3 months	15%			
Total		20,160	65,240	148,820

(W2) Materials cost

		Month 1	Month 2	Month 3	Month 4
Production units		1,450	1,650	2,120	2,460
+ Closing inventory		330	424	492	
		1,780	2,074	2,612	
– Opening inventory		0	(330)	(424)	(492)
Units purchased		1,780	1,744	2,188	
Purchases	(@ $60)	106,800	104,640	131,280	
Payments		0	106,800	104,640	131,280

(W3) Labour cost

		Month 1	Month 2	Month 3	Month 4
Production units		1,450	1,650	2,120	2,460
Wages	(@ $10)	14,500	16,500	21,200	

(W4) **Variable overhead cost**

		Month 1	*Month 2*	*Month 3*	*Month 4*
Production units		1,450	1,650	2,120	2,460
Cost	(@ $20)	29,000	33,000	42,400	
Paid					
– 0 months	65%	18,850	21,450	27,560	
– 1 month	35%		10,150	11,550	
Payments		18,850	31,600	39,110	

(W5) **Fixed overhead cost**

		Month 1	*Month 2*	*Month 3*	*Month 4*
Cost	(excl dep'n)	52,500	52,500	52,500	
Paid					
– 0 months		42,000	42,000	42,000	
– 1 month			10,500	10,500	
Payments		42,000	52,500	52,500	

(b) **Revised component cost**

(i) Cost = $32 per Trackit (or 32 × 1.5 = $48 per unit)

Units purchased		1,780	1,744	2,188
Saved cost	(@ $12)	21,360	20,928	26,256
Savings		0	21,360	20,928

	$
Original net cash flow	(15,980)
Total savings (21,360 + 20,928)	42,288
Revised cash flow	12,212

(ii) Cost = $50 per Trackit (or 50 × 1.5 = $75 per unit)

Units purchased		1,780	1,744	2,188
Extra cost	(@ $15)	26,700	26,160	32,820
Extra payments		0	26,700	26,160

	$
Original net cash flow	(15,980)
Extra costs (26,700 + 26,160)	(52,860)
Revised cash flow	(68,840)

(c)   **REPORT**

To: The shareholders of Q

From: Management Accountant

Date:

Subject: Company Profitability

This report discusses the company's overall profitability and issues raised by the business plan.

Overall Profitability

Overall the Trackit is a profitable product. It will make a contribution of $50 per unit. First year's profits will therefore be:

		$
Contribution	($50 × 27,700 units)	1,385,000
Fixed costs		(840,000)
Bad debts	(5% × 27,700 × $140)	(193,900)
		$351,100

Based on monthly fixed overheads of $70,000 it has a breakeven point of only ($70,000/ $50 contribution per unit) 1,400 units per month. This is achieved as quickly as month two.

Even if the component price rose to $50 so that contribution fell to $40, the breakeven point would be ($70,000/ $40 contribution per unit) 1,750 units which would be achieved by month three.

Cash Position

The problem facing Q is that profitability and cash flow are not the same thing. The company's cash flow forecast shows that the owners' initial $250,000 investment will be completely wiped out within three months of operations. In fact, Q will be overdrawn and may need either further short-term investment or other sources of finance.

The main cause of this problem is in the management of working capital. Materials are paid for within one month of purchase, whereas it takes three months to receive all monies from sales.

This problem will create bigger negative outflows as the company grows – but by month five growth will stop and the cash flow problems will start to ease up. So this is a short term problem and not a long term one.

Impact of changing component prices

It can be seen that the component price could have a significant impact on Q's cash position. If the cost is at the lower end of the scale then the overdrawn position disappears.

Q plans to purchase and pay for 3,524 units in the first three months so that each $1 reduction/increase in the component price will save/cost it 3,524 × 1.5 = $5,286. Therefore to wipe out the original planned overdraft of $15,980 the price would have to fall by:

$$\frac{\$15,980}{\$5,286} = \$3.03 \text{ per component}$$

Q should look for ways to achieve this reduction from the component manufacturer.

Conclusion

It can be seen that the company has short-term cash flow problems. But if it can solve this by either injecting some extra short-term finance or reducing the component cost, long-term profitability is good.

275 THIRTEEN WEEKS (MAY 09 EXAM)

Key answer tips

There are some tricks in almost every part of this question so it is important to be careful in your approach and to ensure you understand all the data that has been provided. However, a lot of marks will be awarded for technique – so if you make a mistake you will not be punished for it more than once.

In part (a) the trick is to account for the bad debts and the loan interest. Recognise that the former is a variable cost and should be included in the calculation of contribution, and the latter is a fixed cost that should be included with other fixed costs. Also, the question asks for the answers in units so there is no need to calculate the margin of safety percentage.

In part (b), the trick is to identify the axis for the diagram. These are given in the question: "budgeted profit to.....the price of raw materials". Draw the relationship as a straight line. We already have one point (the current profit position, so you need to calculate profit from another material cost in order to plot the line required.

For part (c) the trickiest element will be in dealing with a 13 week period and the unusual sums that gives as a result. But the format and style should be familiar to students. The stock adjustment is the hardest part of the requirement, but it should not make the difference between a pass and a fail.

Part (d) is more straightforward – though you should attempt to relate it to part (c) where possible.

(a) **Break even point**

Contribution per unit:	£
Selling price	30.00
Bad debts (2% x 30.00)	(0.60)
Variable selling costs	(1.60)
Raw materials	(9.50)
Production wages	(8.20)
Variable expenses	(1.10)
Contribution	9.00

Fixed costs:		£
Depreciation	(2.70 x 860,000)	2,322,000
Fixed expenses	(3.20 x 860,000)	2,752,000
Loan interest	(9% x 10,000,000)	900,000
		5,974,000

Break even point:

$$= \frac{\text{Fixed costs}}{\text{Contrib'n/unit}}$$

$$= \frac{5,794,000}{9.00}$$

$$= 663,777.8$$

$$= \textbf{663,778 units}$$

Margin of safety

$$= \text{Budgeted sales} - \text{break even point}$$

$$= 810,000 - 663,778$$

$$= \textbf{146,222 units}$$

(b) **Sensitivity analysis**

Current profit (with materials price @ £9.50 per unit)	=	£1,611,000
Change in profit for every £2 change in materials	=	£2 x 810,000 units
	=	£1,620,000

If price is reduced by £2 per unit the revised profit will be:

	=	1,611,000 + 1,620,000
	=	£3,231,000

If price is reduced by £2 per unit the revised profit will be:

	=	1,611,000 - 1,620,000
	=	£(9,000)

Diagram:

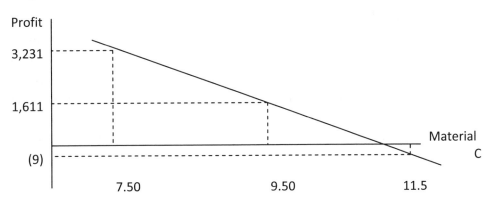

(c)   **Cash Budget**

	Period 1 £	Period 2 £
Receipts		
Sales (W1)	5,143,846	5,314,616
Payments		
Variable selling costs (W2)	240,000	320,000
Materials (W3)	2,139,071	2,201,509
Wages (W4)	1,719,538	1,722,000
Variable expenses (W5)	231,000	231,000
Fixed expenses (W6)	1,376,000	
Loan interest (W7)		450,000
Total payments	5,705,609	4,924,509
Net inflow/(outflow)	(561,763)	390,107
Balance b/f	76,000	(485,763)
Balance C/f	(485,763)	(95,656)

Workings

(W1) Sales Receipts

		Period 1	Period 2
Units		150,000	200,000
Revenue	(@ £30)	4,500,000	6,000,000
Bad debts (@ 2%)		(90,000)	(120,000)
Net sales		4,410,000	5,880,000
Receipts			
– in period	8/13	2,713,846	3,618,462
– in next period	5/13		1,696,154
– brought forward		2,430,000	
Total		5,143,846	5,314,616

(W2) Variable Selling Costs

	Period 1	Period 2
Sales units	150,000	200,000
Cost per unit	£1.60	£1.60
Total cost	£240,000	£320,000

(W3) Materials Cost

	Period 1	Period 2	Period 3
Production Units	210,000	210,000	220,000
	£	£	£
Total cost (@ £9.50 / unit)	1,995,000	1,995,000	2,090,000
+ Closing Inventory			
(Period 1 = 6/13 x £1995k)	920,769		
(Period 2 = 7/13 x £2090k)		1,125,385	
	2,915,769	3,120,385	
– Opening Inventory	(710,000)	(920,769)	
Purchases	2,205,769	2,199,616	
Payments			
brought forward	612,000		
9/13ths in period	1,527,071	1,522,811	
4/13ths in next period		678,698	
Total payments	2,139,071	2,201,509	

(W4) **Labour cost**

	Period 1	Period 2
Production Units	210,000	210,000
	£	£
Wages (@ £8.20)	1,722,000	1,722,000
Payments		
brought forward	130,000	
12/13^{ths} in period	1,589,538	1,589,538
1/13th in next period		132,462
Total payments	1,719,538	1,722,000

(W5) **Variable expenses**

	Period 1	Period 2
Production Units	210,000	210,000
	£	£
Expenses (@ £1.10)	231,000	231,000

(W6) **Fixed expenses**

Depreciation is ignored as it is not a cash flow.

Total fixed expenses = £3.20 x 860,000 = £2,752,000

Half are paid at the beginning of period 1 = £1,376,000

(W7) **Loan interest**

Total interest = £10m x 9% = £900,000

Half are paid at the end of period 2 = £450,000

(d) **Possible problems**

Three areas that may cause concerns for management are:

- The company is overdrawn in the first two quarters of the year. Management may need to consider arranging an overdraft or organising a capital injection into the company

- These figures could be made worse if some cash flows have not been included. For example, tax payments have not been considered nor have dividends from previous years.

- The change in stock policy requires over £200,000 of extra investment — perhaps this could be delayed until cash flows are more stable/positive.

FINANCIAL INFORMATION FOR LONG-TERM DECISION MAKING

276   REGIONAL AIRPORT (MAY 10 EXAM)   Walk *in the footsteps of a top tutor*

Top tutor tips

You should begin questions by reading the requirement first (in the exam hall this can be done during the reading time at the start of the exam). From reading the requirement to this question you can determine that in part (a) you need to calculate the NPV of a project (which can be a time consuming requirement), and that part (b), the discursive element of the question, does not relate in any way to part (a). So this would allow you to attempt part (b). This means that you can pick up a few marks here that you may otherwise miss if you spend too long on part (a).

Part (b) refers to standard deviation – a topic that many students would have struggled with and is likely to be the area that distinguishes the outstanding students from the average students. So don't worry if you are not familiar with this concept. There are still plenty of easy marks available for explaining expected values, NPV, IRR etc. Remember to make points that are relevant to the scenario rather than simply answer in very general terms. But even a mark of only 3 or 4 out of 9 in this section might be enough to distinguish between those students who pass the question and those who fail due to spending too long on part (a).

It will be important to have a methodical approach to part (b). Start by determining whether the question includes tax and/or inflation, the length of the project and the cost of capital. These will influence which proforma is used to answer the question. As is normal in section C questions we discover that it is a short project (4/5 years) and includes both tax and inflation so that we need the columnar NPV proforma. You should therefore set up this proforma and insert the discount factors (which should score an easy mark to get you going).

Now try to deal with the remainder of the information in a logical order. Begin with the initial investment and disposal (putting these in the proforma will gain another easy mark or two). The writing down allowances should come next. These appear very regularly in these types of exam question and you should have practiced lots of them before you enter the exam hall. They are typically worth 4 or 5 marks and you really should aim to achieve as many of these marks as possible by practicing the technique a number of times. It should mean that by this stage you will have around 7 marks for part (a), and if you've already picked up 4 marks for part (b) you've almost got enough marks to pass the question overall.

You are now left with revenue (the toughest part of the calculation), variable costs and overheads. Salaries and overheads are probably the easiest of these elements to deal with so do these first which should be enough to push you up over the pass mark overall. Any reasonable attempt at the remaining, trickier areas should then boost your marks to well over the required target to pass.

(a)

Year	0	1	2	3	4	5
	$000	$000	$000	$000	$000	$000
Sales (W2)		1,620,000	1,782,000	1,960,200	2,156,220	
Variable costs (W3)		(900,000)	(990,000)	(1,089,000)	(1,197,900)	
Lost revenue (W4)		(432,000)	(475,200)	(522,720)	(574,992)	
Salaries		(80,000)	(80,000)	(100,000)	(100,000)	
Increased overheads		(70,000)	(70,000)	(70,000)	(70,000)	
Net operating CF		138,000	166,800	178,480	213,328	
Taxation						
Current Year		(20,700)	(25,020)	(26,772)	(31,999)	
Previous Year			(20,700)	(25,020)	(26,772)	(31,999)
Initial investment	(350,000)				30,000	
Tax depreciat'n (W1)		13,125	22,969	17,227	25,031	17,648
Net CF Post Tax	(350,000)	130,425	144,049	143,915	209,588	(14,351)
DF @8%	1.000	0.926	0.857	0.794	0.735	0.681
Present Value	(350,000)	120,774	123,450	114,269	154,047	(9,773)

NPV   **$152,767**

As the NPV is positive, the project is worthwhile and should be accepted.

Workings

(W1) **Tax depreciation allowances**

Year	Written-down value	Tax saving at 30%	Saving in year	Saving in following year	Cash flow
0	350,000				
1	(87,500)	26,250	13,125		13,125
	262,500				
2	(65,625)	19,688	9,844	13,125	22,969
	196,875				
3	(49,219)	14,766	7,383	9,844	17,227
	147,656				
4	(30,000)				
BA	117,656	35,297	17,648	7,383	25,031
5				17,648	17,648

(W2) Revenue

Year	1	2	3	4
Passenger numbers	180,000	198,000	217,800	239,580
Revenue per customer	$9	$9	$9	$9
Total revenue ($)	1,620,000	1,782,000	1,960,200	2,156,220

(W3) Variable costs

Year	1	2	3	4
Passenger numbers	180,000	198,000	217,800	239,580
Revenue per customer	$5	$5	$5	$5
Total revenue ($)	900,000	990,000	1,089,000	1,197,900

(W4) Lost revenue from cold food

Year	1	2	3	4
Lost passengers (1,200 x 40% x 360)	172,800	190,080	209,088	229,997
Lost contribution	$2.5	$2.5	$2.5	$2.5
Total revenue ($)	432,000	475,200	522,720	574,992

(b)   **Interpretation of project information**

Expected NPV

Net Present Value (NPV) represents the increase in shareholders wealth that should arise if the project is accepted. The project with the biggest NPV, in this case Projects B and C have equal value, will be the most beneficial for shareholders and should be accepted. Because B and C are of equal weighting they are equally preferable.

The 'expected' part of the data provided highlights that the project includes a number of chance points and that probabilities have been allocated to these different potential outcomes to allow a weighted average to be calculated for each set of possibilities. These calculations will ignore any attitudes to risk that the managing director might have – and therefore different risk attitudes might result in different calculations and different decisions by the managing director.

Standard Deviation of Expected NPV

This set of figures aims to give an indication of the risk of each project. It shows how much variation there is from the average. So, the higher the standard deviation, the higher the perceived risk. It can be seen from the data that Project B has the highest standard deviation – this indicates that the expected NPV could typically be up to $50,000 different (either higher or, more importantly, lower). This indicates that Project B is more risky than the other projects (and, likewise, that Project A is the least risky). When coupled with the expected NPV data, a risk averse investor is likely to prefer Project C to B as it has a lower standard deviation.

IRR

The internal rate of return (IRR) gives another indicator of risk. It tells us how high the company's cost of capital (i.e. the cost at which it obtains finance) would have to rise before the expected NPV would fall to zero. Generally, the higher this figure is then the more risky the project becomes. Using this data, Project C now becomes the most risky and least attractive investment.

Deciding factors

The managing director needs to make a decision between the projects. What we know is that B and C are best for investors, A is the least risky, and that Project C would be much less attractive if the cost of capital was to rise. Therefore in order to make his decision, the managing director must determine a number of issues:

- An attitude to risk – a risk seeker might take on project B but an investor who is risk averse might prefer project A.

- The likelihood of a change in the cost of capital – if the cost of capital as been arranged and fixed in advance, then the risk to project C is reduced.

- The validity of the data used – all of this data will be based on predictions about the future and the managing director may want to investigate some of the underlying assumptions that have been made.

277 GYMNASIUM (SEP 2010 EXAM)

Key answer tips

In this question it may be easiest to start with part (c) if you are comfortable with the two techniques for dealing with inflation. Part (b) requires an IRR calculation (this may catch out a lot of students) and cannot be completed until after part (a). In part (a) it is best to use a methodical approach whereby you perform the calculations in the easiest order, for example, putting in the discount factors first, the investment and proceeds next, then doing the tax depreciation, before moving on to the salaries and overheads, before attempting the difficult revenue calculations last.

(a) **Net Present Value**

Year	0	1	2	3	4	5
	$000	$000	$000	$000	$000	$000
New revenue (W2)		3,099,600	3,223,584	3,352,527	3,486,628	
Old revenue (W3)		(2,880,000)	(2,995,200)	(3,115,008)	(3,239,608)	
Salaries		(120,000)	(124,800)	(129,792)	(134,984)	
Increased overheads		(42,000)	(43,680)	(45,427)	(47,244)	
Net operating CF		57,600	59,904	62,300	64,792	
Taxation						
Current Year		(8,640)	(8,986)	(9,345)	(9,719)	
Previous Year			(8,640)	(8,985)	(9,345)	(9,719)
Installation	(100,000)					
Equipment	(50,000)				15,000	
Tax depreciat'n (W1)		5,625	9,844	7,383	10,406	7,242
Net CF Post Tax	(150,000)	54,585	52,122	51,353	71,134	2,477
DF @12%	1.000	0.893	0.797	0.712	0.636	0.567
Present Value	(150,000)	48,744	41,541	36,563	45,241	(1,404)

NPV   **$20,685**

As the NPV is positive, the project is worthwhile and should be accepted.

Workings

(W1) **Tax depreciation allowances**

Year	Written-down value	Tax saving at 30%	Saving in year	Saving in following year	Cash flow
0	150,000				
1	(37,500)	11,250	5,625		5,625
	112,500				
2	(28,125)	8,438	4,219	5,625	9,844
	84,375				
3	(21,094)	6,328	3,164	4,219	7,383
	63,281				
4	(15,000)				
	48,281				
BA	48,281	14,484	7,242	3,164	10,406
5				7,242	7,242

(W2) **Revenue**

Year	1	2	3	4
Occupancy @ 82%	11,808	11,808	11,808	11,808
Average room rate ($)	262.50	273.00	283.92	295.277
Total revenue ($)	3,099,600	3,223,584	3,352,527	3,486,628

Note: Total capacity = 40 rooms x 360 nights = 14,400 room rentals per annum.

(W3) **Old revenue**

Year	1	2	3	4
Occupancy @ 80%	11,520	11,520	11,520	11,520
Average room rate ($)	250.00	260.00	270.40	281.22
Total revenue ($)	2,880,000	2,995,200	3,115,008	3,239,608

(b) **Point of indifference**

The cost of capital at which the hotel will be indifferent to the project will the internal rate of return (IRR) of the project.

This can be calculated as follows:

If we calculate the present values of the cashflows at, say 15%, we get the following:

Net CF Post Tax	(150,000)	54,585	52,122	51,353	71,134	(2,477)
DF @15%	1.00C	0.870	0.756	0.658	0.572	0.497
Present Value	(150,000)	47,489	39,404	33,790	40,689	(1,231)

NPV =$10,141

We can then use this along with the earlier NPV to calculate the IRR:

$$\text{IRR} = 12\% + \frac{20,685}{20,685-10,141} \ (15\% - 12\%)$$

$$\text{IRR} = 12\% + \frac{20,685}{10,544} \ (3\%)$$

$$\text{IRR} = 12\% + 1.96 \ (3\%)$$

$$\text{IRR} = 17.9\%$$

This is the post-tax money cost of capital at which the hotel will be indifferent to accepting/rejecting the project.

(c) **Treatment of inflation**

An alternative approach to dealing with inflation would be to leave the cash flows in present day terms (i.e. do not inflate them), and instead adjust the cost of capital to an effective cost of capital.

This would be calculated as follows:

$$\text{Effective cost of capital} = \frac{1+\text{money cost of capital}}{1+\text{inflation rate}} -1$$

$$\text{Effective cost of capital} = \frac{1.12}{1.04} -1$$

$$\text{Effective cost of capital} = 7.7\%$$

However, a major problem with this method is in dealing with taxation. The tax charges calculated above will be in 'money' terms – that is, they will include an element of inflation. This is particularly true of the tax depreciation charges. Therefore this inflation needs to be 'stripped out' of the money flows to find their equivalent flow in 'real terms'. This matter is further complicated by the fact that the tax is paid over two years.

Overall, this effective method would make the calculation much more difficult. Therefore it would be normal to use the 'money method' illustrated in part (a) to keep the calculation more straightforward.

278   SQ (NOV 07 EXAM)   *Walk in the footsteps of a top tutor*

Tutors top tips

Initially it is not clear from the question whether the new facility is a replacement for or in addition to the existing one – however if there is to be a saving in maintenance costs then the new investment must be a replacement.

What follows is a step by step approach to the question:

1   *Read the requirement – we discover that we are only interested in incremental contribution.*

2   *Read and annotate the question trying to pick up the key pieces of information – is there tax? Inflation? How long will the project last?*

3   *Because it mentions savings in maintenance costs this is what tells us that the new machine will be a replacement for the existing machine.*

4   *Set up workings for corporation tax and WDA's.*

5   *Set up the NPV proforma – you are likely to find it easiest if you set this up in landscape form with the years going across the top of your page. But the answer provides a tabular layout if you find that more comfortable.*

6   *Deal with the section headed 'Proposed new production facility' as this is likely to be a big mark scorer and reasonably easy to deal with. You should be able to put in:*

   ● *the initial investment*

   ● *the scrap proceeds*

   ● *now attempt the capital allowances working. This is a common area in NPV questions and you should practice a lot of these until you can consistently get them right.*

   ● *produce a working for the increase in production capacity (W1)*

   ● *produce a working for the increased contribution per unit (W2)*

   ● *produce a working for the overall net benefit for the investment (W3)*

   ● *transfer the values from this working to the face of the NPV calc.*

7   *Next deal with the maintenance costs – putting them straight onto the face of the NPV calc.*

> 8   *Add together additional contribution and the maintenance cost savings and multiply this by 30% to calculate the tax we will pay on this saving. These savings will have a one year time lag – though this is something that only the very top students are likely to spot and deal with properly. You will need an extra column for your NPV calc now. This shows that when setting up proformas in NPV calculations you should always leave a spare column for just this kind of scenario.*
>
> 9   *Now all that's left is to apply the discount factors and add up the NPV – but leave this final step out if you are short of time.*

(a)   (i)   Relevant cash flows are:

- Investment and residual value
- Increase in contribution due to investment
    - (i)   Increased sales
    - (ii)   Change in variable costs
- Change in tax payment
    - (i)   Change in contribution
    - (ii)   Depreciation/ capital allowances
- Saving in maintenance costs

Fixed overheads are not relevant with the exception of the change in maintenance costs

Year 0 is 2007

Yr	Investment ($)	Contribution + cost saving ($) (W1, W2, W3)	Corporation tax ($) (W3)	Change in tax due to depreciation adjustment ($) (W4)	Net cash flow ($)	DF 12%	Present value ($)
0	(4,000,000)				(4,000,000)	1.000	(4,000,000)
1		1,850,000	(277,500)	150,000	1,722,500	0.893	1,538,193
2		2,320,000	(625,500)	262,500	1,957,000	0.797	1,559,729
3		2,642,000	(744,300)	196,875	2,094,575	0.712	1,491,337
4		2,994,000	(845,400)	147,657	2,296,257	0.636	1,460,419
5	400,000	3,106,000	(915,000)	193,125	2,784,125	0.567	1,578,599
6			(465,900)	129,843	(336,057)	0.507	(170,381)

| | | | | | | NPV | 3,457,896 |

Net present value = $3,457,896

Workings

(W1)   **Sales revenue**

New facility will increase capacity to 130% of previous level

New capacity = 130% × 120,000 = 156,000 units

Sales for next five years

Year	Sales	Increase on previous level	Comment
2008	130,000	10,000	Limited by demand
2009	140,000	20,000	Limited by demand
2010	147,000	27,000	Limited by demand
2011	154,000	34,000	Limited by demand
2012	156,000	36,000	Limited by capacity

(W2) **Change in contribution per unit**

	Existing equipment	New facility
Selling price	150	150
Direct material	(50)	(50)
Direct labour	(30)	(24)
Variable production overhead	(25)	(20)
Variable selling overhead	(10)	(10)
Contribution per unit	35	46

(W3) **Additional contribution, maintenance cost saving, corporation tax on additional contribution**

	Existing equipment	New facility					
		2008	2009	2010	2011	2012	2013
		Year 1	Year 2	Year 3	Year 4	Year 5	Year 6
Sales (units)	120,000	130,000	140,000	147,000	154,000	156,000	–
Contribution per unit ($)	35	46	46	46	46	46	–
Total contribution ($000)	4,200	5,980	6,440	6,762	7,084	7,176	–
Additional contribution ($000)		1,780	2,240	2,562	2,884	2,976	–
Maintenance cost saving		70	80	80	110	130	
Contribution + cost saving		1,850	2,320	2,642	2,994	3,106	
Additional tax (30% of contribution + saving)		555	696	792.6	898.2	931.8	
Payment of tax ($000)							
50% in year		277.5	348	396.3	449.1	465.9	
b/f			277.5	348	396.3	449.1	465.9
Cash flow		277.5	625.5	744.3	845.4	915	465.9

(W4) **Tax depreciation/capital allowances**

It is assumed that the existing facility has no residual value

Year	Written-down value	Tax saving at 30%	Saving in year	Saving in following year	Cash flow
	4,000,000				
2008	(1,000,000)	300,000	150,000		150,000
	—————				
	3,000,000				
2009	(750,000)	225,000	112,500	150,000	262,500
	—————				
	2,250,000				
2010	(562,500)	168,750	84,375	112,500	196,875
	—————				
	1,687,500				
2011	(421,875)	126,563	63,282	84,375	147,657
	—————				
	1,265,625				
2012	(865,625)	259,688	129,844	63,281	193,125
scrap	400,000				
2013				129,843	129,843

(ii)

Tutorial note

You are only asked for two factors. More are included here for completeness.

Other factors which SQ should consider before making decision:

- SQ should consider the validity of the estimates – this calculation is based on forecasts of changes in revenue and costs over a five year period which may not materialise. The company should consider undertaking sensitivity analysis to test how sensitive the NPV is to changes in estimates.

- This analysis is based purely on financial considerations. There may be non-financial risks associated with the project which should also be considered. One possible way of accounting for an element of any risks would be by using a risk-adjusted discount rate.

- If access to capital funding is limited SQ may need to consider alternative used for the $4 million it plans to invest in this project. There may other opportunities which provide a better or less risky return than this proposal which should be considered alongside this.

- SQ should also marketing issues and possible changes in the market in which it operates, for example increased competition from companies producing similar products. This may have an impact on the future demand for the product and the price which can be charged.

- There will be excess capacity in the facility for the first four years if sales volume estimates are accurate. The company should consider whether there are other ways of utilising this additional capacity which could generate additional contribution and improve the returns from the project.

(b) (i) The IRR can be estimated using the formula:

$$IRR \approx A + (B - A)\frac{N_A}{N_A - N_B}$$

where   A   =   lower discount rate

B   =   higher discount rate

NA   =   NPV at rate A

NB   =   NPV at rate B

Calculating an NPV at 20%

Annual net cash flow from project = cash inflow – cash outflow

= $(30,000 – $22,500)

= $7,500

NPV = annual net cash flow × cumulative discount factor at 20% – investment

NPV = $7,500 × 2.106 – $15,000

NPV = $795

Substituting in formula:

A   =   10%

B   =   20%

NA   = $3,652.50

NB   = $795.00

IRR   ≈ 10 + ((10 × 3,652.50) / (3,652.50 – 795.00))

IRR   ≈ 10 + 12.78

IRR   ≈ 22.78 %

(ii) The sensitivity to changes in annual cash inflows is the percentage change in the cash inflows which would change the investment decision, that is which would produce an NPV of $0.

Sensitivity of project   = NPV of project / PV of cash inflow × 100%

Cumulative discount factor for three years at 10% = 2.487

PV of cash inflow   = $30,000 × 2.487   = $74,610

Sensitivity of project   = 3,652.50 / 74,610 × 100%   = 4.90%

279   FRANTISEK COMPANY

Key answer tips

For part (b), in order to get an accurate diagram, the NPV of costs of all three options over periods of 5, 6, 7, 8, 9 and 10 years would need to be calculated, incorporating appropriate residual values and penalty charges. However, it is unlikely this is required given the mark allocation. The diagram provided has been drawn up on the basis of NPVs at 5, 8 and 10 years (see workings) assuming (as an approximation) linearity between these points.

(a)   The approach taken will be to evaluate the NPV of each option over a period of 20 years, assuming the lathes will be sold/returned at the end of that period (see tutorial note for alternative approach using equivalent annual costs).

Purchase A

Time	Cashflow	$	12% discount factor	PV
0	Purchase	(60,000)	1	(60,000)
1–5	Maintenance	(2,000)	3.605	(7,210)
6–10	Maintenance	(2,800)	5.650-3.605	(5,726)
11–15	Maintenance	(3,900)	6.811-5.650	(4,528)
15	Residual value (W1)	6,400	0.183	1,171
15	Purchase	(60,000)	0.183	(10,980)
16–20	Maintenance	(2,000)	3.605×0.183	(1,319)
20	Residual value (W1)	30,400	0.104	3,162
				————
				(85,430)
				————

Purchase B

Time	Cashflow	$	12% discount factor	PV
0	Purchase	(45,000)	1	(45,000)
1–5	Maintenance	(3,100)	3.605	(11,176)
6–10	Maintenance	(5,300)	5.650 – 3.605	(10,839)
10	Residual value (W2)	5,700	0.322	1,835
				(65,180)
+ NPV of cycle repeated in period 10-20 ($65,180 \times 0.322$)				(20,988)
				————
				(86,168)
				————

Rent B

Time	Cashflow	$	12% discount factor	PV
0	Rental	(10,200)	1	(10,200)
1 – 4	Rental	(10,250)	3.037	(31,129)
5 – 9	Rental	(10,995)	5.328 – 3.037	(25,190)
				(66,519)

+ NPV of cycle repeated in period 10–19 ($66,519 × 0.322)   (21,419)

(87,938)

Over a period of 20 years, the option to purchase model A lathes is the most economic, having the lowest NPV of costs.

Tutorial note

An alternative approach would be to calculate the PV of costs of one 'cycle' for each option (of length 15 years, 10 years and 5 years respectively) and divide the result by the appropriate annuity factor to determine the equivalent annual cost. This does, however, assume continual replacement, not taking into account the fact that, for example, the model option is likely to be stopped mid-cycle. PV of costs will not necessarily accrue evenly throughout the cycle.

If valve production is to continue for only five years, the five year PV of cost calculations would be:

Purchase A: $(60,000) + $(7,210) + $30,400 (W1) × 0.567 = $(49,973)

Purchase B: $(45,000) + $(11,176) + $19,200 (W2) × 0.567 = $(45,290)

Rent B: $(10,200) + $(31,129) + $5,000 × 0.567 = $(44,164)

Thus the option to rent model B would now be the most economical.

Workings

(W1) **Residual values – model A**

	$
Purchase price	60,000
First year drop ($\frac{1}{3}$)	(20,000)
Next 4 years drop ($2,400 pa)	(9,600)
Residual value after 5 years	30,400
Next 10 years drop ($2,400 pa)	(24,000)
Residual value after 15 years	6,400

(W2) **Residual values – model B**

		$
Purchase price		45,000
First year drop (1/3)		(15,000)
Next 4 years drop ($2,700 pa)		(10,800)
Residual value after 5 years		19,200
Next 10 years drop ($2,700 pa)		(13,500)
Residual value after 10 years		5,700

(b)

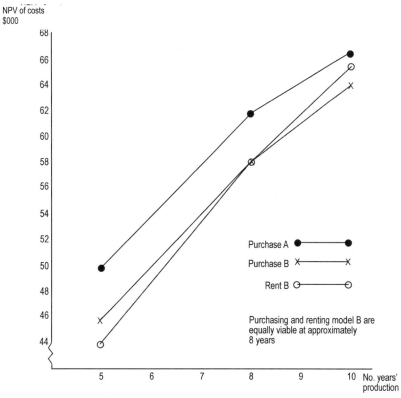

Workings

NPVs at 5 years – as in (a)

NPVs at 10 years – using figures from (a)

Purchase A: $(60,000) + $(7,210) + $(5,726) + [$30,400 − 5 × 2,400] × 0.322 = $(67,011)

Purchase B: $(65,180) [as in (a)]

Rent B: $(66,519) [as in (a)]

NPVs at 8 years

Purchase A: $(60,000) + $(7,210) + $[(2,800) × (4.968 − 3.605)] + [30,400 − 3 × 2,400] × 0.404 = $(61,654)

Purchase B: $(45,000) + $(11,176) + $[(5,300) × (4.968 − 3.605)] + [19,200 − 3 × 2,700] × 0.404 = $(58,916)

Rent B: $(10,200) + $(31,129) + $[(10,995) × (4.564 − 3.037)] + $(2,000) × 0.404 = $(58,926)

(c)   In the above evaluation the decision on which lathe to buy/hire has been based upon expected cash flows and possible lifetimes - the latter being one of the most significant non-financial factors influencing the decision.   As the above analysis shows, over the short time span envisaged by the directors for the use of current production facilities (5–10 years) the option to rent the model B lathe is the most economical for the majority of the time. It would therefore appear to be the most suitable choice.

Other non-financial factors that may influence the decision include:

Flexibility − in view of the uncertainty over the length of time the lathes will be needed, before new technology makes the process redundant, it may be considered that renting is the most flexible option. Extraction from a rental agreement will be easier and more certain.

It may also be possible to swap to renting alternative plant/equipment developed under the new technology.

Certainty of costs, etc − the costs associated with the rental option will generally be more predictable; own maintenance costs and residual values involved in the purchasing options can only be estimates, and could vary considerably - the latter in particular if the lathes are being disposed of following technological development, when they will be virtually obsolete.

Productivity − the relative efficiencies of the two models (A and B) over their lifetimes, in terms of valve production rates, should be taken into account.

Reliability − breakdown/repair frequencies for the two models of lathes need to be established if possible (from own/other users' experience, independent tests, etc).

Alternative uses for purchased lathes − it may be possible to use model A or B lathes for other products, making their purchase a worthwhile investment.

280 INVESTMENT APPRAISAL WITH TAX

Key answer tips

Students are more likely in the exam to present their tables with the years going across in a horizontal row at the top of their tables and the cashflows forming each row below. The answers provided here show the cashflows in columns rather than the years. Either approach is acceptable.

(a) **Evaluation of publishing offers**

Publisher A

Date	Year	Advance	Royalty due	Advance repaid	Tax at 30%[1]	Cash flow	Discount factor	NPV
		$000	$000	$000	$000	$000	16%	$000
01/01/X5	0	80				80.0	1.000	80.000
31/08/X5	1	100				100.0	0.862	86.200
31/10/X6	2		40	(40)	(6.0)	(6.0)	0.743	(4.458)
31/10/X7	3		56	(56)	(14.4)	(14.4)	0.641	(9.230)
31/10/X8	4		80	(80)	(20.4)	(20.4)	0.552	(11.261)
31/10/X9	5		32	(4)	(16.8)	11.2	0.476	5.331
31/10/Y0	6				(4.8)	(4.8)	0.410	(1.968)
								144.614

Publisher B

Date	Year	Advance	Royalty due	Advance repaid	Interest added (2)	Tax at 30%(3)	Cash flow	Discount factor	NPV
		$000	$000	$000	$000	$000	$000	16%	$000
01/01/X5	0	90					90.000	1.000	90.000
31/12/X5	1				9.00	1.350	1.350	0.862	1.164
31/10/X6	2		50	(25)	7.40	(5.040)	19.960	0.743	14.830
31/10/X7	3		70	(35)	4.64	(16.194)	18.806	0.641	12.055
31/10/X8	4		100	(50)	0.10	(24.789)	25.211	0.552	13.916
31/10/X9	5		40	(1.1)	–	(20.985)	17.915	0.476	8.528
31/10/Y0	6					(6.000)	(6.000)	0.410	(2.460)
									137.633

Notes:

(1) Tax is paid on the royalty due, with half being paid in the year that the royalty falls due, and the remainder at the end of the following year. E.g., the tax due on year 2 royalties = 30% × $40,000 = $12,000, with $6,000 being paid in year 2 and $6,000 in year 3. However, in year 3, tax will be due on a further $56,000, i.e. $16,800, with $8,400 payable in year 3 and $8,400 in year 4. This means that the total tax due in year 3 = $6,000 + $8,400 = $14,400, etc.

(2) Interest is added at 10% to the balance outstanding on the royalty advance at the end of each year. The interest schedule will look as follows:

Year	Initial advance $000	Repayment $000	Balance owing $000	Interest added $000	Balance c/f $000
0	90		90		90
1			90	9	99
2		25	74	7.4	81.4
3		35	46.4	4.64	51.04
4		50	1.0	0.10	1.10
5		1.1	NIL		

(3) It is assumed that the interest added to the outstanding royalty advance will qualify for tax relief in the year in which the interest is added. Consequently, in year 1, with no royalty income, there will be an interest expense of $9,000, attracting tax relief of $2,700. Assuming that FAL Company has taxable profits in excess of $9,000 in this year from other sources, the tax relief will result in an increase in cashflow of $1,350 in year 1 (i.e. ½ × $2,700), with the remaining $1,350 being credited in year 2. In year 2 the taxable profit will be $50,000 royalty less the interest added of $7,400, i.e. $42,600. This will attract tax of 0.3 × $42,600 = $12,780, with $6,390 payable in year 2 and the remainder in year 3. This means that the net tax payable in year 2 will be $5,040 ($6,390 − $1,350), etc.

Note that the interest added to the outstanding royalty advance does not result in an actual cashflow in the year in which the interest is added, it is simply an accrued expense which attracts tax relief.

Recommendation:

On the basis of the above evaluation, FAL's management is advised to accept the offer from Publisher A, which shows a higher NPV of $6,981 over the four-year sales period.

(b) Assume that X copies of the book are sold in *each* of the three years 20Y0 to 20Y2. The royalty from Publisher B exceeds that of Publisher A by 10p per copy before tax. Therefore the *differential* NPV between Publisher A and B over this period can be calculated as follows:

Year	Differential	Tax revenue	Net at 30%	Discount factor	Differential cash flow NPV 16%
		$	$	$	$
6	0.1X	0.015X	0.085X	0.410	0.03485X
7	0.1X	0.030X	0.070X	0.354	0.02478X
8	0.1X	0.030X	0.070X	0.305	0.02125X
9		0.015X	(0.015X)	0.263	(0.00395X)
					———
					0.07693X
					———

To eliminate the difference in NPVs between the two offers, this differential NPV would need to equal $6,981, i.e. we have:

0.07693X = 6,981

$$\therefore \quad X \quad = \frac{6,981}{0.07693}$$

$$\therefore \quad X \quad = \textbf{90,745} \cong 91,000 \text{ copies}$$

i.e. to justify changing the advice given in part (a), sales would need to average 91,000 copies in each of the three years 20Y0 to 20Y2. This seems unlikely given that the sales in 20X9 were only forecast to be 80,000 copies.

281 RESTAURANT (NOV 08 EXAM)

Key answer tips

In (a) Calculating the NPV, an average student, who would have omitted price increases and not dealt with variable costs and fixed costs separately, should have been able to layout the proformas and fill in enough information to almost pass this section –6 or 7 marks is a realistic target.

In (b) any attempt at calculating an IRR, even based on incorrect values from a), would have got credit. The actual formula would have got one mark, and the result of around 15% would have enabled the candidate to score full marks here.

In (c), the sensitivity calculation would have been challenging without the right results in a) but any attempt would have got credit. The skill here is in identifying the right cash flows for the sensitivity calculation.

(a)   The approach taken will be to evaluate the NPV of the increases in the relevant cash flows.

Relevant cash Flows:

- Sales

    Incremental cash flows   = £330,000 × 30%   = £99,000

    Applying a 3% price increase year-on-year, the following cash flows will be relevant:

    20X9 : £99,000 × 1.03 = £101,970

    20Y0 : £99,000 × 1.03² = £105,029

    20Y1 : £99,000 × 1.03³ = £108,180

    20Y2 : £99,000 × 1.03⁴ = £111,425

- Costs

  Food and Drink costs incremental cash outflows = (£125,000 + £70,000) × 30%

  = £58,500

  Staff costs incremental cash outflows = £55,000 × 20%

  = £11,000

  Variable costs = 30% × £45,000 ×30%

  = £4,050

  Fixed Costs increases = £10,000

  Total Cost increase = £83,550

Applying a 4% inflation rate year-on-year, the following cash flows will be relevant :

20X9 : £83,550 × 1.04 = £86,892   20Y0 : £83,550 × 1.04² = £90,368

20Y1 : £83,550 × 1.04³ = £93,982   20Y2: £83,550 × 1.04 4 = £97,742

	t=0	20X9	20Y0	20Y1	20Y2	20Y3
		£	£	£	£	£
Investment	(40,000)					
Increase in Cash flows (W1)		15,078	14,661	14,198	13,683	
Tax Savings from Capital Allowances (W2)			6,400	320	256	1,024
additional CT to pay 20%			3,016	2,932	2,840	2,737
Net operating CF	(40,000)	15,078	18,045	11,586	11,099	(1,713)
DF at 8%	1	0.926	0.857	0.794	0.735	0.681
Discounted Cash flows	(40,000)	13,962	15,465	9,199	8,158	(1,167)
NPV	**5,617**					

As the proposed investment yields a positive NPV, it is worthwhile on financial grounds.

Workings

(W1) **Net increases in Cash Flows**

	20X9	20Y0	20Y1	20Y2
Total Revenue increases	101,970	105,029	108,180	111,425
Total Cost Increases	86,892	90,368	93,982	97,742
Increase in Cash flows	15,078	14,661	14,198	13,683

(W2) **Capital Allowances**

Year	Written-down value	Tax saving at 20%
	£30,000	
20X9	£(30,000)	£6,000

Year	Written-down value	Tax saving at 20%
	£10,000	
20X9	£(2,000)	£400
	£8,000	
20Y0	£(1,600)	£320
	6,400	
20Y1	£(1,280)	£256
	£5,120	
20Y2 Bal. Allowance	£5,120	£1,024

(b)　(i)　The IRR can be estimated using the formula:

$$IRR \approx A + (B - A)\frac{N_A}{N_A - N_B}$$

where

	A	=	lower discount rate
	B	=	higher discount rate
	NA	=	NPV at rate A
	NB	=	NPV at rate B

Calculating an NPV at 15%:

Net CF	(40,000)	15,078	18,045	11,586	11,099	(1,713)
DF at 15%	1	0.870	0.756	0.658	0.572	0.497
PV	(40,000)	13,118	13,642	7,624	6,349	(851)
NPV			**(£118)**			

Substituting in formula:

A　=　8%

B　=　15%

NA　=　£5,617

NB　=　(£118)

IRR ≈ 8 + ((7 × 5,617) / (5,617+118))

IRR ≈ 8 + 6.86

IRR ≈ 14.86 %

Interpretation

The IRR can be thought of as the return generated by the project. As the return (around 15%) is greater than the company's cost of capital (8%), then the project should be accepted.

(ii)   The sensitivity to changes in the percentage capacity utilisation is the percentage change in the cash inflows which would change the investment decision.

Sensitivity of project = NPV of project / PV of cash inflow × 100%

Here, the cash inflow under consideration is the total post-tax increase in contribution, as a variation in capacity utilisation will affect our contribution (i.e. revenues less variable costs.)

	20X9	20Y0	20Y1	20Y2	20Y3
Sales Revenue increases (from (a))	£101,970	£105,029	£108,180	£111,425	
Total Variable costs (from (a))	£65,052	£67,654	£70,360	£73,175	
Increased Contribution from investment	£36,918	£37,375	£37,820	£38,250	
Corporation tax 20%		£7,384	£7,475	£7,564	£7,650
Net Post-tax contribution	£36,918	£29,991	£30,345	£30,686	(£7,650)
Discount Factor 8%	0.926	0.857	0.794	0.735	0.681
Discounted Cash flows	£34,186	£ 25,702	£24,094	£22,554	(£5,210)
Total Discounted Cash Flows		**£ 101,326**			

282   CAF COMPANY

Key answer tips

There is a lot of information in this question and it is important that you set out clearly the options that are open to the company and that you will be analysing. This will ensure that you do not become mixed up as you proceed through the question. Clear layout of your NPV calculations will also help, so that you can include earlier calculations in later computations.

(a)   The three options open to CAF Company are:

- Produce Product A for the next two years, then produce Product AA for the subsequent eight years in the UK.

- Produce Product A for the next two years, then sell the UK factory and produce Product AA for the subsequent eight years in Eastern Europe.

- Produce Product A for the next year in the UK, then produce Product X for the subsequent three years in the UK and Product AA in Eastern Europe for the next eight years.

Produce Product A for the next two years, then produce Product AA for the subsequent eight years in the UK.

Year			DF @ 5%	$m
1	Product A sales revenue	$3.0m	0.952	2.856
2	Product A sales revenue	$2.3m	0.907	2.086
				4.942
2	Training and equipment for Product AA introduction	$6m	0.907	(5.442)
3–10	Sales of Product AA	$25 × 200,000 = $5m	7.722 – 1.859	29.315
10	Sell factory	$5.5m + $0.35m − $2m = $3.850	0.614	2.364
	NPV			31.179

Produce Product A for the next two years, then sell the UK factory and produce Product AA for the subsequent eight years in Eastern Europe.

Year			DF @ 5%	$m
−2	Product A sales revenue	See above		4.942
2	Sell factory	$5.5m + $0.35m - $2m = $3.850	0.907	3.492
2	Training and equipment for Product AA introduction	See above		(5.442)
3–10	Sales of Product AA with transport costs	$15 × 200,000 = $3m	7.722 – 1.859	17.589
	NPV			20.581

It would be better therefore to produce Product AA at the UK factory than at the factory in Eastern Europe.

Produce Product A for the next year in the UK, then produce Product X for the subsequent three years in the UK and Product AA in Eastern Europe for the next eight years.

Year			DF @ 5%	$m
1	Product A sales revenue	See above		2.856
1	Buy equipment for Product X	$4m	0.952	(3.808)
2	Product A sales revenue	$3m × 12.5% = $0.375	0.907	0.340
2	Training and equipment for Product AA introduction	See above		(5.442)
2	Product X sales revenue	$70 × 50,000 = $3.5m	0.907	3.175
3	Product X sales revenue	$70 × 75,000 = $5.25m	0.864	4.536
4	Product X sales revenue	$70 × 75,000 = $5.25m	0.823	4.321
4	Sell factory	$5.5m + $0.35m – $2m = $3.850	0.823	3.169
3–10	Sales of Product AA with transport costs	$15 × 200,000 = $3m	7.722 – 1.859	17.589
	NPV			26.736

The best option overall is to produce Product A for the next two years, then produce Product AA for the subsequent eight years in the UK.

(b) (i) Since transport costs only affect the second and third options, the sensitivity of the decision will be tested between the preferred option and the best of the other two, that is the third option.

The NPV of the first option exceeds that of the third option by $31.179m – $26.736m = $4.443m.

Year			Disc factor @ 5%	$m
3–10	Extra transport costs in Option 3	$10 × 200,000	7.722 – 1.859 = 5.863	11.726
	They would have to drop by the amount of the excess NPV for the decision to change			4.443
	Transport costs in Years 3–10 would have to be			7.283

Assuming that this accrues evenly over Years 3–10, this implies an annual transport cost of $7.283m/5.863 = $1.242m instead of $2m, which is a decrease of 38% Hence the decision to choose the first option is not sensitive since transport costs would have to decrease by so much for the decision to change

(ii) A change in the selling price of the factory would be most likely to affect the attractiveness of the second option, since it is sold early in that scenario. However, since this option is so much less attractive than the other two the change would have to be enormous and so the sensitivity of it need not be analysed.

The incremental NPV of the first option is $4.443m whereas the difference between the two options for the selling price at different times is $5.5m × (0.823 − 0.614) = $1.15m. Thus the third option would have to see an increase in the selling price that would make its NPV higher by $4.443m + $1.15m = $5.593m.

(c)   Before relocating to a different country, CAF Company should consider a variety of business issues rather than just financial ones. These are:

- proximity to customer markets
- ease of supply to the factory
- transport links
- availability of skilled staff
- how the remote location should be controlled
- cultural differences
- possible political instability
- taxation rates
- currency risks.

283   PK GLASS COMPANY

Key answer tips

This was a fairly tricky question.   There are several ways in which part (a) could be presented.   It is important to establish your approach and then stick with it.   To reduce the work, the suggested answer below only considers Alternatives 1 and 2.   There is no financial evaluation of continuing with the current situation.

(a)   **Alternative 1**

	Year				
	0	1	2	3	4
	$000	$000	$000	$000	$000
Annual fee		(950)	(950)	(950)	
Saving in rent		10	10	10	
Redundancy (W1)	(21)				
Sale of material	20				
Machinery scrap	70				
Cash before tax	69	(940)	(940)	(940)	
Corporation tax (W2)		156.15	297.15	282	141
Capital allowances (W3)		73.875	73.875		
Net cash flow	69	(709.975)	(568.975)	(658.0)	141
Discount factors		0.893	0.797	0.712	0.636
Present values	69	(634.00)	(453.47)	(468.50)	89.68

Net present value = ($1,397,290)

Alternative 2

	Year 0 $000	1 $000	2 $000	3 $000	4 $000
Prime cost		(700)	(700)	(700)	
Supervisor's salary		(70)	(70)	(70)	
Rent		(50)	(50)	(50)	
Maintenance		(80)	(80)	(80)	
Machine scrap				50	
		(900)	(900)	(850)	
Corporation tax		135	270	270	135
Capital allowances (W3)		21.094	36.915	55.782	39.961
Net cash flows		(743.906)	(593.085)	(524.218)	174.961
Discount factor		0.893	0.797	0.712	0.636
Present value		(664.31)	(472.69)	(373.24)	111.28

Net present value = ($1,398,960)

Alternative 1 is cheaper than Alternative 2. This first alternative should be adopted by the company.

Workings

(W1) **Redundancy payments**

Labour is 30% of $700,000 = $210,000. 10% of this is paid as redundancy.

(W2) **Corporation tax – a net saving**

- Years 1 to 3 cash

   Tax on $940,000 is 30%, i.e. $282,000.

   Half saved in the current year, half saved in the following year.

- Considering the year 0 cash:

	$000
Tax will be saved with the redundancy payment	21
Loss written off on raw material is $100,000 – $20,000	80
	101
30% corporation tax	30.3

   Half saved in year 1, half saved in year 2.

   In summary:

	Year 1 $000	2 $000	3 $000	4 $000
Tax saving	141	282	282	141
Plus	15.15	15.15		
Total	156.15	297.15	282	141

(W3) **Capital allowance schedule**

Year of new alternatives	Year of machine life	Written down value $	30% corporation tax	Cash flows for alternative 2
		1,000,000		
–	1	(250,000)	75,000	Sunk
		750,000		
–	2	(187,500)	56,250	Sunk
		562,500		
1	3	(140,625)	42,188	$(56,250 \times 0.5)$ sunk
				$(42,188 \times 0.5)$ = 21,094
		421,875		
2	4	(105,469)	31,641	$(42,188 \times 0.5) + (31,641 \times 0.5)$
				= 36,915
		316,406		
3	5	(266,406)	79,922	$(31,641 \times 0.5) + (79,922 \times 0.5)$
				= 55,782
	Scrap	50,000		
4	6			$(79,922 \times 0.5)$ = 39,961

In Alternative 1

When machine is sold its written down value was $562,500.

If it is sold for $70,000 then the balancing allowance would be:

$562,500 – $70,000 = $492,500

  $\times$ 30%

Saving in corporation tax $147,750

Half saved in Year 1 and half saved in Year 2, i.e. $73,875 each year.

(b) There is very little financial difference between outsourcing the work to X Packaging Company and keeping the work in-house with a new maintenance company.

Other factors that should be considered include:

If the existing packaging department is closed down, several staff will be made redundant. This will adversely affect morale at W Company. Remaining staff may become unsettled and start looking for work elsewhere.

It is very important to check the reliability of X Packaging Company. W Company will need a reliable, high quality service from X Company. Any problems that arise with the packaging will incur costs for W Company.

Also the customers of W Company will hold W Company responsible for any problems that may in fact have been caused by X Packaging Company.

If X Packaging Company do provide a high quality service then W Company will have the release of valuable resources within the firm that can then be redeployed within the company.

284 H (MAY 08 EXAM)

Key answer tips

In Part (a), calculating the NPV, an average student, who would have omitted indexation and not dealt with variable costs and fixed costs separately, should have been able to layout the proformas and fill in enough information to almost pass this section – 6 or 7 marks is a realistic target.

In (b) any attempt at calculating an IRR, even based on incorrect values from a), would have got credit. The actual formula would have got one mark, and the result of around 13% would have enabled the candidate to score full marks here.

In (c), the alternative calculation involving the real cost of capital is independent from numerical answers in a) and b); Students should have been able to grab 2/3 marks here from a theoretical point well covered in class.

(a)

	20X8	20X9	20Y0	20Y1	20Y2	20Y3	20Y4
	$000	$000	$000	$000	$000	$000	$000
Sales (W1)		578.45	613.27	662.09	675.94	722.69	
Variable prod^n costs (W2)		(259.56)	(277.83)	(302.83)	(312.14)	(336.94)	
Fixed prod^n costs		(105.00)	(110.25)	(115.76)	(121.55)	(127.63)	
Non-production costs		(82.40)	(84.87)	(87.42)	(90.04)	(92.74)	
Net operating CF		131.49	140.32	156.09	152.21	165.38	
Taxation							
Current Year		(19.72)	(21.05)	(23.41)	(22.83)	(24.81)	
Previous Year			(19.72)	(21.05)	(23.41)	(22.83)	(24.81)
Investment in machinery	(500)					100.00	
Tax savings wrt CAs (W3)							
Current Year		15.00	12.00	9.60	7.68	15.72	
Previous Year			15.00	12.00	9.60	7.68	15.72
Net CF Post Tax	(500)	126.76	126.54	133.23	123.25	241.14	(9.09)
Discount Factor @14%	1.000	0.877	0.769	0.675	0.592	0.519	0.456
Present Value	(500)	111.17	97.31	89.92	72.96	125.15	(4.14)
NPV	**(7.62)**						

The NPV calculations show that the project should not be undertaken, as it shows a negative result of around $7,600.

(W1) **Sales revenue**

Growth in price **and** volume need to be incorporated:

		$000
		$000
20X9	$540 \times 103\% \times 1.04$	578.45
20Y0	$540 \times 105\% \times 1.04^2$	613.27
20Y1	$540 \times 109\% \times 1.04^3$	662.09
20Y2	$540 \times 107\% \times 1.04^4$	675.94
20Y3	$540 \times 110\% \times 1.04^5$	722.69

(W2) **Variable Production Cost**

		$000
20X9	$240 \times 103\% \times 1.05$	259.56
20Y0	$240 \times 105\% \times 1.05^2$	277.83
20Y1	$240 \times 109\% \times 1.05^3$	302.83
20Y2	$240 \times 107\% \times 1.05^4$	312.14
20Y3	$240 \times 110\% \times 1.05^5$	336.94

(W3) **Tax Savings and Capital Allowances**

Year		Written-down value	Tax saving at 30%	Saving in year	Saving in next year
		$	$	$	$
		500,000			
20X9	CA@20%	(100,000)	30,000	15,000	
		———			
		400,000			
20Y0	CA@20%	(80,000)	24,000	12,000	15,000
		———			
		320,000			
20Y1	CA@20%	(64,000)	19,200	9,600	12,000
		———			
		256,000			
20Y2	CA@20%	(51,200)	15,360	7,680	9,600
		———			
		204,800			
20Y3	BA	(104,800)	31,440	15,720	7,680
		———			
	Proceeds	100,000			
20Y4					15,720

(b)   The post-tax money cost of capital at which H would be indifferent to accepting or rejecting the project is the Internal Rate of Return. With another discount factor of, say, 5%:

Net CF	(500)	126.76	126.54	133.23	123.25	241.14	(9.09)
DF @14%	1.000	0.952	0.907	0.864	0.829	0.784	0.746
PV	(500)	120.68	114.78	115.10	102.17	189.06	(6.78)
NPV	**135.01**						

NPV is now positive.

IRR = 14% – (7.62 / (7.62 + 135)) × 9% = 13.52%

(c)   In (a) above, each of the annual sales revenues and cost cash flows have been inflated using their respective inflation rates and then, the money cost of capital has been used to discount the resulting cash flow.

An alternative method would have been the calculate the real cost of capital, using the following formula: (1+ money cost of capital)/(1+ inflation) = (1+ real cost of capital)

And then, discount each of the un-inflated cash flows by the real post-tax of capital.

285   PRINTING COMPANY (MAY 05 EXAM)

Key answer tips

Common errors

*   Not appreciating that the calculations needed to reflect the 'additional contribution' ($896K), rather than the new contribution ($2,496K).

*   Phasing incorrectly both the tax relief and the tax on the incremental contribution.

*   Calculating an incorrect figure for the balancing charge.

*   Not discounting the contribution figures.

*   Not realising that the answer to part (a) needed to be the numerator for the sensitivity tests (the principle of the 'own figure' rule would have gained marks for many students).

(a)

Year	Old machine	New machine	Contrib'n (W1)	Corp'n tax (W2)	Tax dep'n (W3)	Net cash flow	Discount factor	Present value
	$000	$000	$000	$000	$000	$000		$000
0	400	(3,000)				(2,600)		(2,600)
1			896	(134.4)	90	851.6	0.877	746.9
2			896	(268.8)	174.4	801.6	0.769	616.4
3			896	(268.8)	147.7	774.9	0.675	523.1
4			896	(268.8)	110.7	737.9	0.592	436.8
5		300	896	(268.8)	144.8	1,072	0.519	556.4
6				(134.4)	97.4	(37)	0.450	(16.7)
								263.0

Net present value = $263,000. Hence the new machine is worthwhile.

Workings

(W1) **Contribution**

	Original		New
Revenue	$4m	× 1.20	$4.8m
Less variable costs	($2.4m)	× 0.80 × 1.20	($2.304m)
Contribution	$1.6m		$2.496m

Increase in contribution = $2.496m − $1.6m = $896,000

(W2) **Corporation tax**

30% of $896,000 = $268,800

50% paid in the current year, and 50% paid in the following year

(W3) **Tax depreciation / capital allowances**

Year	Written down value	Tax saving	Cash timing	Total cash
	$	$	$	$
	3,000,000			
1	(750,000)	** 180,000	90,000	90,000
	2,250,000			
2	(562,500)	168,750	90,000 + 84,375	174,375
	1,687,500			
3	(421,875)	126,563	84,375 + 63,282	147,657
	1,265,625			
4	(316,406)	94,922	63,281 + 47,461	110,742
	949,219			
5	(649,219)	194,766	47,461 + 97,383	144,844
scrap	300,000			
			97,383	97,383

** Capital allowance in Year 1 must be adjusted to reflect the balancing charge arising on the sale of the existing machine.

Balancing charge is $400,000 − $250,000 = $150,000

Hence, capital allowance is $750,000 − $150,000 = $600,000

Tax saving is 30% of $600,000 = $180,000

(b)   Sensitivity analysis is part of uncertainty and risk analysis.

It typically involves posing 'what if" questions. The NPV may be recalculated under different conditions, for example, what would happen if demand fell by 10%? How would the result be affected if variable costs are 5% higher, etc?

Alternatively, it is possible to discover the maximum possible change in one of the parameters before the opportunity becomes non-viable. This maximum possible change is usually expressed as a percentage. It is called the sensitivity margin.

$$\text{Sensitivity margin} = \frac{\text{NPV}}{\text{PV of flow under consideration}}$$

Each variable is tested independently. The smaller the change required to change the initial decision, then the more sensitive is that variable and the more justified is a manager in taking more care over the value of that variable.

(i)   **Contribution**

The PV of contribution can reduce by $263,000 before the proposal has a zero NPV.

Contribution from new project is $2,496,000 per annum. When contribution changes, the tax liability will also change – this should also be considered.

Year		Cash ($000)	Discount factor	Present value
1 – 5	Contribution	2,496	3.433	8,568.8
1 – 5	Tax	(374.4)	3.433	(1,285.3)
2 – 6	Tax	(374.4)	3.012	(1,127.7)
				6,155.8

Tax = 30% of 2,496 = $748,800 (split 50:50)

$$\text{Sensitivity margin} = \frac{\$263,000}{\$6,155,800} \times 100 = 4.3\%$$

Contribution can fall by just 4.3% before the project ceases to be viable.

(ii)   **Tax rate**

The PV of the tax cash flow:

Year		Cash ($000)	Discount factor	Present value
1	Tax depreciation	90	0.877	78.93
2	Tax depreciation	174.4	0.769	134.1
3	Tax depreciation	147.7	0.675	99.7
4	Tax depreciation	110.7	0.592	65.5
5	Tax depreciation	144.8	0.519	75.2
6	Tax depreciation	97.4	0.450	43.8
1 – 5	Corp tax	(134.4)	3.433	(461.4)
2 – 6	Corp tax	(134.4)	3.012	(404.8)
				(368.97)

$$\text{Sensitivity margin} = \frac{\$263,000}{\$368,970} \times 100 = 71.3\%$$

Tax rates would have to increase by 71.3% before the project would cease to be viable.

286 HOTEL GROUP (NOV 09 EXAM)

Key answer tips

This can be a difficult question at first glance. But if you use your exam technique well there should be enough marks available that any well prepared student should be able to gain a pass. There are 'easy' marks in part (a) for standard areas such as the discount factors, the investment, the tax depreciation (which with lots of practice you should be well prepared for in time for the real exam) etc. Part (b) on sensitivity analysis is a part of the syllabus that many students can find difficult. But, again, there will be easy marks for available for providing the formula and making any reasonable progress towards an answer – even if your answer to part (a) is incorrect you will not get punished again in part (b).

(a)   **Net Present Value of the proposed hotel investment ($000)**

$000	1 Jan 20X0	Year 1 20X0	Year 2 20X1	Year 3 20X2	Year 4 20X3	Year 5 20X4	Year 6 20X5
Sales revenue (W3)		130	234	252	284	306	
Guest related costs (W4)		(20)					
Other fixed costs (W2)		(65)	(68)	(68)	(70)	(72)	
Net taxable flows		45	166	184	214	234	
Tax on profit							
Paid in year		(14)	(25)	(28)	(32)	(35)	
Paid in following year			(13)	(25)	(27)	(32)	(35)
Investment in building	(650)					650	
Investment in equipment	(250)					100	
Tax relief on equipment (W1)		7	14	11	9	4	
Net cash flow	(900)	38	142	142	164	921	(35)
Discount factor at 8%	1.000	0.926	0.857	0.794	0.735	0.681	0.630
Present value	(900)	35	122	113	121	627	(22)

Net present value = $96,000.

Since the investment has a positive NPV it is financially worthwhile.

Workings

(W1) WDA's on equipment

	$000	Tax relief	Year 1	Year 2	Year 3	Year 4	Year 5
Yr 0 Cost	250						
Yr 1 tax depreciation	(50)	15	7	8			
	────						
NBV	200						
Yr 2 tax depreciation	(40)	12		6	6		
	────						
NBV	160						
Yr 3 tax depreciation	(32)	10			5	5	
	────						
NBV	128						
Yr 4 tax depreciation	(26)	8				4	4
	────						
NBV	102						
Yr 4 sale	(100)						
	────						
Balancing allowance	2	0*					
Total tax relief			7	14	11	9	4

* the total tax relief on the balancing allowance will be $2,000 x 30% = £600, paid in two instalments of £300. But as figures are being rounded to the nearest £1,000 these have been ignored in the calculation of the NPV. It should not materially affect the decision to invest.

(W2) Fixed costs

Base cost = $40,000 (guest related costs) + $25,000 (other fixed costs)

Year	Base cost	Indexation	Money cost
	$		$
1	65,000	100	65,000
2	65,000	104	67,600
3	65,000	105	68,250
4	65,000	107	69,550
5	65,000	110	71,500

(W3) Sales revenue

Year	Base revenue	Increase in guest numbers (index)	Indexation	Money cost
	$			$
1	130,000	100	100	130,000
2	130,000	180	100	234,000
3	130,000	190	102	251,940
4	130,000	210	104	283,920
5	130,000	220	107	306,020

(W4) **Guest related costs**

Year	Base cost	Increase in guest numbers (index)	Indexation	Money cost
	$			$
1	20,000	100	100	20,000
2	20,000	180	104	37,440
3	20,000	190	105	39,900
4	20,000	210	107	44,940
5	20,000	220	110	48,400

(b) **Sensitivity analysis**

Sensitivity analysis $= \dfrac{NPV}{PV \text{ of fixed charges}} \times 100\%$

$= \dfrac{96,000}{73,470 \text{(W1)}} \times 100\%$

$= 131\%$

(W1) **Present value of other fixed charges**

Year	Base cost	Index-ation	Money cost	Tax relief (year)	Tax relief (next)	Net flows	DF @ 8%	PV
	$		$	$	$	$		$
1	25,000	100	25,000	(3,750)		21,250	0.926	19,677
2	25,000	104	26,000	(3,900)	(3,750)	18,350	0.857	15,726
3	25,000	105	26,250	(3,938)	(3,900)	18,412	0.794	14,619
4	25,000	107	26,750	(4,013)	(3,937)	18,800	0.735	13,818
5	25,000	110	27,500	(4,125)	(4,102)	19,273	0.681	13,125
6					(4,125)		0.630	(3495)
								73,470

287 X COMPANY

Key answer tips

Part (a) is deceptively straightforward. The six notes given in the question may suggest complicated relevant cost concepts. In actual fact, they simply explained timing of cash flows and inflation implications.

Layout in part (a) is important. Consider how to show the cash flows at the beginning of your answer.

Part (b). Many candidates may struggle to answer this part. One approach is to let 'x' represent the number of delegates. Then consider the point of indifference.

(a) **Current training costs**

Year	Travel and accommodation	Course costs	Cash	14%	PV
	$000	$000	$000		$000
1	548.1	72.3	620.4	0.877	544.1
2	575.5	74.1	649.6	0.769	499.5
3	604.3	75.9	680.2	0.675	459.1
4	634.5	77.8	712.3	0.592	421.7
5	666.2	79.8	746.0	0.519	387.2
					2,311.6

| Variable costs | Fixed costs |

NPV = $2,311,600

Travel and accommodation

$870 × 100 people × 6 courses = $522,000 in Year 0

× 1.05

∴ Cost in Year 1 (+ 5%) $548,100

Course costs

$11,750 × 6 courses = $70,500 in Year 0

× 1.025

∴ Cost in Year 1 (+ 2.5%) $72,263

Alternative method

In real terms:

Travel and accommodation – variable cost

Year	Real cash	Annuity factor	Present value
	$000		$000
1 – 5	522.0	3.933	2,053

Real rate = $\dfrac{1.14}{1.05}$ = 1.0857

Year 5 annuity factor = $\dfrac{1 - 1.0857^{-5}}{0.0857}$ = 3.933

Course costs – fixed cost

Year	Real cash $000	Annuity factor	Present value $000
1 – 5	70.5	3.6755	259.1

Real rate = $\dfrac{1.14}{1.025}$ = 1.1122

Year 5 annuity factor = $\dfrac{1 - 1.1122^{-5}}{0.1122}$ = 3.6755

∴ NPV = 2,053 + 259.1 = 2,312.1

i.e. $2,312,100

E-learning

Year	Hard-ware $000	Licences $000	Tech Mgr $000	Camera $000	Trainers $000	Broad-band $000	Net $000	DF	PV $000
0	1,500	35					1,535		1,535.0
1		35	30	24	12	30	131	.877	114.9
2		35	31.8	24	12.7	28.5	132	.769	101.5
3		35	33.7	25.4	13.5	27.1	134.7	.675	90.9
4		35	35.7	27.0	14.3	25.7	137.7	.592	81.5
5	(50)		37.9	28.6	15.1	24.4	56	.519	29.1
									1,952.9

Fixed costs   Variable cost

PV = $1,952,900

Therefore, assuming a 100% take-up of training courses, the e-learning option should be selected.

(b)

Tutorial note

To score marks, some attempt to divide costs into variable cost per delegate and fixed cost must be demonstrated.

(i)

	Current courses $000	E-learning $000	Change in cost $000
PV of Fixed cost	259.1	1,858.5 (W1)	1,599.4
PV of Variable cost per delegate	20.53 (W2)	0.944	19.586

Workings

(W1) E-learning PV of Broadband = 94.4 ($000)

∴ PV of fixed cost = 1,952.9 − 94.4 = 1,858.5

(W2) **Current courses**

PV of variable cost = 2,053 for 100 delegates

∴ Variable cost per delegate = 20.53

(W3) **E-learning**

PV of variable cost = 94.4 for 100 delegates

∴ Variable cost per delegate = 0.944

∴ Point of indifference = $\dfrac{1,599.4}{19.586}$ = 81.7 i.e. 82 delegates

Alternative method (i)

At point of indifference, let x	=	Number of delegates
PV of current courses	=	PV of e-learning
i.e. 259.1 + 20.53x	=	1,858.5 + 0.944x
20.53x − 0.944x	=	1,858.5 − 259.1
19.586x	=	1,599.4
∴ x	=	81.7

∴ Require minimum of 82 delegates

Alternative method (ii)

Using annual equivalents (AE):

$$AE = \frac{PV \text{ of costs}}{Annuity \text{ factor}}$$

AE of current courses $= \dfrac{259.1 + 20.53x}{3.433}$ =   75.47 + 5.98x

AE of e-learning $= \dfrac{1,858.5 + 0.944x}{3.433}$ =   541.36 + 0.275x

Then let 75.47 + 5.98x = 541.36 + 0.275x

When solved, x = 81.7

(ii) Only 100 employees, so a BEP of 82 seems fairly high.

If switch to e-learning, there are very high fixed costs and relatively negligible variable costs. Hence, e-learning costs are not very sensitive to volume. If the number of delegates increases significantly, training costs will become more attractive with e-learning.

The variable cost of current courses is $20,530 (PV) per person, however e-learning is only $944 (PV) per person.

288 JK (NOV 06 EXAM)

Key answer tips

The numbers used in this question are very large and it is advisable to work to the nearest $m. Remember to be consistent with your rounding and work to 1 decimal place greater than your final answer.

(a)

$m	Year 0	Year 1	Year 2	Year 3	Year 4	Year 5
Capital	(50)				1	
Sales revenue (W1)		120.00	132.30	145.53	150.03	
Variable cost (W2)		(85.00)	(96.18)	(108.55)	(114.89)	
Fixed production cost		(4.00)	(4.32)	(4.67)	(5.04)	
Fixed selling and distribution cost		(2.00)	(2.12)	(2.25)	(2.38)	
Fixed administration cost		(1.00)	(1.05)	(1.10)	(1.16)	
Cash flow before tax (excl. capital)		28.00	28.63	28.96	27.56	
Tax on profit		(4.20)	(4.20)	(4.29)	(4.34)	(3.98)
			(4.29)	(4.34)	(3.98)	
Tax relief on capital (W3)		1.88	3.28	2.46	4.07	3.01
Net cash flow	(50)	25.68	23.42	22.79	23.31	(0.97)
Discount factor at 12%	1	0.893	0.797	0.712	0.636	0.567
Present value	(50)	22.93	18.67	16.23	14.83	(0.55)
Net present value (to 1 d.p.)	22.1					

Since the investment has a positive NPV it is financially worthwhile.

Workings

(W1)

	Year 1	Year 2	Year 3	Year 4
Sales price	1,200	1,260	1,323	1,389.15
Sales units	100,000	105,000	110,000	108,000
Sales revenue ($m to 2 d.p.)	120.00	132.30	145.53	150.03

(W2)

	Year 1	Year 2	Year 3	Year 4
Variable production cost/ unit	750	810	874.8	944.784
Variable selling cost per unit	100	106	112	119
Total variable cost per unit	850	916	986.8	1,063.8
Sales units	100,000	105,000	110,000	108,000
Variable cost ($m to 2 d.p.)	85.00	96.18	108.55	114.89

(W3)

	$000	Tax relief	Year 1	Year 2	Year 3	Year 4	Year 5
Yr 0 Cost	50,000						
Yr 1 tax depreciation	12,500	3,750	1,875	1,875			
NBV	37,500						
Yr 2 tax depreciation	9,375	2,812.5		1,406.25	1,406.25		
NBV	28,125						
Yr 3 tax depreciation	7,031.25	2,109.375			1,054.69	1,054.69	
NBV	21,093.75						
Yr 4 sale	1,000						
Balancing allowance	20,093.75	6,028.125				3,014.06	3,014.06
Total tax relief			1,875	3,281.25	2,460.94	4,068.75	3,014.06
In $m to 2 d.p.			1.88	3.28	2.46	4.07	3.01

(b)

Tutorial note

The NPV is positive at 12% and the IRR must be considerably higher than this rate. The highest discount figure given in the tables is 20% and this can be used to find a second NPV. Alternatively a higher discount rate, such as 40% could be calculated to find an NPV closer to the actual IRR. Both answers would be acceptable and as there are only 3 marks available no time should be wasted recalculating to find negative NPVs. Hence extrapolation is used here.

Net cash flow	(50)	25.68	23.42	22.79	23.31	(0.97)
Discount factor at 20%	1	0.833	0.694	0.579	0.482	0.402
Present value	(50)	21.39	16.25	13.20	11.24	(0.39)
Net present value (to 1 d.p.)		11.7				

The IRR $= 12\% + [22.1/(22.1 - 11.7)] \times (20 - 12)\%$

$= 12\% + 17\%$

$= 29\%$

(c) The real rate of return excludes the impact of inflation and can be used to discount cash flows shown at a common price level (usually today's prices).

The money rate of return includes the effect of inflation and can be used to discount money cash flows which include the effect of inflation.

The relationship between the two is given by:

$(1+m) = (1+r)(1+i)$ where m = money rate of return, r = real rate of return and i = the rate of inflation.

The real rate of return can be used if inflation applies to all cash flows equally as the real rate of return can be found by taking the money rate given in the present value tables and adjusting for the rate of inflation. This can then be applied to the real cash flows in each year. In this way each cash flow does not need to be adjusted for inflation.

If cash flows are affected by different rates of inflation, as is the case for JK plc, then to use the real rate would mean using a different discount rate for each cash flow. This is very cumbersome so it is normally preferred to inflate the cash flows to their money equivalent. Discount rates given in the PV tables can then be used to discount the net cash flows to arrive at present values.

THE TREATMENT OF UNCERTAINTY IN DECISION MAKING

289   A BANK (MAY 08 EXAM)

Key answer tips

A long and complex question on relevant cash flows, but the Examiner helps by splitting requirements into sizeable chunks.

In part (a) , calculating bank balances for all types of customers should have been feasible by most students, however the calculation of investment revenue foregone would only have been incorporated by the best prepared. Nevertheless, 2 marks would have been given for the calculation of transaction charges under each option, with one mark for interest revenue and a couple for opportunity costs – the savings income at 3%. (2 marks for the calculation of net balances under the existing option.)

In part (b), even if filled up incorrectly, the two-way data table should have been setup by most and grabbed a mark. Correct calculations could have marked as much as a mark each, and the correct working would also have got the students well over the 4 marks required to pass this question. There would also be marks on the marking scheme for mentioning the need to obtain probabilities for the forecasts of demand and level of loan balance, and how this would enable the decision maker to calculate the probability that the advertising campaign will generate a profit that is higher than the existing profit.

In part (c) a couple of marks were available for general comments on other factors. Follow-through marks from the options in the two-way data table could have been as many as 3. This should remind students that easy marks are available in each requirement and that even a poor performance in the previous requirements should not discourage candidates to attempt all parts of questions.

(a)   (i)   **Continuing with existing bank account**

	Workings	Profit £
Business Customers	1 million × (1–20%) = 800,000	
Routine Transactions per year	800m	
Transaction charges	800m × 0.60	480,000,000
Customers with positive bank balances	45% × 800,000 = 360,000	
Interest paid to 'positive' customers	£2,000 average balance × 0.1% × 360,000	(720,000)
Customers with negative bank balances	55% × 800,000 = 440,000	
Interest charged to overdrawn customers	£4,000 average balance × 20% × 440,000	352,000,000
Current profit		**£831,280,000**

Note: Current business customers net balances:

(360,000 × £2000 average balance) – (440,000 × £4000 average overdraft) = £(1,040,000,000)

Account Option One

	Workings	Profit £
Business Customers	1 million × 1.05 = 1,050,000	
Charges	£10 × 12 months × 1,050,000 customers	126,000,000
Customers with positive bank balances	45% × 1,050,000 = 472,500	
Interest paid to 'positive' customers	£2,000 average balance × 0.5% × 472,500	(4,725,000)
Customers with negative bank balances	55% × 1,050,000 = 577,500	
Interest charged to overdrawn customers	£4,000 average balance × 20% × 577,500	462,000,000
Business Customers net balances	(472,500 × £2000 average balance) – (577,500 × £4000 average overdraft) = £(1,365,000,000)	
Opportunity cost	(£1,365,000,000 – £1,040,000,000) × 3%	(£9,750,000)
Option 1 annual profit		**£573,525,000**

Account Option Two

	Workings	Profit
		£

Business Customers	1 million × 1.10 = 1,100,000	
Customers with positive bank balances	45% × 1,100,000 = 495,000	
Interest paid to 'positive' customers	NIL	
Customers with negative bank balances	55% × 1,100,000 = 605,500	
Interest charged to overdrawn customers	£4,000 average balance × 20% × 605,500	484,000,000
Business Customers net balances	(495,000 × £2000 average balance) – (605,000 × £4000 average overdraft) = £(1,430,000,000)	
Opportunity cost	(£1,430,000,000 – £1,040,000,000) × 3%	(11,700,000)

Option 2 annual profit	**£472,300,000**

Conclusion

On the basis of the above calculations, the bank should keep its existing charging structure.

(b) (i) **Profit matrix**

Average Balance	Number of loans	250,000	280,000	300,000
£7,500		£106,750,000 (see working)	£133,000,000	£150,500,000
£14,000		£188,000,000	£224,000,000	£248,000,000
£15,000		£200,500,000	£238,000,000	£263,000,000

Example Working

250,000 loans × arrangement fee £500	£125,000,000
Add:	
Interest income 5% × £7500 × 250,000 loans	£93,750,000
Less: Advertising campaign cost	(£112,000,000)
Profit	£106,750,000

(ii) The bank needs to calculate whether going ahead with the advertising campaign makes financial sense, i.e. whether there are incremental profits to be gained compared to its existing profits.

Existing profits =

Arrangement fees £500 × 200,000 loans	=	£100,000,000
Add: Revenue from Interest charges		
£5000 × 5% × 200,000 loans	=	£50,000,000
Total	**=**	**£150,000,000**

The two-way table shows that two of the three options at the £7500 increase level do not result in incremental profit for the bank, and that the third only increases this value by £500,000.

However, as there are seven options out of nine that do give a positive incremental profit, the bank should be advised to proceed with the campaign.

For decision making, we need to obtain probabilities for the forecasts of Demand and level of loan balance. Having obtained this information it will be possible to calculate the probability that the advertising campaign will generate a profit that is higher than the existing profit, in other words, the probability that we will benefit from the campaign. This information will help the management understand some of risks involved in the decision.

Other considerations include:

- Extra staff level and / or training to support the increase in business due to the higher number of loans;

- The bank's attitude to risk in view of the conclusions in i), particularly with an analysis of the probability of each outcome occurring.

290 TICKET AGENT

Key answer tips

Note that for part(b) of the question you are only asked to assess scenario 2 – so don't waste time applying the analysis to scenario 1. The mark allocation is generous for part (b) considering the small amount of work required. It is therefore important that you attempt this part of the question, even if part (a) goes badly. As long as you carry forward your answer from part (a) and use the correct technique, you will score well in part (b) and not be punished again for any mistakes made in part (a).

(a)   **Scenario 1**

Expected demand = 350 tickets per concert

Scenario 2

	Probability	Demand	EV
Popular artistes	0.45	500	225
Lesser known artistes	0.30	350	105
Unknown artistes	0.25	200	50
			380

Expected demand = 380 tickets per concert

Pay-off table showing profit (W1, W2, W3)

Demand

		200	350	500
	200	120	120	120
Purchase	300	(57)	225	225
Level	400	(204)	219	360
	500	(246)	177	600

Expected values

		EV
200 tickets	120×1	120
300 tickets	$(57) \times 0.25 + 225 \times 0.75$	154.5
400 tickets	$(204) \times 0.25 + 219 \times 0.3 + 360 \times 0.45$	176.7
500 tickets	$(246) \times 0.25 + 177 \times 0.3 + 600 \times 0.45$	261.6

Scenario 1

If demand is 350 tickets on average, the ticket agent can purchase 200, 300, 400 or 500 tickets. The expected profits would be $120, $225, $219 or $177 respectively.

Optimum purchase level is 300 tickets per concert. This would give an expected profit of $225 per concert.

Scenario 2

The optimum purchase level is 500 tickets per concert, which will give an expected profit of $261.60 per concert.

(b)   If demand is going to be 200 tickets for a concert then the optimum purchase level would be 200 tickets and the expected profit would be $120 per concert.

Similarly, if demand is going to be 350 tickets then the best profit would be $225 and if demand is going to be 500 tickets then the best profit would be $600.

If the ticket agent has perfect information he will always make the best decision.

Expected profit	$=$	$120 \times 0.25 + 225 \times 0.3 + 600 \times 0.45$
	$=$	$367.50 given perfect information.

Value of perfect information = $367.50 - 261.60$	$=$	$105.90 per concert
Annual value = 105.90×60 concerts	$=$	$6,354

Workings

(W1) Profit per ticket at different purchase levels

Purchase level	Discount			Profit per ticket sold
200	20%	20% × $3	=	60p
300	25%	25% × $3	=	75p
400	30%	30% × $3	=	90p
500	40%	40% × $3	=	$1.20

(W2)

Purchase level	Demand	Sales
200	200	200
200	350	200
200	500	200
300	200	200
300	350	300
300	500	300
400	200	200
400	350	350
400	500	400
500	200	200
500	350	350
500	500	500

(W3) Each profit calculation consists of up to three elements:

1 the profit on the units sold;

2 the cost of the units which are unsold and returned;

3 the value of the returns

Value of returns = $3.00 × 60% × 10% = 18p per return

e.g.

Buy 200   Demand 200   Sales 200 tickets × 60p   = $120

Buy 200   Demand 350   Sales 200 tickets × 60p   = $120

Buy 300   Demand 200   Sales 200 tickets and returns 100 tickets

	$
Sales 200 tickets × (3.00 – 2.25)	150
Returns 100 tickets × 18p	18
	168
Cost of returns 100 tickets × $2.25 (30% discount)	(225)
	(57)

291   THE RS GROUP

Key answer tips

You should attempt parts (b) and (c) first as they will be less time pressured and easier overall. If you can score a good mark in these parts of the question you can afford to do less well in part (a). It also means that if you run out of time you will be doing so on the tougher part of the question. For decision trees it is often useful to turn your page on its side so that it is less cramped and easier to mark.

(a)

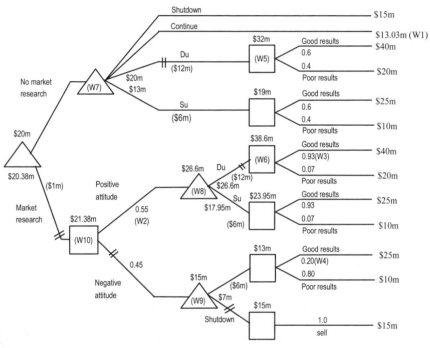

Key

☐	=	Outcome point
Δ	=	Decision point
Du	=	Deluxe upgrade
Su	=	Standard upgrade

Workings

(W1) Profits total if decline at rate of 10% pa =

$$2 + 2 \times 0.9 + 2 \times 0.9^2 + 2 \times 0.9^3 + \ldots + 2 \times 0.9^9$$

This may be worked out in full, or using the sum of a geometric progression:

$$S = \frac{a(1 - r^n)}{1 - r}$$

where

a	=	1st term	=	2
r	=	common ratio	=	0.9
n	=	no of terms	=	10

$$\therefore \text{Sum} = \frac{2(1-0.9^{10})}{1-0.9} = \$13.03m$$

(W2), (W3) & (W4)

A probability tree is the best way of understanding the dependent probabilities given in the question.

The probability of the prediction depends upon whether the results are good or poor.

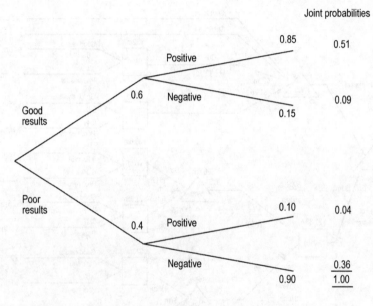

(W2) p(positive attitude) = 0.51 + .04 = 0.55

(W3) p(good results/positive attitude) = $\dfrac{p\,(\text{good results and positive attitude})}{p\,(\text{positive attitude})}$

$$= \frac{0.51}{0.55} = 0.93$$

(W4) p(good results/negative attitude) = $\dfrac{p\,(\text{good results and negative attitude})}{p\,(\text{negative attitude})}$

$$= \frac{0.09}{0.45} = 0.20$$

(W5) Expected profit = $40m × 0.6 + $20m × 0.4 = $32m

(W6) Expected profit = $40m × 0.93 + $20m × 0.07 = $38.6m

(W7) The deluxe upgrade provides an expected profit of ($32m – $12m) $20m. This is the best option if market research is not undertaken.

(W8) Deluxe upgrade profit = $38.6m – $12m = $26.6m

Standard upgrade profit = $23.95 – $6m = $17.95m

∴ Deluxe upgrade is recommended.

(W9) Standard upgrade profit = $7m

Shutdown and sell site = $15m

∴ Shutdown and sell is recommended.

(W10) Expected profit = $26.6m × 0.55 + $15m × 0.45 = $21.38m

(b) In order to maximise expected profit:

- Undertake the market research.
- If the attitude is positive upgrade deluxe.
- If the attitude is negative shutdown and sell the site.

(c) **Comment**

(i) This assumes that all estimates are correct; sensitivity analysis could be carried out on each estimate.

(ii) It is assumed that the RS Group are risk neutral since expected values have been used – although the highest ENPV has a lower risk than the next highest.

(iii) Ten years is a long time period over which to predict profits – a reasonable period for the life of the store but this makes estimation difficult.

(iv) Comments on the courses of action open to the RS Group have been made in (a).

292 EHI COMPANY

Key answer tips

This question combines three syllabus areas – basic investment appraisal, sensitivity analysis and expected values. This reinforces the principle that, in order to do well in this exam, you will need a broad syllabus coverage. But it is still a difficult question overall and you should only attempt it when you are fully comfortable with these three topics.

Assumption: all receipts are at the end of the year to which they relate.

(a) (i) Low technology route

Present value of development costs is $800,000 \times \dfrac{1}{1.1}$ = $727,273

to be viable, the present value of receipts must be at least $727,273.

Contribution from each treatment is $43,000 – $40,000 i.e. $3,000 with the first receipt at time 2 and continuing to time 10. The discount factor for time 2 to 10 at 10% is:

$t_1 \to 10$	6.1446
$(t_1 \quad)$	0.9091
$t_2 \to 10$	5.2355

minimum number of treatments (t) is:

$$t = \frac{727,273}{3,000 \times 5.2355} = \frac{727,273}{15,706.5} = 46.3 \text{ treatments}$$

(ii)   High technology route

Present value of development cost is:

$$\frac{\$6.3m}{3} \times \text{annuity factor } 1 \rightarrow 3 \text{ at } 10\%$$

$$= \$2.1m \times 2.487 = \$5,222,700$$

To be viable the present value of receipts must be at least $5,222,700.

The contribution from each treatment is $43,000 − $18,000 i.e. $25,000 with the first receipt at time 4 continuing to time 10.

The discount factor for time 4 to 10 at 10% is:

$$
\begin{array}{ll}
t_1 \rightarrow 10 & 6.1446 \\
\underline{(t_1 \rightarrow 3)} & \underline{(2.487)} \\
t_4 \rightarrow 10 & 3.6576
\end{array}
$$

minimum number of treatments (t) is:

$$t = \frac{5,222,700}{25,000 \times 3.6576} = \frac{5,222,700}{91,440} = 57.11 \text{ treatments}$$

(iii)   For high and low technology to be equally viable they must have the same net present value

i.e. $3,000 \times 5.2355t - 727,273 = 25,000 \times 3.6576t - 5,222,700$

$15,706.5t = 91,440t + 4,495,427$

$75,733.5t = 4,495,427$

$t = 59.36$

i.e. 59.4 treatments per annum

(b)   To draw the sensitivity diagram we need to calculate NPV at 2 levels of demand, and connect the points with straight lines.

Demand level	PV of receipts		PV of development cost		NPV	
	Low tech	High tech	Low tech	High tech	Low tech	High tech
0	0	0	−727,273	−5,222,700	−727,273	−5,222,700
50	15,706.5× 50	91,440× 50				
	= 785,325	= 4,572,000	−727,273	−5,222,700	58,052	−650,700

Sensitivity diagram for the low and high tech operations

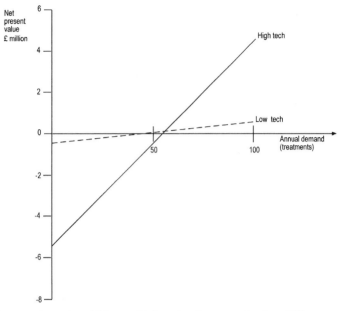

(c)   The maximum that should be paid for the forecast is the difference the information makes to the expected NPV.

Expected NPV without information

The expected number of treatments = $0.4 \times 30 + 0.6 \times 65 = 51$

From the graph in (b) it can be seen that if demand is 51 treatments then the low technology treatment should be developed and the expected NPV of the project is $15,706.5 \times 51 - 727,273 = \$73,759$.

Expected NPV with information

Forecast	Actual	(W1) Probability	Decision	NPV	Probability $\times NPV$
weak	weak	0.368	do nothing	0	0
	strong	0.048	do nothing	0	0
strong	weak	0.032	high tech	−2,479,500 (W2)	−79,344
	strong	0.552	high tech	720,900 (W3)	397,937
				Expected NPV	318,593

gain from forecast = 318,593 − 73,759 = $244,834 which is the maximum that should be paid.

Workings

(W1) Probability

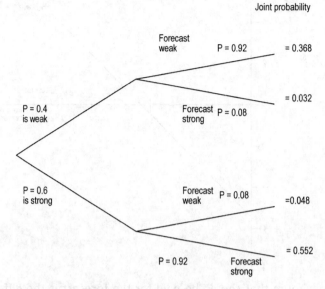

Joint probability

(W2) NPV = 91,440 × 30 − 5,222,700 = −2,479,500

(W3) NPV = 91,440 × 65 − 5,222,700 = 720,900

293   H PRINTING (MAY 07)

Key answer tips

Although part (b) does not specifically ask you to give examples from the scenario in part (a), as there are 10 marks allocated to part (b) it is not sufficient just to make general points. Also, using specific examples may make it easier to put across the points than just using general arguments.

(a)

	$	
Relevant costs		
Material A	15,000	10,000 sheets @ $1.50/sheet.
		Material is in regular use so must be costed at market price
Material B	2,000	250l @ $8 per litre.
		Cost of entire order as surplus is unlikely to be used.
Direct labour	500	50 hours @ $10/hr.
		Overtime only as 100 hours idle time already paid for un guaranteed minimum wage.
Machine A	240	20 hrs @ $12/hr.
		Opportunity cost of lost income.

Machine B	100	25 hrs @ $4/hr.
		Cost of overtime as machine fully utilised in normal hours.
Despatch	400	Additional cost which will be incurred due to this contract
Total relevant costs	18,240	
Not relevant		
Technical report	0	This is a sunk cost.
Supervisor	0	This cost will be incurred irrespective of decision on project.
Overhead	0	This cost is not specific to the project and will be incurred irrespective of decision.
Profit mark-up	0	Profit mark-up is not a relevant cost of the project.

(b) Relevant costs are those costs that are appropriate to a specific management decision.

It is appropriate to use relevant costs when considering the best use of resources at a particular point in time, and to base prices on relevant costs on a one-off basis to win a contract to utilise spare capacity if fixed costs are unchanged by the decision and there is no other profitable work. However, in the long run it is important to ensure that prices are set at a level which covers the underlying fixed costs of the organisation.

When routinely reporting profit within an absorption costing system, the costs will be attributed to the work based on the time taken, overhead absorption rates and inventory levels. These costs will be different from those used in the relevant cost calculation.

For example, in the case of the direct labour costs in this scenario, under absorption costing the labour cost would be reported as 150 hours at a rate of $8 per hour, that is $1,200 rather than the relevant cost of $500. In addition, fixed overheads of $20 per hour of direct labour will be allocated to the work even though the actual level of fixed costs will not be changed by undertaking the contract. In both cases the costs reported for the contract will be greater than the additional costs incurred, thus decreasing the reported profit on the contract.

In the case of machine A, the cost allocated to the contract will be 20 hours at the running cost of $5 per hour. This is lower than the relevant cost which took account of the impact on the overall profitability of the company of not selling spare machine hours. This means that reported profit on the contract is higher, but the income reported elsewhere in the company will be lower.

If the total costs allocated to the contract under the absorption costing system are greater than the relevant costing on which the price is based, it is possible that a contract which was worthwhile from a decision-making perspective may appear to make a loss. This could present a problem to a manager whose performance is measured based on the results from the absorption costing system.

294 D RESCUE (MAY 07 EXAM)

(a)

Tutorial note

As all members pay the same fee it is also possible to calculate the expected number of members and multiply that by the fee.

Number of members	Income $	Probability	Probability × income $
20,000	2,000,000	0.3	600,000
30,000	3,000,000	0.5	1,500,000
40,000	4,000,000	0.2	800,000
		Expected value	2,900,000

(b)

Tutorial note

As the variation in possible costs is even, the expected value is equal to the expected average cost.

Expected value of call-out costs

= $(⅓×50 + ⅓×50×0.8 +⅓×50×1.2) = $50

Since the variation is these costs is equally distributed their expected values will equal the values given.

Expected value of call-out costs = $50

Expected value of admin costs = $10

Expected contribution per member = $100 – $50 – $10 = $40

Fixed costs = $1,100,000

Breakeven point = 1,100,000 / 40 = 27,500 members

(c)

	Call-out cost $ per member	Admin cost $ per member	Contribution $ per member
Costs 20% higher than expected	60	12	28
Costs as expected	50	10	40
Costs 20% lower than expected	40	8	52

Profit = Contribution – Fixed costs, so the two-way data table is as follows:

	Contribution per member		
	$28	$40	$52
Number of members			
20,000	($540,000)	($300,000)	($60,000)
30,000	($260,000)	$100,000	$460,000
40,000	$20,000	$500,000	$980,000

(d) The table above shows managers the possible values of profit and loss which could occur depending on the number of members and the level of costs. The addition of probabilities to the analysis gives an indication of the likelihood of the outcome as follows:

Profit/(loss)	Probability	
$980,000	⅓×0.2 = 0.067	
$500,000	⅓×0.2 = 0.067	–
$460,000	⅓×0.5 = 0.167	
$100,000	⅓×0.5 = 0.167	
$20,000	⅓×0.2 = 0.067	Probability of a profit = 0.535
($60,000)	⅓×0.3 = 0.100	
($260,000)	⅓×0.5 = 0.167	
($300,000)	⅓×0.3 = 0.100	
($540,000)	⅓×0.3 = 0.100	Probability of a loss = 0.467

This shows that, although at the most likely level of members the expected profit is $100,000, the business could make a profit of $980,000 or a loss of $540,000. In fact there is a 47% chance that a loss will be made.

The decision of the managers will depend on their attitude to risk. As there is a high possibility of making a loss, risk averse managers might be reluctant to undertake any activity which results in such a high probability of loss.

(e)

Tutorial note

To gain full marks from this section you will need to illustrate your answer with a number of examples from the scenario.

The analysis of cost data based on the factors which drive particular costs as proposed by the managers is an example of activity based costing (ABC). ABC was developed in response to criticisms of traditional costing systems which analyse all costs purely in terms of the level of activity, in this case the number of members.

The collection of further data and the analysis of costs against other variables should give managers an improved understanding of the factors which affect the costs of the service provided, enabling better planning and control and making it possible to develop a pricing strategy based on the actual costs of providing a service to specific categories of members. For example:

- The age of the vehicle will probably affect the annual cost as older vehicles are likely to break down more often.

- The make and model of the vehicle may affect the level of difficulty of repairs and the time taken.

- More experienced drivers may maintain their cars better, leading to fewer breakdowns. They may also be able to resolve minor problems without the need for a call-out.

- The average annual mileage will probably affect the number of breakdowns – for example a high annual mileage is likely to mean more breakdowns per year.

295 MP ORGANISATION (NOV 05 EXAM)

Key answer tips

Part (a) of the question asks for each combination of cost and revenue values and so was looking for nine combinations. Look carefully at the question requirements because the level of uncertainty and time horizon of the various revenues and costs differ. Remember to discuss your analysis, however briefly, and state a recommendation. In this question very little discussion was possible because the NPVs of all combinations were positive but, as a minimum, state why you have made your recommendation.

Ten marks were available for part (b) and so your answer should be detailed. State how probabilities can be used in (i) and (ii) in general and then illustrate your explanation with data from the scenario where possible. Any discussion of the usefulness of the two approaches should have earned marks.

(a) **Production costs**

Script writing and travel costs of $14,000 have already been incurred. These are sunk and not relevant.

Other costs are:

	Most likely $000	Optimistic $000	Pessimistic $000
Production director's fee	100	100	100
Other costs	120	108	132
	220	208	232
Incurred in year 1 so discount at 15%	0.870	0.870	0.870
Present value	191.4	180.96	201.84

Advertising/promotion/marketing costs.

No uncertainty

$000	Year 0	Year 1	Year 2	Year 3	Year 4	Year5
Cash flow	15	10	10	5	5	5
Discount factor	1	0.870	0.756	0.658	0.572	0.497
Present value	15	8.7	7.56	3.29	2.86	2.484
Total present value	$39.894					

The total present value of costs is:

Most likely = $191.4 + $39.9 = $231.3

Optimistic = $181.0 + $39.9 = $220.9

Pessimistic = $201.8 + $39.9 = $241.7

Revenues

Year	Gross revenue	Most likely	Discount factor	Present value
	$000	$000		$000
1	400	100	0.870	87
2	600	150	0.756	113.4
3	450	112.5	0.658	74.025
4	50	50	0.572	28.6
5	30	30	0.497	14.91
				317.935

This could be 20% lower, $381,522, or 20% lower, $254,348.

The combinations are:

Revenues	Costs	NPV
PVs in $000	PVs in $000	
381.5	231.3	150.2
317.9	231.3	86.6
254.3	231.3	23.0
381.5	220.9	160.6
317.9	220.9	97.0
254.3	220.9	33.4
381.5	241.7	139.8
317.9	241.7	76.2
254.3	241.7	12.6

The NPVs of all combinations are positive and MP Organisation should continue with the production of the film.

(b) **Notes for the management meeting**

(i) If probabilities can be assigned to the most likely, optimistic and pessimistic revenues and costs, then the expected NPV can be calculated by finding the joint probability of each revenue and cost combination, multiplying this with the NPV, and then adding all of the resulting figures.

For example, if the probability of most likely revenue is 0.5 and the probability of most likely cost is 0.6, the joint probability is $0.5 \times 0.6 = 0.3$. The NPV of this combination is $86,600 so the probability $\times$ NPV = $25,998. This is done for each combination given in the table calculated in (a) and summed to find the expected NPV.

Probabilities may be determined by considering data available on past films but there is likely to be some degree of subjectivity. This is because each film is unique and past information may not be a good predictor of future performance.

The expected value may give useful information when a decision is being repeated many times and reliable probabilities can be calculated. For one-off decisions, as in this case, the expected value may be misleading as the actual NPV will range from $12,600 to $160,600.

(ii) Simulation models identify key variables in a decision and assign random numbers to each variable in a proportion which is thought to be in accordance with the underlying probability distribution. For example, if the most likely outcomes are thought to have a 50% probability, optimistic outcomes a 30% probability and pessimistic outcomes a 20% probability, random numbers, representing those attributes, can be assigned to costs and revenues in those proportions.

A powerful computer is then used to repeat the decision many times and give management a view of the likely range and level of outcomes. Depending on the attitude to risk, a more informed decision can be taken.

This approach may help to model what is essentially a one-off decision using many possible repetitions. It is only of any real value, however, if the underlying probability distribution can be estimated with some degree of confidence and this may be difficult for MP Organisation.

296 HEALTH CLINIC (MAY 06 EXAM)

Key answer tips

There are 6 marks available for producing a decision tree. Each branch should represent the possible options. Do not forget to include an option of no investment.

(a) See decision tree below.

Health clinic

Requirement (a)

Year 1 Demand

Years 2 & 3 Demand

Investment B

Investment A

No Investment

Low
Medium
High

Low
Medium
High

Low
Medium
High

Low
Medium
Low
Medium
High
Medium
High

Low
Medium
Low
Medium
High
Medium
High

Low
Medium
Low
Medium
High
Medium
High

(b)   Three options are available. With no investment, facilities will have to be bought in to satisfy medium and high demand in all three years.

The probabilities of low, medium or high demand in years 2 and 3 are dependent on the level of demand in year 1, so a good place to start may be to calculate joint probabilities.

Year 1 demand	Year 2 and 3 demand	Probability		
Low	Low	0.3×0.4	0.12	
Medium	Low	0.5×0.3	0.15	
High	Low	0.2×0.0	0.00	**Total 0.27**
Low	Medium	0.3×0.6	0.18	
Medium	Medium	0.5×0.4	0.20	
High	Medium	0.2×0.3	0.06	**Total 0.44**
Low	High	0.3×0.0	0.00	
Medium	High	0.5×0.3	0.15	
High	High	0.2×0.7	0.14	**Total 0.29**

No further investment

Year 1	Annual cost ($)	Additional facilities ($)	Total cost ($)	Probability	Expected cost
Low	300,000	0	300,000	30%	$90,000
Medium	300,000	100,000	400,000	50%	$200,000
High	300,000	250,000	550,000	20%	$110,000
					$400,000

Years 2 & 3	Annual cost ($)	Additional facilities ($)	Total cost ($)		
Low	300,000	0	300,000	27%	$81,000
Medium	300,000	100,000	400,000	44%	$176,000
High	300,000	250,000	550,000	29%	$159,500
					$416,500
					$\times$ 2 years =
					$833,000

Total present value of cost $1,233,000

Investment in facility A requires additional facilities to be bought in for high demand. Don't forget to include the fixed and variable cost for high demand. The additional facility cost only represents the cost of the *additional* facilities.

Investment in facility A	Annual fixed cost ($)	Annual variable cost ($)	Additional facility cost ($)	Total cost ($)	Probability	Expected cost ($)
Year 0 cost						500,000
Year 1						
Low	100,000	150,000		250,000	30%	75,000
Medium	100,000	250,000		350,000	50%	175,000
High	100,000	250,000	150,000	500,000	20%	100,000
						350,000
Years 2 & 3 expected cost per year:						
Low	100,000	150,000		250,000	27%	67,500
Medium	100,000	250,000		350,000	44%	154,000
High	100,000	250,000	150,000	500,000	29%	145,000
						$366,500 × 2 years = $733,000

Total present value of cost $1,583,000

Investment in facility B provides sufficient capacity to cover all levels of demand so there are no additional facility costs.

Investment in facility B	Fixed cost ($)	Variable cost ($)	Total cost ($)	Probability	Expected cost ($)
Year 0 cost					800,000
Year 1 expected cost:					
Low	200,000	100,000	300,000	30%	90,000
Medium	200,000	150,000	350,000	50%	175,000
High	200,000	200,000	400,000	20%	80,000
					345,000
Years 2 & 3 expected cost per year:					
Low	200,000	100,000	300,000	27%	81,000
Medium	200,000	150,000	350,000	44%	154,000
High	200,000	200,000	400,000	29%	116,000
					$351,000 × 2 years = $702,000
Total present value of cost					**$1,847,000**

The expected cost of the three options are:

- No investment $1,233,000
- Facility A $1,583,000
- Facility B $1,847,000

So on financial grounds the decision would be not to invest and to use existing facilities.

(c) Non-financial factors may be important and include:

- The health clinic will have to use additional facilities to satisfy demand which are not under its direct control. This may lead to quality and reliability issues.
- Demand has only been estimated for the forthcoming three years. A longer time period may need to be considered. By not carrying out investment now it may be more difficult to expand facilities in three years' time if required.
- Reliance on outside contractors may mean that the health clinic is vulnerable to price rises which would be out of its control.
- Employees may become demotivated if there is a perception that the health clinic is unwilling to invest in new facilities.

Users of the health clinic may prefer to be treated in a known environment.

297 THEATRE (NOV 06 EXAM)

Key answer tips

The key to success in this question is to recognise that there are nine possible outcomes – three different audience sizes times three different levels of contribution.

(a)

Ticket sales revenue ($)	Confectionery sales revenue ($)	Total sales revenue ($)	Joint × probability	Sales revenue × probability ($)
7,500	900	8,400	.5 × .3 = .15	1,260
7,500	1,500	9,000	.5 × .5 = .25	2,250
7,500	3,000	10,500	.5 × .2 = .10	1,050
10,000	1,200	11,200	.3 × .3 = .09	1,008
10,000	2,000	12,000	.3 × .5 = .15	1,800
10,000	4,000	14,000	.3 × .2 = .06	840
12,500	1,500	14,000	.2 × .3 = .06	840
12,500	2,500	15,000	.2 × .5 = .10	1,500
12,500	5,000	17,500	.2 × .2 = .04	700
Total			1.00	11,248

The expected value is $11,248 – $10,000 = $1,248. Therefore it is worthwhile engaging MS for the concert.

(b) The data table shows profit values from each combination of ticket sales revenue and contribution from confectionery sales revenue. So, for example, for 300 people and $3 per person total sales revenue is $8,400 (from (a)) – $10,000 fee = $1,600 loss.

Confectionery sales revenue	$3 per person	$5 per person	$10 per person
Ticket sales revenue			
300 people	(1,600)	(1,000)	500
400 people	1,200	2,000	4,000
500 people	4,000	5,000	7,500

(c) The probabilities can be applied to the data in the table to calculate expected values for each combination of outcomes.

People/contribution	Profit/loss ($)	Joint probability	Profit $\times$ probability ($)
300/$3	(1,600)	$.5 \times .3 = .15$	(240)
300/$5	(1,000)	$.5 \times .5 = .25$	(250)
300/$10	500	$.5 \times .2 = .10$	50
400/$3	1,200	$.3 \times .3 = .09$	108
400/$5	2,000	$.3 \times .5 = .15$	300
400/$10	4,000	$.3 \times .2 = .06$	240
500/$3	4,000	$.2 \times .3 = .06$	240
500/$5	5,000	$.2 \times .5 = .10$	500
500/$10	7,500	$.2 \times .2 = .04$	300
		1.00	1,248

It can be seen that the expected value of the decision is $1,248 but the actual possible outcomes range from a loss of $1,600 to a profit of $7,500. The probability of making a loss is 0.4 and the probability of making a profit is 0.6. There is a probability of 0.26 of making a profit above $2,000.

Depending on the management's attitude to risk the decision may be different. A risk averse management may choose not to proceed as there is a substantial risk of making a loss. If management are risk seekers or risk neutral, then they are likely to proceed despite this risk of loss as there is the opportunity to make a good profit and the expected value is positive.

(d) The value of perfect information is given by the expected value of the best strategy when the information is possessed less the expected value of the best strategy when the information is not possessed.

If it were known that ticket sales were for 300 people and contribution from confectionery sales were $3 or $5, then the management would choose not to proceed. Otherwise the management would proceed. The expected value would be $490 higher ($240 + $250 which are the values of the loss-making outcomes) with perfect information and this is its value.

MANAGING SHORT TERM FINANCE

298   MERTON INC

Key answer tips

To answer part (a), you need to review each of the elements of the working capital cycle, doing calculations to enable a comparison with the average data for the media sector before reaching a conclusion on whether there is room for improvement. To reach a conclusion in part (b) on whether the factor's offer is recommended, you will need to calculate both the costs and benefits to Merton. This is best done by comparing a "before" and "after" position, remembering that we have information relating to both the immediate reduction in receivables days with a further reduction over the next two years. Both will need to be examined to be able to form an opinion.

(a)   (i)   **Discussion of working capital management**

The Finance Director believes that substantial improvement in the area of working capital is needed. It should be noted that sales revenue increased by 10.3% in 20X6 and 9.8% in 20X5, so an increase in working capital to support this growth is to be expected. This discussion will focus on the year ending 30 April 20X6, but balance sheets (statements of financial position) for earlier periods would allow a more complete analysis.

Inventory management

The average inventory days for the sector are 100 days and Merton Inc has marginally improved inventory days from 111 days in 20X5 to 110 days in 20X6. The increase in inventory (12.5%) is similar to the increase in cost of sales (14%) and therefore greater than the increase in sales revenue (10.3%). The reasons why the inventory days are higher than the sector, and the reason why inventory has increased at a greater rate than sales revenue, should be investigated. There may be no cause for concern in the area of inventory management.

Receivables management

The increase in receivables of 71% is much greater than the increase in sales revenue (10.3%) and it is therefore not surprising to find that receivables days have deteriorated from 61 days in 20X5 to 94 days in 20X6. This compares unfavourably with the sector average of 60 days, which the factoring company believes is achievable for Merton Inc. It is possible that the increase in sales revenue has been achieved in part by relaxing credit terms, but poor management of receivables is also a possibility.

Cash management

The cash balance has declined from $16m to $1m due to financing an increase in current and non-current assets. The optimum level of cash needs to be found from cash flow forecasts and the expected transactions demand for cash. The increased reliance on overdraft finance is unwelcome, since the company is now carrying a total of $46m of debt and incurring annual interest of $3.6m: it is not clear how this debt is going to be repaid. Comments on the cash management of Merton Inc are not very useful in the absence of benchmark data.

Payables management

Merton Inc is just over the sector average payables period of 50 days, having experienced an increase in payables days from 38 days to 52 days. This is not a cause for alarm, unless the increasing trend continues due to the company's increasing reliance on short-term financing. In fact, taking full advantage of offered trade credit is good working capital management, in the absence of any incentives for early settlement.

Operating cycle and other ratios

The operating cycle of Merton Inc has lengthened from 134 days to 152 days and remains greater than the operating cycle for the sector, which is 110 days (100 + 60 − 50). If the receivables days were reduced from 94 days to 60 days, the current operating cycle would fall to 118 days, which is similar to the sector average.

The current ratio of 3.1 is less than the sector average of 3.5, but in 20X5 it was almost twice the sector average at 6. This could indicate that in 20X5 the company was holding too much cash ($16m), but cash reserves might have been built up in preparation for the purchase of non-current assets, which have increased substantially.

The movement from a substantial cash surplus to a substantial overdraft has been the main factor causing the quick ratio to decline from 3.3 to 1.7, substantially below the sector average of 2.5.

Working capital financing

Merton Inc is increasingly relying on short-term finance from trade credit and a large overdraft. An increase in long-term finance to support working capital is needed. It would be interesting to know what limit has been placed on the overdraft by the lending bank.

Conclusion

Only in the area of receivables management is there clear evidence to support the Finance Director's view that substantial improvement is needed in the area of working capital management. It is possible that this could be achieved by accepting the factor's offer. Attention also needs to be directed toward the company's financing strategy, which from a working capital perspective has become increasingly aggressive.

Analysis of key ratios and financial information

	20X6			20X5	
Inventory days	(365x36/120) =	110 days	(365x32/105.3) =		111 days
Receivables days	(36x41/160) =	94 days	(365x24/145) =		60 days
Payables days	(365x17/120) =	52 days	(365x11/105.3) =		38 days
Current ratio	(78/25) =	3.1	(72/12) =		6.0
Quick ratio	(42/25) =	1.7	(40/12) =		3.3
Operating cycle	(110+94−52) =	152 days	(111+61−38) =		134 days
Turnover/NWC	160/53 =	3.0	145/60 =		2.4
Growth rates:	20X6		20X5		
Sales revenue	160/145 =	10.3%	145/132 =		9.8%
Cost of sales	120/105.3 =	14.0%	105.3/95.7 =		10.0%
Op expenses	30/26.0 =	15.4%	26.0/23.5 =		10.6%
Inventory	36/32 =	12.5%			
Receivables	41/24 =	71%			

(b)   **Evaluation of offer made by factoring company**

	$	$
Current level of receivables	41,000,000	
Proposed level of receivables = $160m x 75/365 =	32,876,712	
Decrease	8,123,288	
Saving in overdraft interest = $8,123,288 x 0.04 =	324,931	
Reduction in irrecoverable debts = $500,000 x 0.8 =	400,000	
Reduction in administration costs	100,000	
		824,931
Interest cost of advance = $32,876,712 x 0.8 x 0.01 =	263,014	
Annual fee of factor = 0.005 x $160m =	800,000	
		1,063,014
Net cost of factoring		238,083

The factor's offer is not financially acceptable on the basis of this analysis.

However, the factor believes that receivables' days can be reduced to the sector average of 60 days over two years, so the analysis can be repeated using this lower value.

	$	$
Current level of receivables	41,000,000	
Proposed level of receivables = $160m × 60/365 =	26,301,370	
	————	
Decrease	14,698,630	
	————	
Saving in overdraft interest = $14,698,630 × 0.04 =	587,945	
Reduction in irrecoverable debts = $500,000 × 0.8 =	400,000	
Reduction in administration costs	100,000	
	————	
		1,087,945
Interest cost of advance = $26,301,370 × 0.8 × 0.01 =	210,411	
Annual fee of factor = 0.005 × $160m =	800,000	
	————	
		1,010,411
		————
Net benefit of factoring		77,534
		————

On this basis, the factor's offer is marginally acceptable, but benefits will accrue over a longer time period. A more accurate analysis, using expected levels of sales revenue and forecast interest rates, should be carried out.

299   FLG CO *Walk in the footsteps of a top tutor*

Key answer tips

Parts (a) and (b) are both standard textbook material. In part (a), for six marks you should discuss at least three factors. Don't forget the requirement is to "discuss" not "state" so you must give some commentary: 'the length of the working capital cycle' will not get the full marks available.

In part (b) the requirement is again to "discuss". Given the emphasis is on how both factoring and invoice discounting can assist in the ***management*** of accounts receivable, there should be more discussion on factoring than invoice discounting (the latter being a tool for managing cash flow rather than managing accounts receivable). Don't forget to define each of the terms to collect some easy marks.

The calculation in part (c) requires some "out of the box" thinking in order to see how the brief information provided can be used to work out the size of the overdraft. Not only does it involve re-arranging the usual working capital ratios we're used to seeing, it also requires a disaggregation of the operating cycle to reveal the inventory holding period.

In contrast, part (d) is a fairly straightforward application of the EOQ model which shouldn't pose many difficulties. The highlighted words are key phrases that markers are looking for.

(a) There are a number of factors that determine the level of investment in current assets and their relative importance varies from company to company.

Length of working capital cycle

The working capital cycle or operating cycle is the period of time between when a company settles its accounts payable and when it receives cash from its accounts receivable. Operating activities during this period need to be financed and as the operating period lengthens, the amount of finance needed increases. Companies with comparatively longer operating cycles than others in the same industry sector, will therefore require comparatively higher levels of investment in current assets.

Terms of trade

These determine the period of credit extended to customers, any discounts offered for early settlement or bulk purchases, and any penalties for late payment. A company whose terms of trade are more generous than another company in the same industry sector will therefore need a comparatively higher investment in current assets.

Policy on level of investment in current assets

Even within the same industry sector, companies will have different policies regarding the level of investment in current assets, depending on their attitude to risk. A company with a comparatively conservative approach to the level of investment in current assets would maintain higher levels of inventory, offer more generous credit terms and have higher levels of cash in reserve than a company with a comparatively aggressive approach. While the more aggressive approach would be more profitable because of the lower level of investment in current assets, it would also be more risky, for example in terms of running out of inventory in periods of fluctuating demand, of failing to have the particular goods required by a customer, of failing to retain customers who migrate to more generous credit terms elsewhere, and of being less able to meet unexpected demands for payment.

Industry in which organisation operates

Another factor that influences the level of investment in current assets is the industry within which an organisation operates. Some industries, such as aircraft construction, will have long operating cycles due to the length of time needed to manufacture finished goods and so will have comparatively higher levels of investment in current assets than industries such as supermarket chains, where goods are bought in for resale with minimal additional processing and where many goods have short shelf-lives.

(b) Factoring involves a company turning over administration of its sales ledger to a factor, which is a financial institution with expertise in this area. The factor will assess the creditworthiness of new customers, record sales, send out statements and reminders, collect payment, identify late payers and chase them for settlement, and take appropriate legal action to recover debts where necessary.

The factor will also offer finance to a company based on invoices raised for goods sold or services provided. This is usually up to 80% of the face value of invoices raised. The finance is repaid from the settled invoices, with the balance being passed to the issuing company after deduction of a fee equivalent to an interest charge on cash advanced.

If factoring is without recourse, the factor rather than the company will carry the cost of any bad debts that arise on overdue accounts. Factoring without recourse therefore offers credit protection to the selling company, although the factor's fee (a percentage of credit sales) will be comparatively higher than with non-recourse factoring to reflect the cost of the insurance offered.

Invoice discounting is a way of raising finance against the security of invoices raised, rather than employing the credit management and administration services of a factor. A number of good quality invoices may be discounted, rather than all invoices, and the service is usually only offered to companies meeting a minimum turnover criterion.

(c)   Calculation of size of overdraft

Inventory period = operating cycle + payables period − receivables period = 3 + 1 − 2 = 2 months

Inventory = 1·89m × 2/12 = $315,000

Accounts receivable = 4·2m × 2/12 = $700,000

Current assets = 315,000 + 700,000 = $1,015,000

Current liabilities = current assets/current ratio = 1,015,000/1·4 = $725,000

Accounts payable = 1·89m × 1/12 = $157,500

Overdraft = 725,000 − 157,500 = $567,500

Net working capital = current assets − current liabilities = 1,015,000 − 725,000 = $290,000

Short-term financing cost = 567,500 × 0·07 = $39,725

Long-term financing cost = 290,000 × 0·11 = $31,900

Total cost of financing current assets = 39,725 + 31,900 = $71,625

(d)   (i)   Economic order quantity = (2 × 6 × 60,000/0·5)0·5 = 1,200 units

Number of orders = 60,000/1,200 = 50 order per year

Annual ordering cost = 50 × 6 = $300 per year

Average inventory = 1,200/2 = 600 units

Annual holding cost = 600 × 0·5 = $300 per year

Inventory cost = 60,000 × 12 = $720,000

Total cost of inventory with EOQ policy = 720,000 + 300 + 300 = $720,600 per year

(ii)   Order size for bulk discounts = 10,000 units

Number of orders = 60,000/10,000 = 6 orders per year

Annual ordering cost = 6 × 6 = $36 per year

Average inventory = 10,000/2 =5,000 units

Annual holding cost = 5,000 × 2 = $10,000 per year

Discounted material cost =12 × 0·99 = $11·88 per unit

Inventory cost = 60,000 × 11·88 = $712,800

Total cost of inventory with discount = 712,800 + 36 + 10,000 = $722,836 per year

The EOQ approach results in a slightly lower total inventory cost

300   PKA CO *Walk in the footsteps of a top tutor*

Key answer tips

Within the reading time, you should have managed a detailed read of the requirement and perhaps a quick skim read of the scenario. This will have highlighted that the question is a good balance of words and calculations and that parts (a) & (c) give an opportunity to capture some easy marks. You should consider doing these sections first.

Part (a) covers two aspects; the objectives of working capital management and the conflicts between them. Use the requirement to help structure your answer by picking out words that can be used as sub-headings. Any discussion on working capital can be reduced to a balance between profitability and liquidity, these being the overriding objectives. You will need to give definitions for both before moving on to talk about how they might conflict. Giving examples can be an easy way to explain things and will make the topic come to life.

Part (b) will require a bit more thought. This is a fairly common exam question but the complexity of it can change depending on the information given. Your starting point should be to work out the economic order quantity (EOQ). We're given the formula in the exam so it's really just a case of finding the three pieces of information required, all of which are clearly stated in the scenario. Having calculated the EOQ, you are now equipped to work out the relative costs of the current policy compared to a potential new policy based on the EOQ. You will need to calculate:

– Total order costs (using annual demand, order size and cost per order)

– Total holding costs (using the cost of holding one unit and the average level of inventory)

Four of these five things are given to us in the scenario or have already been calculated. The tricky one is the average level of inventory as we need to consider not only the size of the order but also the level of buffer stocks held. You would be forgiven for thinking the buffer stock is 35,000 units, however you would be wrong. Some of these units would in fact be used in the two weeks it takes for the order to arrive. The information provided on annual demand will enable us to calculated how many units would be used in those two weeks, from which we can work out the level of inventory just prior to the order being delivered. This is by far the trickiest part of this question and it's important to keep it in context. Had you not spotted this, you would only have lost 2 marks. Don't forget, the requirement asks for the saving – be sure that you specifically calculate this to get all the marks.

A quick read of the scenario for accounts receivable management gives us some ideas for sub-headings to use to answer part (c); accounts receivable period and bad debts. For 7 marks you should be aiming for a couple of points under each heading.

The key learning points from this question are the importance of doing the easy parts of the question first and making sure you maintain good time discipline to ensure you don't get bogged down in one part of the question at the expense of another part. The highlighted words are key phrases that markers are looking for.

(a) The objectives of working capital management are profitability and liquidity. The objective of profitability supports the primary financial management objective, which is shareholder wealth maximisation. The objective of liquidity ensures that companies are able to meet their liabilities as they fall due, and thus remain in business.

However, funds held in the form of cash do not earn a return, while near-liquid assets such as short-term investments earn only a small return. Meeting the objective of liquidity will therefore conflict with the objective of profitability, which is met by investing over the longer term in order to achieve higher returns.

Good working capital management therefore needs to achieve a balance between the objectives of profitability and liquidity if shareholder wealth is to be maximised.

(b) **Cost of current ordering policy of PKA Co**

Ordering cost = €250 × (625,000/100,000) = €1,563 per year

Weekly demand = 625,000/50 = 12,500 units per week

Consumption during 2 weeks lead time = 12,500 × 2 = 25,000 units

Buffer stock = re-order level less usage during lead time = 35,000 – 25,000 = 10,000 units

Average stock held during the year = 10,000 + (100,000/2) = 60,000 units

Holding cost = 60,000 × €0.50 = €30,000 per year

Total cost = ordering cost plus holding cost = €1,563 + €30,000 = €31,563 per year

Economic order quantity = $((2 \times 250 \times 625,000)/0.5)_{1/2}$ = 25,000 units

Number of orders per year = 625,000/25,000 = 25 per year

Ordering cost = €250 × 25 = €6,250 per year

Holding cost (ignoring buffer stock) = €0.50 × (25,000/2) = €0.50 × 12,500 = €6,250 per year

Holding cost (including buffer stock) = €0.50 × (10,000 + 12,500) = €11,250 per year

Total cost of EOQ-based ordering policy = €6,250 + €11,250 = €17,500 per year

Saving for PKA Co by using EOQ-based ordering policy = €31,563 – €17,500 = €14,063 per year

(c) The information gathered by the Financial Manager of PKA Co indicates that two areas of concern in the management of domestic accounts receivable are the increasing level of bad debts as a percentage of credit sales and the excessive credit period being taken by credit customers.

Reducing bad debts

The incidence of bad debts, which has increased from 5% to 8% of credit sales in the last year, can be reduced by assessing the creditworthiness of new customers before offering them credit and PKA Co needs to introduce a policy detailing how this should be done, or review its existing policy, if it has one, since it is clearly not working very well. In order to do this, information about the solvency, character and credit history of new clients is needed. This information can come from a variety of sources, such as bank references, trade references and credit reports from credit reference agencies. Whether credit is offered to the new customer and the terms of the credit offered can then be based on an explicit and informed assessment of default risk.

Reduction of average accounts receivable period

Customers have taken an average of 75 days credit over the last year rather than the 30 days offered by PKA Co, i.e. more than twice the agreed credit period. As a result, PKA Co will be incurring a substantial opportunity cost, either from the additional interest cost on the short-term financing of accounts receivable or from the incremental profit lost by not investing the additional finance tied up by the longer average accounts receivable period. PKA Co needs to find ways to encourage accounts receivable to be settled closer to the agreed date.

Assuming that the credit period offered by PKA Co is in line with that of its competitors, the company should determine whether they too are suffering from similar difficulties with late payers. If they are not, PKA Co should determine in what way its own terms differ from those of its competitors and consider whether offering the same trade terms would have an impact on its accounts receivable. For example, its competitors may offer a discount for early settlement while PKA Co does not and introducing a discount may achieve the desired reduction in the average accounts receivable period. If its competitors are experiencing a similar accounts receivable problem, PKA Co could take the initiative by introducing more favourable early settlement terms and perhaps generate increased business as well as reducing the average accounts receivable period.

PKA Co should also investigate the efficiency with which accounts receivable are managed. Are statements sent regularly to customers? Is an aged accounts receivable analysis produced at the end of each month? Are outstanding accounts receivable contacted regularly to encourage payment? Is credit denied to any overdue accounts seeking further business? Is interest charged on overdue accounts? These are all matters that could be included by PKA Co in a revised policy on accounts receivable management.

301 FRANTIC CO (PART I)

Key answer tips

The highlighted words are key phrases that markers are looking for.

(a) (i) **Payables policy**

Tutorial note

By paying suppliers after one month instead of after two months, the company will earn a discount of 1.5%. This means that by 'investing' $98.50 one month earlier in the payment of creditors, it will 'earn' $1.50, by not having to pay $100 one month later. The question is asking what the 'return on investment' would be from earning $1.50 by investing $98.50 for one month, expressed as an annualised yield.

The establishment of a payables payment policy involves a comparison of interest rates with the number of days' credit in relation to the cash discount available.

Taking the discount yields a return of:

$$\frac{\text{Discount \%}}{(100 - \text{Discount \%})} \times \frac{365}{(\text{Final date} - \text{Discount date})}$$

$$\frac{1.5}{98.5} \times \frac{365\,\text{days}}{(60\,\text{days} - 30\,\text{days})}$$

= 0.1853 or 18.53%. This is more than the discount rate the company uses (i.e. the company's cost of capital). A one-month payment policy should therefore be preferred.

(ii)   **Receivables**

Tutorial note

This part of the question is similar to (a)(i), except here the question is whether to offer an early settlement discount, whereas in (a)(i) the question was whether to accept an early settlement discount.

Offering the discount implies an interest cost of:

$$\frac{\text{Discount \%}}{(100 - \text{Discount \%})} \times \frac{365}{(\text{Final date} - \text{Discount date})}$$

$$\frac{2}{98} \times \frac{365\,\text{days}}{(60\,\text{days} - 30\,\text{days})}$$

= 24.8%

This is more than the discount rate the company uses (i.e. more than the company's cost of capital). It is therefore **not worthwhile**.

Alternative method of solution

For every $100 worth of receivables:

	No discount	With discount
	$	$
Receipt from debtor	100.0	98.0
Interest on investing $98 for (60 − 30) = 30 days:		
= 98 × (30/365) × 15%	–	1.2
Total income	100.0	99.2

Hence, it is not worthwhile to offer the discount.

(b) **REPORT**

To:	Managing Director and Senior Management Team
From:	
Date:	xx/xx/xx
Subject:	Cash budgeting

Introduction

This report addresses a number of key issues concerning Frantic's cash flow position and has four elements which are of immediate concern to Frantic.

How cash flow problems arise

It is important first to **distinguish between profitability and cash availability**. The key idea relates to insolvency since even profitable companies can face insolvency if cash positions are not properly managed.

Thus cash positions require management to avoid the difficulties associated with cash shortages. Cash shortages are likely to arise in a number of situations. The following is not an exhaustive list, but is likely to represent the most common. Cash flow problems can arise due to:

(i)   Sustained losses in the business such that cash resources have been drawn-down

(ii)   Difficulties in dealing with inflating costs combined with an inability to raise sales prices proportionately

(iii)   Overtrading and inadequate financing of growth. This is very common with new businesses which are not able to finance working capital requirements sufficiently. Generally, such problems are associated with under-capitalised businesses and a lack of recognition that working capital requirements require a large base of long-term capital funding

(iv)   Seasonal trading against ongoing costs. This situation arises where income from sales is variable according to the time of year but fairly even monthly outgoings have to be met;

(v)   Unplanned one-off large items of expenditure. This may arise, for example, as a result of a break down of a large piece of machinery, and

(vi)   Poor credit management.

The importance and impact of each item will depend on a number of factors.

Thus, losses may be sustained for a period without a liquidity problem, depending on how large cash resources are, whether in the form of positive bank balances or the availability of overdraft facilities.

Suffering cost inflation at a higher rate than prices can be raised is not sustainable in the long-run. The importance of this may depend on the capability of the business to implement cost savings, or to diversify markets where prices could be increased.

Overtrading is a problem of forecasting and planning for adequate long-term capital. The idea is that growth should be within available resources.

Seasonal trading requires careful cash management and the extent to which cash resources can be smoothed over the year.

Unplanned major items of expenditure may be important if alternative sources of finance are not available, such as leasing.

Methods of easing cash shortages

There are several techniques for offsetting the short-term effects of cash shortages. In the long-term, however, the adequacy of cash has to be addressed. Thus, for example, cash shortages may be alleviated by the following:

(i) **Postponement of expenditure** where feasible. This would not be feasible in the payment of staff wages, but might be in relation to replacing an old piece of equipment that is still working.

(ii) **Accelerating cash inflows**. For example, by more effective use of credit collection, better credit control, improved early payment incentives, or even the factoring of receivables.

(iii) **Sale of redundant assets** either before or after any necessary re-organisation. This may involve the sale of a building where accommodation can be centralised. Other assets may be sold on a sale and lease-back basis, although careful consideration will have to be given to the net benefits arising from this.

(iv) **Re-negotiation of supplier terms or overdraft arrangements**. In particular, bank debt may be mortgaged or secured to access lower rates. Suppliers may agree to lower prices or longer terms if negotiated agreements can be formalised such that a certain level of purchases are made over a period of time.

The importance of each item will depend on the degree of flexibility that Frantic has in its financial structure and agreements. The room for manoeuvre may be limited, but a thorough review of all possibilities is likely to yield at least a number of options. Furthermore, the impact of each potential response depends on how efficient Frantic has been in arranging its affairs in the first place. Finally, none of the items listed will have a sustained impact if the core problem is not identified and dealt-with.

Managing cash resources

A variety of methods might be of use in managing resources. The particular tool chosen will depend on its reliability and appropriateness. Appropriateness, in turn, will be governed by the underlying assumptions of the technique employed. Some of the methods that may be used to manage cash resources are listed below:

(i) **Inventory approach to cash management**. This method views cash in the same way as engine inventory such that EOQ models may be employed. In such circumstances, cash is viewed as an asset with costs associated with it that should be minimised so as to determine what level of cash balances should be held. Thus, decreases or increases in cash balances can be determined according to planned growth, the time value of money and the costs of obtaining new funds.

(ii) **Probability approaches** recognise a degree of uncertainty in predicting cash balances and allow for a range of outcomes to occur. If the assessment of such probabilities is accurate then cash resources can be put in place in readiness for the predicted events. The method is not wholly reliable in situations where the number of potential outcomes is small, since unfeasible expected outcomes may be predicted by using a probability approach.

(iii) Cash management is also about managing **surplus** cash. The response of management should depend on whether the surplus is large and how long it is likely to exist. If the balance is large and is likely to remain, then management have a duty to look for appropriate investment opportunities or else refund the investors with a special dividend, for example. Smaller cash balances can be actively managed via short term deposits.

A centralised treasury function

Treasury departments are normally a feature of larger companies than Frantic, although it is perhaps beneficial to consider the benefits of such departments to assess what practices might reasonably be adopted. Essentially, treasury centralisation is an issue concerned with economies of scale. The benefits of treasury departments are numerous and include the following:

(i) Consolidating bank accounts to create either a single account through which all cash resources are managed or a virtual single account with automatic offset between different accounts. Such an approach maximises deposit interest, which is typically higher on larger cash balances for positive balances whilst minimising overdraft costs for negative balances.

(ii) Borrowings can be arranged in bulk thus accessing lower rates.

(iii) Foreign exchange management is improved. In the same way that cash balances are effectively consolidated, foreign currency payments and receipts of all the divisions in the company can be amalgamated, and cash inflows and outflows in each currency set off against each other. This can reduce the need for expensive hedging agreements. Foreign exchange risk consolidation is common in practice.

(iv) Treasury expertise can be developed within a single department, thus enhancing the quality of resource management generally.

(v) Precautionary cash balances, when centralised, are likely to be lower than when considered on an individual account basis.

302 FRANTIC CO (PART II)

Key answer tips

Part (a) is a fairly straightforward application of the economic order quantity model. Part (b) is slightly more challenging and a methodical approach, with good use of supporting workings / notes is essential to completing the question on time.

(a) **Inventory evaluation without early settlement discounting**

Annual production (demand) = 800 cars = 800 engines.

Cost of ordering = cost of delivery = $1,200.

Annual inventory holding cost = 22% × $1,300 = $286.

$$\text{EOQ ignoring discounts} = \sqrt{\frac{2C_oD}{C_H}} = \sqrt{\frac{2 \times 1,200 \times 800}{286}} = 81.93 \text{ or } 82 \text{ whole units.}$$

At this batch ordering level, a quantity discount of 2% would apply. The annual holding cost would therefore be 22% × 98% x $1,300 = $280.28. Re-working the previous calculation with the quantity discount gives:

$$EOQ = \sqrt{\frac{2C_oD}{C_H}} = \sqrt{\frac{2 \times 1,200 \times 800}{280.28}} = 82.77 \text{ or } 83 \text{ whole units.}$$

Hence the choice facing Frantic Co is between ordering 83 units and getting a 2% discount, or 250 units, which is the minimum purchase quantity needed to get a 3% discount.

Evaluation for an order quantity of 83:

		$
Total purchase costs:	$1,300 × 98% × 800 =	1,019,200
Holding costs:	83/2 × $280.28 =	11,632
Order costs:	(800/83) × $1,200 =	11,566
Total annual costs:		1,042,398

Evaluation for an order quantity of 250:

		$
Total purchase costs:	$1,300 × 97% × 800 =	1,008,800
Holding costs:	250/2 × 22% × 97% × $1,300 =	34,678
Order costs:	(800/250) × $1,200 =	3,840
Total annual costs:		1,047,318

Difference in costs: Buying in quantities of 250 is more expensive by $4,920 each year. **The optimal policy** is to order in quantities that minimises total costs, which in this case is to **order in batches of 83 engines**.

Tutorial note

An alternative answer takes an incremental cost approach, and compares the incremental costs or savings from ordering in batches of 250 compared to ordering in batches of 83. The initial assumption is that the company orders in batches of 83. This approach is shown on the next page.

	$	$
Saving in purchase price by buying 250: (800 × 1% × $1,300)		10,400
Saving in ordering costs by buying in batches of 250:		
[(800 × 1,200)/83] − [(800 × 1,200)/250]		7,726
Total cost savings		18,126
Holding costs with order quantity of 250 (above)	34,678	
Holding costs with order quantity of 83 (above)	11,632	
Additional holding costs from ordering in batches of 250		23,046
Increased costs arising from ordering 250 units		4,920

The same conclusion is reached as above. The optimal policy is to order 83 engines at a time.

(b) As stated in solution (a) the optimal policy is to order 83 engines at a time. This involves ordering 800/83 = 9.64 times per year. A production schedule can be drawn-up to assess when the orders would be made. If this is undertaken the following ordering schedule would result:

Month	1	2	3	4	5	6
Car production[1]	66.7	66.7	66.7	66.7	66.7	66.7
Engine orders placed[2]	83	83	83	83	83	
Inventory at month-end	16	32	48	64	80	13

[1] Fractional production allowed and reflected in work in progress

[2] No orders are placed in the sixth month due to the ordering policy and the resulting inventory build up. This does not have any implications for the six month cash flow since creditors will be paid with one month delay.

Cash flow for first six months:

Month	1	2	3	4	5	6
Receipts						
Cash sales (Note 1)	1,416,667	1,416,667	1,416,667	1,416,667	1,416,667	1,416,667
Credit sales (Note 1)	1,062,500	1,062,500	1,416,667	1,416,667	1,416,667	1,416,667
Total income	2,479,167	2,479,167	2,833,334	2,833,334	2,833,334	2,833,334

Payments

Capital costs			3,200,000			
Engine costs (Note 2)	97,500	104,156	104,156	104,156	104,156	104,156
Other expenses (Note 3)	1,841,667	1,841,667	1,841,667	1,841,667	1,841,667	1,841,667
Fixed costs	18,000	18,000	18,000	22,000	22,000	22,000
Costs net of overdraft	1,957,167	1,963,823	5,163,823	1,967,823	1,967,823	1,967,823
Receipts less payments	522,000	515,344	(2,330,489)	865,511	865,511	865,511
Opening bank balance	(25,000)	496,687	1,012,031	(1,318,458)	(469,428)	390,215
Interest (Note 4)	(313)	–	–	(16,481)	(5,868)	–
Closing bank balance	496,687	1,012,031	(1,318,458)	(469,428)	390,215	1,255,726

Notes:

(1) Monthly sales = 800/12 units. Cash sales are 50% of 800/12 × $42,500 = $1,416,667. Credit sales are the same in each month, but customers take two months' credit. Receipts from credit sales in months 1 and 2 are as stated in the question.

(2) Engine cost payments. Month 1 payment is given in the question. The company will take a bulk purchase discount of 2% and an early settlement discount of 1.5%. Cash paid in subsequent months = quantity purchased in previous month × 98.5% of 98% of $1,300 = $104,156 per month.

(3) Other expenses are 65% × monthly sales = 65% × (800/12) × $42,500 = $1,841,667.

(4) Assumption = Overdraft costs are calculated as (1/12) × 15% × opening bank balance. (Other bases of calculation are acceptable such as interest calculated on average balances.)

303 JACK GEEP

Key answer tips

The scenario in this question is very long so it's important that you read the requirement first and think about the sort of information you will need. For example, for cash inflows you will be expecting sales data (the requirement tells us there will be some probabilities given) together with some details on credit terms with customers. Make notes in the margin as you read it to flag up what each piece of information can be used for. Ensure you also highlight easy marks; cash flows that can be immediately entered into your pro-forma. You should start writing your answer by putting in the easy numbers before doing any more complex workings.

(a)

	High demand	Medium demand	Low demand	Expected demand
	$	$	$	$
February	22,000 × 0.05	20,000 × 0.85	19,000 × 0.1	20,000
March	26,000 × 0.05	24,000 × 0.85	23,000 × 0.1	24,000
April	30,000 × 0.05	28,000 × 0.85	27,000 × 0.1	28,000
May	29,000 × 0.05	27,000 × 0.85	26,000 × 0.1	27,000
June	35,000 × 0.05	33,000 × 0.85	32,000 × 0.1	33,000

	January	February	March	April	May	June
	$	$	$	$	$	$
Receipts						
Capital	150,000					
Cash sales (W1)		2,000	2,400	2,800	2,700	3,300
Credit sales (W1)			8,775	10,530	12,285	11,846
				9,000	10,800	12,600
	150,000	2,000	11,175	22,330	25,785	27,746
Payments						
Non-current assets		200,000		50,000		
Labour (W3)	6,300	7,560	8,820	8,505	10,395	10,395
Materials (W3)		4,200	5,040	5,880	5,670	6,930
Overheads (W3)			2,100	2,520	2,940	2,835
Fixed costs	7,000	7,000	7,000	7,000	7,000	7,000
Consultant		12,000				
	13,300	230,760	22,960	73,905	26,005	27,160
Net cash flow	136,700	(228,760)	(11,785)	(51,575)	(220)	586
Opening balance	0	136,700	(92,060)	(103,845)	(155,420)	(155,640)
Closing balance	136,700	(92,060)	(103,845)	(155,420)	(155,640)	(155,054)

(W1) Cash from sales

	January	February	March	April	May	June
	$	$	$	$	$	$
Cash sales (10%)		2,000	2,400	2,800	2,700	3,300
Credit sales:						
(90% × 0.5 × 0.975)			8,775	10,530	12,285	11,846
(90% × 0.5)				9,000	10,800	12,600

(W2) Variable production costs ($600 per $1,000 of sales)

	January	February	March	April	May	June
	$	$	$	$	$	$
Cost of sales	12,000	14,400	16,800	16,200	19,800	19,800
Defects (5%)	600	720	840	810	990	990
Total	12,600	15,120	17,640	17,010	20,790	20,790

(W3) Production cash flows (see (W2))

	January	February	March	April	May	June
	$	$	$	$	$	$
Labour (3/6 of total)	6,300	7,560	8,820	8,505	10,395	10,395
Materials (2/6 of total)		4,200	5,040	5,880	5,670	6,930
Overheads (1/6)			2,100	2,520	2,940	2,835

Tutorial note

Materials paid one month in arrears and variable overheads two months in arrears.

(b) The introduction of just-in-time inventory management for finished goods has a number of benefits:

(1) It significantly improves the short-term liquidity of the business with a maximum financing requirement of $138,533 rather than $155,640. There is also a more rapidly improving deficit thereafter, with the balance falling to $134,986 by the end of June. In the longer term, however, there is continued loss of profitability due to lost sales when demand is high.

The primary reason for this is the reduced investment in inventory that is tying up cash. Under the original proposal there is surplus inventory amounting to the next month's sales which means production is necessary at an earlier stage thereby using up cash resources.

(2) Interest costs and inventory holding costs are saved by reduced inventory levels, thereby adding to profit.

(3) There already appears to be a just-in-time inventory management policy with respect to raw materials and work in progress and such a policy for finished goods would be consistent with this.

There are, however, a number of problems with just-in-time inventory management in these circumstances:

(1) When demand is higher than expected, the additional sales are lost as there is insufficient production to accommodate demand above the mean expected level. This is because no inventory is carried. This, however, amounts to a potential shortfall of $2,000 sales in a particular month, which will occur 5% of the time. This is only $100 per month of sales on average, which may be a price worth paying in return for improved liquidity in terms of a reduced cash deficit.

(2) In addition to losing contribution there may be a loss of goodwill and reputation if customers cannot be supplied. They may go elsewhere not just for the current sale but also for future sales if Mr Geep is seen as an unreliable supplier. This results from the fact that customers demand immediate delivery of orders.

(3) Just-in-time management of inventory relies upon not just reliable timing and quantities but also reliable quality. The number of defects can be planned if it is constant, but if they occur irregularly this presents an additional problem.

(4) If production in each month is to supply demand in the same month, this relies on the fact that demand parallels production within the month. If the majority of demand is at the beginning of each month this would cause problems without a level of safety inventory, given that prompt delivery is expected by customers.

A number of compromises between the two positions would be possible:

(1) Inventory could be held sufficient to accommodate demand when it was high. This amounts to only an extra $2,000 at selling values thus an extra $1,200 at variable cost. This is significantly lower than a whole month's production but would accommodate peak demand.

(2) Liquidity is very important initially as the business attempts to become established. Therefore minimal inventories could be held in the early months, with perhaps slightly increased inventory once the business and its cash flows become established.

304 ANJO

Key answer tips

This is a fairly straightforward question with some easier written marks within part (c). Tackle these first to ensure you give yourself the most amount of time for the calculations.

(a) **Calculation of ratios**

Inventory days	20X6:	(3,000/9,300) x 365	= 118 days
	20X5:	(1,300/6,600) x 365	= 72 days
		Sector average: 90 days	

Receivables days	20X6:	(3,800/15,600) x 365	= 89 days
	20X5:	(1,850/11,100) x 365	= 61 days
		Sector average: 60 days	
Payables days	20X6:	(2,870/9,300 x 0.95) x 365	= 119 days
	20X5:	(1,600/6,600 x 0.95) x 365	= 93 days
		Sector average: 80 days	

In each case, the ratio in 20X6 is higher than the ratio in 20X5, indicating that deterioration has occurred in the management of inventories, receivables and payables in 20X6.

Inventory days have increased by 46 days or 64%, moving from below the sector average to 28 days – one month – more than it. Given the rapid increase in sales revenue (40%) in 20X6, Anjo Inc may be expecting a continuing increase in the future and may have built up inventories in preparation for this, i.e. inventory levels reflect future sales rather than past sales. Accounting statements from several previous years and sales forecasts for the next period would help to clarify this point.

Receivables days have increased by 28 days or 46% in 20X6 and are now 29 days above the sector average. It is possible that more generous credit terms have been offered in order to stimulate sales. The increased sales revenue does not appear to be due to offering lower prices, since both gross profit margin (40%) and net profit margin (34%) are unchanged.

In 20X5, only management of payables was a cause for concern, with Anjo Inc taking 13 more days on average to settle liabilities with trade payables than the sector. This has increased to 39 days more than the sector in 20X6. This could lead to difficulties between the company and its suppliers if it is exceeding the credit periods they have specified. Anjo Inc has no long-term debt and the balance sheet (statement of financial position) indicates an increased reliance on short-term finance, since cash has reduced by $780,000 or 87% and the overdraft has increased by $850,000 to $1 million. Perhaps the company should investigate whether it is undercapitalised (overtrading). It is unusual for a company of this size to have no long-term debt.

(b)   Cash operating cycle (20X5) = 72 + 61 – 93 = 40 days
Cash operating cycle (20X6) = 118 + 89 – 119 = 88 days

The cash operating cycle or working capital cycle gives the average time it takes for the company to receive payment from receivables after it has paid its trade payables. This represents the period of time for which payables require financing. The cash operating cycle of Anjo Inc has lengthened by 48 days in 20X6 compared with 20X5. This represents an increase in working capital requirement of approximately $15,600,000 x 48/365 = $2.05 million.

(c)   The objectives of working capital management are liquidity and profitability, but there is a tension between these two objectives. Liquid funds, for example cash, earn no return and so will not increase profitability. Near-liquid funds, with short investment periods, earn a lower return than funds invested for a long period. Profitability is therefore decreased to the extent that liquid funds are needed.

The main reason that companies fail, though, is because they run out of cash and so good cash management is an essential part of good working capital management. Business solvency cannot be maintained if working capital management in the form of cash management is of a poor standard.

In order to balance the twin objectives of liquidity and profitability in terms of cash management, a company needs to decide on the optimum amount of cash to hold at any given time. There are several factors that can aid in determining the optimum cash balance.

First, it is important to note that cash management is a forward-looking activity, in that the optimum cash balance must reflect the expected need for cash in the next budget period, for example in the next month. The cash budget will indicate expected cash receipts over the next period, expected payments that need to be made, and any shortfall that is expected to arise due to the difference between receipts and payments. This is the transactions need for cash, since it is based on the amount of cash needed to meet future business transactions.

However, there may be a degree of uncertainty as to the timing of expected receipts. Receivables, for example, may not all pay on time and some may take extended credit, whether authorised or not. In order to guard against a possible shortfall of cash to meet future transactions, companies may keep a 'buffer inventory' of cash by holding a cash reserve greater than called for by the transactions demand. This is the precautionary demand for cash and the optimum cash balance will reflect management's assessment of this demand.

Beyond this, a company may decide to hold additional cash in order to take advantage of any business opportunities that may arise, for example the possibility of taking over a rival company that has fallen on hard times. This is the speculative demand for cash and it may contribute to the optimum cash level for a given company, depending on that company's strategic plan.

	$000
Current receivables =	3,800
Receivables under factor = 3,800 x 0.7 =	2,660
Reduction in receivables =	1,140
Finance cost saving = 1,140 x 0.08 =	91.2
Administration cost saving = 1,000 x 0.02 =	20.0
Interest on advance = 2,660 x 0.8 x 0.01 =	(21.3)
Factor's annual fee = 15,600 x 0.005 =	(78.0)
Net benefit of accepting factor's offer	11.9

Although the terms of the factor's offer are financially acceptable, suggesting a net financial benefit of $11,900, this benefit is small compared with annual sales revenue of $15.6 million. Other benefits, such as the application of the factor's expertise to the receivables management of Anjo Inc, might also be influential in the decision on whether to accept the offer.

305 BLIN

Key answer tips

Parts (a) and (c) of this question should be fairly straightforward. For part (a), your answer should give some emphasis to the yield curve. Part (b) is probably more difficult, because it is not necessarily easy to see what the examiner had in mind with 'approaches'. Thinking about the question logically might help you to construct an answer. You are asked to comment on approaches to the mix of long-term and short-term funding to finance working capital. Logically, the approaches are (1) to have mainly long-term capital and not much short-term capital, (2) to have mainly short-term capital and not much long-term capital, and (3) to have a more balanced mixture of short-term and long-term capital. These are the approaches in the solution.

However, the distinction between 'permanent' levels of current assets and 'fluctuating' levels of current assets is a useful distinction, which the solution in part (b) uses as a basis for analysis. A company's current assets are continually changing in total amount, up and down, but there is usually a 'permanent' amount below which the total of current assets does not fall. Fluctuating current assets are current assets in excess of the minimum level.

(a) The following factors will influence the rate of interest charged on the new bank loan.

General level of interest rates

Interest rates charged on loans will depend on the general level of interest rates. Typically, interest rates on a bank loan are set at a margin above a 'base rate' or 'prime rate' or at a margin above a money market benchmark rate such as LIBOR. Similarly, longer-term fixed interest rates are at a margin above either a government bond rate or the swap rate. When the general level of interest rates goes up, rates on new lending will also rise.

Risk of default

The bank providing the loan to Blin will make an assessment of the risk that the company might default on its loan commitments and charge an interest rate that reflects this risk. Since Blin is listed on a stock exchange it will be seen as less risky than an unlisted company and will pay a lower interest rate as a result. The period of time that the company has been listed may also be an influential factor.

Since Blin has expanded sales significantly and relies heavily on overdraft finance, it may be overtrading. This could increase the risk of default and so increase the rate of interest charged on the loan. The bank would need to be convinced through financial information supporting the loan application, such as cash flow forecasts, that Blin would be able to meet future interest payments and repayments of principal.

Security offered

The rate of interest charged on the loan will be lower if the debt is secured against an asset or assets of the company. It is likely in Blin's case that the loan will carry a fixed charge on particular assets, such as land or buildings. In the event of default by the company, the bank can recover its loan by selling the secured assets.

Duration of loan

The longer the period of the loan taken out by Blin, the higher the interest rate that will be charged. This reflects the shape of the normal yield curve.

The normal yield curve shows that the yield required on debt increases in line with the term to maturity. One reason for this is that loan providers require compensation for deferring their use of the cash they have lent, and the longer the period for which they are deprived of their cash, the more compensation they require. This is described as the liquidity preference explanation for the shape of the normal yield curve.

Other explanations for the shape of the normal yield curve are expectations theory and market segmentation theory. Expectations theory suggests that interest rates rise with maturity because rates of interest are expected to rise in the future, for example due to an expected increase in inflation. Market segmentation theory suggests that the market for long-term debt differs from the market for short-term debt.

Amount borrowed

The rate of interest charged on the new loan could be lower if the amount borrowed is not a small sum. It is more convenient from an administrative point of view for a bank to lend a large sum rather than several small amounts.

(b)   The approaches that Blin could adopt regarding the relative proportions of long- and short-term finance to meet its working capital needs could be described as conservative, moderate and aggressive.

The assets of a business are categorised into current and non-current assets. Current assets are used up on a regular basis within a single accounting period and non-current assets benefit a business for several accounting periods. Current assets can be further categorised into permanent current assets and fluctuating current assets. Permanent current assets represent the core level or minimum level of investment in current assets needed for a given level of business activity, and arise from the need for businesses to carry inventory and to extend credit. Fluctuating current assets represent a variable need for investment in current assets, arising from either seasonal or unpredictable variations in business activity.

With a *conservative* approach to the financing mix, long-term finance is the main source of working capital funds. Long-term finance is used to finance non-current assets, permanent current assets and some fluctuating current assets.

Long-term debt finance is less risky to a company than short-term debt finance, since once in place it is not subjected to the dangers of renewal or immediate repayment. However, it is more expensive in that the rate of interest charged normally increases with maturity. A conservative approach would therefore increase the amount of lower-risk long-term debt finance used by the company, but would also incur higher total interest payments than an approach emphasizing the use of short-term debt.

This approach will therefore lead to relatively lower profitability. A similar argument can be made when equity finance is used as long-term finance; equity requires an even higher return than long-term debt finance.

With an *aggressive* approach to the financing mix, short-term finance is the main source of working capital funds. This approach, which is currently being used by Blin, uses short-term finance for fluctuating current assets and some permanent current assets, with long-term finance being used for the balance of permanent current assets and non-current assets. This increases the relative amount of higher-risk short-term finance used by the company, but will also incur lower total interest payments than the conservative approach discussed above, leading to relatively higher profitability.

Between these two approaches lies a moderate or matching approach. This approach applies the matching principle, whereby the maturity of the funding is matched with life of the assets financed. Here, long-term finance is used for permanent current assets and non-current assets, while short-term finance is used for fluctuating current assets.

The repayment of the overdraft will result in Blin adopting a conservative approach to the mix of long- and short-term finance. This will resolve an overtrading situation, if it exists. However, it may reduce profitability more than necessary. If Blin continues to expand sales, or reintroduces overdraft finance, the conservative position will only be temporary and a moderate position may arise in the future. The speed with which this happens will depend on the size of the loan taken out, and whether a moderate position is desirable will depend on the company's attitude to risk and return. It may be preferable to reduce the overdraft to a lower level rather than repaying it completely. A clearer picture would emerge if we knew the intended use for, and the amount of, the balance of the loan not being used to repay the overdraft.

(c) The cash operating cycle is the length of time between paying trade payables and receiving cash from receivables. It can be calculated by adding together the average inventory holding period and the average time for receivables to pay, and then subtracting the average time taken to pay trade payables. The inventory holding period may be subdivided into the holding periods for raw materials, work-in-progress and finished goods. Using accounting ratios, the cash operating cycle can be approximated by adding together inventory days and receivables days and subtracting payables days.

The significance of the cash operating cycle in determining the level of investment in working capital is that the longer the cash operating cycle, the higher the investment in working capital.

The length of the cash operating cycle varies between industries: for example, a service organization may have no inventory holding period, a retail organization will have an inventory holding period based almost entirely on finished goods and a very low level of receivables, and a manufacturing organization will have an inventory holding period based on raw materials, work-in-progress and finished goods. The level of investment in working capital will therefore depend on the nature of business operations.

The cash operating cycle and the resulting level of investment in working capital does not depend only on the nature of the business, however. Companies within the same business sector may have different levels of investment in working capital, measured for example by the accounting ratio of sales/net working capital, as a result of adopting different working capital policies. A relatively aggressive policy on the level of investment in working capital is characterised by lower levels of inventory and receivables: this lower level of investment increases profitability but also increases the risk of running out of inventory, or of losing potential customers due to better credit terms being offered by competitors. A relatively conservative policy on the level of investment in working capital has higher levels of investment in inventory and receivables: profitability is therefore reduced, but the risk of inventory stock-outs is lower and new credit customers may be attracted by more generous terms.

It is also possible to reduce the level of investment in working capital by reducing the length of the cash operating cycle. This is achieved by reducing the inventory holding period (for example by using JIT methods), by reducing the average time taken by receivables to pay (for example by improving receivables management), or by increasing the length of credit period taken from suppliers (for example by settling invoices as late as possible). In this way an understanding of the cash operating cycle can assist in taking steps to improve working capital management and profitability.

306 PNP PLC

Key answer tips

Parts (a) and (b) of this question both require a significant amount of workings. Laying your workings out neatly and clearly cross referencing them to your answer will ensure you have the best chance of scoring all the marks available. When laying out your answer to part (c), use plenty of sub-headings to clearly indicate to your marker the points you are making.

(a) **Effect on profitability of implementing the proposal**

	£	£
Benefits:		
Increased contribution (W1)	200,000	
Decrease in irrecoverable debts (W2)	6,300	
		206,300
Costs:		
Increase in current Class 1 discount (W3)	12,167	
Discount from transferring Class 2 receivables (W4)	11,498	
Discount from new Class 1 receivables (W5)	3,750	
Increase in irrecoverable debts, new Class 2 receivables (W6)	2,055	
Increase in financing cost from new receivables (W7)	4,932	34,402
Net benefit of implementing the proposal		171,898

The proposed change appears to be financially acceptable and so may be recommended. Uncertainty with respect to some of the assumptions underlying the financial evaluation would be unlikely to change the favourable recommendation.

Workings

Contribution/sales ratio = $100 \times (5{,}242 - 3{,}145)/5{,}242 = 40\%$

Irrecoverable debts ratio for Class 2 receivables = $100 \times (12{,}600/252{,}000) = 5\%$

Increase in Class 1 receivables from new business = $250{,}000 \times 30/365 = £20{,}548$

Increase in Class 2 receivables from new business = $250{,}000 \times 60/365 = £41{,}096$

(W1) Contribution from increased business = $500{,}000 \times 40\% = £200{,}000$

(W2) Decrease in irrecoverable debts for transferring current Class 2 receivables = $12{,}600 \times 0.5 = £6{,}300$

(Note that other assumptions regarding irrecoverable debts are possible here)

(W3) Current sales of Class 1 receivables = $200{,}000 \times (365/30) = £2{,}433{,}333$

Rise in discount cost for current Class 1 receivables = $2{,}433{,}333 \times 0.005 = £12{,}167$

(W4) Current sales of Class 2 receivables = $252{,}000 \times (365/60) = £1{,}533{,}000$

Discount cost of transferring Class 2 receivables = $1{,}533{,}000 \times 0.5 \times 0.015 = £11{,}498$

(W5) Discount cost for new Class 1 receivables = $250{,}000 \times 0.015 = £3{,}750$

(W6) Irrecoverable debts arising from new Class 2 receivables = $41{,}096 \times 0.05 = £2{,}055$

(Note that other assumptions regarding irrecoverable debts are possible here)

(W7) Increase in financing cost from new receivables = $(20{,}548 + 41{,}096) \times 0.08 = £4{,}932$

(Note that it could be assumed that transferring receivables pay after 30 days rather than 60 days)

Examiner's Note: because of the various assumptions that could be made regarding irrecoverable debts and payment period, other approaches to a solution are also acceptable.

(b) **Current cash operating cycle**

Inventory days = $(603/3{,}145) \times 365 = 70$ days
Payables days = $(574.5/3{,}145) \times 365 = 67$ days
Average receivables days = $(744.5/5{,}242) \times 365 = 52$ days
Cash operating cycle = $70 + 52 - 67 = 55$ days

After implementation of the proposal, it is reasonable to assume that inventory days and payables days remain unchanged. Total receivables have increased by £61,644 to £806,144 and sales revenue has increased to £5.742m. Average receivables days are now $365 \times (806/5{,}742) = 51$ days. The cash operating cycle has marginally decreased by one day to 54 days $(70 + 51 - 67)$.

(c) The key elements of a receivables management system may be described as establishing a credit policy, credit assessment, credit control and collection of amounts due.

Establishing credit policy

The credit policy provides the overall framework within which the receivables management system of PNP plc operates and will cover key issues such as the procedures to be followed when granting credit, the usual credit period offered, the maximum credit period that may be granted, any discounts for early settlement, whether interest is charged on overdue balances, and actions to be taken with accounts that have not been settled in the agreed credit period. These terms of trade will depend to a considerable extent on the terms offered by competitors to PNP plc, but they will also depend on the ability of the company to finance its receivables (financing costs), the need to meet the costs of administering the system (administrative costs) and the risk of irrecoverable debts.

Credit assessment

In order to minimise the risk of irrecoverable debts, PNP plc should assess potential customers as to their creditworthiness before offering them credit. The depth of the credit check depends on the amount of business being considered, the size of the client and the potential for repeat business. The credit assessment requires information about the customer, whether from a third party as in a trade reference, a bank reference or a credit report, or from PNP itself through, for example, its analysis of a client's published accounts. The benefits of granting credit must always be greater than the cost involved. There is no point, therefore, in PNP plc paying for a detailed credit report from a credit reference agency for a small credit sale.

Credit control

Once PNP plc has granted credit to a customer, it should monitor the account at regular intervals to make sure that the agreed terms are being followed. An aged receivables analysis is useful in this respect since it helps the company focus on those clients who are the most cause for concern. Customers should be reminded of their debts by prompt despatch of invoices and regular statements of account. Customers in arrears should not be allowed to take further goods on credit.

Collection of amounts due

The customers of PNP plc should ideally settle their accounts within the agreed credit period. There is no indication as to what this might be, but the company clearly feels that a segmental analysis of its clients is possible given their payment histories, their potential for irrecoverable debts and their geographical origin. Clear guidelines are needed over the action to take when customers are late in settling their accounts or become irrecoverable debts, for example indicating at what stage legal action should be initiated.

Overseas receivables

PNP plc will need to consider the ways in which overseas receivables differ from domestic receivables. For example, overseas receivables tend to take longer to pay and so will need financing for longer. Overseas receivables will also give rise to exchange rate risk, which will probably need to be managed. The credit risk associated with overseas customers can be reduced in several ways, however, for example by using advances against collection, requiring payment through bills of exchange, arranging documentary letters of credit or using export factoring.

Section 7

SPECIMEN EXAM PAPER QUESTIONS

OBJECTIVE TEST QUESTIONS

1.1 The original budgeted profit statement for a product is as follows:

	$
Revenue	200,000
Variable costs	100,000
Fixed costs	36,000
Profit	64,000

It has now been realised that sales volume will be 10% higher than budgeted volume with no change in selling price. The product has also been redesigned to lower variable costs by 20% per unit.

The percentage increase in the budgeted profit as a result of the two changes will be:

A   2.0%

B   30.0%

C   50.0%

D   62.5%   **(2 marks)**

1.2 A project has the following present values when discounted at the company's cost of capital of 8% per annum:

	$
Initial investment	250,000
Cash inflows	500,000
Cash outflows	200,000

The sensitivity of the project to changes in the cash inflows is:

A   8%

B   10%

C   20%

D   50%   **(2 marks)**

The following data is for questions 1.3 and 1.4

D provides a motorist rescue service to its members. It has been proposed to change the annual membership fee to $120 for the next year. The impact of this on the number of members is uncertain but the following estimates have been made:

Number of members	Probability
20,000	0.1
30,000	0.6
40,000	0.3

It is thought that the variable operating costs vary in relation to the number of members but the cost per member is uncertain. The following estimates have been made:

Variable cost per member	Probability
$70	0.3
$60	0.5
$40	0.2

D expects to incur annual fixed costs of $1,100,000.

1.3 **Calculate, based on expected values, the profit for the next year**

(2 marks)

1.4 **The Management Accountant of D has produced a two-way data table.**

(i) Calculate the value that would be shown in that table in the cell for the profit from 40,000 members with a variable cost per member of $40. **(2 marks)**

(ii) Calculate the joint probability of having 20,000 members and a variable cost per member of $40. **(2 marks)**

1.5 **GF wants to sell an unquoted bond. The bond has a coupon rate of 5% and will repay its face value of $1,000 at the end of four years.**

GF estimates that the market requires a yield to maturity of 11% from this type of bond. GF has asked you to recommend a selling price for the bond.

Calculate the selling price for the bond. **(4 marks)**

1.6 **A company has the following information:**

	Actual 31 December 2009	Forecast 30 June 2010
Balances	$000	$000
Trade receivables	75	80
Trade payables	47	40
Inventory of raw materials	29	31

The production budget for the six month period to 30 June 2010 shows that the cost of raw materials to be used in that period will be $331,000.

Calculate the cash that will be paid to suppliers during the six month period to 30 June 2010. **(3 marks)**

1.7   **A company's trade payables days outstanding at 30 September 2009 were 45 days. Purchases for the year to 30 September 2009 were $324,444 occurring evenly throughout the year.**

The company's budgeted purchases for the year ending 30 September 2010 are $356,900 occurring evenly throughout the year.

Calculate the budgeted trade payables days outstanding at 30 September 2010.

(Assume that the trade payables outstanding balance at 30 September 2010 will be the same amount as at 30 September 2009.)   **(3 marks)**

(Total: 20 marks)

Section 2

2

(a)   A company manufactures office equipment in England but sells it in the UK and to overseas customers.

Current situation UK customers (£2·1m annual revenue)

The company offers a cash discount of 3% for payment within 10 days to UK customers. Approximately 40% of customers take advantage of the early payment discount whilst the remainder pay in 30 days.

Overseas customers (£0.9m annual revenue)

All sales are on credit but customers are required to pay a 20% deposit when they place their orders and the balance in 60 days.

Debt factoring

The company is thinking about debt factoring. Investigations have revealed that a non-recourse factor will accept 85% of the company's UK customers. It is assumed that the remaining 15% will not take advantage of the early settlement discount.

Required:

Calculate, based on a 365-day year, the total debtors' days if

(i)   the current situation continues

(ii)   debt factoring is introduced   **(5 marks)**

(b)   Discuss the non-financial factors that a company would need to consider before making a decision to factor its debts.   **(5 marks)**

(c)   The manager of a hotel is deciding if he should carry out repairs to the hotel immediately or postpone them for a year. He has made the following estimates for the coming year:

The cost of the repairs would be £90,000.

If the repairs are started immediately there is only a two-in-three chance of them being completed in time. If the repairs are completed in time the contribution for the hotel could be any one of the three levels below with equally probability. If the repairs are not completed on time some rooms will be unavailable and consequently demand could be either medium or low, with equal probability.

Contribution for the coming year if the repairs are undertaken could be:

       £200,000 if there is high demand

       £150,000 if there is medium demand

       £100,000 if demand is low

If the repairs are not undertaken the contribution for the coming year is estimated to be £37,500.

Required:

Demonstrate, using a decision tree, if the repairs should be started immediately or postponed for a year. **(5 marks)**

(d)   A fast food outlet served the following number of burgers in the past 13 quarters:

	2007				2008				2009				2010
	Q1	Q2	Q3	Q4	Q1	Q2	Q3	Q4	Q1	Q2	Q3	Q4	Q1
Burgers (000)	75	80	110	175	92	96	122	210	111	116	164	259	135

Regression analysis was used to determine the following equation for the trend of sales:

$S = 134.23 + 7.945Q$ where

S = quarterly sales ('000)

Q = quarter number. (The 13 quarters in the period Q1 2007 to Q1 2010 were coded from -6 through to $+6$).

Previous research has established that the sales follow a seasonal pattern:

Quarter	1	2	3	4
Seasonality	−25%	−25%	0	+50%

Required:

Calculate the number of burgers that are forecast to be sold in quarters 2, 3 and 4 of 2010. **(5 marks)**

(e)   **Explain how a budget can cause conflict between "motivation" and "control".** **(5 marks)**

(f)   **Two classifications of environmental costs are "environmental internal failure costs" and "environmental external failure costs".**

Explain each one of the two classifications of environmental costs mentioned above. Your answer should include, for each classification, an example of an activity that would cause such costs. **(5 marks)**

(Total: 30 marks)

3

The Board of Directors of a company are considering two mutually exclusive projects. Both projects necessitate buying new machinery and both projects are expected to have a life of five years.

Project One

This project has already been evaluated. Details of the project are:

Initial investment needed	£500,000
Net present value	£41,000
Accounting rate of return	31%

Project Two

Details of Project Two are:

Year	1	2	3	4	5
Revenue (£000)	370	500	510	515	475
Operating costs (£000)	300	350	380	390	400
Depreciation (£000)	90	90	90	90	90

The figures for revenue and operating costs in the table above are cash flow estimates, have been stated at current values and are assumed to occur at the year end. However differential inflation is expected: 8% per annum for revenue and 6% per annum for operating costs.

The machinery will cost £500,000 and will be sold for £50,000 cash at the end of year 5.

Additional information

The company pays tax at 30%. Tax is paid and / or received one year in arrears.

The machines qualify for tax depreciation at the rate of 25% per annum on a reducing balance basis.

The company's cost of capital is 12% per annum. The current rate of return on investments in the money market is 7%.

The project chosen will be funded by internal funds.

The target accounting rate of return is 30%. The company defines "Accounting rate of return" as the average profit before tax divided by the average investment.

Required:

(a) (i) Calculate the Net Present Value and the Accounting Rate of Return of Project Two. **(12 marks)**

(ii) Prepare a report for the Board of Directors which

- recommends which of the projects, if any, they should invest in;
- identifies two non-financial factors that are relevant to the decision;
- explains the strengths and weaknesses of net present value and accounting rate of return. **(8 marks)**

(b) A government organisation has a fixed interest ten-year loan. The interest rate on the loan is 8% per annum. The loan is being repaid in equal annual instalments at the end of each year. The amount borrowed was £250,000. The loan has just over 4 years to run.

Ignore taxation.

Required:

Calculate the present value of the amount outstanding on the loan. **(5 marks)**

(Total: 25 marks)

4

A hospital specialises in the provision of a particular surgical procedure. The hospital seeks to provide a value-for-money service. In order to do this it hires teams of specialist staff on a sub-contract basis and pays them only for the hours that they have worked. The hospital uses a standard marginal costing system.

Overhead costs are attributed to the procedures based on direct labour cost.

Budget for November

Budgeted number of procedures to be performed: 20 procedures Standard marginal cost per procedure:

		$
Team fee	2 hours @ $1,500 per hour	3,000
Variable overheads	65% of team fee	1,950
		4,950

The budgeted fixed overheads for November were $48,000

Actual results for November

Procedures performed: 22 procedures

Costs incurred:

Team fees: the team worked 47 hours and were paid a total of $75,400.

Variable overheads: $48,000

Fixed overheads: $46,000

Required:

(a) **Prepare a statement which reconciles the original budget cost for November and the actual costs incurred, in as much detail as possible.** **(14 marks)**

(b) **It has now been realised that the budgeted rate for the team should have been $1,625 per hour.**

Calculate the planning variance and the operational rate and efficiency variances for the team fees for November. **(6 marks)**

(c) **Explain why budgetary control and standard costing are most effective when used together as a means of cost control in service-based organisations.** **(5 marks)**

(Total: 25 marks)

Section 8

ANSWERS TO SPECIMEN PAPER

OBJECTIVE TEST QUESTIONS

1.1   C

Contribution after reduction in variable cost = $120,000

Contribution following volume increase = $132,000

Increase in contribution = increase in profit = $32,000

Original profit was $64,000 therefore increase = 50%

1.2   B

Net present value = $50,000

Present value of cash inflows = $500,000

Sensitivity = 50,000/500,000 = 10%

1.3   EV of variable cost = $(70*0.3) + (60*0.5) + (40*0.2) = $59

Therefore the expected contribution is $61 per member

EV of number of members = (20,000*0.1) + (30,000*0.6) + (40,000*0.3) = 32,000

Expected total contribution = $61*32,000 = $1,952,000

Expected profit = $1,952,000 – 1,100,000 = **$852,000**

1.4

(i)   If VC = $40 then the contribution per member will be $80

Total contribution = 40,000*$80 = $3,200,000

Profit = $2,100,000

(ii)   Joint probability of 20,000 members and $40 variable cost = 0.1*0.2 = 0.02

1.5 Selling price= ($50 × (annuity factor t = 4, r = 11) + ($1,000 × (disc factor t = 4, r = 11)

From tables:

Selling price = $(50 × 3.102) + (1,000 × 0.659) = 155.1 + 659 = $814.10

GF should sell the bond for $814.10

1.6

	$000
Inventory used in production	331
Adjustment for increase in inventory	2
	333
Add reduction in trade payables	7
Forecast cash required	340

1.7 **The outstanding balance of trade payables in 2008 is $40,000. This is calculated as shown below:**

$$\frac{\chi}{324,444} \times 365 = 45$$

$$\chi = 45 \times \frac{324,444}{365}$$

$$\chi = 40,000$$

Days outstanding = 41 days

2

(a) (i)

		£
UK non-discount	60%*£2.1m*30/365	103,561
UK discount	40%*£2.1m*10/365	23,014
Overseas	80%*£0.9m*60/365	118,356
Total debtors		**244,931**

Debtors days = £244,931 * 365/£3m = **29.8 days**

(ii)

		£
UK non factored	15%*£2.1m*30/365	25,890
Overseas	80%*£0.9mm*60/365	118,356
Total debtors		**144,246**

Debtors days = £144,246 * 365/£3m = **17.5 days**

(b) Flexibility – it offers a flexible source of finance, as sales increases with a corresponding demand for finance, so finance from this source increases.

Security – it allows the firm to pledge other assets as security for the finance.

Last resort – it may be the most cost effective lender to a firm that has no assets to offer as security.

Administration – it relieves management of the responsibility for the sales ledger and the factor can probably perform credit checking better than the firm.

Risk of future changes – Management must balance the disruption from cutting back its administrative function with the financial and other advantages of factoring. However, the financial advantage may change and it may be costly to re-establish a sales ledger function.

Reputation – factoring is associated in many people's mind with financial difficulties or at best with small businesses, which may have an impact on the image of the business in the eyes of its suppliers.

Customer relationship – The use of factoring may create a barrier between the firm and its customers.

(c)   EV with repairs = £51,670 Earnings without repairs = £37,500

Therefore do the repairs.

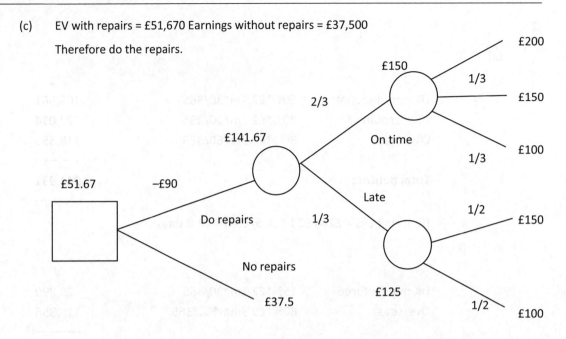

(d)

	Trend values	Seasonal adjustment	Forecast
2009 Q2	134.23 + (7.945 * 7)	0.75	142
2009 Q2	134.23 + (7.945 * 8)	1.00	198
2009 Q2	134.23 + (7.945 * 9)	1.50	309

(e)   When preparing the whole company's budget it is important to have a realistic forecast of what is likely to happen, particularly for cash, purchases, labour and capital budgets. However, for a budget to be effective for motivation, targets must be set that are challenging. It is also argued that for control purposes the budget must be a realistic benchmark against which actual performance can be compared, that is, it must be close to a forecast.

The difficulty is that both of these objectives are valid and beneficial. Thus the issue becomes whether one budget can do both tasks or whether companies need to choose which task the budget will be used for.

(f)   Environmental internal failure costs are costs that are incurred after hazardous materials, waste and / or contaminants have been produced. The costs are incurred in an attempt to comply with expected or enforced standards. Examples include treating and disposing of toxic materials and recycling scrap.

Environmental external failure costs are the most significant costs: they are incurred after the hazardous materials have been introduced into the environment. Examples of costs that an organisation has to pay include decontaminating land and clearing a river after leakage. These costs can give rise to adverse publicity. Some external failure costs may be caused by the organisation but 'paid' by society.

3

(a) *Workings* £000

Year	0	1	2	3	4	5	6
Money Sales		399.600	583.200	642.453	700.652	697.931	
Money costs		318.000	393.260	452.586	492.366	535.290	
Tax profit		81.600	189.940	189.867	208.286	162.641	
Tax		24.480	56.982	56.960	62.486	48.792	
tax offset			24.480	56.982	56.960	62.486	48.792
Capital value		500	375	281.25	210.9375	158.2031	
Allowance		125	93.75	70.3125	52.73438	108.2031	
C/f		375	281.25	210.9375	158.2031		
Tax		37.5	28.125	21.09375	15.82031	32.46094	
offset			37.5	28.125	21.09375	15.82031	32.46094

Cash flows

	0	1	2	3	4	5	6
Investment	−500					50	
Sales-costs		81.600	189.940	189.867	208.286	162.641	
Tax			−24.480	−56.982	−56.960	−62.486	−48.792
Tax allow			37.5	28.125	21.09375	15.82031	32.46094
net cash flow	−500	81.6	202.96	161.01	172.4194	165.9752	−16.3312
Discount factor	1.00	0.893	0.797	0.712	0.636	0.567	0.507
Present Value	−500	72.87	161.76	114.64	109.66	94.11	−8.28

Net present value = £44,760

	1	2	3	4	5
Sales Revenue	399.600	583.200	642.453	700.652	697.931
Operating Costs	318.000	393.260	452.586	492.366	535.290
Depreciation	90.00	90.00	90.00	90.00	90.00
Profit	(8.40)	99.94	99.867	118.286	72.641

Total profit = £382,334.

Average profit = £382,334/5 = £76,467

Average investment = (500,000+50,000)/2 = £275,000

Accounting Rate of Return = £76,467 /£275,000 = 0.278

Accounting Rate of Return = 28%

To: Board of Directors

From: Management Accountant

Date: July 2009

Subject: Investment projects

From a financial perspective based on the information given and that the projects are mutually exclusive the company should invest in Project 2. Investment decisions should be based on Net Present Values as this methodology is consistent with maximising company wealth. However, the company will also need to consider non-financial factors that could affect the decision.

Examples include:

- Consistency with the company's strategy
- Impact on other areas of the business
- Technical compatibility and obsolescence

Accounting rate of return is a simple method of investment appraisal but has many disadvantages. In particular it is based on accounting profit rather than cash flow. Accounting profit is a subjective and dependant on the choice of accounting methods used. Accounting rate of return also ignores the time value of money.

The Net Present Value method is preferable as it ensures that shareholders wealth is maximised and recognises that cash received in the future is less valuable than cash received today. Net present value does suffer from a number of disadvantages as follows:

- The speed of the repayment of the original investment is not highlighted
- Non-financial managers may have difficulty in understanding the concept
- Determination of the correct discount rate can be difficult

(b)   Annual repayments   = £250,000/(10 year 8% annuity factor)

      = £250,000/6.71

      = £37,258

There are just over years remaining therefore the company will be about to make a payment and then will have four more annual payments to make. The value of these five payments is:

£37,258 + (37,258 * 3.312) = **£160,656**

4

(a)   **Surgical procedure – November reconciliation**

Original budget (20 procedures)	$	$	$
Team			60,000
Variable overheads			39,000
Fixed overheads			48,000
Total cost			147,000
Flexed budget (22 procedures)			
Additional variable costs			9,900
Expected total cost of 22 procedures			**156,900**

Variances	F	A	
Team fee rate (47 × 1,500) – 75,400		4,900	
Team efficiency ((22 × 2) – 47) × 1,500		4,500	
Variable overhead expenditure (47 × 975) – 48,000		2,175	
Variable overhead efficiency ((22 × 2) – 47) × 975		2,925	
Fixed overhead expenditure (48,000 – 46,000)	2,000	–	
	2,000	14,500	12,500

Actual cost   **169,400**

(b)   Revised standard cost = $1,625 per hour

        Original standard cost = $1,500 per hour

Original total team cost for 22 procedures (22 * 2 * $1,500)	66,000
Actual cost	75,400
Total variance	**9,400** adverse

Planning variance (22 * 2 * (1,500 – 1,625))	5,500 adverse
Operational team rate variance (75,400 – (47*1,625))	975 favourable
Operational team efficiency variance (3 * 1,625)	4,875 adverse
	9,400

(c)   Budgets are projected cost (and/or revenue) aggregates which quantify expectations about future performance. They are used as comparators against which current performance can be measured and as "authority to spend" within which expenditure will be allowed. A budget is an effective planning and control tool for service based organisation.

        Standards measure performance at a lower, operational, level. Standard costing is extensively used in manufacturing industries but can equally be applied to service based organisations e.g. in the insurance industry, a standard may be the time to process an insurance claim or key in a document.

        Standard costing and budgetary control can be used effectively in both manufacturing and service organisation. They should however be used in combination because together they are more powerful and embrace the organisation more completely than either can do in isolation. It makes little sense to control, or plan, at operational level, without considering impacts at higher levels. Similarly, overall budgets cannot be realistically set without looking at the feasibility of setting operational standards.

Performance Pillar

P1 – Performance Operations

24 November 2010 – Wednesday Morning Session

Instructions to candidates

You are allowed three hours to answer this question paper.
You are allowed 20 minutes reading time **before the examination begins** during which you should read the question paper and, if you wish, highlight and/or make notes on the question paper. However, you will **not** be allowed, **under any circumstances**, to open the answer book and start writing or use your calculator during this reading time.
You are strongly advised to carefully read ALL the question requirements before attempting the question concerned (that is all parts and/or sub-questions).
ALL answers must be written in the answer book. Answers written on the question paper will **not** be submitted for marking.
You should show all workings as marks are available for the method you use.
ALL QUESTIONS ARE COMPULSORY.
Section A comprises 8 sub-questions and is on pages 2 to 5.
Section B comprises 6 sub-questions and is on pages 6 to 8.
Section C comprises 2 questions and is on pages 10 to 13.
Maths tables and formulae are provided on pages 15 to 18.
The list of verbs as published in the syllabus is given for reference on page 19.
Write your candidate number, the paper number and examination subject title in the spaces provided on the front of the answer book. Also write your contact ID and name in the space provided in the right hand margin and seal to close.
Tick the appropriate boxes on the front of the answer book to indicate which questions you have answered.

P1 – Performance Operations

TURN OVER

[You are advised to spend no longer than 36 minutes on this question.]

ANSWER *ALL* EIGHT SUB-QUESTIONS IN THIS SECTION

Instructions for answering Section A:

The answers to the eight sub-questions in Section A should ALL be written in your answer book.

Your answers should be clearly numbered with the sub-question number then ruled off, so that the markers know which sub-question you are answering. **For multiple choice questions, you need only write the sub-question number and the letter of the answer option you have chosen.** You do not need to start a new page for each sub-question.

For sub-questions **1.6** to **1.8** you should show your workings as marks are available for the method you use to answer these sub-questions.

Question One

1.1   Invoice discounting is:

A   Reducing or discounting the amount owed by a customer in order to ensure payment.

B   Writing off a debt because the customer is not expected to pay.

C   Selling invoices to a finance company that then collects the cash from the customer.

D   Selling invoices to a finance company for less than their face value while continuing to collect the cash from the customer.

(2 marks)

1.2 A project with a five year life requires an initial investment of $120,000 and generates a net present value (NPV) of $50,000 at a discount rate of 10% per annum.

The project cash flows are as follows.

	$000 per annum
Variable material cost	30
Variable labour cost	10
Incremental fixed cost	5

The costs and activity levels are expected to remain the same for each year of the project.

Ignore taxation and inflation.

The sensitivity of the investment decision to changes in the variable costs is:

A   131.9%

B   44.0%

C   33.0%

D   29.3%

(2 marks)

1.3 The data in the table below has been extracted from a company's cost accounting records. It shows the total costs and the inflation index for the periods in which the costs were incurred. Cost behaviour patterns are the same in both periods.

Output level	Total cost	Inflation index
6,000 units	$10,500	1.05
8,000 units	$13,390	1.03

The variable cost per unit, to the nearest $0.01, at an inflation index of 1.06 is:

A $1.45

B $1.59

C $1.53

D $1.50

(2 marks)

Section A continues on the next page

TURN OVER

The budgeted selling price of one of C's range of chocolate bars was $6.00 per bar. At the beginning of the budget period market prices of cocoa increased significantly and C decided to increase the selling price of the chocolate bar by 10% for the whole period. C also decided to increase the amount spent on marketing and as a result actual sales volumes increased to 15,750 bars which was 5% above the budgeted volume. The standard contribution per bar was $2.00 however a contribution of $2.25 per bar was actually achieved.

1.4 The sales price variance for the period was:

A $9,450 A

B $9,450 F

C $9,000 A

D $9,000 F

(2 marks)

1.5 The sales volume contribution variance for the period was:

A $1,500.00 F

B $3,937.50 F

C $3,750.00 F

D $1,687.50 F

(2 marks)

1.6 H has a budgeted production for the next budget year of 12,000 units spread evenly over the year. It expects the same production level to continue for the next two years. Each unit uses 4kg of material.

The estimated opening raw material inventory at the start of the next budget year is 3,000kg. H's future policy will be to hold sufficient raw material inventory at the end of each month to cover 110% of the following month's production.

The budgeted material cost is $8 per kg for purchases up to 49,000kg. The excess of purchases over 49,000kg in a year will be at a cost of $7.50 per kg.

Calculate the material purchases budget for the year in $.

(3 marks)

1.7 An unquoted bond has a coupon rate of 6% per annum and will repay its face value of $100 on its maturity in 4 years' time. The yield to maturity on similar bonds is estimated to be 3% per annum. The annual interest has just been paid for the current year.

Calculate the current expected market value of the bond.

(3 marks)

1.8 A company has to choose between three mutually exclusive projects. Market research has shown that customers could react to the projects in three different ways depending on their preferences. There is a 30% chance that customers will exhibit preferences 1, a 20% chance they will exhibit preferences 2 and a 50% chance they will exhibit preferences 3. The company uses expected value to make this type of decision.

The net present value of each of the possible outcomes is as follows:

	Probability	Project A	Project B	Project C
		$000	$000	$000
Preferences 1	0.3	400	800	500
Preferences 2	0.2	500	300	600
Preferences 3	0.5	700	200	400

A market research company believes it can provide perfect information about the preferences of customers in this market.

Calculate the maximum amount that should be paid for the information from the market research company.

(4 marks)

(Total for Section A = 20 marks)

Reminder

All answers to Section A must be written in your answer book.

Answers to Section A written on the question paper will **not** be submitted for marking.

End of Section A

Section B begins on page 6

TURN OVER

SECTION B – 30 MARKS

[You are advised to spend no longer than 9 minutes on each sub-question in this section.]

ANSWER ALL SIX SUB-QUESTIONS. YOU SHOULD SHOW YOUR WORKINGS AS MARKS ARE AVAILABLE FOR THE METHOD YOU USE.

Question Two

(a)   **Explain** the stages in the budget setting process for a company that uses a zero-based budgeting system.

(5 marks)

(b)   AP sells fruit in a market where the level of demand is uncertain. AP has to order the fruit before the demand level is known.

The payoff table below shows the profits AP can expect depending on the level of order that is placed and the level of demand that occurs.

Demand level	Level of order		
	High	*Medium*	*Low*
Good	$600	$300	$100
Average	$200	$400	$100
Poor	$(100)	$300	$200

Required:

(i)   **Identify** which order level would be selected if AP applied:

 a.   the maximin decision criterion
 b.   the maximax decision criterion

(2 marks)

(ii)   **Identify,** using a minimax regret table, the order level that would be selected if AP applied the minimax regret decision criterion.

(3 marks)

(Total for sub-question (b) = 5 marks)

(c) "Decision rules based on expected values assume that the decision maker is risk neutral".

Required:

(i) **Explain** the above statement.

(2 marks)

(ii) **Describe** TWO other attitudes to risk.

(3 marks)

(Total for sub-question (c) = 5 marks)

(d) RX has a balance outstanding on its trade receivables account at the start of the year of $83,000 after allowing for bad debts. RX forecasts sales revenue for the next year of $492,750. All sales are on credit.

Based on past experience, RX anticipates that bad debts will represent 5% of sales for the year. Trade receivable days at the end of the year are expected to be 60 days.

Required:

(i) **Calculate** the expected receipts from customers during the year.

(3 marks)

(ii) **Describe** TWO methods that RX could use to reduce the possibility of bad debts occurring.

(2 marks)

(Total for sub-question (d) = 5 marks)

(e) A company has forecast that it will have surplus funds to invest for a 12 month period. It is considering two investments as follows:

Investment 1
Invest in a bank deposit account that has a variable rate of interest. The current rate of interest on the account is 1.1% per quarter.

Investment 2
Buy a 12 month fixed dated government bond. The bond has a coupon rate of 2.5% payable every six months.

Required:

Explain the advantages AND disadvantages to the company of each of the investments.

You should consider the return offered and the level and type of risk involved with each investment.

You should assume that there are no other investments available and that these investments are only available now.

(5 marks)

TURN OVER

(f) An extract from WCC's trial balance at the end of its financial year is given below:

	$000
Sales revenue (80% on credit)	1,400
Cost of sales	1,215
Purchases of materials (95% on credit)	915
Inventories at end of year	
Raw materials	85
Finished goods	90
Trade receivables	185
Trade payables	125

Required:

Calculate the length of WCC's working capital cycle to the nearest 0.1 of a day.

(5 marks)

(Total for Section B = 30 marks)

End of Section B

Section C begins on page 10

This page is blank

TURN OVER

SECTION C – 50 MARKS

[You are advised to spend no longer than 45 minutes on each question in this section.]

ANSWER *BOTH* QUESTIONS IN THIS SECTION. EACH QUESTION IS WORTH 25 MARKS. YOU SHOULD SHOW YOUR WORKINGS AS MARKS ARE AVAILABLE FOR THE METHOD YOU USE.

Question Three

A healthcare company specialises in hip, knee and shoulder replacement operations, known as surgical procedures. As well as providing these surgical procedures the company offers pre operation and post operation in-patient care, in a fully equipped hospital, for those patients who will be undergoing the surgical procedures.

Surgeons are paid a fixed fee for each surgical procedure they perform and an additional amount for any follow-up consultations. Post procedure follow-up consultations are only undertaken if there are any complications in relation to the surgical procedure. There is no additional fee charged to patients for any follow up consultations. All other staff are paid annual salaries.

The company's existing costing system uses a single overhead rate, based on revenue, to charge the costs of support activities to the procedures. Concern has been raised about the inaccuracy of procedure costs and the company's accountant has initiated a project to implement an activity-based costing (ABC) system.

The project team has collected the following data on each of the procedures.

Procedure Information	Hip	Knee	Shoulder
Fee charged to patients per procedure	$8,000	$10,000	$6,000
Number of procedures per annum	600	800	400
Average time per procedure	2.0 hours	1.2 hours	1.5 hours
Number of procedures per theatre session	2	1	4
In-patient days per procedure	3	2	1
Surgeon's fee per procedure	$1,200	$1,800	$1,500
% of procedures with complications	8%	5%	10%
Surgeon's fee per follow up consultation	$300	$300	$300
Cost of medical supplies per procedure	$400	$200	$300

The project team has obtained the following information about the support activities.

Activity	Cost Driver	Overheads $000
Theatre preparation for each session	Number of theatre preparations	864
Operating theatre usage	Procedure time	1,449
Nursing and ancillary services	In-patient days	5,428
Administration	Sales revenue	1,216
Other overheads	Number of procedures	923

Section C continues on the next page

Question Four

A car manufacturer has been experiencing financial difficulties over the past few years. Sales have reduced significantly as a result of the worldwide economic recession. Costs have increased due to quality issues that led to a recall of some models of its cars.

Production volume last year was 50,000 cars and it is expected that this will increase by 4% per annum each year for the next five years.

The company directors are concerned to improve profitability and are considering two potential investment projects.

Project 1 – implement a new quality control process
The company has paid a consultant process engineer $50,000 to review the company's quality processes. The consultant recommended that the company implement a new quality control process. The new process will require a machine costing $20,000,000. The machine is expected to have a useful life of five years and no residual value.

It is estimated that raw material costs will be reduced by $62 per car and that both internal and external failure costs from quality failures will be reduced by 80%.

Estimated internal and external failure costs per year without the new process, based on last year's production volume of 50,000 cars, and their associated probabilities are shown below:

Internal Failure Costs		External Failure Costs	
$	Probability	$	Probability
300,000	50%	1,300,000	60%
500,000	30%	1,900,000	30%
700,000	20%	3,000,000	10%

Internal and external failure costs are expected to increase each year in line with the number of cars produced.

The company's accountant has calculated that this investment will result in a net present value (NPV) of $1,338,000 and an internal rate of return of 10.5%.

Project 2 – in-house component manufacturing
The company could invest in new machinery to enable in-house manufacturing of a component that is currently made by outside suppliers. The new machinery is expected to cost $15,000,000 and have a useful life of five years and no residual value. Additional working capital of $1,000,000 will also be required as a result of producing the component in-house.

The price paid to the current supplier is $370 per component. It is estimated that the in-house variable cost of production will be $260 per component. Each car requires one component. Fixed production costs, including machinery depreciation, are estimated to increase by $5,000,000 per annum as a result of manufacturing the component in-house.

Depreciation is calculated on a straight line basis.

Additional Information
The company is unable to raise enough capital to carry out both projects. The company will therefore have to choose between the two alternatives.

Taxation and inflation should be ignored.

The company uses a cost of capital of 8% per annum.

Required:

(a) **Calculate** for Project 1 the relevant cash flows that the accountant should have used for year 1 when appraising the project.

All workings should be shown in $000.

(6 marks)

(b) **Calculate** for Project 2:

(i) the net present value (NPV)
(ii) the internal rate of return (IRR)

All workings should be shown in $000.

(10 marks)

(c) **Advise** the company directors which of the two investment projects should be undertaken.

(4 marks)

(d) A company is considering two alternative investment projects both of which have a positive net present value. The projects have been ranked on the basis of both net present value (NPV) and internal rate of return (IRR). The result of the ranking is shown below:

	Project A	Project B
NPV	1st	2nd
IRR	2nd	1st

Discuss potential reasons why the conflict between the NPV and IRR ranking may have arisen.

(5 marks)

Total for Question Four = 25 marks)

(Total for Section C = 50 marks)

End of question paper
Maths tables and formulae are on pages 15 to 18

This page is blank

PRESENT VALUE TABLE

Present value of $1, that is $(1+r)^{-n}$ where r = interest rate; n = number of periods until payment or receipt.

Periods	Interest rates (r)									
(n)	1%	2%	3%	4%	5%	6%	7%	8%	9%	10%
1	0.990	0.980	0.971	0.962	0.952	0.943	0.935	0.926	0.917	0.909
2	0.980	0.961	0.943	0.925	0.907	0.890	0.873	0.857	0.842	0.826
3	0.971	0.942	0.915	0.889	0.864	0.840	0.816	0.794	0.772	0.751
4	0.961	0.924	0.888	0.855	0.823	0.792	0.763	0.735	0.708	0.683
5	0.951	0.906	0.863	0.822	0.784	0.747	0.713	0.681	0.650	0.621
6	0.942	0.888	0.837	0.790	0.746	0705	0.666	0.630	0.596	0.564
7	0.933	0.871	0.813	0.760	0.711	0.665	0.623	0.583	0.547	0.513
8	0.923	0.853	0.789	0.731	0.677	0.627	0.582	0.540	0.502	0.467
9	0.914	0.837	0.766	0.703	0.645	0.592	0.544	0.500	0.460	0.424
10	0.905	0.820	0.744	0.676	0.614	0.558	0.508	0.463	0.422	0.386
11	0.896	0.804	0.722	0.650	0.585	0.527	0.475	0.429	0.388	0.350
12	0.887	0.788	0.701	0.625	0.557	0.497	0.444	0.397	0.356	0.319
13	0.879	0.773	0.681	0.601	0.530	0.469	0.415	0.368	0.326	0.290
14	0.870	0.758	0.661	0.577	0.505	0.442	0.388	0.340	0.299	0.263
15	0.861	0.743	0.642	0.555	0.481	0.417	0.362	0.315	0.275	0.239
16	0.853	0.728	0.623	0.534	0.458	0.394	0.339	0.292	0.252	0.218
17	0.844	0.714	0.605	0.513	0.436	0.371	0.317	0.270	0.231	0.198
18	0.836	0.700	0.587	0.494	0.416	0.350	0.296	0.250	0.212	0.180
19	0.828	0.686	0.570	0.475	0.396	0.331	0.277	0.232	0.194	0.164
20	0.820	0.673	0.554	0.456	0.377	0.312	0.258	0.215	0.178	0.149

Periods	Interest rates (r)									
(n)	11%	12%	13%	14%	15%	16%	17%	18%	19%	20%
1	0.901	0.893	0.885	0.877	0.870	0.862	0.855	0.847	0.840	0.833
2	0.812	0.797	0.783	0.769	0.756	0.743	0.731	0.718	0.706	0.694
3	0.731	0.712	0.693	0.675	0.658	0.641	0.624	0.609	0.593	0.579
4	0.659	0.636	0.613	0.592	0.572	0.552	0.534	0.516	0.499	0.482
5	0.593	0.567	0.543	0.519	0.497	0.476	0.456	0.437	0.419	0.402
6	0.535	0.507	0.480	0.456	0.432	0.410	0.390	0.370	0.352	0.335
7	0.482	0.452	0.425	0.400	0.376	0.354	0.333	0.314	0.296	0.279
8	0.434	0.404	0.376	0.351	0.327	0.305	0.285	0.266	0.249	0.233
9	0.391	0.361	0.333	0.308	0.284	0.263	0.243	0.225	0.209	0.194
10	0.352	0.322	0.295	0.270	0.247	0.227	0.208	0.191	0.176	0.162
11	0.317	0.287	0.261	0.237	0.215	0.195	0.178	0.162	0.148	0.135
12	0.286	0.257	0.231	0.208	0.187	0.168	0.152	0.137	0.124	0.112
13	0.258	0.229	0.204	0.182	0.163	0.145	0.130	0.116	0.104	0.093
14	0.232	0.205	0.181	0.160	0.141	0.125	0.111	0.099	0.088	0.078
15	0.209	0.183	0.160	0.140	0.123	0.108	0.095	0.084	0.079	0.065
16	0.188	0.163	0.141	0.123	0.107	0.093	0.081	0.071	0.062	0.054
17	0.170	0.146	0.125	0.108	0.093	0.080	0.069	0.060	0.052	0.045
18	0.153	0.130	0.111	0.095	0.081	0.069	0.059	0.051	0.044	0.038
19	0.138	0.116	0.098	0.083	0.070	0.060	0.051	0.043	0.037	0.031
20	0.124	0.104	0.087	0.073	0.061	0.051	0.043	0.037	0.031	0.026

Cumulative present value of \$1 per annum, Receivable or Payable at the end of each year for n years $\frac{1-(1+r)^{-n}}{r}$

Periods (n)	Interest rates (r)									
	1%	2%	3%	4%	5%	6%	7%	8%	9%	10%
1	0.990	0.980	0.971	0.962	0.952	0.943	0.935	0.926	0.917	0.909
2	1.970	1.942	1.913	1.886	1.859	1.833	1.808	1.783	1.759	1.736
3	2.941	2.884	2.829	2.775	2.723	2.673	2.624	2.577	2.531	2.487
4	3.902	3.808	3.717	3.630	3.546	3.465	3.387	3.312	3.240	3.170
5	4.853	4.713	4.580	4.452	4.329	4.212	4.100	3.993	3.890	3.791
6	5.795	5.601	5.417	5.242	5.076	4.917	4.767	4.623	4.486	4.355
7	6.728	6.472	6.230	6.002	5.786	5.582	5.389	5.206	5.033	4.868
8	7.652	7.325	7.020	6.733	6.463	6.210	5.971	5.747	5.535	5.335
9	8.566	8.162	7.786	7.435	7.108	6.802	6.515	6.247	5.995	5.759
10	9.471	8.983	8.530	8.111	7.722	7.360	7.024	6.710	6.418	6.145
11	10.368	9.787	9.253	8.760	8.306	7.887	7.499	7.139	6.805	6.495
12	11.255	10.575	9.954	9.385	8.863	8.384	7.943	7.536	7.161	6.814
13	12.134	11.348	10.635	9.986	9.394	8.853	8.358	7.904	7.487	7.103
14	13.004	12.106	11.296	10.563	9.899	9.295	8.745	8.244	7.786	7.367
15	13.865	12.849	11.938	11.118	10.380	9.712	9.108	8.559	8.061	7.606
16	14.718	13.578	12.561	11.652	10.838	10.106	9.447	8.851	8.313	7.824
17	15.562	14.292	13.166	12.166	11.274	10.477	9.763	9.122	8.544	8.022
18	16.398	14.992	13.754	12.659	11.690	10.828	10.059	9.372	8.756	8.201
19	17.226	15.679	14.324	13.134	12.085	11.158	10.336	9.604	8.950	8.365
20	18.046	16.351	14.878	13.590	12.462	11.470	10.594	9.818	9.129	8.514

Periods (n)	Interest rates (r)									
	11%	12%	13%	14%	15%	16%	17%	18%	19%	20%
1	0.901	0.893	0.885	0.877	0.870	0.862	0.855	0.847	0.840	0.833
2	1.713	1.690	1.668	1.647	1.626	1.605	1.585	1.566	1.547	1.528
3	2.444	2.402	2.361	2.322	2.283	2.246	2.210	2.174	2.140	2.106
4	3.102	3.037	2.974	2.914	2.855	2.798	2.743	2.690	2.639	2.589
5	3.696	3.605	3.517	3.433	3.352	3.274	3.199	3.127	3.058	2.991
6	4.231	4.111	3.998	3.889	3.784	3.685	3.589	3.498	3.410	3.326
7	4.712	4.564	4.423	4.288	4.160	4.039	3.922	3.812	3.706	3.605
8	5.146	4.968	4.799	4.639	4.487	4.344	4.207	4.078	3.954	3.837
9	5.537	5.328	5.132	4.946	4.772	4.607	4.451	4.303	4.163	4.031
10	5.889	5.650	5.426	5.216	5.019	4.833	4.659	4.494	4.339	4.192
11	6.207	5.938	5.687	5.453	5.234	5.029	4.836	4.656	4.486	4.327
12	6.492	6.194	5.918	5.660	5.421	5.197	4.988	7.793	4.611	4.439
13	6.750	6.424	6.122	5.842	5.583	5.342	5.118	4.910	4.715	4.533
14	6.982	6.628	6.302	6.002	5.724	5.468	5.229	5.008	4.802	4.611
15	7.191	6.811	6.462	6.142	5.847	5.575	5.324	5.092	4.876	4.675
16	7.379	6.974	6.604	6.265	5.954	5.668	5.405	5.162	4.938	4.730
17	7.549	7.120	6.729	6.373	6.047	5.749	5.475	5.222	4.990	4.775
18	7.702	7.250	6.840	6.467	6.128	5.818	5.534	5.273	5.033	4.812
19	7.839	7.366	6.938	6.550	6.198	5.877	5.584	5.316	5.070	4.843
20	7.963	7.469	7.025	6.623	6.259	5.929	5.628	5.353	5.101	4.870

FORMULAE

PROBABILITY

$A \cup B = \textbf{\textit{A}}$ **or** $\textbf{\textit{B}}$. $A \cap B = \textbf{\textit{A}}$ **and** $\textbf{\textit{B}}$ (overlap).

$P(B \mid A)$ = probability of B, **given** A.

Rules of Addition
If A and B are mutually exclusive: $P(A \cup B) = P(A) + P(B)$

If A and B are not mutually exclusive: $P(A \cup B) = P(A) + P(B) - P(A \cap B)$

Rules of Multiplication
If A and B are *independent*:: $P(A \cap B) = P(A) * P(B)$

If A and B are **not** *independent*: $P(A \cap B) = P(A) * P(B \mid A)$

$E(X) = \sum (\text{probability} * \text{payoff})$

DESCRIPTIVE STATISTICS

Arithmetic Mean

$$\overline{x} = \frac{\sum x}{n} \qquad \overline{x} = \frac{\sum fx}{\sum f} \quad \text{(frequency distribution)}$$

Standard Deviation

$$SD = \sqrt{\frac{\sum (x - \overline{x})^2}{n}} \qquad SD = \sqrt{\frac{\sum fx^2}{\sum f} - \overline{x}^2} \quad \text{(frequency distribution)}$$

INDEX NUMBERS

Price relative = $100 * P_1/P_0$ Quantity relative = $100 * Q_1/Q_0$

Price: $$\frac{\sum w * \left(\dfrac{P_1}{P_o} \right)}{\sum w} \times 100$$

Quantity: $$\frac{\sum w * \left(\dfrac{Q_1}{Q_o} \right)}{\sum w} \times 100$$

TIME SERIES

Additive Model

Series = Trend + Seasonal + Random

Multiplicative Model

Series = Trend * Seasonal * Random

FINANCIAL MATHEMATICS

Compound Interest (Values and Sums)
Future Value S, of a sum of X, invested for n periods, compounded at $r\%$ interest

$$S = X[1 + r]^n$$

Annuity
Present value of an annuity of £1 per annum receivable or payable for n years, commencing in one year, discounted at $r\%$ per annum:

$$PV = \frac{1}{r}\left[1 - \frac{1}{[1+r]^n}\right]$$

Perpetuity
Present value of £1 per annum, payable or receivable in perpetuity, commencing in one year, discounted at $r\%$ per annum:

$$PV = \frac{1}{r}$$

LEARNING CURVE

$$Y_x = aX^b$$

where:
Y_x = the cumulative average time per unit to produce X units;
a = the time required to produce the first unit of output;
X = the cumulative number of units;
b = the index of learning.

The exponent b is defined as the log of the learning curve improvement rate divided by log 2.

INVENTORY MANAGEMENT

Economic Order Quantity

$$EOQ = \sqrt{\frac{2C_oD}{C_h}}$$

where: C_o = cost of placing an order
C_h = cost of holding one unit in inventory for one year
D = annual demand

LIST OF VERBS USED IN THE QUESTION REQUIREMENTS

A list of the learning objectives and verbs that appear in the syllabus and in the question requirements for each question in this paper.

It is important that you answer the question according to the definition of the verb.

LEARNING OBJECTIVE	VERBS USED	DEFINITION
Level 1 - KNOWLEDGE What you are expected to know.	List State Define	Make a list of Express, fully or clearly, the details/facts of Give the exact meaning of
Level 2 - COMPREHENSION What you are expected to understand.	Describe Distinguish Explain Identify Illustrate	Communicate the key features Highlight the differences between Make clear or intelligible/State the meaning or purpose of Recognise, establish or select after consideration Use an example to describe or explain something
Level 3 - APPLICATION How you are expected to apply your knowledge.	Apply Calculate Demonstrate Prepare Reconcile Solve Tabulate	Put to practical use Ascertain or reckon mathematically Prove with certainty or to exhibit by practical means Make or get ready for use Make or prove consistent/compatible Find an answer to Arrange in a table
Level 4 - ANALYSIS How are you expected to analyse the detail of what you have learned.	Analyse Categorise Compare and contrast Construct Discuss Interpret Prioritise Produce	Examine in detail the structure of Place into a defined class or division Show the similarities and/or differences between Build up or compile Examine in detail by argument Translate into intelligible or familiar terms Place in order of priority or sequence for action Create or bring into existence
Level 5 - EVALUATION How are you expected to use your learning to evaluate, make decisions or recommendations.	Advise Evaluate Recommend	Counsel, inform or notify Appraise or assess the value of Advise on a course of action

Performance Pillar

Operational Level Paper

P1 – Performance Operations

November 2010

Wednesday Morning Session

Operational Level Paper

P1 –Performance Operations

Examiner's Answers

Answer to Question One

1.1 **The correct answer is D.**

1.2 $40,000 x 3.791 = $151,640
$50,000 / $151,640 = 0.3297 = 33.0%

The correct answer is C.

1.3 $10,500 / 1.05 = $10,000
$13,390 / 1.03 = $13,000

Using the high-low method

($13,000 – $10,000) / (8,000 – 6,000) = $ 1.50 per unit

At inflation index of 1.06 = $1.50 x 1.06 = $1.59

The correct answer is B.

1.4 The sales price variance is:

($6.60 – $6.00) x 15,750 = $9,450 Favourable

The correct answer is B.

1.5 The sales volume contribution variance is:

(15,750 – 15,000) x $2.00 = $1,500 Favourable

Budgeted sales were 15,750/1.05 = 15,000 units

The correct answer is A.

1.6 Materials Usage
12,000 units x 4kg = 48,000kg

Opening inventory = 3,000kg
Closing inventory = 12,000/12 x 4kg x 1.1 = 4,400kg

Material Purchases Budget (kg)

Material usage	48,000kg
Plus closing inventory	4,400kg
Less opening inventory	(3,000)kg
	49,400kg

Material Purchases Budget ($)

49,000kg x $8 =	$392,000
400kg x $7.50 =	$3,000
Total	$395,000

1.7 Yield to maturity of similar bonds is 3%, therefore use 3% as the discount rate.

Year(s)	Description	Cash flow $	Discount Factor (3%)	Present Value $
1-4	Interest	6	3.717	22.3
4	Redemption	100	0.888	88.8
0	Market value			111.1

The current expected market value of the bond is therefore $111.10

1.8

	Probability	Project A	Project B	Project C
		$000	$000	$000
Preferences 1	0.3	400	800	500
Preferences 2	0.2	500	300	600
Preferences 3	0.5	700	200	400
Expected Value		570	400	470

Project A is the best choice (without the benefit of perfect information) as it has the highest expected value (EV) of the NPV of $570k.

With perfect information:

If market research say preferences 1: select B and earn $800k – probability 0.3
If market research say preferences 2: select C and earn $600k – probability 0.2
If market research say preferences 3: select A and earn $700k – probability 0.5

EV (with perfect information) = ($800k x 0.3) + ($600k x 0.2) + ($700k x 0.5) = $710k

Value of perfect information is $710k – $570k = $140,000

Answer to Question Two

(a)

There are three main stages in the budget setting process in a zero based budgeting system:

Description of activities in decision packages
The activities that are being proposed are described in a decision package. There will often be more than one decision package proposed e.g. one based on providing services at a minimum level and others at incremental levels above the minimum.

Some of these packages will be mutually exclusive and will require management to select the best solution to the issue involved. For example options for debt collection could be in-house or outsourced solutions and a decision package will be needed for each.

Evaluation and ranking
Each decision package is evaluated. Its costs are compared to its benefits and net present values or other measures calculated. The non-financial aspects are also considered as some packages might have legal obligations attached e.g. updating accounting systems.

Management will rank each package based on the benefits to the organisation. They may decide to reject packages even though the activity was undertaken last year. In this way the organisation is said to be starting from a zero base with each package given due consideration.

Allocation of resources
Once management decide which packages to accept a budget can be prepared for the resources required. This should include costs, revenues and other resource allocations necessary.

(b)

(i)　　If AP applied the maximin decision criterion it would order at the medium level. The worst result is a profit of $300 and this is the best "worst result".

(ii)　　If AP applied the maximax decision criterion it would order at the high level, since the maximum return of $600 is to be gained at this level.

(iii)

Minimax Regret Table			
Demand level	Level of order		
	High	Medium	Low
Good	0	$300	$500
Average	$200	0	$300
Poor	$400	0	$100

The maximum regret if AP orders at the high level is $400
The maximum regret if AP orders at the medium level is $300
The maximum regret if AP orders at the low level is $500

Therefore if AP wants to minimise the maximum regret it will order at the medium level.

(c)

(i) Expected values represent a long-run average outcome but decisions should not be made solely on expected values as they do not take account of the attitude to risk. In addition to expected value decision makers should consider measures of dispersion and the probability distribution of the outcomes of the various courses of action. A **risk neutral** decision maker will tend to ignore risk and choose the course of action that gives the highest expected value.

(ii) A **risk seeker** is a decision maker that is interested in the best possible outcomes no matter how unlikely they are to occur. They are not put off with the low probability of an outcome but choose to focus on potential large returns instead. A risk seeker faced with a choice between two alternatives with identical expected values will choose the riskier investment with the highest possible outcome and ignore the downside risk. These decision makers are often viewed as optimistic.

A **risk averse** decision maker is one that focuses on the poor results and seeks to avoid high degrees of risk. A risk averse decision maker, faced with a choice between two alternatives with identical expected values will choose the less risky alternative. These decision makers are often viewed as pessimistic.

(d)

(i) Trade receivable at end of the year = $492,750 / 365 x 60 = $81,000

Bad debts = ($492,750 – $81,000) x 5% = $20,587.50

Cash collected = $83,000 + $492,750 - $81,000 - $20,587.50 = $474,162.50

(ii)

Examiner's note: the question asks for two methods. Examples of methods that would be rewarded are given below.

To reduce the incidence of bad debts RX could:

- Ensure that all new customers have a full credit rating check before the granting of credit. This can be achieved by the use of credit rating organisations or by the taking of references from the prospective customer.
- Carry out routine credit ratings checks on existing customers, in particular the slow payers.
- Ensure that debt collection procedures are efficient in chasing up late payers.
- Charge penalties for late payment or offer discounts to encourage customers to pay early.
- Ensure that credit limits are allocated to customers and enforced by the credit control department. No sales should be allowed if credit limits have been exceeded, effectively putting the account on "stop" should this happen.

(e)

The returns given are over different time periods. We need to calculate an annual rate to enable the investments to be compared.

The annual return on the deposit account is $(1.011)^4 = 1.044731$ or 4.47% per annum.

The annual return on the bond is 2.5% x 2 = 5% per annum.

The deposit account has two main types of risk. Firstly, the interest rate could change and this will introduce variability in the return, although this is likely to reflect market rates. Secondly, after the world banking crisis in 2008/2009 it is now conceivable for a bank to fail. This introduces another, albeit small, element of risk in that there is liquidation risk of the bank itself.

A government bond is generally considered to be risk free. However the bonds are fixed dated and cannot be cashed in early. Therefore the bonds lack flexibility. Although the return is fixed, market interest rates may rise with the result that the return on the bond is below market rates. If they are a tradable item, the bonds could be sold to another investor through a broker. However this would incur sales costs and expose the company to price movements which will reflect the change in market interest rates.

The choice of investment will depend on the company's attitude to risk and whether they prefer to have a fixed return. The bond currently offers a higher return but may not continue to do so in the future. It also offers less risk as the return is guaranteed.

(f)   The number of days for each component of the working capital cycle is as follows:

Component	Calculation	Days
Raw material inventory days	85/915 x 365	33.9
Finished goods inventory days	90/1215 x 365	27.0
Receivable days	185/(0.80 x 1,400) x 365	60.3
Payables days	125/(0.95 x 915) x 365	-52.5
Working capital cycle		68.7

The working capital cycle is therefore 68.7 days.

Answer to Question Three

(a)

	Hip	*Knee*	*Shoulder*
	$	$	$
Fee charged to patient	8,000	10,000	6,000
Surgeon's fee	(1,200)	(1,800)	(1,500)
Fee for follow-up consultations	(24)	(15)	(30)
Medical supplies	(400)	(200)	(300)
Overhead cost	(5,200)	(6,500)	(3,900)
Profit per procedure	1,176	1,485	270

Follow-up consultations working:

Hip - $300 per consultation x 8% = $24
Knee - $300 per consultation x 5% = $15
Shoulder - $300 per consultation x 10% = $30

Overhead cost workings:

	Hip	*Knee*	*Shoulder*	*Total*
	$	$	$	$
Sales revenue	$8,000 x 600 = $4,800,000	$10,000 x 800 = $8,000,000	$6,000 x 400 = $2,400,000	$15,200,000
Overheads				$9,880,000
Overheads / sales revenue				65%
Cost per procedure	$8,000 x 65% $5,200	$10,000 x 65% $6,500	$6,000 x 65% $3,900	

(b)

Activity	Cost Driver	Overheads $000	No. of cost drivers	Cost per driver $
Theatre preparation for each session	Number of theatre preparations	864	(600/2 + 800/1 + 400/4) = 1,200	$720 per theatre preparation
Operating theatre usage	Procedure time	1,449	(600 x 2hrs) + (800 x 1.2hrs) + (400 x 1.5hrs) = 2,760	$525 per hour
Nursing and ancillary services	In-patient days	5,428	(600 x 3) + (800 x 2) +(400 x 1) = 3,800	$1,428 per day
Administration	Sales revenue	1,216	15,200,000	$0.08 per $ sales revenue
Other overheads	Number of procedures	923	(600 + 800 + 400) = 1,800	$513 per procedure

Overhead cost per procedure	Hip	Knee	Shoulder
Theatre preparation for each session	$720/2 = $360	$720/1 = $720	$720/4 = $180
Operating theatre usage	($525 x 2) = $1,050	($525 x 1.2) =$630	($525 x 1.5) = $788
Nursing and ancillary services	($1,428 x 3) =$4,284	($1,428 x 2) =$2,856	($1,428 x 1) =$1,428
Administration	(8,000 x $0.08) = $640	(10,000 x $0.08) = $800	(6,000 x$ 0.08) = $480
Other overheads	$513	$513	$513
Total overhead cost per procedure	$6,847	$5,519	$3,389

	Hip	Knee	Shoulder
	$	$	$
Profit per procedure per (a) above	1,176	1,485	270
Add back overhead cost per (a) above	5,200	6,500	3,900
Less overhead cost using ABC	(6,847)	(5,519)	(3,389)
Profit per procedure using ABC	(471)	2,466	781

(c) Under an activity based costing (ABC) system the various support activities that are involved in the process of making products or providing services are identified. The cost drivers that cause a change to the cost of these activities are also identified and used as the basis to attach activity costs to a particular product or service. Through the tracing of costs to product in this way ABC establishes more accurate costs for the product or service.

The identification of cost drivers provides information to management to enable them to take actions to improve the overall profitability of the company. Cost driver analysis will provide information to management on how costs can be controlled and managed. Variance analysis will be more useful as it is based on more accurate costs. The establishment of more accurate procedure costs should also help hospital managers to assess procedure profitability and make better decisions concerning pricing and procedure mix decisions.

In the above example, the use of an ABC system has resulted in different levels of profit for each of the procedures. It is apparent that the knee replacement procedure and the shoulder replacement procedure are more profitable than was thought under the absorption costing system. The shoulder replacement procedure however is making a significantly lower margin that the knee replacement procedure. The hip replacement procedure is now shown to be loss making. This additional information will enable management to make important decisions regarding pricing of the procedures. The price of the knee replacement procedure could potentially be reduced to make it more competitive and increase volumes. The price of both the hip replacement and shoulder replacement procedures could be increased to make these procedures more profitable. Before making any decision regarding pricing however they would need to review market prices and consider the effect any adjustment would have on the company's market position. If market conditions would not allow an increase in price of both hip and shoulder replacement procedures they could look at ways to reduce the costs of these procedures. ABC gives more detailed information about how costs are incurred and the potential for cost reduction by reducing activity levels. Alternatively they may want to consider whether to discontinue the hip replacement procedures altogether and replace them with a more profitable use of resources. This decision may not be appropriate however if part of the marketing strategy is for the company to provide a range of complementary procedures.

An activity based costing system can be extended beyond product and service costing to a range of cost management applications known as activity based management. These include the identification of value added and non value added activities and performance management in terms of measuring efficiency through cost driver rates.

Answer to Question Four

(a) **Project 1**

Internal Failure Cost Savings:
Current Expected Value ($300k x 0.5) + ($500k x 0.3) + ($700k x 0.2) = $440k
Expected Savings Year 1 = $440k x 80% x 1.04 =$366k

External Failure Cost Savings:
Current Expected Value ($1,300k x 0.6) + ($1,900k x 0.3) + ($3,000k x 0.1) = $1,650k
Expected Savings Year 1 = $1,650k x 80% x 1.04 = $1,373k

Raw Material Cost:
Expected savings Year 1 = 50,000 x $62 x 1.04 =$3,224k

Net cash flows Year 1
$366,080 + $1,372,800 + $3,224,000 = $4,963k

(b) **Project 2**

(i) Component Costs:
Expected savings Year 1 = 50,000 x $110 x 1.04 =$5,720k

Depreciation per annum = $15,000,000 / 5 = $3,000k

Additional fixed costs (excluding depreciation) per annum = $5,000k - $3,000k $2,000k

Net Present Value

	Year 0 $000	Year 1 $000	Year 2 $000	Year 3 $000	Year 4 $000	Year 5 $000
Initial Investment	(15,000)					
Working capital	(1,000)					1,000
Cost savings		5,720	5,949	6,187	6,434	6,691
Fixed costs		(2,000)	(2,000)	(2,000)	(2,000)	(2,000)
Net cash flows	(16,000)	3,720	3,949	4,187	4,434	5,691
Discount Factor @ 8%	1.000	0.926	0.857	0.794	0.735	0.681
Present value	(16,000)	3,445	3,384	3,324	3,259	3,876

Net present value = $1,288k

(ii)

	Year 0 $000	Year 1 $000	Year 2 $000	Year 3 $000	Year 4 $000	Year 5 $000
Net cash flows	(16,000)	3,720	3,949	4,187	4,434	5,691
Discount Factor @ 12%	1.000	0.893	0.797	0.712	0.636	0.567
Present value	(16,000)	3,322	3,147	2,981	2,820	3,227

Net present value = - $503k

IRR

NPV at 8% = $1,288k
NPV at 12% = -$503k

By interpolation

8% + (1,288/(1,288 + 503)) x 4% =10.9%

(c)

The general rule in discount cash flow analysis where projects are mutually exclusive is that the project with the highest net present value should be selected. In this case project 1 has a NPV of $1,338K and project 2 has a NPV of $1,288K. Therefore on the basis on NPV alone project 1 should be selected.

Project 2 requires an investment of $16m while project 1 requires an investment of $20m. While project 2 has a marginally lower NPV than alternative 1, if the additional $4m of funds can be invested in other projects with NPVs in excess of this difference, it would be worthwhile investing in project 2.

The company directors will also have to consider the risk of the two projects and other non-financial factors.

(d)

The IRR measures the project return as a percentage whereas NPV measures the absolute amount. This can result in a problem if the IRR is used to select projects where the projects are mutually exclusive. Decisions based on IRR may result in the selection of a project with a lower investment and a higher return, when it may be preferable to invest a greater sum which generates a lower percentage return but produces a greater absolute amount. Where projects are mutually exclusive NPV should be used to select projects.

Even if mutually exclusive projects have the same initial investment, NPV and IRR can give conflicting results due to the assumption regarding the reinvestment of surplus cash flows generated by an investment. The assumption if the NPV method is adopted is that the cash flows generated by an investment will be reinvested at the cost of capital. The IRR method assumes that cash flows generated by the investment will be reinvested at the IRR of the original project. IRR may favour an investment with high early cash flows, reinvested at the IRR, while NPV may prefer a different project with later cash flows. The NPV ranking of the projects depends on the discount rates used. When the discount rate exceeds a certain level the choice of projects will change and the conflict will no longer exist.

Section A – Question One – Compulsory

Question One consists of 8 objective test sub-questions. These are drawn from all sections of the syllabus. They are designed to examine breadth across the syllabus and thus cover many learning outcomes.

Section B – Question Two – Compulsory

Question Two has 6 sub-questions.

(a)   The question assesses learning outcome B3(b) *apply alternative approaches to budgeting*. It examines the candidates' ability to explain the different stages in a budget setting process for a company that uses zero based budgeting.

(b)   The question assesses learning outcome D1(a) *analyse the impact of uncertainty and risk on decision models that may be based on relevant cash flows, learning curves, discounting techniques etc*. It examines candidates' ability to apply various decision making criterion to a particular decision.

(c)   The question assesses learning outcome D1(a) *analyse the impact of uncertainty and risk on decision models that may be based on relevant cash flows, learning curves, discounting techniques etc*. It examines candidates' ability to explain the effect that a decision maker's attitude to risk will have on the chosen decision.

(d)   The question assesses learning outcome E1(e) *analyse trade debtor and creditor information*. Part (i) of the question examines candidates' ability to calculate expected cash receipts from credit customers given information relating to bad debts and trade receivable days. Part (ii) of the question examines candidates' ability to describe methods that a company could use to reduce the occurrence of bad debts.

(e)   The question assesses learning outcome E2(b) *identify alternatives for investment of short-term cash surpluses*. It examines candidates' ability to compare two potential short term Investment opportunities and explain the advantages and disadvantages of each.

(f)   The question assesses learning outcome E1(b) *interpret working capital ratios for business sectors*. It examines candidates' ability to calculate working capital ratios and the working capital cycle.

Section C – Questions Three and Four - Compulsory

Question Three Part (a) of the question assesses learning outcome A1(a) *compare and contrast marginal (or variable), throughput and absorption accounting methods in respect of profit reporting and stock valuation*. It examines candidates' ability to calculate the cost of a service using a traditional method of overhead absorption. Part (b) assesses learning outcome A1(c) *discuss activity-based costing as compared with traditional marginal and absorption costing methods, including its relative advantages and disadvantages as a system of cost accounting*. It requires candidates to be able to apply activity based costing to the calculation of a service costs. Part (c) assesses learning outcome A1(c) *discuss activity-based costing as compared with traditional marginal and absorption costing methods, including its relative advantages and disadvantages as a system of cost accounting*. It examines candidates' ability to explain the potential benefits of the information for management decision making.

Question Four Parts (a) and (b) of the question assess learning outcomes C1(a) *explain the processes involved in making long-term decisions* and C2(a) *evaluate project proposals using the techniques of investment appraisal*. They examine candidates' ability to identify relevant costs and calculate the net present value and IRR of a project. Part (c) of the question assesses learning outcome C2(a) *evaluate project proposals using the techniques of investment appraisal*. It examines candidates' ability to evaluate two investment projects based on their NPV and IRR. Part d) of the question assesses learning outcome C2(c) *prioritise projects that are mutually exclusive, involve unequal lives and/or are subject to capital rationing*. It requires candidates to discuss the reasons why conflicts arise between the ranking of projects based on their IRR and NPV.